Anglo-Saxon Studies 34

PRIESTS AND THEIR BOOKS
IN LATE ANGLO-SAXON ENGLAND

Anglo-Saxon Studies

ISSN 1475-2468

GENERAL EDITORS
John Hines
Catherine Cubitt

'Anglo-Saxon Studies' aims to provide a forum for the best scholarship on the Anglo-Saxon peoples in the period from the end of Roman Britain to the Norman Conquest, including comparative studies involving adjacent populations and periods; both new research and major re-assessments of central topics are welcomed.

Books in the series may be based in any one of the principal disciplines of archaeology, art history, history, language and literature, and inter- or multi-disciplinary studies are encouraged.

Proposals or enquiries may be sent directly to the editors or the publisher at the addresses given below; all submissions will receive prompt and informed consideration.

Professor John Hines, School of History, Archaeology and Religion, Cardiff University, John Percival Building, Colum Drive, Cardiff, Wales, CF10 3EU, UK

Professor Catherine Cubitt, School of History, Faculty of Arts and Humanities, University of East Anglia, Norwich, England, NR4 7TJ, UK

Boydell & Brewer, PO Box 9, Woodbridge, Suffolk, England, IP12 3DF, UK

Previously published volumes in the series are listed at the back of this book

PRIESTS AND THEIR BOOKS
IN LATE ANGLO-SAXON ENGLAND

Gerald P. Dyson

THE BOYDELL PRESS

© Gerald P. Dyson 2019

All Rights Reserved. Except as permitted under current legislation no part of this work may be photocopied, stored in a retrieval system, published, performed in public, adapted, broadcast, transmitted, recorded or reproduced in any form or by any means, without the prior permission of the copyright owner

The right of Gerald P. Dyson to be identified as the author of this work has been asserted in accordance with sections 77 and 78 of the Copyright, Designs and Patents Act 1988

First published 2019
The Boydell Press, Woodbridge
Paperback edition 2021

ISBN 978-1-78327-366-9 hardback
ISBN 978-1-78327-638-7 paperback

The Boydell Press is an imprint of Boydell & Brewer Ltd
PO Box 9, Woodbridge, Suffolk IP12 3DF, UK
and of Boydell & Brewer Inc.
668 Mt Hope Avenue, Rochester, NY 14620–2731, USA
website: www.boydellandbrewer.com

A CIP catalogue record for this book is available
from the British Library

The publisher has no responsibility for the continued existence or accuracy of URLs for external or third-party internet websites referred to in this book, and does not guarantee that any content on such websites is, or will remain, accurate or appropriate

To faithful shepherds, past and present

Contents

List of Illustrations — viii

Acknowledgements — x

Introduction — 1

1   Priests, Books, and Pastoral Care — 17

2   "Ne cunnon þæt leden understandan": Issues of Clerical Literacy — 43

3   Demand and Supply: Production and Provision of Books for Priests — 80

4   Preaching and Homiletic Books for Priests — 110

5   Performing the Liturgy: Priests' Books for the Mass and Office — 146

6   Locating Penitentials, Manuals, and *Computi* — 193

Conclusions — 227

Appendix — 235

Bibliography — 240

Index — 277

Illustrations

Plates

Plate 1. Bern, Burgerbibliothek 671, f. 76v. Reproduced with permission of the Bern Burgerbibliothek — 68

Plate 2. Oxford, Bodleian Library, MS. Auct. D. 2. 19, fol. 168v. Reproduced with permission of the Bodleian Libraries, the University of Oxford — 72

Plate 3. The Taunton Fragment, SHC DD\SAS/C1193/77, p. 7. Reproduced with kind permission of the Somerset Archaeological and Natural History Society — 133

Plate 4. Oxford, Bodleian Library, MS. Junius 85, fol. 19r. Reproduced with permission of the Bodleian Libraries, the University of Oxford — 137

Plate 5. Cambridge, Corpus Christi College 41, p. 482. Reproduced with permission of the Parker Library and the Master and Fellows of Corpus Christi College, Cambridge — 173

Plate 6. Warsaw, Biblioteka Narodowa, I. 3311, f. 17v. Reproduced with permission of the National Library of Poland — 177

Plate 7. Warsaw, Biblioteka Narodowa, I. 3311, f. 38r. Reproduced with permission of the National Library of Poland — 183

Plate 8. Oxford, Bodleian Library, MS. Laud Misc. 482, fol. 28r. Reproduced with permission of the Bodleian Libraries, the University of Oxford — 211

Plate 9. Cambridge, Corpus Christi College 422, p. 41. Reproduced with permission of the Parker Library and the Master and Fellows of Corpus Christi College, Cambridge — 220

The author and publisher are grateful to all the institutions and individuals listed for permission to reproduce the materials in which they hold copyright. Every effort has been made to trace the copyright holders; apologies are offered for any omission, and the publisher will be pleased to add any necessary acknowledgement in subsequent editions.

Illustrations

Tables

Table 1. A comparison of Anglo-Saxon and Carolingian lists of texts for priests — 36
Table 2. Contents of Oxford, Bodleian Library, Junius 85 and 86 — 139
Table 3. The structure of the mass with the liturgical books needed for each section — 156
Table 4. The contents of the Winchester computus — 208
Table 5. Tabulation of pericopes from Warsaw, Biblioteka Narodowa, I. 3311 — 235

Acknowledgements

I must firstly acknowledge Katy Cubitt. I was blessed to have Katy as a doctoral supervisor and benefitted immensely from her critiques and encouragements. This book would not exist were it not for her patient and thoughtful guidance through the challenges of a PhD.

My thanks are also due to Jesse Billett and Mary Blanchard, both of whom were very generous with their time in reading and commenting on drafts of several chapters. In particular, Jesse's comments on the Warsaw Lectionary and other liturgical material have been invaluable.

My parents also deserve my thanks. They instilled in me from an early age the importance of history and helped spark my interest in history as a career. Following them into the field of medicine was never attractive to me (and for this my hypothetical patients breathe a sigh of relief), but they have unfailingly encouraged me in my endeavors. On top of this, my father put his career on hold for more than a decade to give my brother and me a quality education. Now 100 percent of his graduates hold doctorates, so I think he did alright. Thank you to you both.

My wife Aurelia has been very patient through the various phases of preparing this book. I am grateful for her willingness to take up the slack for me when it felt like I was working two full-time jobs to finish the book. On top of this, her editing and proofreading of earlier drafts of these chapters brought them a long way towards completion.

Finally, I'd like to thank the staff of Boydell & Brewer, who have been perennially helpful and responsive. Special thanks are due to Caroline Palmer for all the help, patience, and good suggestions along the way. It was in the Cave du Cochon on Walmgate in York in a meeting with Caroline, catalyzed by Katy Cubitt, that this book project began.

Soli Deo Gloria.

Introduction

Christianity has long been recognized as a religion of the book. Within two or three decades of the death and resurrection of Jesus, accounts of his life were written and circulated, as were pastoral letters to newly founded churches in Europe and Asia Minor. Sources such as the pre-Pauline creed in 1 Corinthians 15 and the description of early Christian worship found in Justin Martyr's *First Apology* attest to frequent use of written liturgy and the texts that eventually formed the biblical canon, both of which are indicative of a strong literate element in these formative centuries.[1] This element was passed on to the medieval church and has persisted to the present day. The dependence of Christianity on written texts necessitates literacy and the availability of books to those who lead its adherents – a need witnessed in the present day by the years of training that ministers undergo prior to ordination and the significant number of publishers whose business depends on the sale of bibles, commentaries, devotional volumes, and books for the liturgy.

Though the advent of printing and the rise of Protestantism stand between us and the books used by the medieval priest in England, the clergy's reliance on books has remained constant. Throughout the Middle Ages, the provision of the rites and services of the church by priests was largely reliant on access to certain texts, such as penitentials, books for the celebration of the mass and Divine Office, books of sermons or homilies, and others. These are frequently one of the very few routes we have into understanding the ministry of the secular clergy to medieval Christians outside of prescriptive sources and thus the study of priests' books is an essential component in understanding the contexts for and practice of pastoral care. Scholarly interest in the study of pastoral care on its own merit has grown in recent decades, but has largely been limited to studies of individual aspects of pastoral care, a specific text, or a single priestly book, and it is my hope that this work will be a constructive addition to an important stage of development in this burgeoning field. To present a more holistic understanding of the practice of pastoral care in late Anglo-Saxon England, this study considers the books of English priests in the tenth

---

[1] Leslie W. Barnard, trans., *St Justin Martyr: The First and Second Apologies* (New York: Paulist Press, 1997), 71; Risto Uro, "Ritual, Memory and Writing in Early Christianity," *Temenos* 47, no. 2 (2011); Harry Gamble, *Books and Readers in the Early Church: A History of Early Christian Texts* (New Haven: Yale University Press, 1995).

and eleventh centuries through both documentary and manuscript evidence as well as through contextual factors, such as clerical literacy and the availability of books.

This book consists of two main sections. The first (chapters 1–3) introduces the material and considers the two main issues related to the use of priestly books and pastoral care: clerical literacy and the availability of books to Anglo-Saxon priests. The second section (chapters 4–6) presents manuscript case studies of the types of books used by the secular clergy and considers both documentary and manuscript evidence. These case studies are illustrative rather than exhaustive; the establishment of a comprehensive corpus of manuscripts used by Anglo-Saxon secular priests has not been attempted here. The final chapter will unify the themes discussed and consider the implications of the evidence presented for pastoral care and the ministry of the Anglo-Saxon secular clergy.

Chapter 1 lays out the historical groundwork for the remainder of the study by giving an overview of the role of the priest in pastoral care and the types of churches in which Anglo-Saxon priests served in the tenth and eleventh centuries. It further discusses the Latin and Old English terminology relating to books and the prescriptive booklists found in Anglo-Saxon and influential Carolingian sources. Chapter 2 deals with the issue of clerical literacy in the late Anglo-Saxon period, arguing that despite the acrimonious nature of monastic writings on the subject, most priests were at least functionally literate with regard to the performance of the liturgy in Latin. This chapter also provides an overview of the avenues through which education was available to the secular clergy and evidence for the literate skills of priests. Chapter 3 discusses the ways in which Anglo-Saxon priests obtained their books, particularly liturgical books, examining the evidence for methods of transmission such as episcopal provision, aristocratic patronage, and commissioning or purchase by individual clerics or communities.

Chapter 4 examines the homiletic tradition in Anglo-Saxon England, preaching and the use of homilies, and the surviving homiletic manuscripts used by secular clerics. I argue that preaching was a major part of the practice of pastoral care in this period and that through homiletic books we can observe pastoral priorities and the wide circulation of preaching texts in secular churches. Furthermore, the chapter looks at evidence suggesting that secular clerics played a significant role in the composition and adaptation of vernacular homilies. Chapter 5 discusses the evidence for priestly books used in the performance of the mass and Divine Office. This chapter draws attention to the fullness of the liturgical celebration of secular minsters, the pastoral relevance of the Office in these churches, and the way in which the move from the sacramentary to the missal in England reflects the changing way pastoral care was delivered. This chapter additionally shows that a

Introduction

heretofore neglected manuscript was used in the liturgy, probably by secular clerics in a small minster or parish church. Chapter 6 considers penitentials, manuals, and the computus. These texts are grouped together due to their similar manuscript context; they rarely survive as discrete volumes and are instead bound with codices containing other texts. This chapter examines penitentials and manuals in light of their function, pastoral significance, and manuscript context. The section on computus discusses the use of these texts in the discernment of liturgically significant days and the wide currency of the Winchester and Leofric-Tiberius *computi*. This chapter also proposes that London, British Library, Cotton Vespasian D. XV is best understood as a pastorally oriented penitential handbook for a priest. The final chapter brings together the themes of pastoral care and priestly books in late Anglo-Saxon England and considers the implications of this study for our understanding of clerical ministry, texts that were available and circulating in this period, and the early medieval clergy.

What makes a priest's book?

Like most medieval books, priests' books rarely state their purpose or users explicitly. Without the luxury of clear statements concerning a book's purpose or users, those studying medieval manuscripts are generally left to make determinations based on a book's contents and physical characteristics. Priests' books have seldom received their due in this regard, but understanding potential identifying features and characteristics of priests' books is essential, particularly in differentiating these from other manuscripts containing Christian texts. To this end, some general statements about these books and their differentiation can be made.

Firstly, at their most general, priests' books are understood here as the books of the secular clergy, particularly those ordained to the priesthood. This would encompass books available for the use of clerics, such as service books that were part of the property of the church, and books that were the property of individual priests.[2] Secondly, most of the books of the secular clergy were pastoral in nature. As is discussed

---

[2] The term priest will be used in its modern English sense in this book. The Old English term *preost* had a wider range of meanings than its modern equivalent and could refer to a priest in the current sense (a cleric ordained to the highest grade) or a cleric in the lower grades. *Mæssepreost* seems to be the Old English equivalent of modern English "priest". Christopher N. L. Brooke, *Churches and Churchmen in Medieval Europe* (London: Hambledon Press, 1999), 240; Thomas Pickles, "*Biscopes-tun, muneca-tun and preosta-tun*: Dating, Significance and Distribution," in *The Church in English Place-Names*, ed. Eleanor Quinton (Nottingham: English Place-Name Society, 2009), 71.

later in this chapter, episcopal expectations for priests' books consist almost wholly of books relating directly to pastoral care, including mass-books, lectionaries, and penitentials. This is of course not to say that priests did not own books for other purposes. Some may indeed have owned collections of poetry, grammatical works, medical texts, classical and early Christian writings, and liturgical or paraliturgical texts not directly related to pastoral ministry. That said, many pastoral books must have been written for late Anglo-Saxon secular priests (or churches) to meet their institutional and ministerial needs. For the historian's purpose, priests' books are one of the clearest windows into pastoral care at a local level, though this vantage point requires careful study and contextualization. Thirdly, these books are to be differentiated from those for monastic and episcopal use. One of the difficulties of studying late Anglo-Saxon priests' books is in fact the large portion of surviving manuscripts that have episcopal or monastic associations. This should not be taken as an indication that the secular clergy did not have access to books, but rather an indication of the ways in which patterns of manuscript survival have narrowed the range of available evidence. With regard to differentiation of manuscripts with monastic associations, the waters are somewhat muddied by the fact that monks also took clerical orders and increasing numbers of monk-priests appear in the historical record during the early medieval period.[3] But monks, even those who also held clerical orders, were by definition not members of the secular clergy, as they ostensibly lived apart from the world and according to a rule. Conversely, bishops and priests were not distinguished from each other in terms of order or clerical grades, as Ælfric points out in his pastoral letter for Bishop Wulfsige, but there is often a clear boundary between liturgical books for episcopal use and those for more general use by secular clerics.[4] For example, pontificals and benedictionals were used solely by bishops and several of the extant mass-books of the Anglo-Saxon period can be firmly associated with episcopal use by virtue of the texts they contain.[5]

Further distinctions have been advanced to differentiate priests' books from those for bishops. Indeed, the study of priests' books as a group largely began with Niels Rasmussen and his attempt to

---

[3] Christopher Jones, "Ælfric and the Limits of 'Benedictine Reform'," in *A Companion to Ælfric*, ed. Hugh Magennis and Mary Swan (Leiden: Brill, 2009), 85.

[4] Dorothy Whitelock, Martin Brett, and Christopher N. L. Brooke, eds., *Councils and Synods, with Other Documents Relating to the English Church, AD 871–1204*, vol. 1 (Oxford: Clarendon Press, 1981), 205.

[5] Well-known examples include the Leofric Missal (Oxford, Bodleian Library, Bodley 579), the Sacramentary of Robert of Jumièges (Rouen, Bibliothèque municipale, 274, Y.6), and the Giso Sacramentary (London, British Library, Cotton Vitellius A. XVIII).

create a typology to distinguish them from episcopal books.[6] This framework was subsequently taken up more recently by Yitzhak Hen, who expanded the original framework to four criteria for identifying priestly books:

1. The "material aspects and layout of a manuscript",
2. The liturgical content,
3. "[T]he combination of canonical material with liturgical prayers", and
4. The combination of different types of liturgical books in one volume.[7]

In essence, these studies suggest that the books used by medieval priests were humble and portable volumes into which liturgy, canon law, homilies, and other types of texts were combined. These criteria are applicable to many books that were used by priests, particularly those serving in small, local churches. However, I offer two caveats to the use of this framework. Firstly, this may encourage confirmation bias in the identification of priestly books. Scholars have often conjectured that books with subpar script and poor-quality materials are those belonging to priests, according with the first criterion, but we will only find priestly manuscripts of the kind we are looking for and in the places we are looking for them. As a result, many books utilized by secular priests may have been passed over due to preconceptions about appearance. There is little reason why priests' books could not have been produced in major monastic scriptoria and manuscript evidence from England and the continent indicates that this did take place.[8] Secondly, building on my first objection, the framework, particularly points 1 and 4, takes too narrow a view of what makes a priestly book. Early medieval priests in general and Anglo-Saxon priests specifically were a diverse group whose status, finances, and education varied dramatically; it would be surprising if their books were not also diverse in their content and physical aspect. The communities of secular cathedrals and minsters certainly possessed high-status books, and royal and aristocratic chaplains may also have owned and had access to high-quality manuscripts. Waltham Holy Cross, a secular minster generously patronized by Harold Godwinson,

---

[6] Niels Rasmussen, "Célébration épiscopale et célébration presbytérale: Un essai de typologie," in *Segni e riti nella Chiesa altomedievale occidentale*, vol. 33, no. 2 of *Settimane di studio del Centro italiano di sull'alto medioevo* (Spoleto: Presso la sede del Centro, 1987).

[7] Yitzhak Hen, "Knowledge of Canon Law among Rural Priests: The Evidence of Two Carolingian Manuscripts from around 800," *The Journal of Theological Studies* 50, no. 1 (1999): 129.

[8] See pages 84–88, 95, and 103.

was gifted eight gospelbooks in the eleventh century, all of which were decorated with gold or silver, and other aristocratic gifts may have been similarly lavish.[9] Books like these might give no material indication of their use by secular priests, nor would these priests have necessarily combined a miscellany of texts into one volume. Both secular minsters and manorial churches were the recipients of aristocratic patronage in the form of books and this patronage was a means by which the Anglo-Saxon nobility could exhibit both their wealth and piety. Without doubt, there is validity to this framework for the identification of priests' books, particularly for those manuscripts produced for use by priests providing pastoral care, and, in that light, it is potentially useful. However, this typology should be used more flexibly and with the diverse contexts in which early medieval priests lived and worked in mind.

That this framework was developed by scholars of the continental church is indicative of a larger trend, namely that the study of priests' books in the early Middle Ages has focused on continental Europe, while studies of priests' books in Anglo-Saxon England have been of limited scope. Some scholarly work has been undertaken concerning the books of Merovingian priests while the books of Carolingian priests have deservedly received a good deal of attention.[10] Studies of this kind have universally recognized the necessity of books to priestly ministry and have credibly identified a significant number of books as produced for, or at least used by, early medieval priests.[11]

---

[9] Leslie Watkiss and Marjorie Chibnall, eds., *The Waltham Chronicle: An Account of the Discovery of Our Holy Cross at Montacute and Its Conveyance to Waltham* (Oxford: Clarendon Press, 1994), 33; David Dumville, "Anglo-Saxon Books: Treasure in Norman Hands?," in *Anglo-Norman Studies XVI: Proceedings of the Battle Conference 1993*, ed. Marjorie Chibnall (Woodbridge: Boydell Press, 1994).

[10] Yitzhak Hen, "Priests and Books in the Merovingian Period," in *Men in the Middle: Local Priests in Early Medieval Europe*, ed. Steffen Patzold and Carine van Rhijn (Berlin: De Gruyter, 2016); Carine van Rhijn, *Shepherds of the Lord: Priests and Episcopal Statutes in the Carolingian Period* (Turnhout: Brepols, 2007); van Rhijn, "The Local Church, Priests' Handbooks and Pastoral Care in the Carolingian Period," in *Chiese locali e Chiese regionali nell'alto medioevo*, vol. 61, no. 2 of *Settimane di studio della Fondazione Centro italiano di studi sull'alto medioevo* (Spoleto: Fondazione Centro italiano di studi sull'alto medioevo, 2014).

[11] Yitzhak Hen and Rob Meens, eds., *The Bobbio Missal: Liturgy and Religious Culture in Merovingian Gaul* (Cambridge: Cambridge University Press, 2004); Hen, "Knowledge of Canon Law among Rural Priests"; Hen, "Educating the Clergy: Canon Law and Liturgy in a Carolingian Handbook from the Time of Charles the Bald," in *De Sion exibit lex et verbum domini de Hierusalem: Essays on Medieval Law, Liturgy and Literature in Honour of Amnon Linder*, ed. Hen (Turnhout: Brepols, 2001); Hen, "A Liturgical Handbook for the Use of a Rural Priest (Brussels, BR 10127–10144)," in *Organizing the Written Word: Scripts, Manuscripts, and Texts*, ed. Marco Mostert (Turnhout: Brepols, forthcoming); Susan Keefe, *Water and the Word: Baptism and the Education of the Clergy in the*

Introduction

Some similar studies of individual books intended for pastoral use also concern Anglo-Saxon manuscripts, with the Red Book of Darley receiving particular attention.[12] Examinations of priests' books from England and continental Europe have at the very least shown that early medieval priests did have access to books, many might have owned books themselves, and that the often humble liturgical books of priests are "unique entities that deserve to be studied on their own merits".[13] Furthermore, they have shown the value of these books in studying pastoral care and challenged traditional views regarding the literacy of secular priests.

But as useful as individual manuscript studies have been, significant limitations have become apparent as a result of this approach. In reference to the Anglo-Saxon material, relatively few books thought to have been used by priests in Anglo-Saxon England have received concerted study. As a result, a great deal of the English manuscript evidence remains inadequately explored in relation to use by the secular clergy. Partially owing to this inadequacy, there has been little effort to study priestly manuscripts intended for use in pastoral care holistically rather than individually. This book attempts to address both of these issues by considering late Anglo-Saxon priestly books as a group in addition to presenting case studies of priestly manuscripts, several of which have received very little attention, in the second half of this volume.

Clergy

Secular priests of the Middle Ages were often the scapegoats of the monastic writer. They were commonly castigated for laziness, ignorance and illiteracy, and for sexual incontinence. In Anglo-Saxon England specifically, the monks of the Benedictine reform were harsh

---

Carolingian Empire, 2 vols. (Notre Dame: University of Notre Dame Press, 2002); Frederick Paxton, "*Bonus liber*: A Late Carolingian Clerical Manual from Lorsch (Bibliotheca Vaticana MS Pal. Lat. 485)," in *The Two Laws. Studies in Medieval Legal History Dedicated to Stephan Kuttner*, ed. Laurent Mayali and Stephanie Tibbetts (Washington, DC: Catholic University of America Press, 1990); Sven Meeder, "The Early Irish Stowe Missal's Destination and Function," *Early Medieval Europe* 13, no. 2 (2005).

[12] Helen Gittos, "Is There Any Evidence for the Liturgy of Parish Churches in Late Anglo-Saxon England? The Red Book of Darley and the Status of Old English," in *Pastoral Care in Late Anglo-Saxon England*, ed. Francesca Tinti (Woodbridge: Boydell Press, 2005); Victoria Thompson, "The Pastoral Contract in Late Anglo-Saxon England: Priest and Parishioner in Oxford, Bodleian Library, MS Laud Miscellaneous 482," in *Pastoral Care in Late Anglo-Saxon England*, ed. Tinti.

[13] Yitzhak Hen, "Review Article: Liturgy and Religious Culture in Late Anglo-Saxon England," *Early Medieval Europe* 17, no. 3 (2009): 337.

critics of their secular counterparts.¹⁴ However, in light of the decline of monastic life and institutions in England in the ninth century, due at least in part to disruption brought on by the Vikings, ecclesiastical institutions seem to have been staffed almost exclusively by secular clerics through much of the ninth century and into the middle of the tenth. Even after this date, monks were comparatively few in number: a recent study has estimated that secular priests outnumbered monks roughly five to one at the time of the Conquest.¹⁵ Priests are therefore a critical area of study in understanding Anglo-Saxon ecclesiastical culture as well as pastoral care. Through uncritical acceptance of monastic accounts however, scholars have until relatively recently shown little interest in the secular clergy, resulting in the marginalization of these figures in academic study and the dominance of monastic narratives.¹⁶

Accordingly, academic studies of priests and the secular clergy more generally are a relatively new development and scholarly interest in the work and careers of the secular clergy has significantly increased in the last two decades.¹⁷ Some studies focusing specifically on the Anglo-Saxon clergy have also appeared since the 1990s, most notably the work of Julia Barrow and Catherine Cubitt.¹⁸ Anglo-Norman secular

---

¹⁴ For an account of this sort of monastic writing and its rationale in Anglo-Saxon England, see Rebecca Stephenson, *The Politics of Language: Byrhtferth, Ælfric, and the Multilingual Identity of the Benedictine Reform* (Toronto: University of Toronto Press, 2015), especially chapter 2.

¹⁵ Olga Timofeeva, "Anglo-Latin Bilingualism before 1066: Prospects and Limitations," in *Interfaces between Language and Culture in Medieval England: A Festschrift for Matti Kilpiö*, ed. Alaric Hall et al. (Leiden: Brill, 2010), 13–14. I suspect the number of secular clerics below the rank of priest is significantly underestimated by Timofeeva.

¹⁶ Part of this is simply because monks seem to have written more than priests. Some defenses of clerical life have survived, but they are rare in comparison to monastic vitriol towards priests and appear from the later eleventh century and after. Julia Barrow, *The Clergy in the Medieval World: Secular Clerics, Their Families and Careers in North-Western Europe c. 800–c. 1200* (Cambridge: Cambridge University Press, 2015), 5, nn. 16, 17; John Ott, *Bishops, Authority and Community in Northwestern Europe, c. 1050–1150* (Cambridge: Cambridge University Press, 2015), 60.

¹⁷ An exception to this would be the interesting but extremely dated Edward Lewes Cutts, *Parish Priests and Their People in the Middle Ages in England* (London: Society for Promoting Christian Knowledge, 1898), which devotes several chapters to the Anglo-Saxon church. However, advances in Anglo-Saxon scholarship, such as the identification of Wulfstan as the author of the *Canons of Edgar* and the *Laws of Edward and Guthrum*, and the largely descriptive nature of this book have rendered it essentially irrelevant to modern scholarship.

¹⁸ Alan Thacker, "Priests and Pastoral Care in Early Anglo-Saxon England," in *The Study of Medieval Manuscripts of England: Festschrift in Honor of Richard W. Pfaff*, ed. George Brown and Linda Voights (Turnhout: Brepols, 2010); Julia Barrow, "Wulfstan and Worcester: Bishop and Clergy in the Early Eleventh Century," in *Wulfstan, Archbishop of York: The Proceedings of the Second Alcuin Conference*, ed.

clerics too have been the subject of significant scholarly interest: Hugh Thomas has emphasized the intellectual aspects of the English secular clergy after the Conquest, devoting several chapters of *The Secular Clergy in England, 1066–1216* to the bookholdings of secular clerics and their place in the intellectual movements of the twelfth century.[19]

The rising tide of studies of the clergy has also led to more interest in the continental European clergy and, as much of the inspiration for the regulation of the secular clergy came to reforming bishops of the late Anglo-Saxon period from Carolingian sources, comparative material on the early medieval clergy of western Europe is particularly apt for this study. Scholars such as Julia Barrow have usefully brought together a wide variety of documentary evidence to shed light on the education, families, and ecclesiastical careers of secular clerics throughout Northern Europe. Prosopographical work of this kind on the medieval clergy has gone far in exploring the relationship between the secular clergy and the societies in which they lived and to which they ministered.[20] More specific regional and cultural studies of priests have also been crucial in establishing the study of the medieval clergy in its own right, particularly the work of Wendy Davies on local priests in early medieval Brittany.[21] Similarly, Robert Godding's work on the priests of Merovingian Gaul has resurrected these figures out of near-total obscurity and further developed the prosopography of the medieval clergy, while studies by Carine van Rhijn have shed further light on the lives and work of early medieval priests, with van Rhijn utilizing episcopal statutes to emphasize the importance of the local priest in the implementation of Carolingian *correctio*.[22] The fact

---

Matthew Townend (Turnhout: Brepols, 2004); Barrow, "Clergy in the Diocese of Hereford in the Eleventh and Twelfth Centuries," in *Anglo-Norman Studies XXVI: Proceedings of the Battle Conference 2003*, ed. John Gillingham (Woodbridge: Boydell Press, 2004); Barrow, *Who Served the Altar at Brixworth? Clergy in English Minsters c. 800–c. 1100* (Brixworth: Friends of All Saints Church, Brixworth, 2013); Barrow, "The Clergy in English Dioceses c. 900–c. 1066," in *Pastoral Care in Late Anglo-Saxon England*, ed. Tinti; Catherine Cubitt, "Bishops, Priests and Penance in Late Saxon England," *Early Medieval Europe* 14, no. 1 (2006); Cubitt, "The Clergy in Early Anglo-Saxon England," *Historical Research* 78 (2005); Cubitt, "Images of St Peter: The Clergy and the Religious Life in Anglo-Saxon England," in *The Christian Tradition in Anglo-Saxon England: Approaches to Current Scholarship and Teaching*, ed. Paul Cavill (Cambridge: D. S. Brewer, 2004).

[19] Hugh Thomas, *The Secular Clergy in England, 1066–1216* (Oxford: Oxford University Press, 2014), particularly chapters 10 to 12; David Spear, "The Norman Empire and the Secular Clergy, 1066–1204," *Journal of British Studies* 21, no. 2 (1982).

[20] Barrow, *Clergy in the Medieval World*.

[21] Wendy Davies, "Priests and Rural Communities in East Brittany in the Ninth Century," *Études Celtiques* 20 (1983); Davies, *Small Worlds: The Village Community in Early Medieval Brittany* (Berkeley: University of California Press, 1988).

[22] Robert Godding, *Prêtres en Gaule mérovingienne* (Brussels: Société des Bollandistes, 2001); van Rhijn, *Shepherds of the Lord*.

that studies of early medieval clergy in their own right have appeared in the last few decades signals a noteworthy change in the scholarly perception of the secular clergy and one that has furnished this book with a relative wealth of comparative evidence.

Pastoral care

Giles Constable has asserted that pastoral care may be defined as "the performance of those ceremonies that were considered central to the salvation of the individual Christian and that were the primary responsibility of ordained priests working in parish churches under the supervision of the diocesan bishop or his representative."[23] This definition for the most part describes the structures and individuals involved in pastoral care, but what did pastoral care in the early medieval period consist of and how was it provided? In the earlier centuries of Anglo-Saxon Christianity, most pastoral care was provided by *monasteria*, religious communities that varied significantly in size and consisted of secular clerics, monks, or a mix of both.[24] By the tenth and eleventh centuries, the range of institutions providing pastoral care had significantly expanded. Pastoral care in these later centuries might have been provided by a manorial church with a single priest, a community of secular clerics, a local monastery, or for those in towns, a cathedral community, which, like the early *monasteria*, may have been monastic, secular, or, less commonly, mixed.[25] One of the primary ways in which pastoral care was practiced was through the celebration of the mass. For those able and willing to attend services regularly, this was likely the most commonly experienced form of pastoral care and one in which priests played an indispensable role, though the mass itself as a key aspect of pastoral care has seen limited scholarly attention.[26] The Divine Office may also have played a role in the services in

---

[23] Giles Constable, "Monasteries, Rural Churches and the *Cura Animarum* in the Early Middle Ages," in *Cristianizzazione ed organizzazione ecclesiastica delle campagne nell'alto medioevo: Espansione e resistenze*, vol. 28, no. 1 of *Settimane di studio del Centro italiano di studi sull'alto medioevo* (Spoleto: Presso la sede del Centro, 1982), 353.

[24] C. E. Cubitt, "Pastoral Care and Conciliar Canons: The Provisions of the 747 Council of *Clofesho*," in *Pastoral Care before the Parish*, ed. John Blair and Richard Sharpe (Leicester: Leicester University Press, 1992), 204–9.

[25] Blair and Sharpe, introduction to *Pastoral Care before the Parish*, 1–3. The types of institutions providing pastoral care in the tenth and eleventh centuries in England will receive more detailed treatment in chapter 1.

[26] John Romano, "Priests and the Eucharist in the Middle Ages," in *A Companion to Priesthood and Holy Orders in the Middle Ages*, ed. Greg Peters and C. Colt Anderson (Leiden: Brill, 2016) is naturally very broad, but useful. *A Companion to the Eucharist in the Middle Ages*, ed. Ian Christopher Levy, Gary Macy, and Kristen Van Ausdall (Leiden: Brill, 2012) devotes almost no attention to the mass as a form of pastoral care. Compare this with the perspective taken

which the laity participated during certain liturgical seasons, despite the common conception of the Office as solely an internal service of monasteries and clerical communities.

Anglo-Saxon pastoral care has not been wholly neglected within the field, the most notable contribution being an edited volume by Francesca Tinti, the seven chapters of which address pastoral provision and lay participation in the church at the lowest levels.[27] It is significant that this is the only volume published to date that focuses solely on late Anglo-Saxon pastoral care. Two of the seven studies presented examine individual books used by the secular clergy, showing the potential of this type of study for Anglo-Saxon pastoral care. Considerations of the Red Book of Darley (Cambridge, Corpus Christi College 422) and Oxford, Bodleian Library, Laud Misc. 482, both of which were studied in the above volume, have been incorporated into this book, which goes further by more broadly contextualizing them within the wider group of Anglo-Saxon priestly books. Conversely, other recent works, such as Sarah Hamilton's *Church and People in the Medieval West, 900–1200*, have contributed a somewhat broader perspective to the study of pastoral care by reinterpreting the interrelationship of the church and the laity and revisiting the functions and mechanics of pastoral care in this period.[28]

Additionally, many of the individual aspects of pastoral care have been well served in recent scholarship. In particular, the assignment of penance, the practice of baptism, and rites for the sick and dying – texts for which commonly appear together in their manuscript context – have been fruitful areas of scholarly inquiry. Rob Meens has been instrumental in analyzing the manuscript evidence for penitentials in Western Europe from the eighth to the tenth century and Hamilton's monograph on penance has endeavored to establish the forms and distribution of penitential practice in the tenth and eleventh centuries.[29] These studies and others have recognized the practice of penance at

---

by Josef Jungmann in his seminal *The Mass of the Roman Rite: Its Origins and Development*, trans. Francis A. Brunner, 2 vols. (New York: Benziger, 1951–55).

[27] Francesca Tinti, ed., *Pastoral Care in Late Anglo-Saxon England* (Woodbridge: Boydell Press, 2005).

[28] Sarah Hamilton, *Church and People in the Medieval West, 900–1200* (London: Routledge, 2013); Catherine C. E. Cubitt, "Pastoral Care and Religious Belief," in *A Companion to the Early Middle Ages: Britain and Ireland, c.500–c.1100*, ed. Pauline Stafford (Oxford: Wiley-Blackwell, 2009).

[29] Rob Meens, "The Frequency and Nature of Early Medieval Penance," in *Handling Sin: Confession in the Middle Ages*, ed. Peter Biller and A. J. Minnis (York: York Medieval Press, 1998); Meens, "Penitentials and the Practice of Penance in the Tenth and Eleventh Centuries," *Early Medieval Europe* 14, no. 1 (2006); Sarah Hamilton, *The Practice of Penance, 900–1050* (London and Woodbridge: The Royal Historical Society and Boydell Press, 2001). Also see Abigail Firey, ed., *A New History of Penance* (Leiden: Brill, 2008).

a low level by local priests and the availability of penitential texts for continental priests in the ninth century; the practice of penance in England may be witnessed particularly in the composition and circulation of vernacular penitentials from the later tenth century, despite the relatively few manuscript copies of penitentials that have survived outside episcopal collections of canon law.

By the same token, the performance of occasional offices in the Middle Ages, both in England and elsewhere, has also seen interest in recent years. Many studies, particularly the recent *Understanding Medieval Liturgy: Essays in Interpretation*, have relied on the rites found in medieval liturgical books to understand contemporary usage, an approach that has been particularly applied in studies of baptism.[30] Furthermore, it has been shown in studies by Victoria Thompson that there were developed rites for the care of the dying and dead in the late Anglo-Saxon period not only for those in religious communities, but also for laypeople served by the clergy in parish churches.[31] Thompson has shown this in part through the witness of Oxford, Bodleian Library, Laud Misc. 482, which she argues was used to train the secular clergy at Worcester in care for the dying, though I suggest that this view perhaps places too much specificity on the potential function of this volume. Many of these studies have usefully focused on the books employed in pastoral care, often by the secular clergy, and provided detailed analysis of the rites contained in these books, laying groundwork for a more wide-ranging examination of the significance of these rites to the manuscripts and practice of pastoral care.

Anglo-Saxon priests and their books

A great deal of episcopal legislation from the early medieval period acknowledged the need for priests to have access to certain books in order to be effective in the delivery of pastoral care.[32] Many of

---

[30] Helen Gittos and Sarah Hamilton, eds., *Understanding Medieval Liturgy: Essays in Interpretation* (Farnham: Ashgate, 2015); Sarah Foot, "'By Water in the Spirit': The Administration of Baptism in Early Anglo-Saxon England," in Blair and Sharpe, *Pastoral Care before the Parish*; Sally Crawford, "Baptism and Infant Burial in Anglo-Saxon England," in *Medieval Life Cycles: Continuity and Change*, ed. Isabelle Cochelin and Karen Smyth (Turnhout: Brepols, 2013). For a longitudinal study of baptism, see Bryan Spinks, *Early and Medieval Rituals and Theologies of Baptism: From the New Testament to the Council of Trent* (Aldershot: Ashgate, 2006).

[31] Victoria Thompson, *Dying and Death in Later Anglo-Saxon England* (Woodbridge: Boydell Press, 2004); Thompson, "The Pastoral Contract," in *Pastoral Care in Late Anglo-Saxon England*, ed. Tinti.

[32] Carolingian examples can be found in the episcopal *capitula* of Haito of Basel, Radulf of Bourges, Theodulf of Orleans, and Waltcaud of Liège. Some form of

Introduction

the episcopal statutes promulgated by Carolingian bishops contain prescriptive lists of books for priests and Anglo-Saxon churchmen of the tenth and eleventh centuries drew on these lists and others, such as that from the *Penitential of Egbert*, to populate their own prescriptive booklists for priests. The scope of these booklists varies widely: the ninth-century episcopal statute of Radulf of Bourges only specifically mentions a mass-book, a lectionary, and a psalter, while the roughly contemporary *Capitula Florentina* prescribes a more extensive list, including a "sacramentarium, evangelium, lectionarium, antiphonarium, psalterium, omelia beati Augustini vel sancti Gregorii, martyrologium sive compotum".[33] The items included in lists such as these were primarily, though not exclusively, liturgical books and would have provided a priest with the texts that he needed to say mass, perform the Office, administer the rites of the church, and calculate the dates of moveable feasts. The frequency with which these books were included in episcopal legislation makes it clear that bishops saw access to these books as an essential prerequisite for the provision of pastoral care by priests. Accordingly, episcopal legislation details the pastoral care that priests were to provide through the use of these books, though our sources rarely connect these so clearly. Archbishop Wulfstan's *Canons of Edgar*, an early eleventh-century set of episcopal guidelines for the clergy of the diocese of York, enjoins priests to preach, baptize children, care for the dying and the dead, say mass, celebrate the Divine Office, hear confession, and assign penance. Likewise, the pastoral letters penned by Ælfric for Wulfstan and Wulfsige III of Sherborne offer a very similar view of the pastoral care that was to be provided by an Anglo-Saxon priest.[34]

---

prescription of books for priests was included in most episcopal statutes from the Frankish empire. As for Anglo-Saxon texts, the *Penitential of Egbert* contains a prescriptive list of books for priests, as do two of the pastoral letters written by Ælfric.

[33] "A sacramentary, gospelbook, lectionary, antiphoner, psalter, the homilies of blessed Augustine or St Gregory, a martyrology or computus". *Capitula episcoporum*, pt. 1, ed. Peter Brommer, *Monumenta Germaniae Historica* (Hanover: Hahnsche Buchhandlung, 1984), 223, 237.

[34] Roger Fowler, ed., *Wulfstan's Canons of Edgar* (London: Oxford University Press, 1972), 5, 11, 13, 15–16, 18; Bernhard Fehr, ed., *Die Hirtenbriefe Ælfrics in altenglischer und lateinischer Fassung* (Hamburg: Henri Grand, 1914), *passim*. The manuscript copies of the *Canons of Edgar* make clear that this text was also known in the diocese of Worcester, which Wulfstan held in plurality with York from 1002 to 1016. It should be noted that there is limited manuscript evidence, particularly outside episcopal collections of canon law, for the circulation of both the *Canons of Edgar* and the pastoral letters written by Ælfric; see Fowler, *Wulfstan's Canons of Edgar*, xi–xvi; Joyce Hill, "Authorial Adaptation: Ælfric, Wulfstan, and the Pastoral Letters," in *Text and Language in Medieval English Prose: A Festschrift for Tadao Kubouchi*, ed. Akio Ōizumi, Jacek Fisiak, and John Scahill (Frankfurt: Peter Lang, 2005), 64–65.

Though there are slight differences in the books prescribed by these pastoral letters (and the *Canons of Edgar* does not provide us with a prescriptive booklist), the group of texts prescribed for Anglo-Saxon priests are fairly static, consisting of a mass-book, a lectionary, a psalter, a minimal number of books for the Office, a book of occasional offices, a penitential, and a computus.[35] The books needed to provide the forms of pastoral care described in these sources precisely correlate with those prescribed in Ælfric's pastoral letters, indicating on some level the standardization of pastoral care that was to be offered by priests and a clear vision on the part of Anglo-Saxon churchmen for the bibliographical resources needed by priests to accomplish these pastoral goals. Some scholars have expressed skepticism about the availability of a complete group of pastoral texts such as this in local churches, but the expectations expressed in these booklists do not exclude the large number of local churches that had sprung up in the tenth century.[36] They may indeed be partially intended to exert more episcopal control over this burgeoning class of churches. Episcopal legislation indicates that these churches were expected to and indeed must have had at least a few books if they were to come close to fulfilling the pastoral expectations placed on them.

A potentially mitigating factor in a priest's need for books is memorization. Through their frequent and long-term participation in the celebration of the liturgy as well as moral and theological instruction of the laity using scripture and homiletic texts, priests would have regularly heard, spoken, sung, and read texts essential to their ministry and vocation. Constant exposure to these texts would inevitably lead to a degree of rote memorization and in turn reduce a priest's reliance on the written word. It is difficult to assess how commonly this might have enabled a priest to perform the liturgy or preach a homily without a written aid, though Archbishop Wulfstan's instruction that

---

[35] For a more detailed discussion of these booklists and their contents, see chapter 1. It should also be noted that the tenth and eleventh centuries were a time of significant change in the form and type of liturgical books produced. The late tenth and early eleventh centuries in England give us the first extant missals or fragments of missals, signaling the beginning of a move away from the sacramentary as well as the changing needs of celebrants. Additionally, books for the Divine Office were also undergoing change, as it is in the later eleventh century that early forms of the breviary begin to appear in both monastic and secular contexts. The evolution of liturgical books has significant relevance to this study, as these changes may be a witness to the way in which strategies for the provision of pastoral care were affected by the shift in the types of ecclesiastical institutions bearing the greater part of the responsibility for ministry to the laity.

[36] For examples of this skepticism, see Sarah Hamilton, "The *Rituale*: The Evolution of a New Liturgical Book," in *The Church and the Book*, ed. R. N. Swanson (Woodbridge: Boydell Press, 2004), 76; Whitelock, Brett, and Brooke, *Councils and Synods*, 292, n. 2.

Introduction

priests always use the book when celebrating mass implies that some could and did perform the liturgy without the text in front of them.[37] Evidence from homiletic manuscripts also points to a role for memorization in the delivery and transmission of vernacular preaching texts.[38] Though these indications are significant, it is very unlikely that an Anglo-Saxon priest, even with an excellent memory, could do without books, particularly in light of the textual resources to which bishops expected priests to have access. That said, an awareness of the potential for memorization of certain types of priestly texts and the effects this could have on the textual needs of the secular clergy is valuable for the purposes of this study.

Though there is a reasonable amount of prescriptive evidence for the books that were to be used by Anglo-Saxon priests, the years have not been kind to Anglo-Saxon books. Liturgical manuscripts have survived in relatively large numbers, but many of these tend to be high-status volumes that were preserved in cathedrals and monasteries due to their deluxe status and, in some cases, because they continued to be practically useful. On the other hand, the survival of books utilized by priests in pastoral care has been far less consistent, as secular minsters and local churches have not been reliable conduits of manuscript transmission. Certainly the number of books produced for the Anglo-Saxon clergy is exponentially greater than the number of surviving manuscripts. The fact that many more mass-books and lectionaries were produced than have survived intact is in part attested by the significant number of fragments of these books, many of which date to the late tenth and eleventh centuries, and have most frequently survived as flyleaves in later medieval and early modern books.[39] Despite destruction and neglect by later generations, a small group of Anglo-Saxon manuscripts thought to have been used by secular priests has survived. The group is diverse: some are well-used and

---

[37] Whitelock, Brett, and Brooke, *Councils and Synods*, 324–25.
[38] Mary Swan, "Memorialised Readings: Manuscript Evidence for Old English Homily Composition," in *Anglo-Saxon Manuscripts and Their Heritage*, ed. Phillip Pulsiano and Elaine Treharne (Aldershot: Ashgate, 1998); Loredana Teresi, "Mnemonic Transmission of Old English Texts in the Post-Conquest Period," in *Rewriting Old English in the Twelfth Century*, ed. Mary Swan and Elaine Treharne (Cambridge: Cambridge University Press, 2000).
[39] Helmut Gneuss, "Liturgical Books in Anglo-Saxon England and Their Old English Terminology," in *Learning and Literature in Anglo-Saxon England: Studies Presented to Peter Clemoes on the Occasion of His Sixty-Fifth Birthday*, ed. Michael Lapidge and Gneuss (Cambridge: Cambridge University Press, 1985), 102, 109; Nicholas Orchard, "An Eleventh-Century Anglo-Saxon Missal Fragment," *Anglo-Saxon England* 23 (1994); K. D. Hartzell, "An Eleventh-Century English Missal Fragment in the British Library," *Anglo-Saxon England* 18 (1989); Rebecca Rushforth, "The Prodigal Fragment: Cambridge, Gonville and Caius College 734/782a," *Anglo-Saxon England* 30 (2001). To these can be added Bloomington, Indiana University, Lilly Library, Poole 41.

roughly made books produced by unknown scribes in unidentified locations, while others are very competent products of cathedral and monastic scriptoria that were clearly intended for parochial use. Furthermore, aside from the surviving manuscripts, documentary evidence can further inform our view of the books of English priests in the tenth and eleventh centuries. At least one booklist provides a record of the service books at an Anglo-Saxon secular church in the eleventh century and accounts of the liturgical life at some secular minsters, such as at Waltham Holy Cross and Holy Trinity, Twynham, can help to elucidate the books available to priests in these institutions.

It is clear that medieval bishops saw books as essential tools for the work of priests and that the books that were prescribed for use by priests align with the pastoral mission envisioned for the secular clergy by the second generation of Benedictine reformers. Therefore, these books, whether attested through manuscript or documentary evidence, are our closest sources to the practice of pastoral care, and in order to understand the context and practical implementation of pastoral care in late Anglo-Saxon England, it is to these books that we must turn.

1
Priests, Books, and Pastoral Care

Priests were ubiquitous figures in the medieval world. The liturgical and pastoral functions they performed necessitated their presence at every level of society. Additionally, the education they received and passed on made them useful teachers, scribes, and agents of royal and diocesan administration, and various sources show priests acting as glossators, buyers and sellers of land, and, less commonly, as thieves and fornicators.[1] Despite the wide variety of functions performed by priests, the provision of pastoral care was one of their primary functions and they served in a variety of institutions and social circumstances to fulfill this role. As this study analyzes priests' books, understanding the context in which these books were used is vital to their interpretation. When one refers to Anglo-Saxon priestly books, one refers to the possessions and "spiritalia arma" of an extremely diverse group of individuals living and working in variable contexts.[2] What follows is a brief discussion of the varied physical and social circumstances of priestly ministry to provide a context for the provision, use, and circulation of priests' books for use in pastoral care. An examination of the institutions and content of pastoral care along with a consideration of the books that were required for priestly ministry will provide an understanding of the circumstances in which pastoral care took place and in turn will inform the discussion of the expectations that governed the use of priests' books.

Settings of pastoral ministry

A well-known passage from VIII Æthelred, a royal law code promulgated in 1014, serves to adumbrate the types of churches in which late Anglo-Saxon priests were working. This passage delineates the "chief

---

[1] See chapters 2 and 3 for a discussion of priestly glossing and scribal activity. For the role of priests in land transactions and illegal activity, see Janet Fairweather, trans., *Liber Eliensis: A History of the Isle of Ely from the Seventh Century to the Twelfth* (Woodbridge: Boydell Press, 2005), 116, 129–31.

[2] Bernhard Fehr, ed., *Die Hirtenbriefe Ælfrics in altenglischer und lateinischer Fassung* (Hamburg: Henri Grand, 1914), 51.

minster", a "minster of the middle class", a smaller minster, and a field church, as well as the monetary penalties to be paid for violations of the sanctuary of each class.[3] The "chief minster" (OE *heafodmynster*) is quite clearly in reference to an episcopal or archiepiscopal seat. Until the Benedictine reform of the mid-tenth century, the clerics serving in cathedral communities were almost invariably secular, as the communities of continental cathedrals were and continued to be in the tenth and eleventh centuries. Secular cathedral communities in England however underwent significant change during these centuries, some through processes of monasticization and others through the institution of rules of life for the secular clergy, though the latter trend is only evident after 1050.[4] The communities of some cathedrals may have been similar to Julia Barrow's characterization of Worcester in the second half of the tenth century, consisting of "one or two priests and one or two deacons and then about eleven or twelve *clerici*".[5] But the number of clerics in these institutions might vary considerably: the secular cathedral community at Hereford in the 1050s almost certainly consisted of more than seven canons, as seven canons were killed resisting the destruction of the church by an Irish and Welsh army in 1055, whereas only four or five canons were serving at Wells at the beginning of Giso's episcopate.[6]

As the size of cathedral communities might vary, so might the proportion of priests to other clerics. The proportion of priests to other clerics at Worcester mentioned above is fairly low, while the smaller secular community at Lichfield in the later eleventh century seems to have been composed only of priests who corporately served in the cathedral and, according to a twelfth-century source, individually in various chapels.[7] In contrast to cathedrals with monastic communities, the secular communities of most English cathedrals seem to have been little affected by reform before the mid-eleventh century.[8] Like their

---

[3] *English Historical Documents*, ed. David C. Douglas, vol. 1, *c. 500–1042*, ed. Dorothy Whitelock (London: Eyre Methuen, 1979), 449.

[4] Julia Barrow, "English Cathedral Communities and Reform in the Tenth and Eleventh Centuries," in *Anglo-Norman Durham, 1093–1193*, ed. David Rollason, Margaret Harvey, and Michael Prestwich (Woodbridge: Boydell Press, 1998), 29–30.

[5] Barrow, "Grades of Ordination and Clerical Careers, c. 900–c. 1200," in *Anglo-Norman Studies XXX: Proceedings of the Battle Conference 2007*, ed. C. P. Lewis (Woodbridge: Boydell Press, 2008), 59.

[6] *The Chronicle of John of Worcester*, vol. 2, *The Annals from 450 to 1066*, ed. R. R. Darlington and P. McGurk, trans. Jennifer Bray and McGurk (Oxford: Clarendon Press, 1995), 576; Mary Frances Giandrea, *Episcopal Culture in Late Anglo-Saxon England* (Woodbridge: Boydell Press, 2007), 79.

[7] C. P. Lewis, "Communities, Conflict and Episcopal Policy in the Diocese of Lichfield, 1050–1150," in *Cathedrals, Communities and Conflict in the Anglo-Norman World*, ed. Paul Dalton, Charles Insley, and Louise Wilkinson (Woodbridge: Boydell Press, 2011), 67–69.

[8] Barrow, "English Cathedral Communities and Reform," 38–39.

monastic counterparts, the members of secular cathedral communities may have been involved in the administration of pastoral care in addition to the observance of mass and the Divine Office. However, the pastoral importance of the cathedral community may have been limited in some areas due to the foundation or movement of bishoprics away from major urban centers and, in those sees which were based in towns, the proliferation of urban parish churches.[9] The more well-attested cathedral communities at Winchester and Worcester, both of which were strongly influenced or dominated by monastic elements from the second half of the tenth century, certainly appear to have been deeply involved in the practice of pastoral care in their respective towns, and a similar state of affairs likely existed in other, less well-attested episcopal seats.[10]

Lower on the ecclesiastical hierarchy are *medemran mynstres*, most often referred to as "minsters" or "secular minsters" in current scholarship. These were collegiate churches that generally seem to have originated in the seventh and eighth centuries, at which time they may have contained both monks and clerics, and by the tenth century typically housed communities of secular clerics.[11] The minster priests who served in these small secular communities likely represented a large proportion of the priests serving in the late Anglo-Saxon period, though this probably fluctuated as the demand for priests in local churches increased. As in cathedrals, the communities of secular minsters varied considerably in size. Domesday's often problematic records reflect this variation, showing many churches with two priests, likely along with a number of other clerics in lower orders, but a minority of secular minsters were home to communities with thirteen or even twenty-four clerics.[12]

---

[9] Ibid., 29; John Blair, *The Church in Anglo-Saxon Society* (Oxford: Oxford University Press, 2005), 500–501. Blair suggests that small urban parishes may have "provide[d] devotional foci for small groups", such as groups of tradesmen or merchants.

[10] Michael Franklin, "The Cathedral as Parish Church: The Case of Southern England," in *Church and City, 1000–1500: Essays in Honour of Christopher Brooke*, ed. David Abulafia, Franklin, and Miri Rubin (Cambridge: Cambridge University Press, 1992), 174–75; Julia Barrow, "The Community of Worcester, 961–c. 1100," in *St Oswald of Worcester: Life and Influence*, ed. Nicholas Brooks and Catherine Cubitt (London: Leicester University Press, 1996), 96; Christopher Riedel, "Praising God Together: Monastic Reformers and Laypeople in Tenth-Century Winchester," *The Catholic Historical Review* 102, no. 2 (2016).

[11] Sarah Foot, *Monastic Life in Anglo-Saxon England, c. 600–900* (Cambridge: Cambridge University Press, 2006), 67–68, 332–33; Blair, *The Church in Anglo-Saxon Society*, 153–58. For an opposing view, see Eric Cambridge and David Rollason, "Debate: The Pastoral Organization of the Anglo-Saxon Church: A Review of the 'Minster Hypothesis'," *Early Medieval Europe* 4, no. 1 (1995).

[12] John Blair, "Secular Minster Churches in Domesday Book," in *Domesday Book:*

Priests serving in minsters also seem to have been of demonstrably higher status than secular priests outside of a clerical community. Some Anglo-Saxon legislation implies that minster priests were more likely to adhere to a rule and have a communal life, though the hereditary succession and separate housing attested in some tenth- and eleventh-century churches indicate that this standard was not universally upheld.[13] But for those priests who did adhere to a rule and remained unmarried, exculpation proceedings were to be significantly less involved than those for other priests, and the wergild for such a priest was to be equivalent to that of a thegn, indicating attempts by bishops to socially incentivize priests to remain celibate and live *regollice*.[14] Just as the adherence of minster churches and their priests to episcopal legislation was mixed, so the wealth of these common institutions and the priests who served them was similarly variable and uneven. Minsters like Waltham Holy Cross were fabulously wealthy on account of aristocratic patronage, but most minster churches probably saw little of this extravagance and relied on tithes and their more modest endowments for support.

Moving further down the hierarchy of VIII Æthelred, we find what the law code refers to as a smaller minster, which seems to be primarily in reference to estate churches. These first appear in English law in the mid-tenth-century law code II Edgar, which refers to "any thegn who has on his bookland a church with which there is a graveyard".[15] There is some ambiguity when it comes to understanding the complex local relationships that precipitated the founding of churches such as these. Small, local churches were founded through various means in the tenth and eleventh centuries, such as by the initiative of aristocratic men and women; by cathedrals, monasteries, or secular minsters; by the shared efforts of a local community; or via a combination of these groups. Despite the multiplicity of ways in which these churches were founded, manorial sites seem to have been the most common locations for the foundation of new Anglo-Saxon local churches from the tenth century and later.[16] The church at Raunds, Northamptonshire has since its excavation served as a prime example of this type of church: a small, tenth-century church with a graveyard

---

A Reassessment, ed. Peter Sawyer (London: Edward Arnold, 1985), 112–14. See pages 162–63 for evidence of large minster communities.

[13] Blair, *The Church in Anglo-Saxon Society*, 361; Leslie Watkiss and Marjorie Chibnall, eds. and trans., *The Waltham Chronicle: An Account of the Discovery of Our Holy Cross at Montacute and Its Conveyance to Waltham* (Oxford: Clarendon Press, 1994), xxiv–xxv, 67, 83.

[14] Felix Liebermann, ed., *Die Gesetze der Angelsachsen*, vol. 1, *Text und Übersetzung* (Halle: Max Niemeyer, 1903), 238.

[15] Whitelock, *English Historical Documents, c. 500–1042*, 431.

[16] See Blair, *The Church in Anglo-Saxon Society*, chapter 7.

directly abutting a manorial site. Even by the standards of medieval churches, manorial churches were often tiny: the interior space of the first church at Raunds, built in wood, totaled a mere 19 square meters (204 square feet), though the subsequent rebuilding and expansion of the structure more than doubled its size.[17] Excavations of churches like the one at Raunds have generally shown that these small structures were first built in wood and later rebuilt in stone and expanded.[18] Furthermore, documentary evidence indicates that churches such as these were probably served by priests appointed by the lay lords that had funded the churches' construction and endowment. For example, we see in the will of the Anglo-Saxon noblewoman Siflæd that she appointed Wulfmær the priest, who may well have already been the priest at her church, and his offspring to serve at her church as long as the members of his family were in holy orders.[19] In cases where a local church was controlled by a larger church, which might have been a minster, cathedral, or monastery, priests may have been assigned to a dependent chapel by the controlling institution.

Finally, the humblest in the church hierarchy was the "field church", a chapel lacking burial rights. These churches are difficult to differentiate from other small, local churches, as they are not necessarily smaller than local churches that had burial rights, and some may have acquired these rights over the lifespan of the church. Odda's Chapel, a stone church built by Odda, earl and relative of Edward the Confessor, may be a surviving example of this type of church, particularly considering its lack of associated burials, though the church's stone construction and direct aristocratic association are exceptional.[20]

As small institutions with little or no documentary evidence for their existence, smaller minsters and field churches, as well as the clergy who served them, rarely come into sharp focus. Despite the difficulty of acquiring detailed information about them, the local priests who served these churches in tenth- and eleventh-century England were integral and normative parts of rural life and the ecclesiastical landscape. This is in part demonstrated by the expectation that, at least in some regions, "every village would be able to provide a priest to serve on the Domesday jury", and the survey itself records more than 2,000 "'churches', 'priests', and 'priests with churches' – an

---

[17] See Andy Boddington, *Raunds Furnells: The Anglo-Saxon Church and Churchyard* (London: English Heritage, 1996), 25.
[18] Helen Gittos, *Liturgy, Architecture, and Sacred Places in Anglo-Saxon England* (Oxford: Oxford University Press, 2013), 180.
[19] Dorothy Whitelock, ed., *Anglo-Saxon Wills* (Cambridge: Cambridge University Press, 1930), 93. Also see Susan Wood, *The Proprietary Church in the Medieval West* (Oxford: Oxford University Press, 2006), 519–30.
[20] David Parsons, "Odda's Chapel, Deerhurst: Place of Worship or Royal Hall?" *Medieval Archaeology* 44, no. 1 (2000).

undoubtedly incomplete list even so".[21] While priests had served in cathedrals and minster churches from the early days of Anglo-Saxon Christianity, the local churches represented by the smaller minster and field church of VIII Æthelred were not widely distributed in England until the tenth century, though the prevalence of these churches varied strongly by region.[22] Additionally, there are indications that the expansion of this class of churches in some ways threatened the status of larger and often older minster communities. Royal legislation from Edgar to Cnut takes care to regulate where tithes could be paid in an attempt to protect minster churches from financial encroachment by other churches, going so far as to allow for the confiscation of the appropriate tithe if necessary.[23]

Though minsters had some legal protection against financial competition, this did not prevent local churches from significantly influencing the role of the minster in pastoral care. In some regions, minsters may have been supplanted as the primary providers of pastoral care in their formerly large *parochiae*. But the changes in the Anglo-Saxon pastoral landscape do not necessarily entail the marginalization of minsters: some parts of England in the late Anglo-Saxon period had relatively few local churches, and minsters there were likely to have still been primarily responsible for the provision of pastoral care.[24] Additionally, minster churches, like reformed monasteries, were major recipients of aristocratic patronage across England and in some cases served as important centers for the veneration of saints such as Oswald, Cuthman, and John of Beverley.[25] Furthermore, a number of major liturgical festivals, such as Ash Wednesday and Rogationtide, seem to have integrally involved the local minster, pointing to secular minsters as focal points for the more complex and theologically significant liturgy of the church year and as continuing hubs of lay partic-

---

[21] Blair, *The Church in Anglo-Saxon Society*, 369.
[22] Ibid., 417–21.
[23] Dorothy Whitelock, Martin Brett, and Christopher N. L. Brooke, eds., *Councils and Synods, With Other Documents Relating to the English Church, AD 871–1204*, vol. 1 (Oxford: Clarendon Press, 1981), 97–99, 391, 475–76.
[24] Julia Barrow, "Survival and Mutation: Ecclesiastical Institutions in the Danelaw in the Ninth and Tenth Centuries," in *Cultures in Contact: Scandinavian Settlement in England in the Ninth and Tenth Centuries*, ed. Dawn Hadley and Julian Richards (Turnhout: Brepols, 2000), 166–67; Barrow, "Wulfstan and Worcester: Bishop and Clergy in the Early Eleventh Century," in *Wulfstan, Archbishop of York: The Proceedings of the Second Alcuin Conference*, ed. Matthew Townend (Turnhout: Brepols, 2004), 146.
[25] Blair, "Secular Minster Churches in Domesday Book," 120–21. For the cult of saints and Anglo-Saxon secular minsters, see David Rollason, "Lists of Saints' Resting-Places in Anglo-Saxon England," *Anglo-Saxon England* 7 (1978): 87; John Blair, "St Cuthman, Steyning and Bosham," *Sussex Archaeological Collections* 135 (1997).

ipation.[26] Despite major institutional change in the way that pastoral care was being delivered, minster churches continued to be significant and natural parts of Anglo-Saxon religious life throughout the tenth and eleventh centuries and into the twelfth.

Additionally, it should not be assumed that these minsters and local churches were perpetually at odds and competing for resources. While many of the local churches of the late Anglo-Saxon period were founded by lay lords, others seem to have been founded cooperatively between a local minster and the lord.[27] Yet others, as noted above, were in fact dependent chapels of the minster itself and likely served by its priests. Some local churches may too have been established via the initiative of the *probi homines* of a given community which was inconveniently located relative to a mother church. As Gervase Rosser suggests, the maintenance and repair of these local churches might have been one of the motivating factors for the establishment of parish guilds.[28] Simply put, the founding of local churches was a complex process determined by local need and financial resources and therefore the relationships between minsters and local churches should not be painted as universally adversarial. More important is the effect that local churches had in diversifying and localizing the practice of pastoral care in England and accordingly expanding both the demand for priests and the reach of priestly ministry.

Though most priests would have worked directly in ecclesiastical institutions, others were employed by laymen and their households. Royal priests, the chaplains who served the king and his household, are the clearest examples of this type of service.[29] These priests were probably responsible for the performance of mass, saying of the Office, and the provision of pastoral care to those in the king's household and retinue, as they were at the Carolingian court.[30] In addition, there is some evidence that English priests of the royal household were

---

[26] See Gittos, *Liturgy, Architecture and Sacred Places*, chapter 4; Gervase Rosser, "The Cure of Souls in English Towns before 1000," in *Pastoral Care before the Parish*, ed. John Blair and Richard Sharpe (Leicester: Leicester University Press, 1992), 275–76.

[27] Blair, *The Church in Anglo-Saxon Society*, 517–18.

[28] John Blair, introduction to *Minsters and Parish Churches: The Local Church in Transition, 950–1200*, ed. Blair (Oxford: Oxford University Committee for Archaeology, 1988), 8, 11; Gervase Rosser, "The Anglo-Saxon Guilds," in *Minsters and Parish Churches*, 32.

[29] Royal priests should not be confused with priests who served in minsters and local churches controlled by the king, frequently referred to in Domesday as "king's priests", or indeed with clerics who were at court but were not part of the king's household. Julia Barrow, *The Clergy in the Medieval World: Secular Clerics, Their Families and Careers in North-Western Europe, c. 800–c. 1200* (Cambridge: Cambridge University Press, 2015), 244.

[30] Ibid., 238.

responsible for the relics of the king.[31] Royal priests might also have acted in some cases as royal scribes, producing charters, writs, and other governmental records. A number of individuals who were probably royal priests, including Oda, later archbishop of Canterbury, and Beornstan, later bishop of Winchester, witnessed early charters of Æthelstan; their involvement in these charters may also have extended to participation in their drafting and copying.[32] In the eleventh century we can witness the wealth of many Anglo-Saxon royal priests and the trend of the promotion of royal priests to the episcopate, particularly under Edward the Confessor; notable examples include Leofric at Exeter, Giso at Wells, and Ulf at Dorchester.[33] Regenbald, a royal priest in the reign of Edward the Confessor, held a great deal of land across multiple counties, managed to maintain his holdings after the Conquest, and seems to have retired from royal service to a secular minster community at Cirencester.[34]

Chaplains were also represented in non-royal aristocratic households. A chaplain (OE *hirdpreost*) would certainly have said mass for his patron and household, and may have taken on other functions such as drafting charters and educating the young members of the aristocratic family.[35] It was probably under a priest (described vaguely as a *religiosus vir*) that Oda of Canterbury received his early education in the household of a pious thegn named Æthelhelm, where he studied books as well as "the true pattern of the catholic faith and the sacraments of Holy Mother Church".[36] Aristocratic chaplains appear

---

[31] F. E. Harmer, ed., *Select English Historical Documents of the Ninth and Tenth Centuries* (Cambridge: Cambridge University Press, 1914), 35.

[32] Simon Keynes, "Royal Government and the Written Word in Late Anglo-Saxon England," in *The Uses of Literacy in Early Medieval Europe*, ed. Rosamond McKitterick (Cambridge: Cambridge University Press, 1990), 256–57; Keynes, "The West Saxon Charters of King Æthelwulf and His Sons," *English Historical Review* 109 (1994): 1131–34, 1146–47; Douglas Dales, *Dunstan: Saint and Statesman* (Cambridge: Lutterworth Press, 1988), 18.

[33] Mary Frances Smith, "The Preferment of Royal Clerks in the Reign of Edward the Confessor," *The Haskins Society Journal* 9 (1997). Though Edward's promotion of royal priests to the episcopate was a trend informed by continental practice, it mirrored practices of episcopal election in ninth- and early tenth-century Wessex. See David Pratt, *The Political Thought of King Alfred the Great* (Cambridge: Cambridge University Press, 2007), 56–58.

[34] M. F. Smith, "Regenbald (*fl.* 1050–1086)," in *Oxford Dictionary of National Biography*, Oxford University Press, 2004, accessed February 18, 2018, doi:10.1093/ref:odnb/23312.

[35] It was recorded that Earl Leofric was accustomed to "have two masses each day", likely performed by his chaplain. Peter A. Stokes, "The Vision of Leofric: Manuscript, Text and Context," *The Review of English Studies* 63 (2011): 549.

[36] Michael Lapidge, ed. and trans., *Byrhtferth of Ramsey: The Lives of St Oswald and St Ecgwine* (Oxford: Clarendon Press, 2009), 19. Priests are depicted in several other Anglo-Saxon sources as educators. See Whitelock, Brett, and Brooke, *Councils and Synods*, 318; Richard Marsden, ed., *The Old English Heptateuch*

in several Anglo-Saxon wills receiving estates, churches, weaponry, and other items from their patrons, and in narrative sources they are typically depicted serving legal and administrative functions.[37] From the evidence for both royal and non-royal households, chaplains were valuable not only as providers of pastoral care to lords and their households, but also as literate individuals who could serve educational and administrative roles.

Monks and the Anglo-Saxon secular clergy

Beyond working in institutions with only secular clerics, priests might also work within or alongside monastic or mixed communities. Though sources often portray the conduct of secular priests as antithetical to the monastic life, the availability of priests within monastic communities was just as important as at any other religious institution. However, monks in the early medieval West could and did take clerical orders and become priests, particularly from the ninth century onward, obviating the need for secular priests within a monastic community. For example, of the monks at Fulda in the earlier ninth century, more than two-thirds held major orders.[38] Furthermore, many Anglo-Saxon monks of the tenth and eleventh centuries were ordained as priests, including St Wulfstan, Ælfric, Byrhtferth, Wulfstan Cantor, as well as significant proportions of the monks serving in the Old and New Minsters at Winchester.[39] Nonetheless, there are

---

and Ælfric's Libellus de Veteri Testamento et Novo, vol. 1, *Introduction and Text*, Early English Text Society Original Series 330 (Oxford: Oxford University Press, 2008), 3–4.

[37] S 1503, 1521; Stephen Baxter, *The Earls of Mercia: Lordship and Power in Late Anglo-Saxon England* (Oxford: Oxford University Press, 2007), 202, n. 193, 244–45.

[38] Christopher Jones, "Ælfric and the Limits of 'Benedictine Reform'," in *A Companion to Ælfric*, ed. Hugh Magennis and Mary Swan (Leiden: Brill, 2009), 85; Giles Constable, "Monasteries, Rural Churches and the *Cura Animarum* in the Early Middle Ages," in *Cristianizzazione ed organizzazione ecclesiastica delle campagne nell'alto medioevo: Espansione e resistenze*, vol. 28, no. 1 of *Settimane di studio del Centro italiano di studi sull'alto medioevo* (Spoleto: Presso la sede del Centro, 1982), 361–65; Mayke de Jong, *In Samuel's Image: Child Oblation in the Early Medieval West* (Leiden: Brill, 1996), 139.

[39] Michael Winterbottom and R. M. Thomson, eds. and trans., *William of Malmesbury: Saints' Lives* (Oxford: Oxford University Press, 2002), 22; Peter Clemoes, ed., *Ælfric's Catholic Homilies: The First Series*, Early English Text Society Supplementary Series 17 (Oxford: Oxford University Press, 1997), 174; Peter Baker and Michael Lapidge, eds. and trans., *Byrhtferth's Enchiridion*, Early English Text Society Supplementary Series 15 (Oxford: Oxford University Press, 1995), 150; Michael Lapidge and Michael Winterbottom, eds. and trans., *Life of St Æthelwold* (Oxford: Clarendon Press, 1991), xiii; London, British Library, Stowe 944, ff. 18r–22r.

indications that non-monastic priests and monks might in some cases have lived together in the same community, with the priests filling the role of celebrants within the community. Certainly priests and monks lived together in early Anglo-Saxon minsters and Canterbury monks and secular priests of the ninth century were said to have corporately celebrated the Divine Office.[40] While the corporate celebration of the liturgy by monks and priests at Canterbury was the product of exceptional circumstances, and the source that depicts it is late and potentially questionable, it may still reflect a situation that was considered entirely appropriate by contemporaries. Additionally, the coexistence of monks and secular priests in ecclesiastical institutions can be witnessed even after the Benedictine reform. Though the cathedral communities of Canterbury and Worcester eventually became wholly monastic, these communities included both monks and secular clerics into the eleventh century. This trend is particularly apparent at Worcester, where a combination of secular clerics and monks comprised the *hired* or *congregatio* of Worcester Cathedral, though the two groups served in separate churches.[41]

The trend of those in the monastic life taking clerical orders and becoming priests also affected how pastoral care might be provided. As a result of the Benedictine reform of the tenth century, several cathedral communities based in major Anglo-Saxon towns were staffed with monks rather than the norm of a community of secular clerics, and monks serving in these towns would have had considerable opportunity to interact pastorally with laypeople. Recent work on monasticism and pastoral care has highlighted the interaction between monks and the laity in these urban areas: Worcester Cathedral in the time of St Wulfstan was involved in preaching, baptism, and administering penance, and at Winchester, monks and laypeople frequently intermingled at the shrine of St Swithun.[42] There is also manuscript evidence of this potential monastic concern for pastoral care, most notably in the problematic example of the Red Book of Darley (Cambridge, Corpus Christi College 422), but also in London, British Library, Cotton Tiberius A. III, which transmits texts related to Benedictine monasticism as well as vernacular homilies and material related to confession.[43] These indications of the blending of monastic

---

[40] Foot, *Monastic Life in Anglo-Saxon England*, 67–68; Jesse D. Billett, *The Divine Office in Anglo-Saxon England, 597–c. 1000* (London and Woodbridge: Henry Bradshaw Society and Boydell Press, 2014), 89–90.

[41] Barrow, "Wulfstan and Worcester," 149–50.

[42] Francesca Tinti, "Benedictine Reform and Pastoral Care in Late Anglo-Saxon England," *Early Medieval Europe* 23, no. 2 (2015): 239–41; Riedel, "Praising God Together".

[43] Tinti, "Benedictine Reform and Pastoral Care," 242–44. For a detailed consideration of Tiberius A. III, see Tracey-Anne Cooper, *Monk-Bishops and the English*

life and work with pastoral concerns further illustrate the changing environment in which late Anglo-Saxon priests – secular or monastic – were involved.

Nevertheless, there were attempts to distance and differentiate monks from the secular clergy by the later tenth century, as is evident from the writings of Byrhtferth and Ælfric. Monastic writers frequently characterized secular clerics as lazy, uneducated, and unchaste. Texts written by monks who held these contemptuous views are often the best or the only sources for the life and work of priests in the late Anglo-Saxon period. As a result, these monastic attempts to demarcate monks from the secular clergy have often colored scholarly views of the interaction between the secular and the monastic in the tenth and eleventh centuries. However, the necessity of the liturgical function of priests and the less strictly defined role of monks prior to the Benedictine reform may point to a degree of integration and flexibility in contemporary views of the roles of monks and priests.

Performance of the liturgy and wider pastoral ministry

The primary duty of the priest and the defining characteristic of priesthood was the celebration of mass. Early medieval theologians held that partaking in the bread and wine, when consecrated in the course of the mass by a priest, thus becoming the body and blood of Christ, was essential for salvation.[44] But the mass was not merely a significant event for theologians with a deep knowledge of doctrine. Rather, it acted for all as a memorial to the sacrificial death and subsequent resurrection of Christ and served to reinforce belief in the core tenets of the Christian faith. This took place not only through acts such as the recitation of the Creed, but also through the ritual and drama played out in the Eucharistic liturgy. It was only through a priest that the mass and the accompanying consecration of the Eucharist could take place, making the presence of a priest indispensable to any medieval church. In addition to its salvific necessity and centrality to Christian belief, the mass was the primary vehicle through which most medieval laypersons would have experienced pastoral care. The expectation for the laity was to attend and participate in mass on Sundays and on certain liturgical days of particular importance, though bishops were aware

---

Benedictine Reform Movement: Reading London, BL, Cotton Tiberius A. iii in Its Manuscript Context (Toronto: Pontifical Institute of Medieval Studies, 2015).

[44] Whitelock, Brett, and Brooke, Councils and Synods, 204; Celia Chazelle, "The Eucharist in Early Medieval Europe," in A Companion to the Eucharist in the Middle Ages, ed. Ian Christopher Levy, Gary Macy, and Kristen Van Ausdall (Leiden: Brill, 2012), 248–49.

of the laity's regular failure to adhere to this standard.[45] Attendance at mass was a vital expression of Christian community and, for many laypeople, it was probably the main point of contact with their local priest or with the members of a local clerical community. In certain liturgical seasons, attendance at mass might also have created opportunities for other forms of pastoral care, such as confession and the assignment of penance or the blessing and anointment of a sick individual.

Furthermore, as will be discussed in greater detail in chapter 4, the mass was the main vehicle for vernacular preaching. Preaching to the laity served two primary purposes: education in the Scriptures and moral exhortation. Surviving Anglo-Saxon homilies are rich in didactic, exhortatory content, and in most homilies, particularly the heterogeneous anonymous homilies and the sermons penned by Archbishop Wulfstan, the intention is the guidance of the hearer to moral rectitude rather than detailed exegesis of the biblical text. Additionally, as the chanting of the readings within the mass took place in Latin, vernacular preaching was not only important for exhortation and scriptural instruction, but was also necessary for providing the meaning of the reading to the majority of those listening. Many surviving Old English homilies indeed provide a brief summary of the given scriptural passage on which they are based, a practice that Ælfric encouraged priests to observe in his pastoral letter for Wulfsige.[46] In short, the mass was the primary component of pastoral care through its affirmation and dramatic retelling of the events that shaped Christian belief, its facilitation and construction of a local Christian community, and the opportunities that attendance at mass provided for other means of pastoral care, particularly vernacular preaching.

The second major liturgical duty of priests was to celebrate the Divine Office, a duty which is made clear in a variety of late Anglo-Saxon episcopal legislation.[47] Though monks sometimes denigrated the celebration of the Office by secular clerics, it is clear from both prescriptive and narrative evidence for the performance of the Office in Anglo-Saxon cathedrals and secular minsters that the observation of the Office was an important part of the duties of the secular clergy.[48] Furthermore, though the Office was first and foremost an internal

---

[45] Whitelock, Brett, and Brooke, *Councils and Synods*, 331–32. For forms of lay participation in the mass, see Josef Jungmann, *The Mass of the Roman Rite: Its Origins and Development*, trans. Francis A. Brunner (New York: Benziger, 1951), 1:233–45.
[46] Whitelock, Brett, and Brooke, *Councils and Synods*, 208.
[47] Ibid., 206, 276–77, 329.
[48] See, for example, indications of this at Waltham and Holy Trinity, Twynham in the eleventh century as well as the evidence from Oxford, Bodleian Library, Junius 27 for performance of the Office at pre-monastic Winchester, all of which is discussed in detail in chapter 5.

liturgical celebration of a religious community and not necessarily a foundational component of pastoral care, attendance by the laity at certain hours, particularly Vespers, was not unusual in the Middle Ages. Some early medieval sources from the continent even exhort laypeople to attend the Office during particularly important liturgical seasons.[49] A more detailed consideration of the Divine Office in reference to the books of the secular clergy is undertaken in chapter 5.

In addition to the regular performance of the liturgy within the church, the performance of occasional offices was a crucial part of pastoral ministry. For example, baptism was a central ritual through which membership in the Christian community was expressed, whether it was performed through the volition of an individual or, more usually in the late Anglo-Saxon period, through the initiative of one's parents and godparents. Ælfric wrote that "a child without speech is baptized through the belief of his father and mother and the godfather who speaks for the child, and pledges God that the child will keep to the Christianity of God's teaching" and furthermore asserted that "no unbaptized man may attain eternal life".[50] As such, baptism was the primary indicator of who was inside or outside the Christian community. Infants who died unbaptized were ostensibly, though not always practically, excluded from burial in consecrated ground, as were others who were considered separate from the community for grave sins, such as oath-breaking.[51] Thus baptism was singularly meaningful as a profession of faith, whether in the present or the future, and as the primary signification of belonging in a Christian community.

Anglo-Saxon priests would also have been called upon to hear confession and summarily assign penance. Homilies and episcopal legislation regularly explicate the duty of the priest in this regard and the need of the laity to confess; one version of Wulfstan's *Canons*

---

[49] *Capitula episcoporum*, pt. 1, ed. Peter Brommer, Monumenta Germaniae Historica (Hanover: Hahnsche Buchhandlung, 1984), 137; Jacques-Paul Migne, ed., *Buchardi vormatiensis episcopi opera omnia* ..., Patrologia Latina 140 (Paris: Garnier, 1880), 962. Laypeople seem to have been present at Vespers at both Waltham and Twynham in the late eleventh or early twelfth century. Watkiss and Chibnall, *The Waltham Chronicle*, 67, 69; Patrick Hase, "The Mother Churches of Hampshire," in *Minsters and Parish Churches*, 59. For an example of lay attendance in the High Middle Ages, see Augustine Thompson, *Cities of God: The Religion of the Italian Communes, 1125–1325* (University Park, PA: Pennsylvania State University Press, 2005), 243–45.

[50] Malcolm Godden, ed., *Ælfric's Catholic Homilies: The Second Series*, Early English Text Society Supplementary Series 5 (Oxford: Oxford University Press, 1979), 26; Sally Crawford, "Baptism and Infant Burial in Anglo-Saxon England," in *Medieval Life Cycles: Continuity and Change*, ed. Isabelle Cochelin and Karen Smyth (Turnhout: Brepols, 2013), 57.

[51] Crawford, "Baptism and Infant Burial," 70–72, 76; Whitelock, *English Historical Documents, c. 500–1042*, 422.

of *Edgar* requires priests to "shrive and impose penance on him who confesses to him, and also help him to make atonement".[52] It is less clear how often laypeople were expected to confess, though some sources intimate that it would have taken place at least once a year. The tenth-century *Ecclesiastical Institutes,* derived from the Carolingian episcopal statute Theodulf I, exhorts the priest to gather his congregation in the week beginning Lent and assign penance to those who confess. Ælfric similarly calls for confession by the laity in either the first week of Lent (the week of Ash Wednesday) or the following week.[53] Other events of the liturgical year with a penitential theme, such as Rogationtide, may also have served as opportunities for lay confession. Though the form of confession by the laity might have varied to some degree depending on the priest and the penitential texts he had access to, the Anglo-Saxon vernacular penitentials present a relatively static picture of the confessional process, consisting of the humble confession of sins by the penitent, an inquiry by the priest about what the individual believes and if he regrets his wrongdoing, and finally the assignment of an appropriate penance.[54] Confession on one's deathbed was also a common practice in the early medieval period, with rituals for deathbed penance appearing in Europe from at least the seventh century.[55] The practice of deathbed confession was not only encouraged by writers such as Bede, Ælfric, and Wulfstan, but episcopal legislation also prohibited priests from refusing confession and penance to anyone.[56] The Worcester monk Hemming claimed that St Wulfstan attended Godwine, brother to Leofric of Mercia, at the time of his death, anointing the nobleman with oil and ostensibly

---

[52] Whitelock, Brett, and Brooke, *Councils and Synods,* 335.
[53] Hans Sauer, ed., *Theodulfi Capitula in England: Die altenglischen Übersetzungen, zusammen mit dem lateinischen Text* (Munich: Wilhelm Fink, 1978), 376–77; Clemoes, *Ælfric's Catholic Homilies: The First Series,* 265; Walter Skeat, ed., *Ælfric's Lives of Saints,* Early English Text Society Original Series 76 and 82 (London: Oxford University Press, 1966), 282.
[54] See, for example, the instructions to the confessor in the *Old English Introduction,* ed. Allen J. Frantzen, "Corpus 190 (S) 368," in *Anglo-Saxon Penitentials: A Cultural Database,* accessed February 20, 2018, http://anglo-saxon.net/penance/?p=TOEI190_368; *Old English Handbook,* ed. Frantzen, "Corpus 201 (D) 114," in *Anglo-Saxon Penitentials,* accessed February 20, 2018, http://anglo-saxon.net/penance/index.php?p=TOEH201_114; Ibid., "Corpus 201 (D) 115," http://anglo-saxon.net/penance/index.php?p=TOEH201_115.
[55] Frederick Paxton, *Christianizing Death: The Creation of a Ritual Process in Early Medieval Europe* (Ithaca: Cornell University Press, 1990), 104–5.
[56] Ananya Jahanara Kabir, *Paradise, Death and Doomsday in Anglo-Saxon Literature* (Cambridge: Cambridge University Press, 2001), 105; Whitelock, Brett, and Brooke, *Councils and Synods,* 335–36 and 454. The *Canons of Edgar* does not explicitly invoke deathbed confession, but canon 68 includes confession at the beginning of an admonition concerned with the care for the sick and dying.

convincing him to accept penance.[57] The practice of confession and penance on the eve of death was not an isolated practice, however. Rather, confession to a priest by a sick or dying parishioner could be accompanied by unction – blessing the individual and anointing him with oil – as well as the administration of the Eucharist. As is evident from Laud Misc. 482, considered in detail in chapter 6, liturgical rites other than the administration of the Eucharist and confession could be performed in the home of the penitent, such as the sprinkling of holy water and ashes, the recitation of liturgical prayers, and even the performance of mass for up to seven days in the home. In the case of death, the priest also had a role in the preparation of the body for burial as well as the rites that would have taken place at the time of burial.[58]

In summation, the pastoral care provided by Anglo-Saxon priests consisted of regular liturgical services in which the laity participated and occasional offices which might have been provided at times of liturgical significance, such as confession at Lent, or indeed personal significance, such as baptism after the birth of a child or spiritual care for a sick or dying individual. These practices were not simply imposed on laypeople by bishops and priests, but were instead essential to the construction of the Anglo-Saxon Christian's belief and experience of faith. Additionally, we should not underestimate the value of rites such as the corporate celebration of mass and baptism as a signification and reinforcement of the bonds and bounds of membership in the Christian community. In short, the provision of pastoral care to the early medieval laity, in which the secular clergy played the most visible role, served to define the Christian community, shape the layperson's experience of belief, and, less tangibly, provide both spiritual and emotional support through the course of an individual's life.

The provision of the forms of pastoral care discussed above typically involved the use of written texts – a mass-book (either a missal or a sacramentary) was needed to perform the mass, a penitential was needed to assign appropriate penances for particular sins, and a *manuale* guided the priest through the administration of occasional offices. These collections of texts in many ways enabled pastoral ministry. Furthermore, prescriptive booklists from episcopal legislation present a picture of priests' bookholdings that aligns with the liturgical services and occasional offices discussed here.

---

[57] Francesca Tinti, *Sustaining Belief: The Church of Worcester from c.870 to c.1100* (Farnham: Ashgate, 2010), 4, n. 6.
[58] Victoria Thompson, *Dying and Death in Later Anglo-Saxon England* (Woodbridge: Boydell Press, 2004), 77, 81–82.

The vocabulary of books and book storage

Before analyzing prescriptive lists of books for priests, it is useful to discuss in brief the Old English and Latin vocabulary related to books and their storage, which will serve to illustrate the potential range of meaning for terms commonly used to describe priestly books. The Old English word for "book" is *boc*, a word that enjoyed a significantly wider range of meaning in Old English than its Modern English descendant. The semantic range of the term *boc* is illustrated by its use not only in reference to codices, but also to legal documents such as charters. David Porter rightly points out that the Latin *liber* is essentially synonymous with *boc* and that the semantic range of both terms could encompass a single sheet, a quire, or a codex. Considering the wide range of meaning for *boc*, it too may have been used to refer to booklets, a number of which have been identified in Anglo-Saxon manuscripts.[59] In common with words from most Germanic languages, *boc* could also be used to form compound words denoting the use of a book, such as the liturgical *mæsseboc* or *pistolboc*, or could indicate ownership, as with the onomastically derived "Oddan boc" of an Anglo-Saxon booklist.[60] Like *boc*, *liber* could also refer to a document, a charter, or indeed any written work or "subdivision of written text".[61] Other Latin vocabulary related to books is similarly broad. The Latin *libellus*, which originally referred to the inner bark of a tree used for writing, might too have had a significant range of meanings. While not as broad as *boc* or *liber*, a *libellus* could refer to a short theological treatise or homiletic booklet. The term could also be used for any relatively small book, as it was around the turn of the eleventh century in reference to Warsaw, Biblioteka Narodowa, I. 3311, a small-format gospel lectionary of more than 100 folios. Medieval writers also used

---

[59] Pamela R. Robinson, "Self-Contained Units in Composite Manuscripts of the Anglo-Saxon Period," *Anglo-Saxon England* 7 (1978); Phillip Pulsiano, "Jaunts, Jottings, and Jetsam in Anglo-Saxon Manuscripts," *Florilegium* 19 (2002); Jonathan Wilcox, "The Use of Ælfric's Homilies: MSS Oxford, Bodleian Library, Junius 85 and 86 in the Field," in *A Companion to Ælfric*, ed. Hugh Magennis and Mary Swan (Leiden: Brill, 2009).

[60] Jane Roberts and Christian Kay, with Lynne Grundy, *A Thesaurus of Old English in Two Volumes*, vol 1, *Introduction and Thesaurus* (London: King's College London, Centre for Late Antique and Medieval Studies, 1995), 694–95; Michael Lapidge, "Surviving Booklists from Anglo-Saxon England," in *Learning and Literature in Anglo-Saxon England: Studies Presented to Peter Clemoes on the Occasion of His Sixty-Fifth Birthday*, ed. Michael Lapidge and Helmut Gneuss (Cambridge: Cambridge University Press, 1985), 63.

[61] *Dictionary of Medieval Latin from British Sources*, s.v. "līber"; Scott Gwara, ed., *Anglo-Saxon Conversations: The Colloquies of Ælfric Bata*, trans. David Porter (Woodbridge: Boydell Press, 1997), 54.

the term *libellus* to refer to a short or small document, such as a charter or episcopal profession.[62]

As opposed to the wide range of meaning evident for the terms commonly used to refer to books, the vocabulary of book storage is more limited and its range of meaning is relatively narrow. Few Anglo-Saxon libraries had the bibliographical resources to require a great deal of book storage, and it seems that the bookholdings of churches and monasteries, and probably individuals as well, were kept in chests. Diverse sources in both Latin and Old English from the beginning of the Anglo-Saxon period to the eleventh century record the use of these chests, referred to as *armaria* (or *arca libraria* in the case of Aldhelm) in Latin and in Old English as *boccest*. *Bibliotheca* also came into Old English as a Latin loanword and was sometimes used to mean a library or collection of books, but more commonly referred to the books of the Bible.[63] A further word from Anglo-Saxon England used to describe the storage of books is the Latin *scrinium*, simply meaning a chest or a box for books, which was used in the *Enucleatio libelli* to refer to the chest in which the community of Worcester kept important documents.[64] Another term for book storage that may have special relevance to priests and bishops who made rounds of their respective areas of authority is the Anglo-Latin term *scetha*, which was used in an eighth-century riddle to refer to a pouch or case for a single volume or a few volumes, possibly in reference to a satchel, intended to keep books clean and undamaged while traveling.[65] It has been suggested that some Anglo-Saxon stone carvings depict such a satchel and one early medieval example of this type of object has been found in excavations at Loch Glashan in Scotland.[66] The wide range of meaning in the terms for books and the relatively narrow vocabulary

---

[62] The text of f. 1v of this manuscript, a gospel lectionary written around 1000, reads, "In christi nomine incipit pars sanctorum evangeliorum qvedam hoc in libello causa necessitatis descripta". For more on this manuscript, see chapter 5. *Dictionary of Medieval Latin from British Sources*, s.v. "libellus".

[63] Michael Lapidge, *The Anglo-Saxon Library* (Oxford: Oxford University Press, 2005), 61–62; David Ganz, "Anglo-Saxon England," in *The Cambridge History of Libraries in Britain and Ireland Volume 1: To 1640*, ed. Elisabeth Leedham-Green and Teresa Webber (Cambridge: Cambridge University Press, 2006), 91–92.

[64] Stokes, "The Vision of Leofric," 542; Tinti, *Sustaining Belief*, 125. The term *scrinium* can also refer to a reliquary.

[65] Ganz, "Anglo-Saxon England," 92. Sharpe has discussed the etymology of the word *scetha* with special attention to its use in medieval Irish texts and a brief discussion of its use in England. See Sharpe, "Latin and Irish Words for 'Book-Satchel'," *Peritia* 4 (1985).

[66] James Lang, *York and Eastern Yorkshire*, vol. 3 of *Corpus of Anglo-Saxon Stone Sculpture*, ed. Rosemary Cramp (Oxford: Published for the British Academy by Oxford University Press, 1991), 88–89, illustration 254; Ibid., 189–93, illustrations 710 and 728; Ibid., 215–17, illustration 833; Bernard Meehan, "Book Satchels in Medieval Scotland and Ireland," in *A Crannog of the First Millennium*

for book storage may help us to think about the physical aspects of priestly books and their use within early medieval churches.

The priest's toolkit: episcopal expectations of priestly books

It is frequently observed that the texts produced by the Carolingian reformers of the ninth century had a profound intellectual influence on Anglo-Saxon churchmen of the following two centuries. The observation is well founded, and one readily apparent but infrequently explored aspect of this relationship is the connection between the expectations of priests' books in late Anglo-Saxon and Carolingian sources. The episcopal statutes of ninth-century Francia are an early witness to attempts by bishops to regulate the lives of the clergy under their control and one facet of this attempt was the regulation of basic priestly texts. Regino of Prüm, Riculf of Soissons, and others penned prescriptive lists of this kind, but only a few seem to have gained currency in Anglo-Saxon England.[67] The first episcopal statute of Theodulf of Orléans was certainly the most influential of these in late Anglo-Saxon England, but it provides no explicit list of books for priests to own. Conversely, the episcopal statutes of Haito of Basel and Radulf of Bourges as well as the *Rule of Chrodegang* in its various interpolations were all known in England at least by the time of the Benedictine reform and all provide lists of basic texts for priests. With the influence of sources such as these, late Anglo-Saxon episcopal legislation also provides lists of books that priests were to own. Sometime between 992 and 1002, Ælfric, then a monk and priest at Cerne Abbey, wrote a pastoral letter in Old English for the clergy of the diocese of Sherborne at the request of Bishop Wulfsige III. In 1005, Ælfric produced two additional pastoral letters in Latin, which he later loosely translated into Old English for Archbishop Wulfstan of York. These letters give an account of church history, instruct priests on their role and responsibilities within the church, and are an important source for contemporary expectations for Anglo-Saxon priests. Along with this material, Ælfric's pastoral letters provide lists of the books that a mass-priest should own. These lists of books vary slightly and the Old English letter for Wulfsige is slightly fuller:

AD: Excavations by Jack Scott at Loch Glashan, Argyll, 1960, by Anne Crone and Ewan Campbell (Edinburgh: Society of Antiquaries of Scotland, 2005).

[67] Wilfried Hartmann, ed. and trans., *Das Sendhandbuch des Regino von Prüm* (Darmstadt: Wissenschaftliche Buchgesellschaft, 2004), 26; *Capitula episcoporum*, pt. 2, ed. Rudolf Pokorny and Martina Stratmann, *Monumenta Germaniae Historica* (Hanover: Hahnsche Buchhandlung, 1995), 103.

He sceal habban eac þa wæpna to þam gastlicum weorce, ær þan þe he beo gehadod þæt synd þa halgan bec: saltere 7 pistolboc, godspellboc 7 mæsseboc, sangboc 7 handboc, gerim 7 passionalem, penitentialem 7 rædingboc. Þas bec sceal mæssepreost nede habban, 7 he ne mæg butan beon, gif he his had on riht healdan wyle 7 þam folce æfter rihte wisigan, þe him to locað. 7 beo he æt þam wær þæt hi beon wel gerihte.

(He shall have also the weapons for that spiritual work, before he is ordained, namely, the holy books: a psalter and a book with the epistles, an evangeliary and a missal, songbooks and a manual, a computus and a passional, a penitential and a reading-book. These books the priest must needs have and he cannot be without them, if he wishes to observe his order rightly and to direct correctly the people who belong to him. And he is to be careful that they are well corrected.)[68]

This list and the list for Wulfstan have been variously discussed by Bernhard Fehr and Milton Gatch, and more recently by Helmut Gneuss, Christopher Jones, and Joyce Hill.[69] In his edition of Ælfric's pastoral letters, Fehr argues that the origin of the Wulfsige list is to be found in the *Penitential of Egbert* on the grounds of some essentially identical phrases and similarities in the booklists themselves. Jones, while largely accepting Fehr's attribution, has convincingly posited a connection between the *Capitula* of Radulf of Bourges and Ælfric's booklists; Gneuss too has lent tacit support to this position.[70] Table 1 compares these with other influential lists and the late Anglo-Saxon lists found in Ælfric's pastoral letters.

---

[68] Whitelock, Brett, and Brooke, *Councils and Synods*, 206–7. The letter for Wulfstan reads similarly, but diverges slightly in wording and content. "Ge sceolan beon gebocade, swa swa eower hade gebyrað. Mæssepreost sceal habban mæsseboc 7 pistelboc 7 sangboc 7 rædingboc 7 saltere 7 handboc 7 penitentialem 7 gerim; 7 þa beon wel gewrihte" (You must be equipped with books as befits your order. A mass-priest must have a missal and a book of the epistles and a hymn-book and a reading-book and a psalter and a manual and a penitential and a computus; and they are to be well-corrected). Ibid., 291–92.
[69] Fehr, *Die Hirtenbriefe Ælfrics*, lxxxvi–xcii; Milton Gatch, *Preaching and Theology in Anglo-Saxon England: Ælfric and Wulfstan* (Toronto: University of Toronto Press, 1977); Helmut Gneuss, "Liturgical Books in Anglo-Saxon England and Their Old English Terminology," in *Learning and Literature in Anglo-Saxon England*; Christopher Jones, "Ælfric's Pastoral Letters and the Episcopal *Capitula* of Radulf of Bourges," *Notes and Queries* 42, no. 2 (1995); Joyce Hill, "Monastic Reform and the Secular Church: Ælfric's Pastoral Letters in Context," in *England in the Eleventh Century: Proceedings of the 1990 Harlaxton Symposium*, ed. Carola Hicks (Stamford, UK: Paul Watkins, 1992).
[70] Jones, "Ælfric's Pastoral Letters," 149–54; Gneuss, "Liturgical Books," 95.

Table 1. A comparison of Anglo-Saxon and Carolingian lists of texts for priests

	Ælfric's OE Letter for Wulfsige	Ælfric's Latin Letter for Wulfstan	Ælfric's OE Letter for Wulfstan	OE Enlarged Rule of Chrodegang[a]	Haito's Capitula	Penitential of Egbert	Radulf's Capitula ecclesiastica[b] (expanded)
Compotus / Gerim							
Missale / sacramentarium / mæsseboc							
Penitentialem / dædbote tæcan							
Psalterium / Saltere							
Lectionarium / evangelium / godspel an rædan							
Rædingboc / uhtan rædan							
Antiphonarium							
Baptisterium / fulluhtian							
Manualem / handboc							
Martirlogium							
Passionalem							
Pistolboc							
Sangbec / Sangboc							

Epistolas / Pistel					
Gradalem					
Godspellboc					
Homiliae					
Liber cum lectionibus ad nocturnas					
Nocturnalem					

[a] Brigitte Langefeld, ed. and trans., *The Old English Version of the Enlarged Rule of Chrodegang* (Frankfurt: Peter Lang, 2003), 317.

[b] The original list from Radulf's *Capitula* contains only three specific items, namely a psalter, a missal, and a lectionary, as well as "aliquos libellos sibi necessarios bene correctos". The items listed here come from an expanded version of the list found in Cambridge, Corpus Christi College 265, a manuscript associated with Archbishop Wulfstan. This manuscript also contains Ælfric's pastoral letters. Jones, "Ælfric's Pastoral Letters," 151–52.

Terminology for liturgical books

Before making a determination concerning the books that Anglo-Saxon priests were generally expected to own, it is helpful to consider the precise meaning of the terms used to refer to specific types of priestly books in these lists. The sometimes difficult nature of terminology for liturgical books and the evolution of this terminology over time makes direct comparison between some of these lists difficult at first glance, but a careful and contextualized reading aids in making sense of these lists, as does the correspondence of Latin and Old English terms in the pastoral letters of Ælfric.

Ælfric's second Latin letter for Wulfstan lists *nocturnalem* and *gradalem* in place of the Old English *sangbec*, indicating this Old English term is referring not to hymnals, but to books containing the sung portions of the mass and Office.[71] These books correspond to what the earlier lists (Haito, Radulf, and the *Penitential of Egbert*) refer to as antiphoners, as the use of the Latin *antiphonarius* in Old English generally denoted a gradual, while Ælfric's term *nocturnale* has been thought to refer to an antiphoner for the Night Office.[72] Ælfric's "lectionarium quod quidam vocant epistolarium" corresponds in sequence to the *pistolboc* of Ælfric's Old English letters. Ursula Lenker has argued that the term *pistolboc* refers to a "full lectionary", a volume containing both the first and second readings for mass, rather than simply an epistolary. This line of argument is supported by the *Monasterialia indicia*, which refers to the purpose of the *pistolboc* in an indirect way, noting that "one reads the gospel in there and likewise in the gospelbooks", indicating that this term does not refer to a book that only contains the epistle readings.[73] Similarly, the equivalent of the "librum cum lectionibus ad nocturnas" in the Old English lists appears to be the *rædingboc*, found in both the vernacular pastoral letters listed above.

---

[71] Whitelock, Brett, and Brooke, *Councils and Synods*, 207, n. 3; Jesse Billett, "The Divine Office and the Secular Clergy in Later Anglo-Saxon England," in *England and the Continent in the Tenth Century: Studies in Honour of Wilhelm Levison (1876–1947)*, ed. David Rollason, Conrad Leyser, and Hannah Williams (Turnhout: Brepols, 2010), 433; Gneuss, "Liturgical Books," 103. The reading *sangbec* appears in two of the three manuscripts containing the letter for Wulfsige (Whitelock's Gg and X) and one of three manuscripts containing, in varying versions, the second Old English letter for Wulfstan. Intriguingly, this is the version apparently edited by Archbishop Wulfstan (Whitelock's D).

[72] Gneuss, "Liturgical Books," 103–4, 117. It should be noted however that the term antiphoner can refer to a book that only contains mass chants or a book containing chants for both the mass and Office. See Billett, *The Divine Office in Anglo-Saxon England*, 100–101, n. 80.

[73] Ursula Lenker, "The West Saxon Gospels and the Gospel-Lectionary in Anglo-Saxon England: Manuscript Evidence and Liturgical Practice," *Anglo-Saxon England* 28 (1999): 158–59. Gneuss suggested this prior to Lenker, but with little certainty; see Gneuss, "Liturgical Books," 110.

Though the term *rædingboc* is vague, it is most likely that Ælfric had in mind a volume containing homilies or biblical lections for the secular Night Office.[74] However, not all of the books from Ælfric's lists can be matched. The second Latin letter for Wulfstan and the Old English letter for Wulfsige both include a *passionalem*, which does not appear in the relevant Old English letter for Wulfstan. This term almost certainly refers to a book containing the stories of Christian saints and martyrs that could be used to read out a saint's *vita* on a given feast day.[75] The Wulfsige letter also includes a *godspellboc*, which is not attested in any of the letters for Wulfstan. It seems most likely here that the term simply means a gospelbook rather than a homiliary.[76]

More correspondence between the earlier lists and the lists from the pastoral letters is apparent in closely examining the *baptisterium* of Egbert and Haito's lists and the equivalent *fulluhtian* from the Old English translation of the *Enlarged Rule of Chrodegang*. Though we are unsure of the exact contents of these books, their names reveal that they contained rituals for at least one of the occasional offices – baptism – and may have contained all the rites for the occasional offices. Whether they contained *ordines* for baptism alone or for multiple occasional offices, the *baptisterium* of the early lists can in either case be placed broadly within the category of a manual. Furthermore, while the passional of two of the Ælfrician lists and the martyrology listed by the *Penitential of Egbert* and Radulf's expanded *Capitula* are not necessarily synonymous, both types of books served a similar function as both could be employed for reading in the Office on an appropriate day or possibly as edifying material to be read at the common table of a clerical community.[77]

---

[74] Gneuss, "Liturgical Books," 121; Billett, "The Divine Office and the Secular Clergy," 433.

[75] A passional may also refer to a short volume with the liturgical texts needed for the celebration of the mass and Office during Holy Week, but this use of the term passional does not seem to have been in use in England in the tenth and eleventh centuries; see Jane Hardie, "Salamanca to Sydney: A Newly Discovered Manuscript of the *Lamentations of Jeremiah*," in *Music in Medieval Europe: Studies in Honour of Bryan Gillingham*, ed. Terence Bailey and Alma Santosuosso (Aldershot: Ashgate, 2007), 14.

[76] Gneuss, "Liturgical Books," 108.

[77] Richard Gameson, "St Wulfstan, the Library of Worcester and the Spirituality of the Medieval Book," in *St Wulfstan and His World*, ed. Barrow and Brooks (Aldershot: Ashgate, 2005), 88. A passional or martyrology might have been one of the "edifying books" that was read at the common table of the minster at Hawkesbury where St Wulfstan served prior to his tenure as bishop of Worcester. For the liturgical use of these books, see Thomas J. Heffernan, "The Liturgy and the Literature of Saints' Lives," in *The Liturgy of the Medieval Church*, ed. Heffernan and E. Ann Matter (Kalamazoo: Published for the Consortium for the Teaching of the Middle Ages, by Medieval Institute Publications, Western Michigan University, 2005).

When linguistic differences between Latin and Old English are accounted for, as well as chronological differences in terminology for liturgical books, the lists given in Table 1 present a fairly static core of priestly texts. This includes a mass-book, a lectionary, a psalter, a minimal number of books for the Office, a book of occasional offices, a penitential, and a computus. Possession of or access to these books was designed to equip priests to carry out their pastoral duties, namely to say mass, celebrate the Office, perform occasional offices, impose penance, and calculate the date of Easter. The content of these prescriptive booklists also has relevance to the availability of pastoral texts and the liturgical competence of Anglo-Saxon priests. The pastoral letters themselves take for granted the familiarity of the reader with what appear to be fairly inferential references to certain books or groups of books, such as *sangbec*, which have been interpreted here as specific books for the sung portions of the mass and Office in light of the Latin version of Ælfric's letter to Wulfsige. Hill has written that Ælfric's pastoral letters "assume that priests ... have access to liturgical texts and an ability to identify and employ readings, antiphons and the like, which are often referred to in familiar and thus rather cryptic ways"; these assumptions apparently applied to both priests in minster communities and local, single-priest churches.[78] In the Old English text Whitelock termed *On the Examination of Candidates for Ordination*, found only in Oxford, Bodleian Library, Junius 121, an eleventh-century manuscript containing a great deal of material related to Archbishop Wulfstan, we find no mention of books. However, certain portions of the text instruct the examiner to direct his inquiries to subjects which strongly imply access to books, such as a potential candidate's knowledge of the symbolic meaning of baptism and mass as well as his familiarity with computus and canon law. Interestingly, both Theodulf I and the *Interrogationes examinationis*, the first certainly a source for Wulfstan and the other suggested by Whitelock as a possible source for *On the Examination of Candidates for Ordination*, are similar in that they assume knowledge of certain texts without mentioning them explicitly.[79] The D version of the *Canons of Edgar* provides slightly more specificity in requiring that priests "to ælcon synoðe habban ælce geare becc and reaf to godcundre þenunge" in addition to ink, parchment, and food, but still lacks a clear description of the books to be brought to the synod.[80]

---

[78] Hill, "Monastic Reform and the Secular Church," 109.
[79] Whitelock, Brett, and Brooke, *Councils and Synods*, 422–26; Carine van Rhijn, *Shepherds of the Lord: Priests and Episcopal Statutes in the Carolingian Period* (Turnhout: Brepols, 2007), 108.
[80] Roger Fowler, ed., *Wulfstan's Canons of Edgar* (London: Oxford University Press, 1972), 2. "At each synod every year they are to have books and vestments

The relatively high level of knowledge assumed in Ælfric's letters and other sources is balanced by a certain degree of condescension and outlining of fairly basic priestly duties. Nonetheless, the group of texts prescribed for priests, the expected standards of liturgical observance, and inferential references to liturgical material set a relatively high benchmark for priestly performance of the mass and the Office and access to the books needed to perform these services. This is certainly not proof that Anglo-Saxon priests owned or had access to every book in Ælfric's lists. However, the fact that Ælfric and assumedly his episcopal backers presumed their audience's familiarity with a range of ambiguous references to liturgical books and competence in relatively complex liturgical practices – even in a letter largely aimed at priests whose knowledge of Latin was said to be deficient – may be some indication of the ability of priests to actually fulfill these expectations.[81]

As providers of pastoral care and as literate figures, priests were present at every level of Anglo-Saxon society. In cathedrals and secular minsters, priests formed a vital part of the clerical community, were essential to daily liturgical celebrations, and, depending on the church in which they served, were involved in providing pastoral care to the laity. Priests were as great a necessity in the local church as they were in cathedrals: the liturgical forms of these institutions were unquestionably divergent, but the indispensable nature of the priestly office to liturgical celebrations necessitated their presence at every church. As local churches numbered in the thousands by the end of the eleventh century, this trend must have precipitated an increase in the number of priests who were ordained. There are no documents from the late Anglo-Saxon period recording the number of ordinands in any given diocese, so this hypothesis is a difficult one to prove. However, the spate of church-building must have increased demand for priests and it is unlikely that a large proportion of cathedral or minster clergy would have left institutions with comfortable endowments to serve

---

for the divine service," translated by Whitelock, Brett, and Brooke, *Councils and Synods*, 316.

[81] Further evidence for high expectations of the ability of priests to both perform the liturgy and have access to books comes from Cambridge, Corpus Christi College 265, one of the surviving Wulfstanian "handbooks" and the only surviving Anglo-Saxon manuscript to contain Radulf's *Capitula*. The minimal list of three books necessary for priests to own, specifying only a missal, psalter, and lectionary, is the reading found in every manuscript of Radulf's *Capitula* other than Corpus 265. The list more than doubles in size in the Corpus manuscript, adding an antiphoner, a martyrology, a computus, and a penitential to the original list. Similarly, Allen Frantzen seems to suggest that the booklist in the *Penitential of Egbert* was a later addition as it "does not suggest the English church of Egbert's time", though the addition may be continental in origin. Jones, "Ælfric's Pastoral Letters," 151–52; Frantzen, *The Literature of Penance in Anglo-Saxon England* (New Brunswick, NJ: Rutgers University Press, 1983), 74.

one-celled or two-celled churches, which were no doubt challenging and unglamorous environments for pastoral ministry. We can also see significant priestly involvement outside the church, often recorded in noble and royal households, where priests served religious, administrative, and educational functions.

Furthermore, the pastoral landscape in England in the tenth and eleventh centuries was diverse and dynamic, consisting of various classes of churches ministering to laypeople through liturgical services and the performance of occasional offices that were central to the lives of medieval Christians. As minster churches continued to be important parts of this landscape, the number of local churches increased exponentially, precipitating the legal involvement of the state in order to protect the rights of minsters in light of the threat the growing number of small churches posed to the traditional rights and income of minsters. This move toward local churches diversified and localized the way in which pastoral care was provided, practically improving the accessibility of pastoral care and over time devolving much of the responsibility for pastoral care from minsters and clerical communities to local churches and individual priests. Through the course of the late Anglo-Saxon period, this change must have had a significant effect on the relationship between the laity and the church and on the position of a large proportion of Anglo-Saxon priests.

Finally, the importation of Carolingian episcopal statutes into England helped set standards for the lives and work of the clergy, including basic collections of priestly texts. These Carolingian *capitula* were adapted, synthesized, and, in at least one case, expanded by their tenth- and eleventh-century Anglo-Saxon readers to meet the liturgical and pastoral demands placed upon priests of their time.[82] These new expectations probably developed as demands on and for priests increased in the tenth and eleventh centuries and as greater numbers of priests engaged in ministry apart from clerical communities.[83] Greater numbers of local churches required priests to perform the mass with limited assistance and the burgeoning local church likewise prompted figures such as Archbishop Wulfstan and Bishop Wulfsige III, who were concerned for the liturgical and moral integrity of the secular clergy, to use the intellectual resources available to them to make clear episcopal expectations of priests for both behavior and liturgy.

---

[82] See note 81.
[83] Cyrille Vogel, *Medieval Liturgy: An Introduction to the Sources*, ed. and trans. William George Storey and Niels Rasmussen (Washington, DC: Pastoral Press, 1986), 105.

2

"Ne cunnon þæt leden understandan": Issues of Clerical Literacy[1]

Faciendi plures libros nullus est finis;
frequensque meditatio, carnis afflictio est.
– Ecclesiastes 12:12b

In 1222, the dean of Salisbury Cathedral visited and examined six priests who were serving in churches controlled by the dean and chapter. One priest was exempt from the examination as the examiners seem to have had prior knowledge or testimony of his ability, but the other five were asked about their ordination and tested on their liturgical and linguistic abilities. One of the examined priests was Simon, the chaplain serving at the village of Sonning, who had been ordained by Hugh, Bishop of Lincoln four years previously. When tested, he was able to read the passage from the gospel for the first Sunday in Advent, but was unable to understand what he had read. When tested on the text of the mass, he was familiar with it, but was unable to parse "Te igitur, clementissime Pater". When pressed by the examiners to give an answer as to which word governs "Te", he replied that "Pater" does, because the Father governs everything.[2]

Though the events told in this historical anecdote took place a century and a half after the Norman Conquest, the concerns of ecclesiastical authorities in regard to the abilities of the parochial clergy changed little in the intervening period. Several monastic writers of the tenth and eleventh centuries, such as Ælfric and Byrhtferth of Ramsey, appear pessimistic about the ability of the secular clergy to use Latin. But if priests were to fulfill duties as basic as celebrating

---

[1] "Cannot understand the Latin". This quotation is taken from Ælfric's first Old English pastoral letter for Archbishop Wulfstan. Dorothy Whitelock, Martin Brett, and Christopher N. L. Brooke, eds., *Councils and Synods, with Other Documents Relating to the English Church, AD 871–1204*, vol. 1 (Oxford: Clarendon Press, 1981), 261.

[2] W. H. Rich Jones, ed., *Vetus registrum Sarisberiense alias dictum registrum S. Osmundi Episcopi: The Register of S. Osmund*, vol. 1, Rerum Britannicarum medii aevi scriptores (Rolls Series) 78 (Millwood, NY: Kraus Reprint, 1965), 304–5; William Dohar, "*Sufficienter litteratus*: Clerical Examination and Instruction for the Cure of Souls," in *A Distinct Voice: Medieval Studies in Honor of Leonard E. Boyle, O.P.*, ed. Jacqueline Brown and William Stoneman (Notre Dame: University of Notre Dame Press, 1997), 312.

mass and baptizing children, this required the use and performance of texts in Latin. There is a clear tension between characterizations of priests' literacy (or lack thereof) and the pastoral responsibilities they were to carry out on a regular basis. Understanding this tension and moving towards a clearer view of late Anglo-Saxon clerical literacy requires a concise look at scholarly thought on literacy and the issues surrounding it and, most crucially, the contemporary evidence.

Issues of priestly literacy

The literacy of medieval priests has often been questioned and disparaged, with many twentieth-century scholars accepting a view of priests as "barely literate, barely celibate, barely sober bumpkins", largely resulting from uncritical acceptance of monastic barbs aimed at the secular clergy.[3] Attempts have been made to contextualize these monastic statements, prompting some scholars to re-evaluate their views of the medieval priesthood, but as Matthew Wranovix has noted, the rehabilitation of the intellectual abilities of even the later medieval priest has been met with mixed success.[4] However, a large proportion of the literature has made conflicting assumptions regarding the literacy of priests. Many scholars have assumed clerical illiteracy or literacy of only the most rudimentary sort, while simultaneously accepting that secular clerics were capable of performing complex liturgical texts and responsible to some degree for the interpretation of religious texts.[5] As a result of these assumptions and the generally poor survival of priests' books in the Anglo-Saxon period, studies of lay and monastic literacy have dominated, further skewing scholarly perceptions of the literacy and literate skills of the secular clergy.[6]

---

[3] John Shinners and William Dohar, eds., *Pastors and the Care of Souls in Medieval England* (Notre Dame: University of Notre Dame Press, 1998), xiii.

[4] Matthew Wranovix, "Ulrich Pfeffel's Library: Parish Priests, Preachers, and Books in the Fifteenth Century," *Speculum* 87, no. 4 (2012): 1125–26.

[5] Christopher Hohler, "Some Service Books of the Later Saxon Church," in *Tenth-Century Studies: Essays in Commemoration of the Millennium of the Council of Winchester* and *Regularis Concordia*, ed. David Parsons (London: Phillimore, 1975), 74; Roy Liuzza, "Who Read the Gospels in Old English?," in *Words and Works: Studies in Medieval English Language and Literature in Honour of Fred C. Robinson*, ed. Peter S. Baker and Nicholas Howe (Toronto: University of Toronto Press, 1998), 6–7.

[6] For studies of literacy in Anglo-Saxon England, see George Brown, "The Dynamics of Literacy in Anglo-Saxon England," in *Textual and Material Culture in Anglo-Saxon England: Thomas Northcote Toller and the Toller Memorial Lectures*, ed. Donald Scragg (Cambridge: D. S. Brewer, 2003); Kathryn Lowe, "Lay Literacy in Anglo-Saxon England and the Development of the Chirograph," in *Anglo-Saxon Manuscripts and Their Heritage*, ed. Phillip Pulsiano and Elaine Treharne (Aldershot: Ashgate, 1998); Susan Kelly, "Anglo-Saxon Lay Society

Issues of Clerical Literacy

Specifically addressing clerical literacy in an Anglo-Saxon context is important for several reasons. Firstly, priests needed to be literate in Latin to fulfill their liturgical and pastoral role. The importance of Latin literacy should not be understood as a marginalization of the vernacular, the unique importance of which to the literate culture of England has been increasingly recognized. However, while some early medieval English liturgy contained rubrics and notations in Old English, liturgical books and services were predominately in Latin.[7] Additionally, early medieval mandates calling for the ownership of certain books by priests, discussed in the previous chapter, presupposed that priests were able to read and perform the content of certain texts, particularly liturgical texts in Latin. Secondly, secular priests must have been by far the largest literate group in late Anglo-Saxon England. As mentioned previously, Olga Timofeeva has estimated the number of secular priests in England in 1066 to be slightly over 4,000 based on Domesday records and extrapolation from these records for regions in which the recorded number of priests and churches is known to be low. This estimate can be contrasted with the fewer than 1,000 monks thought to be in England in the same period.[8] I suspect that Timofeeva's numbers may be slightly low, particularly in reference to the number of those in clerical orders below the office of priest, but they presumably at minimum give a sense of the relative size of the English priesthood. The size of this group suggests that there were established means of education and training for secular clerics and further that in such a large group, individual priests would have spanned a wide range of linguistic proficiency, particularly in Latin. Finally, much has been made of monastic indictments of the literacy

---

and the Written Word," in *The Uses of Literacy in Early Medieval Europe*, ed. Rosamond McKitterick (Cambridge: Cambridge University Press, 1990); Patrick Wormald, "The Uses of Literacy in Anglo-Saxon England and Its Neighbours," *Transactions of the Royal Historical Society*, 5th ser., 27 (1977); M. Godden, "Literacy in Anglo-Saxon England," in *The Cambridge History of the Book in Britain Volume 1: c.400–1100*, ed. Richard Gameson (Cambridge: Cambridge University Press, 2011); Katherine O'Brien O'Keeffe, *Visible Song: Transitional Literacy in Old English Verse* (Cambridge: Cambridge University Press, 1990).

[7] For Old English in liturgical books, see Helen Gittos, "Is There Any Evidence for the Liturgy of Parish Churches in Late Anglo-Saxon England? The Red Book of Darley and the Status of Old English," in *Pastoral Care in Late Anglo-Saxon England*, ed. Francesca Tinti (Woodbridge: Boydell Press, 2005); David Dumville, *Liturgy and the Ecclesiastical History of Late Anglo-Saxon England: Four Studies* (Woodbridge: Boydell Press, 1992), 127–32.

[8] Olga Timofeeva, "Anglo-Latin Bilingualism before 1066: Prospects and Limitations," in *Interfaces between Language and Culture in Medieval England: A Festschrift for Matti Kilpiö*, ed. Alaric Hall et al. (Leiden: Brill, 2010), 14; Giles Constable, "Religious Communities, 1024–1215," in *The New Cambridge Medieval History Volume 4: c.1024–c.1198*, ed. David Luscombe and Jonathan Riley-Smith (Cambridge: Cambridge University Press, 2004), 1:335.

of clerics, but little effort has been made to marshal the evidence that would allow an analysis of priestly literacy. This evidence is scattered across a variety of sources, but assembling the available evidence for analysis will present a more detailed picture of the education and literate skills of Anglo-Saxon secular priests.

The definition of literacy has been widely disputed among scholars, but the current and intuitive definition is that literacy, at its core, consists of the ability to read and write.[9] This becomes somewhat problematic when assessing literacy in different periods, however, as many individuals throughout the medieval period who were wholly capable of reading complex texts did little in the way of writing.[10] Much early literature pertaining to the Middle Ages has understood literacy simply as the ability to use Latin, but recent scholarship has rightly found this understanding increasingly untenable, especially for England in the late Anglo-Saxon period. Though Latin obviously had a great deal of cultural importance, the exclusion of the vernacular from discussions of literacy overlooks two crucial issues: the social function of literacy and the relationships between Latin and the vernacular.[11] A more inclusive definition of literacy that encompasses both the ability to read and potentially write in the vernacular and the ability to use Latin is more appropriate and better represents the function of literate skills in the medieval period.[12] This is particularly apposite for tenth- and eleventh-century England, where there existed "an astonishing confidence in the potential of the vernacular to be developed as a medium for scholarly and religious discourse on a par with Latin".[13]

Our understanding of literacy must also consider the degree of variability in literate skills. George Brown has noted that the level of literacy among individual members of the Anglo-Saxon clergy varied considerably, from "the ability to read with (or without) understand-

---

[9] Anne Campbell, Irwin S. Kirsch, and Andrew Kolstad, *Assessing Literacy: The Framework for the National Adult Literacy Survey* (Washington, DC: US Department of Education, 1992), 9–10; Brett Elizabeth Blake and Robert W. Blake, *Literacy and Learning: A Reference Handbook* (Santa Barbara, CA: ABC-CLIO, 2002), 11.

[10] Hugh Magennis, "Audience(s), Reception, Literacy," in *A Companion to Anglo-Saxon Literature*, ed. Phillip Pulsiano and Elaine Treharne (Oxford: Blackwell, 2001), 86.

[11] Franz Bäuml, "Varieties and Consequences of Medieval Literacy and Illiteracy," *Speculum* 55, no. 2 (1980): 237–39.

[12] This has been recognized in a number of studies of medieval literacy: Bäuml, "Varieties and Consequences"; Seth Lerer, *Literacy and Power in Anglo-Saxon Literature* (Lincoln: University of Nebraska Press, 1991).

[13] Mechthild Gretsch, "Winchester Vocabulary and Standard Old English: The Vernacular in Late Anglo-Saxon England," *Bulletin of the John Rylands University Library of Manchester* 83, no. 1 (2001): 87.

ing such texts as simple prayers and the psalms to the ability to read and write the convoluted, sophisticated, and artificed Latin termed 'hermeneutic'".[14] A secular cleric's level of Latin literacy would in general have depended on a priest's status and prior education; a local priest may well have been liturgically competent, but it is unlikely that the literate skills of most priests serving small village churches were equivalent to those of priests in royal service or cathedral canons who had reached the priesthood. On the other hand, the elite literacy represented by the use of hermeneutic Latin in late Anglo-Saxon England was the reserve of a small minority and is typically associated with the proponents of reformed monasticism. The use of hermeneutic Latin in late Anglo-Saxon England has been well studied and though most often associated with monks, one identifiable secular priest, the biographer and probable secretary of St Dunstan, adopted this style in his own writing.[15] While this register of Latin was accessible to a limited number of secular clerics, hermeneutic Latin was by its nature impractical owing to its use of obscure words, Grecisms, and an intentional lack of linguistic accessibility. Use of Latin at this level would require an individual to possess a wide vocabulary in their second language, probably consisting of several thousand words. But in attempting to assess the ability of Anglo-Saxon priests to use the books prescribed for them, we are not pursuing a definition that would necessitate what one might call elite literacy. Instead, the uses of Latin for most priests were eminently practical, namely their performance of liturgical services and the use of other pastoral texts in Latin. Texts like the Psalms, performed daily in the Office, are relatively simple and grammatically straightforward, and the texts used in the mass were performed utilizing a limited, formulaic Latin vocabulary. Additionally, priests brought a degree of what Katherine O'Brien O'Keeffe has called "predictive knowledge" to the performance of the liturgy, shaped by both their education in Latin and their practical liturgical experience.[16] More advanced texts would have required a sophisticated knowledge of Latin grammar and vocabulary, but, for example, the vocabulary

---

[14] Brown, "The Dynamics of Literacy," 186.
[15] Michael Lapidge, "The Hermeneutic Style in Tenth-Century Anglo-Latin Literature," *Anglo-Saxon England* 4 (1975); Rebecca Stephenson, "Byrhtferth's *Enchiridion*: The Effectiveness of Hermeneutic Latin," in *Conceptualizing Multilingualism in England, c.800–c.1250*, ed. Elizabeth Tyler (Turnhout: Brepols, 2011). The priest referred to here is known as B. See Lapidge, "B. and the *Vita Sancti Dunstani*," in *Anglo-Latin Literature, 900–1066* (London: Hambledon Press, 1993); Stephenson, *The Politics of Language: Byrhtferth, Ælfric, and the Multilingual Identity of the Benedictine Reform* (Toronto: University of Toronto Press, 2015), 21–22. Stephenson argues that B.'s association with Dunstan and the context of the *Vita Sancti Dunstani* are further indications of the explicit association of the hermeneutic style with monasticism.
[16] O'Brien O'Keeffe, *Visible Song*, 21.

necessary to perform the liturgy probably encompassed several hundred words as opposed to the few thousand that would have been required for fluent reading of complex Latin works.[17] Therefore the definition of literacy required here is one concerned with the ability of Anglo-Saxon priests to use specific texts to administer the sacraments, perform the liturgy, and engage in other forms of pastoral care. For the late Anglo-Saxon priest and the bishops who attempted to regulate priests' lives, literacy was not an intangible and nebulous collection of academic skills, but a degree of education that enabled priests to ably perform their duties, not unlike the conception of *sufficienter litteratus* found in texts concerning ordination from the later Middle Ages.[18] Thus a study of clerical literacy in the early Middle Ages is in essence a study of functional literacy.

Functional literacy is by its nature situational in that an individual requires specific literate skills to accomplish given ends in "structured, patterned contexts" and the Latin content that priests were called on to perform, primarily as part of the liturgy, was repetitious, heavily structured, and relied on a limited and specialized vocabulary.[19] The accomplishment of these given ends for priests necessitated sufficient knowledge to utilize specific, formulaic texts in Latin (in the performance of the mass, Divine Office, and occasional offices, such as baptism and burial) and the spoken and written vernacular (in preaching, the assignment of penance, and general interaction with those in a priest's care). Therefore, we may define literacy in this context as proficiency in the use of Latin and the vernacular in structured and familiar ecclesiastical and pastoral contexts.

However, questions of priestly literacy have been complicated by monastic accounts of low standards of literacy among the clergy. Many of the sources that are relied upon for information about priests and their books in this period were penned by monks, many of whom held low opinions of the state of the secular clergy, and a lack of similar sources by the secular clergy has allowed little room for an alternate perspective. For example, Ælfric notes that in the previous generation, no priest was able to write or translate a letter in Latin, though it seems that this statement is an echo of Alfred's probably hyperbolic statement in the preface to the Old English *Pastoral Care*.[20]

---

[17] For a useful overview of the Latin terminology used in the liturgy, see Daniel Sheerin, "The Liturgy," in *Medieval Latin: An Introduction and Bibliographical Guide*, ed. F. A. C. Mantello and A. G. Rigg (Washington, DC: Catholic University of America Press, 1996).

[18] Dohar, "*Sufficienter litteratus*," 315–16.

[19] David Barton and Mary Hamilton, "Literacy Practices," in *Situated Literacies: Reading and Writing in Context*, ed. Barton, Hamilton, and Roz Ivanič (London: Routledge, 2000), 11.

[20] Robert Stanton, *The Culture of Translation in Anglo-Saxon England* (Cambridge:

Similarly, Ælfric claims in his first Old English letter for Wulfstan that he has written the letter in Old English because not all of his audience could understand Latin and hopes that evil priests "may be ashamed of their stupidity".[21] Other English Benedictine writers take equally harsh positions towards secular clerics: after accusing the clerics of Winchester Cathedral of drunkenness, gluttony, and illicit marriage, Wulfstan of Winchester refers to them as "detestable blasphemers against God", while Byrhtferth of Ramsey's *Enchiridion* frequently chastises secular clerics for their laziness and ignorance of computus.[22] Much of the monastic evidence against clerical literacy was taken at face value by previous generations of scholars, but others have more recently attempted to provide context for these statements. The most prominent among these voices is Rebecca Stephenson, who has shown these writers promoted a monastic, Latinate identity through criticism of the laziness and lack of education of secular clerics, taking pains to demarcate between Benedictine monks and their inferior secular counterparts. Byrhtferth of Ramsey in particular caricatures the secular clergy, demonstrating how "writing hermeneutic Latin reinforces and reinscribes those boundaries, by creating a discourse accessible only to a monastic elite".[23] Furthermore, the monks of some institutions saw the clergy of secular minsters and even cathedrals as rivals for resources, status, and patronage.[24] Understanding that English monks were concerned to differentiate themselves from the secular clergy and were in some ways in competition with them for resources and patronage does not necessarily discredit these sources. However, we should recognize the implications of this monastic bias and accordingly treat

---

D. S. Brewer, 2002), 116, n. 59; Magennis, "Audience(s), Reception, Literacy," 88.

[21] Whitelock, Brett, and Brooke, *Councils and Synods*, 261.

[22] Michael Lapidge and Michael Winterbottom, eds. and trans., *Life of St Æthelwold* (Oxford: Clarendon Press, 1991), 30–31; P. Baker and Lapidge, eds. and trans., *Byrhtferth's* Enchiridion, Early English Text Society Supplementary Series 15 (Oxford: Oxford University Press, 1995), 13, 19, 47, 53, 105.

[23] Stephenson, *The Politics of Language*, 101; Stephenson, "Scapegoating the Secular Clergy: The Hermeneutic Style as a Form of Monastic Self-Definition," *Anglo-Saxon England* 38 (2009). For others who have recognized this trend in the late Anglo-Saxon period, see Joyce Hill, "Monastic Reform and the Secular Church: Ælfric's Pastoral Letters in Context," in *England in the Eleventh Century: Proceedings of the 1990 Harlaxton Symposium*, ed. Carola Hicks (Stamford, UK: Paul Watkins, 1992), 108–11; Frank Barlow, *The English Church, 1000–1066: A History of the Later Anglo-Saxon Church*, 2nd ed. (London: Longman, 1979), 25; Lapidge and Winterbottom, *Life of St Æthelwold*, xlv; Emma Cownie, *Religious Patronage in Anglo-Norman England, 1066–1135* (London and Woodbridge: The Royal Historical Society and Boydell Press, 1998), 12–13.

[24] Paul Dalton, Charles Insley, and Louise Wilkinson, introduction to *Cathedrals, Communities and Conflict in the Anglo-Norman World*, ed. Dalton, Insley, and Wilkinson (Woodbridge: Boydell Press, 2011), 21–22, 24.

these sources with caution. Furthermore, it must be recognized that what erudite Benedictine monks saw as an appropriate level of literacy was probably significantly removed from the literacy needed by priests to fulfill their pastoral function.[25] In short, monastic declamations against secular clerics, particularly concerning their ability to use Latin, should be considered prudently and in context, particularly in light of the potential expectations of priestly literacy that may have far exceeded practical Latin literacy for use in the liturgy and pastoral care.

The acquisition of literate skills in Anglo-Saxon England

To the Anglo-Saxons, Latin was a foreign language. Though it was a language of great cultural and religious importance, the general population spoke English and learning Latin took instruction and practice. Considering the necessity of a priesthood literate in Latin, how did aspiring Anglo-Saxon secular clerics acquire the necessary skills to, at the very least, read Latin so as to perform the liturgy? To understand this requires an examination of the educational avenues available to aspiring clerics and the content of a clerical education.

Though passed over in most accounts of medieval education, the acquisition of the vernacular would have then as now occurred in the home in a child's first few years. At home children learned to construct sentences, built a rudimentary vocabulary, and, in imitating their parents, began to use distinctly regional pronunciation. The majority of Anglo-Saxon households would not have contained an individual who was capable of reading either Latin or the vernacular, but many Anglo-Saxon children must have grown up listening to and reciting vernacular poetry.[26] The form and influence of this oral tradition are clearly seen in many of the most noted writers of the Anglo-Saxon period and priests of this period were no less influenced by it, as is indicated by injunctions against priests acting as *scops* or singers in taverns, places in which traditional poetry and song were performed.[27] Though literate Anglo-Saxon households were certainly the excep-

---

[25] An example of the potentially lofty literate standards of Benedictine monks can be seen in the education of early medieval child oblates. See Mayke de Jong, *In Samuel's Image: Child Oblation in the Early Medieval West* (Leiden: Brill, 1996), 127–28, 232–36.

[26] Including secular clergy, monks, and a conservative number of laymen, the percentage of free men literate in Latin in eleventh-century England has been calculated at slightly more than two percent, approximately 5,000 men. The proportion of those able to read and possibly write in the vernacular must have been higher. See Timofeeva, "Anglo-Latin Bilingualism before 1066," 15.

[27] Whitelock, Brett, and Brooke, *Councils and Synods*, 333; Gabriele Knappe, "The

tion rather than the rule, there were likely some lay households that resembled that of Dhuoda, a Carolingian countess and mother who authored the *Liber Manualis* as a guide for her son in the ninth century. King Alfred's mother played a role in his early education, teaching her sons Old English poetry and encouraging them to memorize the poetry they heard. Famously, when the boy Alfred heard that his mother would give him a book of poetry if he could memorize its contents, he took it to his master, apparently to have the poems read to him, memorized the poems, and recited them to his mother to receive the book.[28] Thus some aristocratic lay households may have had a literate dimension which helped to develop literate skills in children and adolescents being fostered in royal or aristocratic households. Mothers, and indeed aristocratic women whose households fostered children, may have played a vital role in this type of early education.[29] As we see in England and on the continent, some of those who went on to distinguished ecclesiastical careers, such as Oda of Canterbury, were brought up in aristocratic households and benefitted from the education available in them.[30]

A type of family environment outside the aristocratic household in which children must have had greater access to education than most has been largely ignored: the clerical household. Celibacy was ostensibly required for those in major orders (the priesthood and the diaconate) in the early medieval period, but priestly marriage and clerical families were common in England in the tenth and eleventh centuries.[31] The priest at Great Bedwyn at the time of the Domesday survey had inherited the church from his father and some of the canons at Waltham Holy Cross in the eleventh century had inherited their

---

Rhetorical Aspect of Grammar Teaching in Anglo-Saxon England," *Rhetorica: A Journal of the History of Rhetoric* 17, no. 1 (1999): 15.

[28] Simon Keynes and Michael Lapidge, trans., *Alfred the Great: Asser's Life of King Alfred and Other Contemporary Sources* (London: Penguin Books, 1983), 75.

[29] Julia Barrow, *The Clergy in the Medieval World: Secular Clerics, Their Families and Careers in North-Western Europe, c. 800–c. 1200* (Cambridge: Cambridge University Press, 2015), 159; Michael Clanchy, "Did Mothers Teach Their Children to Read?," in *Motherhood, Religion, and Society in Medieval Europe, 400–1400: Essays Presented to Henrietta Leyser*, ed. Conrad Leyser and Lesley Smith (Farnham: Ashgate, 2011).

[30] Michael Lapidge, ed. and trans., *Byrhtferth of Ramsey: The Lives of St Oswald and St Ecgwine* (Oxford: Clarendon Press, 2009), 19; Barrow, *The Clergy in the Medieval World*, 159–60.

[31] Catherine Cubitt, "Images of St Peter: The Clergy and the Religious Life in Anglo-Saxon England," in *The Christian Tradition in Anglo-Saxon England: Approaches to Current Scholarship and Teaching*, ed. Paul Cavill (Cambridge: D. S. Brewer, 2004), 48–53; Barrow, *The Clergy in the Medieval World*, 142–45. Some men may have married and had children while in minor orders and separated from their wives upon attaining major orders, but there is evidence for a significant number of married priests in the late Anglo-Saxon period.

positions from their fathers; even at higher levels in the ecclesiastical hierarchy, marriage was not unheard of.[32] At least two late Anglo-Saxon bishops fathered children and the father of St Wulfstan of Worcester – Æthelstan – was a member of the cathedral clergy at Worcester in the late tenth century.[33] Sometime between 996 and 1008, Wulfstan's father seems to have taken a church at Itchington in Warwickshire, married, and fathered a son who would not only become bishop of Worcester, but would carry on what appears to have been a clerical line at Worcester which lasted for nearly a century.[34] Sons with clerical fathers must have often been at an educational advantage, not only from the tutoring that many must have received, but also from their liturgical experience, gained by spending time in the church with their fathers and assisting in the liturgy. Ælfric specifically instructs priests who had no assistants to take on boys and young men and teach them the ropes of clerical ministry and the sons of priests were surely among those who assisted in the performance of the liturgy.[35] Osbern, son of the priest Brihtric, assisted with the liturgy in the church at Haselbury as a boy in the twelfth century and eventually took charge of the church there, succeeding his father as priest.[36] Additionally, all priests were assumed even by more pessimistic writers to be able to read English. Even when Latin literacy was "at a low ebb", the reason that priests were unable to understand certain books was that they were not written in Old English.[37] Clerical sons would thus probably have been, at minimum, literate in the vernacular – their spoken language and a language that their fathers were able to read – and would have had a significant degree of liturgical experience by adulthood.

---

[32] D. A. Crowley, *A History of the County of Wiltshire: Volume 16, Kinwardstone Hundred* (Oxford: Oxford University Press, 1999), 30; Leslie Watkiss and Marjorie Chibnall, eds. and trans., *The Waltham Chronicle: An Account of the Discovery of Our Holy Cross at Montacute and Its Conveyance to Waltham* (Oxford: Clarendon Press, 1994), xxix.

[33] Barrow, *The Clergy in the Medieval World*, 141–42. Peter, one of the royal priests of Edward the Confessor and a bishop after the Conquest, also fathered a son. See C. P. Lewis, "Communities, Conflict and Episcopal Policy in the Diocese of Lichfield, 1050–1150," in Dalton, Insley, and Wilkinson, *Cathedrals, Communities and Conflict*, 70.

[34] Nicholas Brooks, "Introduction: How Do We Know about St Wulfstan?," in *St Wulfstan and His World*, ed. Julia Barrow and Brooks (Aldershot: Ashgate, 2005), 18–21. For more on Wulfstan's kin, see Ann Williams, "The Spoliation of Worcester," in *Anglo-Norman Studies XIX: Proceedings of the Battle Conference 1996*, ed. Christopher Harper-Bill (Woodbridge: Boydell Press, 1997), 394–96.

[35] Bernhard Fehr, ed., *Die Hirtenbriefe Ælfrics in altenglischer und lateinischer Fassung* (Hamburg: Henri Grand, 1914), 174–76.

[36] Maurice Bell, ed., *Wulfric of Haselbury, by John, Abbot of Ford* (Frome and London, 1933), lii, 52; Pauline Matarasso, *John of Forde: The Life of Wulfric of Haselbury, Anchorite* (Collegeville, MN: Liturgical Press, 2011), 139, 187.

[37] Magennis, "Audience(s), Reception, Literacy," 89–90.

Though most of these young men may not have been the educational equals of monastic oblates, children brought up in clerical households would have had firsthand knowledge of the skills required to perform the duties of a priest, and many sons indeed followed in their fathers' footsteps.

Though instruction in the household provided some level of education, monastic and cathedral schools are the most well-known and widely attested sources of clerical education in England in the tenth and eleventh centuries, particularly for the study of Latin. The curricula of these schools seem to have been very similar in terms of a lettered education, so they will here be discussed together, particularly as some of the major episcopal seats became and remained monastic in the period under consideration.[38] Michael Lapidge has argued that these schools succeeded education at the royal court as "foyers of learning" in the course of the tenth century and a glance at the alumni of these schools seems to support his notion.[39] The most noted writers and ecclesiastical figures of this period, including Dunstan, Æthelwold, Ælfric, Byrhtferth, and St Wulfstan of Worcester, were educated in schools of this kind. Both Dunstan and Æthelwold were educated in the first half of the tenth century, a time for which there is limited evidence for education in England. At Glastonbury, probably prior to the adoption of Benedictine monasticism, Dunstan was trained as a scribe and illuminator in addition to his "sacra litterarum studia", and Æthelwold, though he began his studies at the royal court, received much of his later education at Winchester and Glastonbury.[40] In the later tenth century and the beginning of the eleventh, we see that the bulk of Ælfric of Eynsham's studies after his early education under a local priest were undertaken at Winchester during Æthelwold's tenure as bishop, while Byrhtferth and St Wulfstan were both educated at monastic schools, though Wulfstan had not yet taken monastic vows at the time of his education.[41] As in Wulfstan's case, it appears that monastic schools were not only open to monks, but to secular clerics as well as laymen.[42] The secular cleric known to us only as B., one of the

---

[38] C. Stephen Jaeger, *The Envy of Angels: Cathedral Schools and Social Ideals in Medieval Europe, 950–1200* (Philadelphia: University of Pennsylvania Press, 1994), 26–27.

[39] Michael Lapidge, "Schools, Learning and Literature in Tenth-Century England," in *Anglo-Latin Literature, 900–1066* (London: Hambledon Press, 1993), 4.

[40] Michael Lapidge and Michael Winterbottom, eds. and trans., *The Early Lives of St Dunstan* (Oxford: Clarendon Press, 2012), 40.

[41] For Ælfric's Latin education at Winchester, see Michael Lapidge, "Ælfric's Schooldays," in *Early Medieval Texts and Interpretations: Studies Presented to Donald Scragg*, ed. Elaine Treharne and Susan Rosser (Tempe: Arizona Center for Medieval and Renaissance Studies, 2002).

[42] Donald A. Bullough, "The Educational Tradition in England from Alfred to Ælfric: Teaching *utriusque linguae*," in *Carolingian Renewal: Sources and Heritage*

biographers of St Dunstan and at some point a member of his retinue, seems to have been educated at Glastonbury without ever taking monastic vows.[43] Byrhtferth, the master of the school at Ramsey, often addresses both clerics and monks in his *Enchiridion*, which envisions a classroom environment for its computistical instruction. Byrhtferth at times refers to both "city clerics" and "rustic priests" in his lessons, typically unfavorably, implying that clerics from a variety of locales came to be schooled at Ramsey.[44] It may be that in regions like the Fenlands, where we know of few secular minsters but an abundance of monasteries, these institutions were the primary centers of education for the secular clergy.[45]

Pupils at monasteries and cathedrals were schooled in letters and in sacred texts, beginning with learning and eventually memorizing the Psalms, particularly for those intending to pursue a clerical or monastic vocation. The ubiquity of the Psalms in worship meant that they were familiar to many students and their regular use served as a constant reminder and reinforcement of their text and message.[46] The musical use of the biblical text in the liturgy may also have led into instruction in church music. As the liturgy was a major part of both the vocation of clerics and daily life in cathedrals and monasteries, a text such as the *Commemoratio breuis de tonis et psalmis modulandis*, a guide to the singing of the psalms surviving in Cambridge, Corpus Christi College 260, copied in the late tenth century at Christ Church

---

(Manchester: Manchester University Press, 1991), 316. Mary Giandrea notes that the children of the aristocracy were educated in cathedral schools, such as Segild of Droitwich's son, who studied under Coleman, biographer of St Wulfstan. See Giandrea, *Episcopal Culture in Late Anglo-Saxon England* (Woodbridge: Boydell Press, 2007), 82.

[43] Lapidge, "B. and the *Vita S. Dunstani*," 288–89, 291. B.'s work not only offers a more personal view of Dunstan, but is also an erudite work by an Anglo-Saxon secular cleric, providing a "valuable counterbalance to the prevalent monkish perspective".

[44] Baker and Lapidge, *Byrhtferth's* Enchiridion, 19, 107, 111, 139, 185.

[45] A map showing the distribution of attested monasteries and secular minsters can be found in John Blair, "Secular Minster Churches in Domesday Book," in *Domesday Book: A Reassessment*, ed. Peter Sawyer (London: Edward Arnold, 1985), 108–9.

[46] The centrality of the Psalms to medieval education, particularly the education of monks and clerics, has been consistently recognized. See G. Brown, "The Psalms as the Foundation of Anglo-Saxon Learning," in *The Place of the Psalms in the Intellectual Culture of the Middle Ages*, ed. Nancy Van Deusen (Albany: State University Press of New York, 1999); Rebecca Rushforth, "Annotated Psalters and Psalm Study in Late Anglo-Saxon England: The Manuscript Evidence," in *Rethinking and Recontextualising Glosses: New Perspectives in the Study of Late Anglo-Saxon Glossography*, ed. Patrizia Lendinara, Loredana Lazzari, and Claudia Di Sciacca (Porto: Fédération Internationale des Instituts d'Études Mediévales, 2011); Joseph Dyer, "The Singing of Psalms in the Early-Medieval Office," *Speculum* 64, no. 3 (1989).

Canterbury, might have been a text used by a cantor for such a purpose.[47] To facilitate training in reading, writing, and the use of Latin, students were taught grammar as well as the rules of poetic meter, as Æthelwold's biographer recalled and as seems to have been the case at Ramsey in the later tenth century.[48] Students were also set to work on the Books of Wisdom such as Job, Proverbs, and Sirach as they became more proficient in Latin, eventually moving on to patristic works, Christian Latin poets of Late Antiquity, and the writings of the early Anglo-Latin masters, such as Bede and Aldhelm.[49] A student availed of such a curriculum, whether clerical or monastic, would certainly have had a solid foundation in the study of the Bible and the Fathers as well as in Latin. Instruction in writing must also have taken place at monasteries and cathedrals, which in addition to acting as centers of learning were frequently involved in book production. Though the evidence for this type of training is slim, many priests educated in these institutions must have received scribal training, as we see secular clerics involved in writing and glossing Anglo-Saxon manuscripts, which will be discussed in due course.

Schools and clerical careers

Boys at these schools who were intended for clerical careers likely took minor orders at a young age and advanced gradually. In Gaul, boys who attended episcopal schools, consisting of family members of the bishop, sons of priests, orphans, those who had attended parish schools, and others, started around the age of ten and Brown has

---

[47] Susan Rankin, "Music Books," in Gameson, *The Cambridge History of the Book in Britain*, 505–6. There is some evidence for books of music theory in cathedrals. The strongest surviving evidence comes from Canterbury, but around the same time as the copying of the *Commemoratio breuis* mentioned above, Wulfstan Cantor wrote a "Breviloquium super musicam" at Winchester, which Rankin suggests was a commentary on the *De institutione musica* of Boethius.

[48] Lapidge and Winterbottom, *Life of St Æthelwold*, 14–17; Baker and Lapidge, *Byrhtferth's Enchiridion*, lxxix–lxxx. Education in Old English may also have taken place at cathedral and monastic schools, as it did at Crowland in the late eleventh century. See Elaine Treharne, "Reading from the Margins: The Uses of Old English Homiletic Manuscripts in the Post-Conquest Period," in *Beatus Vir: Studies in Early English and Norse Manuscripts in Memory of Phillip Pulsiano*, ed. A. N. Doane and Kirsten Wolf (Tempe: Arizona Center for Medieval and Renaissance Studies, 2006), 353.

[49] Michael Lapidge, "Schools," in *The Wiley-Blackwell Encyclopedia of Anglo-Saxon England*, 2nd ed., ed. Lapidge et al. (Oxford: Wiley-Blackwell, 2014), 422; Lapidge, "B. and the *Vita S. Dunstani*," 288. B., in a letter to Bishop Æthelgar, references Aldhelm's *De Virginitate*, which he dismissively calls a "little book in praise of virginity". Lapidge argues that B. had likely studied this work in his time at Glastonbury, possibly along with Æthelgar.

suggested that a similar situation existed in England in the tenth century.[50] The number of clerical grades had been fixed at seven by the mid-third century in Rome, but was not clearly established throughout Western Europe until sometime in the ninth century. These grades were doorkeeper, exorcist, reader, acolyte, subdeacon, deacon, and priest.[51] Ælfric gives a short explication of the clerical grades in his Old English pastoral letter for Wulfsige III in which the number of the grades is set at seven, drawing primarily on the writings of Amalarius and Isidore, though he gives no indication as to how clerics moved through these grades.[52] Though there are some exceptional cases, the minimum age of ordination to the priesthood was thirty in the Middle Ages. Thus a cleric who began moving through the clerical *cursus honorum* as a pre-adolescent would have had approximately twenty years of liturgical and educational experience behind him by the time he was elevated to the priesthood. However, not all ordinands came up through the grades as children. Adult entrants to clerical orders could be fast tracked, with one late fifth-century text suggesting that adults be moved through the grades and into the priesthood in only eighteen months, while other early medieval sources suggest adult laymen might undergo *conversio* for a year.[53] This must have been a very difficult course indeed and those taking orders in adulthood, and struggling with the educational requirements of the presbyterate, may have formed a proportion of Archbishop Wulfstan's "half-educated" (OE *samlæred*) men who at times had to be ordained out of necessity.[54]

Though we know the general shape of the way in which priests moved through the grades, the number or proportion of secular clerics, or indeed any other group, who would have attended monastic and cathedral schools is not known. Assumedly, most that did attend these schools would have been more competent in Latin than their priestly counterparts whose training was less prestigious. But we do know that student cohorts in equivalent continental schools were expected to be small, having not more than a dozen students, though class size may have increased in the tenth and eleventh centuries as secular clerics

---

[50] Brown, "The Dynamics of Literacy," 195; Pierre Riché, *Education and Culture in the Barbarian West, Sixth through Eighth Centuries*, trans. John Contreni (Columbia: University of South Carolina Press, 1976), 283.

[51] As noted by Julia Barrow, by the eleventh century the three lowest grades had essentially lost their liturgical function due to their use as grades for children and adolescents; only the four higher grades had active roles in the mass. Barrow, "Grades of Ordination and Clerical Careers, c. 900–c. 1200," in *Anglo-Norman Studies 30: Proceedings of the Battle Conference 2007*, vol. 30, ed. C. P. Lewis (Woodbridge: Boydell Press, 2008), 47–48.

[52] Whitelock, Brett, and Brooke, *Councils and Synods*, 202–5.

[53] Barrow, "Grades of Ordination and Clerical Careers," 45.

[54] Whitelock, Brett, and Brooke, *Councils and Synods*, 425.

and laymen were educated in English schools of this kind and demand for priests grew to meet the needs of large numbers of local churches.[55] Though some secular priests were certainly educated in these schools, many of the ones able to attend them were likely well born or well connected, as a significant number of the alumni of monastic and cathedral schools went on to notable ecclesiastical careers and, if better records of the backgrounds of secular priests existed, we might be able to add some of the royal priests of the late Anglo-Saxon period to their list of alumni. Not all pupils were members of the aristocracy, however. Ælfric himself was probably of relatively humble birth and Eadmer of Canterbury records that St Oswald of Worcester took "twelve poor men" under his wing who were fed by the church and wished to "all know their letters and all hold orders".[56] This account of education for the poor at Worcester might wisely be accepted with caution, as the number of poor men reads as a biblically inspired topos and Eadmer's account is relatively late. However, the church's role in feeding the poor in this way should not be doubted and it may be that a clerical education was provided to certain poor individuals, as was the case for some medieval orphans.[57] The implied mix of "rustic" and "city" clerics in Byrhtferth's classroom at Ramsey too points to a fairly plebian student body.[58] It is perhaps unwise to conjecture too strongly on the socio-economic and political positions of the students in these schools, but certainly a large proportion of those with notable ecclesiastical careers, many of whom were of noble birth, were educated at monastic and cathedral schools, but there is also evidence for the education of secular clerics and those of low birth in the same institutions.

Aside from monastic and cathedral schools, the royal court appears to have provided education for some high-born and well-connected clerics. Though education for clerics at the royal court had died out in Francia by the later ninth century, it seems to have remained common in England at least through the first half of the tenth century and

---

[55] Lapidge, "Schools," 421.
[56] Catherine Cubitt, "Ælfric's Lay Patrons," in *A Companion to Ælfric*, ed. Hugh Magennis and Mary Swan (Leiden: Brill, 2009), 177; Andrew Turner and Bernard Muir, ed. and trans., *Eadmer of Canterbury: Lives and Miracles of Saints Oda, Dunstan, and Oswald* (Oxford: Clarendon Press, 2006), 233.
[57] Riché, *Education and Culture in the Barbarian West*, 283. A significant portion of the alms received by Anglo-Saxon churches was earmarked for the poor, particularly for their sustenance. For more information on almsgiving in the early Middle Ages, see Aleisha Olson, "Textual Representations of Almsgiving in Late Anglo-Saxon England" (PhD thesis, University of York, 2010), http://etheses.whiterose.ac.uk/1111/1/Textual_Representations_of_Almsgiving_-_Aleisha_Olson.pdf; Eric Schuler, "Almsgiving and the Formation of Early Medieval Societies, A.D. 700–1025" (PhD thesis, University of Notre Dame, 2010), https://curate.nd.edu/downloads/j9601z42v32.
[58] Baker and Lapidge, *Byrhtferth's* Enchiridion, 19, 107, 111.

fostering of the king's relatives was still taking place at the English royal court in the mid-eleventh century.⁵⁹ Most famously, King Alfred established a school at his court at which both English and Latin were taught. According to Asser, most of the children of the Anglo-Saxon nobility were educated in this school, as was Alfred's son Æthelweard.⁶⁰ Æthelwold spent some of his early years at the court of Æthelstan, and though his education was completed at Winchester and Glastonbury, he may well have gained a lettered education of some sort in the king's household. Similarly, Dunstan, after taking minor orders, spent time at the king's court, where he "excelled in the arts of writing, of painting, [and] of sculpting", in addition to other handicrafts.⁶¹ The details on the content of education at the royal court are slim, but the royal court housed a great deal of educational resources, particularly under kings such as Alfred and Æthelstan, and must have served as both an academic and political proving ground for those clerics in royal favor.

Education in secular minsters

The evidence for English clerical education in this period on the whole is thin and when we turn to clerical education outside of a monastery or cathedral, the evidence becomes more so. Despite this, several understudied and largely unknown records point to a pedagogical milieu outside that of major ecclesiastical centers. Though relatively little is known of their educational activities, some minsters certainly operated schools in the eleventh century, and education in minsters may well extend back into the tenth century and earlier.

Waltham Holy Cross is one of the minsters for which clear evidence of a school survives. Thanks to aristocratic patronage first from Tovi the Proud, a Danish thegn of Cnut, and later from King Harold, Waltham was a very wealthy house of secular canons in the late eleventh century. We know something of the church and the clergy that served it partially due to its wealth and to an anonymous twelfth-century writer who penned *The Waltham Chronicle*, which itself was based on a lost eleventh-century history and other contemporary documents.⁶² The author of *The Waltham Chronicle* refers briefly to those who were teach-

---

[59] Barrow, *The Clergy in the Medieval World*, 159, 164. For practices at the Carolingian court, see Matthew Innes, "'A Place of Discipline': Carolingian Courts and Aristocratic Youth," in *Court Culture in the Early Middle Ages: The Proceedings of the First Alcuin Conference*, ed. Catherine Cubitt (Turnhout: Brepols, 2003).
[60] Keynes and Lapidge, *Alfred the Great*, 90–91.
[61] Turner and Muir, *Eadmer of Canterbury*, 57–59.
[62] Rosalind Ransford, ed., *The Early Charters of the Augustinian Canons of Waltham Abbey, Essex, 1062–1230* (Woodbridge: Boydell Press, 1989), xxiii, n. 2; Watkiss and Chibnall, *The Waltham Chronicle*, xxxiii.

ing at Waltham in the eleventh and early twelfth centuries, namely a learned Lotharingian named Adelard, recruited by Harold, and subsequently his son Peter. In addition, one of the canons who ostensibly retrieved the body of King Harold after the Battle of Hastings is named as Æthelric Childemaister, which, along with Harold's recruitment of Adelard, implies the existence of a school at Waltham by at least the 1060s.[63] The *Chronicle* even allows us a glimpse into the daily life of a young student at the minster school:

> Indeed a rich spring of instruction in the disciplines flowed from Peter himself in accordance with the methods of the Germans for the study and reading of Latin and the composition of verses did not prevent singing being learnt and constantly practised in the church. The mien of the boys was so strictly controlled that, like their 'regular' brethren, they would walk, stand, read, and sing in a becoming and dignified manner, and whatever they had to sing on the step of the choir, or in the choir itself, one or two boys, or more, would sing or chant by heart without the help of a book. Once in his place in the choir one boy did not look at another unless, perhaps, askance, and then rarely, nor did he utter a single word to him. The boys did not run through the choir unless they had been ordered to do so by the master for the purpose of transferring books or copes, or for some other reason. They remained in the choir in the order they walked in procession, and as they entered the choir from the schools, so they entered the schools when leaving the choir, like canons rising in the night.[64]

As the passage makes clear, the school at Waltham instructed its students in Latin, meter and poetic composition, and provided training in the liturgy. Though the chronicler's account of education at the minster was probably primarily based on his own experiences in the twelfth century, the academic instruction offered at Waltham was probably similar under Master Adelard, Peter's father, and the practical liturgical training for boys at Waltham likely also remained unchanged. Susan Boynton has described liturgical education as the

---

[63] Watkiss and Chibnall, *The Waltham Chronicle*, 29, 47.
[64] "Fons enim uberrimus disciplinis doctrine tunc scaturiebat ab ipso Petro secundum modum Teutonicorum, non enim obstantibus lectionibus uel litteris et uersibus componendis minus addiscebatur et frequentabatur in ecclesia cantus. Et ordinatissima distinctio puerilis habitudinis ita ut, more religiosorum fratrum, honeste et non sine grauitate incederent, starent, legerent, et cantarent, et quicquid ad gradum chori uel in ipso choro cantare oportebat, corde tenus unus uel duo, uel plures, absque libri solatio cantarent et psallerent. In choro constituti, non respiciebat puer alterum, nisi forte ex obliquo tamen raro, nec faceret ei uerbum unum; non discurrebant per chorum nisi quibus fuisset iniunctum a magistro pro cappis aut pro libris transferendis uel aliis quibuslibet causis; manentes in choro, sicut processione procedentes, a scolis intrant chorum sic exeuntes intrant scolas ad modum canonicorum de nocte surgentium." Ibid., 66–67.

"primary form" of early education for monks, one in which students would constantly have been involved as they were acquainted with the forms and hierarchy of monastic life.⁶⁵ Liturgical education for secular clerics must have been similarly emphasized. The chronicler further shows the participation of the boys in the liturgy of the minster in a later miracle story in which the young chronicler and "the other boys" were present at and presumably participating in Vespers.⁶⁶ The prominence placed on the behavior and decorum of the boys training at Waltham is also of interest as it likely bears resemblance to the instruction that Master Adelard received in cathedral schools on the Continent, where *ecclesiasticae disciplinae* was stressed.⁶⁷

The Waltham Chronicle is a unique source in that it directly addresses the education of students at a minster school and it is likely that many of these students were destined for clerical careers. But while our source material may be unique, Waltham was not unique in terms of its wealth nor in its operation of a school. As for wealth, the collegiate church at Bosham, Sussex held 147 hides of land in the late Anglo-Saxon period and enjoyed the patronage of King Harold and possibly Earl Godwin. Considering that it was "probably the richest unreformed minster left in England" at the time of the Conquest, Bosham would also have had the financial resources to operate a school and attract scholars as Waltham Holy Cross did.⁶⁸ Other secular minsters that were recipients of aristocratic and royal patronage may have also housed schools, but it may not have only been wealthy ministers that educated up-and-coming clerics. Even schools in local churches at times played a role in education, as will later be discussed in detail, and secular minsters without generous benefactors may have taught basic literacy skills and provided liturgical training for students.

Post-Conquest documentary evidence further illuminates the availability of schools in secular minsters of the late Anglo-Saxon period. In the early 1120s, Henry I granted All Saints, Warwick the same rights and privileges that it had enjoyed under Edward the Confessor, which

---

⁶⁵ Susan Boynton, "Training for the Liturgy as a Form of Monastic Education," in *Medieval Monastic Education*, ed. George Ferzoco and Carolyn Muessig (Leicester: Leicester University Press, 2000), 16.

⁶⁶ Watkiss and Chibnall, *The Waltham Chronicle*, 66–69. The chronicler's recollection of the performance of the *Ad cenam agni prouidi* and *Te Deum* as well as the antiphon being sung at the time might indicate that the boys were participating in the Office.

⁶⁷ Jaeger, *Envy of Angels*, passim.

⁶⁸ Richard Gameson, *The Role of Art in the Late Anglo-Saxon Church* (Oxford: Clarendon Press, 1995), 247; Blair, "Bosham," in Lapidge et al., *The Wiley-Blackwell Encyclopedia of Anglo-Saxon England*, 75.

included the operation of a school.⁶⁹ Similarly, it was recorded that the minster at Twynham, Hampshire (now known as Christchurch and located within the modern county of Dorset) had a school in the general charter of Earl Baldwin de Redvers, dated to about 1140.⁷⁰ The existence of a pre-Conquest school there is plausible, as the minster community in the period of the 1080s was large, consisting of twenty-five members, the liturgical life of the church was reportedly vibrant, and the church had a number of "outbuildings and domestic offices", one of which could have housed a school.⁷¹ Additionally, some have argued that schools were set up in the new minsters founded in the *burhs* constructed by Alfred and his offspring in the late ninth and early tenth centuries. This argument was first made in 1915 by A. F. Leach and has more recently been independently suggested by Jeremy Haslam for St Mary Magdalen's in London, which later became Holy Trinity Priory, where, a little more than a century after the Conquest, William Fitzstephen claimed the school there was one of three in London of "privilegio et antiqua dignitate".⁷² Similarly, St Oswald's was founded at Gloucester in the earliest years of the tenth century in the same period as Æthelred and Æthelflæd of Mercia's construction of *burhs*. Michael Hare has asserted that this new minster may have had an educational function, as it is certain that by the early twelfth century the new minster had a strong association with schools: it is then that we find "a confirmation by Henry I to St Oswald's of all the schools of Gloucester".⁷³ Furthermore, Archbishop Ælfheah was educated at Deerhurst in the tenth century, which was ostensibly monastic during his time there, but as Patrick Wormald suggests, the minster

---

⁶⁹ C. R. Fonge, ed., *The Cartulary of St Mary's Collegiate Church, Warwick* (Woodbridge: Boydell Press, 2004), 21–22.

⁷⁰ Robert Bearman, ed., *Charters of the Redvers Family and the Earldom of Devon, 1090–1217*, Devon and Cornwall Record Society Publications, n.s. 37 (Exeter: Devon and Cornwall Record Society, 1994), 64–65.

⁷¹ P. H. Hase, "The Mother Churches of Hampshire," in *Minsters and Parish Churches: The Local Church in Transition, 950–1200*, ed. John Blair (Oxford: Oxford University Committee for Archaeology, 1988), 52, 59.

⁷² A. F. Leach, *The Schools of Medieval England* (London: Methuen, 1915), 76–79; Haslam, "Parishes, Churches, Wards and Gates in Eastern London," in Blair, *Minsters and Parish Churches*, 38; Henry Thomas Riley, ed., *Munimenta Gildhallæ Londoniensis*, vol. 2, pt. 1, *Liber Custumarum with Extracts from the Cottonian MS. Claudius, D. II*, Rerum Britannicarum medii aevi scriptores (Rolls Series) 12 (London: Longman, Green, Longman, and Roberts, 1860), 5.

⁷³ Michael Hare, *The Two Anglo-Saxon Minsters of Gloucester* (Gloucester: Friends of Deerhurst Church, 1993), 5–6. For the church itself, see Carolyn Heighway and Richard Bryant, "A Reconstruction of the Tenth-Century Church of St Oswald, Gloucester," in *The Anglo-Saxon Church: Papers on History, Architecture and Archaeology in Honour of Dr. H. M. Taylor*, ed. Lawrence Butler and Richard Morris (London: Council for British Archaeology, 1986).

may have been secular in the tenth century as it was in the ninth and eleventh centuries.[74]

The sum of the evidence presented above is a significant indication of the availability of education in minsters in the late Anglo-Saxon period. Minster schools like these, which would probably have been available to a much wider segment of the population than monastic and cathedral schools, may be the venues that Alfred envisioned in his preface to the Old English *Pastoral Care* for the education of young, free men as well as those who would go on to take clerical orders.[75] Though these schools are not well known, their pre-Conquest pedigree is not infrequently referenced or implied in the late eleventh and early twelfth centuries, intimating that a sizeable number of minster churches, maybe particularly those with wealthy patrons, were able to operate schools in which students could receive instruction in letters as well as practical liturgical education and provide an educational alternative to cathedral and monastic schools.

Other educational venues

Ælfric's well-known account of his own education under a secular priest, contained in the preface to his translation of Genesis, suggests another potential form of clerical education:

> Hwilon ic wiste þæt sum mæssepreost, se þe min magister wæs on þam timan, hæfde þa boc Genesis and he cuðe be dæle Lyden understandan. Þa cwæþ he be þam heahfædere Iacobe þæt he hæfde feower wif: twa geswustra and heora twa þinena. Ful soð he sæde, ac he nyste, ne ic þa git, hu micel todal ys betweohx þære ealdan æ and þære niwan. [...] Ða ungelæredan preostas, gif hi hwæt litles understandað of þam Lydenbocum, þonne þingð him sona þæt hi magon mære lareowas beon, ac hi ne cunnon swaþeah þæt gastlice andgit þærto and hu seo ealde æ wæs getacnung toweardra þinga, oþþe hu seo niwe gecyþnis æft[er] Cristes menniscnisse [w]æs gefillednys ealra þæra þinga þe seo ealde gecyðnis getacnode towearde, be Criste and be hys gecorenum.

> (I once knew a priest, who was at the time my teacher, and who had the book of Genesis and could understand some Latin; and he declared that the patriarch Jacob had four wives – two sisters and their handmaids. He spoke the truth, certainly, but he did not know – nor as yet did I – what a sharp distinction there is between the Old Law and the New. [...] These ignorant priests, should they understand any small part of books

---

[74] P. Wormald, *How Do We Know So Much about Anglo-Saxon Deerhurst?* (Gloucester: Friends of Deerhurst Church, 1993), 8–9.

[75] *English Historical Documents*, ed. David C. Douglas, vol. 1, *c. 500–1042*, ed. Whitelock, 2nd ed. (London: Eyre Methuen, 1979), 889.

written in Latin, immediately think they can be great teachers; yet, nevertheless, they have no comprehension of the spirituality in these books and that the Old Law was a sign of things to come, or that, after Christ's Incarnation, the New Testament was a fulfillment of all those things, to which the Old Testament had borne witness, about Christ's coming and his chosen ones.)[76]

Though much of the literature on Anglo-Saxon education has centered on formal schools, particularly monastic and cathedral schools, Ælfric's brief explication of his own early education may show a different side to Anglo-Saxon education. This passage has been discussed by a number of historians in light of its significance for Ælfric's education but as his point here is to warn of the dangers of eisegesis and clerical ignorance, he provides few details, leading to a diversity of thought on the exact circumstances of the education Ælfric describes. Mark Griffith has argued that Ælfric's description of his teacher, who Griffith assumes is a priest and teacher at Winchester, as one who "cuðe be dæle Lyden understandan" is actually a form of rhetorical understatement and that this statement should in fact be understood to mean "he knew a thing or two about Latin."[77] Griffith's interpretation of this passage, however, ignores the prevailing conditions at Winchester in the second half of the tenth century as well as the context of Ælfric's other writings. Even if scriptural interpretations supporting clerical marriage would have been accepted at Winchester before 964, it would be very unlikely that such a teacher could remain after the clerics were expelled by Æthelwold. Furthermore, Ælfric associates this sort of ignorance of the orthodox interpretation of the Old and New Testaments with secular priests, implying that this priest was not teaching at Winchester under Æthelwold.[78] Griffith's interpretation has been rejected by other scholars, including Christopher Jones and Joyce Hill, who have accepted a literal reading of this preface: Ælfric's teacher was a secular priest who had "an imperfect knowledge of Latin".[79] As Ælfric was not an oblate and there is no internal evidence

---

[76] Richard Marsden, ed., *The Old English Heptateuch and Ælfric's* Libellus de Veteri Testamento et Novo, vol. 1, *Introduction and Text*, Early English Text Society Original Series 330 (Oxford: Oxford University Press, 2008), 3–4; Alexandra H. Olsen and Burton Raffel, eds., *Poems and Prose from the Old English*, trans. Raffel (New Haven: Yale University Press, 1998), 173–74.

[77] Mark Griffith, "How Much Latin Did Ælfric's Magister Know?," *Notes and Queries* 46, no. 2 (1999): 176, 181; Lapidge, "Ælfric's Schooldays," 309. Lapidge seems to accept Griffith's interpretation of this passage, though he spends very little time discussing this preface.

[78] Whitelock, Brett, and Brooke, *Councils and Synods*, 198–200, 265–67, 269, 278–80. Ælfric's *Letter to Sigefyrth* also significantly concerns itself with these issues, edited in Bruno Assmann, ed., *Angelsächsische Homilien und Heiligenleben* (Kassel: G. H. Wigand, 1889), 13–23.

[79] Joyce Hill, "Ælfric: His Life and Works," in Magennis and Swan, *A Companion*

in this passage for this particular priest's tenure at Winchester, it seems more likely that his teacher was a cleric near to the area where Ælfric grew up, possibly on an estate of one of his later patrons.[80] And despite Ælfric's dim view of this priest's exegetical abilities, we should note that his teacher had access to and was able to read and comprehend the book of Genesis in Latin, even if he did not grasp its theological depth to Ælfric's satisfaction. Similar to the experience described by Ælfric, Orderic Vitalis, who was himself the son of a priest, tells us that "my father gave me into the charge of a noble priest called Siward to learn my letters, and for five years I studied the first rudiments of learning under his instruction".[81]

It is not clear from these firsthand accounts what the environment of Ælfric and Orderic's early education was. Griffith's suggestion that Ælfric's teacher was a priest at Winchester is unlikely, but his teacher may have been a part of the community of a secular minster or, as Catherine Cubitt has suggested, the local priest of a church on or near one of the estates of Æthelweard, the patron of a number of Ælfric's later works.[82] If so, this would afford a closer look at the opportunities for early clerical education in Anglo-Saxon England, potentially along the lines of the local schools mandated by Theodulf's first episcopal statute.[83] Orderic's early education in or near Shrewsbury in the later eleventh century by Siward the priest may also have been a similar sort of arrangement. In this case however, it may instead be that Siward was the teacher at a school operated by a minster, particularly as Shrewsbury had an unusually large number of secular minsters in the eleventh century.[84]

---

to Ælfric, 45; Christopher Jones, "Meatim Sed et Rustica: Ælfric of Eynsham as a Medieval Latin Author," *The Journal of Medieval Latin* 8 (1998): 53–54.

[80] Hill, "Ælfric: His Life and Works," 47; Cubitt, "Ælfric's Lay Patrons," 177.

[81] "Post quinquennium Siwardo nobili presbytero litteris erudiendus a genitore traditus sum. cuius magisterio prima percipiens rudimenta quinque annis subiugatus sum." Marjorie Chibnall, ed. and trans., *The Ecclesiastical History of Orderic Vitalis*, vol. 3, bks. 5 and 6 (Oxford: Clarendon Press, 1972), 7, 9.

[82] Cubitt, "Ælfric's Lay Patrons," 177.

[83] *Capitula episcoporum*, pt. 1, ed. Peter Brommer, *Monumenta Germaniae Historica* (Hanover: Hahnsche Buchhandlung, 1984), 115–16. This episcopal statute was fairly well known in England in the tenth and eleventh centuries: it exists in two independent Old English translations and served as a source for Wulfstan, Ælfric's pastoral letters, and the author of Vercelli Homily III. Hans Sauer, *Theodulfi Capitula in England: Die altenglischen Übersetzungen, zusammen mit dem lateinischen Text* (Munich: Wilhelm Fink, 1978), 509.

[84] See Steven Bassett, "Anglo-Saxon Shrewsbury and Its Churches," *Midland History* 16 (1991); Chibnall, *The Ecclesiastical History*, 146, n. 3. Bassett notes that the Siward responsible for Orderic's early education is "almost certainly" not the Siward son of Æthelgar who founded St Peter and St Paul's minster. Chibnall asserts that the church in which Siward served was St Peter's in Shrewsbury.

Though the autobiographical nature of Ælfric and Orderic's educational experiences is unique, we do find other references to schooling outside monasteries, cathedrals, and other known centers of education in the Anglo-Saxon period. In the late ninth or early tenth century, Oda, later Archbishop of Canterbury and uncle of Oswald of Worcester, joined the household of a thegn named Æthelhelm and was there educated by "a certain man of religion". Oda's teacher was probably a priest serving in the household, as Oda took holy orders while under his tutelage, eventually reaching the priesthood and serving as Æthelhelm's household priest.[85] Archbishop Wulfstan's *Canons of Edgar* seems to refer to this trend of education under a priest in the requirement that "no priest receive the scholar of another without the permission of him who he previously followed".[86] It is possible that this passage refers to a school, but the language here seems to indicate an individual teacher–pupil arrangement rather than a classroom environment. *On the Examination of Candidates for Ordination*, which tells us that a teacher must recommend a student to the bishop for his advancement through the clerical grades, may too imply a comparable educational arrangement.[87]

Education under an individual priest or in a school run by a local priest might have been less formal and potentially less rigorous than that of cathedral and monastic schools, but if education at this level generally resembled that of Orderic, then it was similar in that it consisted of instruction in letters, some liturgical training, and learning the Psalms.[88] Ælfric's early education may have been comparable and he was certainly familiar with his tutor's rudimentary knowledge of Latin, which could indicate that his early Latin instruction took place under this nameless priest. Additionally, the sort of relationship intimated in the *Canons of Edgar* and *On the Examination of Candidates for Ordination* seems to have been a personal one, probably analogous to an apprenticeship, particularly for those embarking on a clerical career. Whether in a cathedral or a minster church, those advancing to the priesthood in the course of a year must have been few in number and well known to their teachers, leading to long-term mentoring relationships and interpersonal connections.

---

[85] Lapidge, *Lives of St Oswald and St Ecgwine*, 19, 21.
[86] "7 riht is þæt ænig preost ne underfo oðres scolere butan þæs leafe þe he ær folgade." Whitelock, Brett, and Brooke, *Councils and Synods*, 318.
[87] Ibid., 426.
[88] Barrow, *The Clergy in the Medieval World*, 179, n. 49.

Writers, scribes, and glossators

Though a clear view of the instruction of the Anglo-Saxon clergy is largely obscured by documentary lacunae, it is apparent that multiple educational avenues were available for those aspiring to clerical careers. Examining the use of literate skills by priests is in some ways significantly more difficult than looking at the ways in which they received education, however. Reading, for example, does not necessarily produce physical evidence of its occurrence and written sources annotated or composed by secular priests are few. Despite this difficulty, some evidence from the late Anglo-Saxon period points to the involvement of secular clerics in literate activities such as producing books and legal documentation, glossing manuscripts, and composing hagiographical texts.

Though we have far fewer extant, readily identifiable examples of writing by priests in the tenth and eleventh centuries than those by monks, a small but significant corpus of material written by secular clerics has survived. Several scholars have identified the production of charters as associated with priests, royal and otherwise, in the Anglo-Saxon period. For example, a number of the scribes at Exeter during Leofric's episcopate, at least some of whom were probably cathedral canons, produced several extant charters and a range of evidence shows the involvement of the secular clergy in charter production.[89] Additionally, priests were common witnesses of charters and some of the priests who witnessed charters presumably had a hand in their composition and copying. Unfortunately, few English charters record the identity of their drafters or copyists, though in one lease related to Reculver minster, the scribe identifies himself as "Amery the priest".[90] More generally, the work of individual priests is difficult to delineate from the mass of charter evidence, but the work of at least one scribe, who was almost certainly a secular cleric and possibly a priest, can be identified in multiple documents on paleographical grounds.

---

[89] Simon Keynes, "Royal Government and the Written Word in Late Anglo-Saxon England," in McKitterick, *The Uses of Literacy in Early Medieval Europe*, 252, 257; Keynes, "The West Saxon Charters of King Æthelwulf and His Sons," *English Historical Review* 109 (1994): 1131–34, 1146–47; Charles Insley, "Charters and Episcopal Scriptoria in the Anglo-Saxon South-West," *Early Medieval Europe* 7, no. 2 (1998): 192. For examples outside England, see Barrow, *The Clergy in the Medieval World*, 246–47; Wendy Davies, *Small Worlds: The Village Community in Early Medieval Brittany* (Berkeley: University of California Press, 1988), 101; Rosamund McKitterick, *The Carolingians and the Written Word* (Cambridge: Cambridge University Press, 1989), 104–5, 109–16.

[90] John Blair, *The Church in Anglo-Saxon Society* (Oxford: Oxford University Press, 2005), 513–14.

Issues of Clerical Literacy

Bern, Burgerbibliothek 671 is a small gospelbook written in southwestern England or Wales in the first half of the ninth century with additions from the early tenth century, including the Bedwyn Guild Statutes and two manumissions. The scribe of the manumissions on f. 76v of this manuscript also penned the will of Wulfgar, which survives in single sheet format, allowing the handwriting of these two documents to be compared.[91]

Judging from the fact that this hand and two other contemporary hands wrote various documents relating to Bedwyn in the final leaves of the manuscript in the first few decades of the tenth century, the scribe of the will and manumissions was probably a member of the community of the royal minster at Bedwyn. The other two hands copying material relating to the church may indicate the presence of additional able scribes in the minster community.[92] The scribe of the manumissions or one of the others who made additions to the manuscript in Old English may in fact have been the priest, named as Ælfheah, who witnessed both manumissions, but this suspicion is impossible to test with the available evidence. It seems probable that the church at Bedwyn in this period was an urban minster, as may be indicated by the presence of statutes for the Bedwyn guild in this same manuscript as well as by a late Anglo-Saxon mint located there. A sizeable royal estate also centered on Bedwyn, and these factors may help to explain the geographical importance of this minster and its usefulness for the production and recording of documents.[93] In addition to indicating scribal activity in an Anglo-Saxon minster, the hand that wrote the will of Wulfgar and the manumissions in Bern 671 practiced a form of Anglo-Saxon Square Minuscule, a relatively new style for writing Old English that was in use at Winchester at the time that these additions were made. From this we can glean that the scribe at Bedwyn was not only literate and a competent scribe, but was also

---

[91] Malcolm Parkes, "A Fragment of an Early-Tenth-Century Anglo-Saxon Manuscript and Its Significance," *Anglo-Saxon England* 12 (1983): 137, n. 51. The will is S 1533.

[92] David Dumville, *Wessex and England from Alfred to Edgar: Six Essays on Political, Cultural, and Ecclesiastical Revival* (Woodbridge: Boydell Press, 1992), 78–82, 94. David Pratt has also accepted that the scribe who produced these documents was probably based at Bedwyn. See Pratt, "Kings and Books in Anglo-Saxon England," *Anglo-Saxon England* 43 (2014): 314–15. Though Dumville has written that "there can be little doubt that they [the additions to Bern 671] were all written at Bedwyn itself", the suggestion that all three scribes were part of the minster community at Bedwyn is my own. For more detailed information on the history of the Bedwyn estate, see Dumville, *Wessex and England from Alfred to Edgar*, 107–12.

[93] Bruce Eagles, "The Area around Bedwyn in the Anglo-Saxon Period," in *The Romano-British Villa at Castle Copse, Great Bedwyn*, ed. Eric Hostetter and Thomas Howe (Bloomington: Indiana University Press, 1997), 386–87, 390.

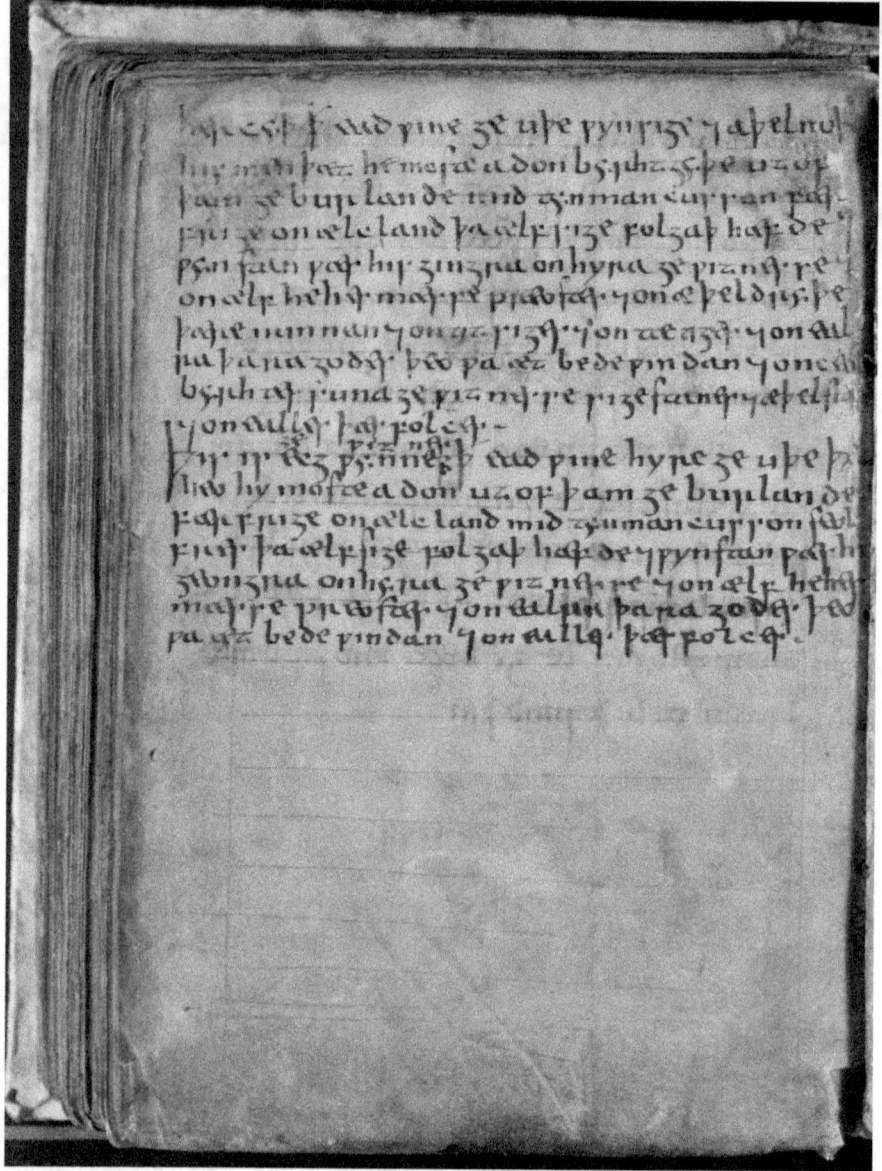

Plate 1: Burgerbibliothek Bern, Cod. 671, f. 76v. Old English manumissions of the early tenth century associated with the minster at Bedwyn.

trained to write in a form consistent with contemporary fashion in larger centers of book production. These practices, namely the production of multiple Old English documents, probably by several clerical scribes, and the practice of a contemporary scribal hand utilized in major centers of book production, constitute significant evidence for the literacy of the minster community at Bedwyn in the first half of the tenth century.

In another form of written output, at least two priests have identified themselves as the glossators of gospelbooks in colophons. The most noted priestly colophon is that of Aldred, who glossed the late seventh- or early eighth-century Lindisfarne Gospels (London, British Library, Cotton Nero D. IV) in Old English, leaving a lengthy record of his work and the work of those who had created the Lindisfarne Gospels. On f. 259r, he describes himself as the "unworthy and most miserable priest" who "glossed [the Lindisfarne Gospels] in English between the lines with the help of God and St Cuthbert".[94] Aldred tells us that he was the son of a certain Alfred and an unnamed "good woman" and from the dialect of the glosses, his origin, and potentially his education, was Northumbrian.[95] Much has been written about Aldred's colophon, its record of the making of the Lindisfarne Gospels more than two centuries earlier, and its relation to the text.[96] Aldred may have had a habit of inserting notes of this kind, as we also find a colophon by him in the Durham Collectar (Durham, Cathedral Library A. IV. 19), in which he notes that he copied four collects into the book while traveling in southern England with Bishop Ælfsige.[97] The language of the colophon in the Lindisfarne Gospels has led some scholars to interesting conclusions about the literacy of Aldred and the Chester-le-Street community in which he served. Aldred here references both Carolingian and Latin poetry, primarily Ovid, but with allusions to Alcuin and Theodulf of Orleans as well. Aldred's knowledge of Ovid is remarkable, as the influence of this Latin poet on Anglo-Saxon authors is almost wholly conjectured by the verbal reminisces of a handful of writers and only a single, fragmentary Anglo-

---

[94] Richard Gameson, "Why Did Eadfrith Write the Lindisfarne Gospels?," in *Belief and Culture in the Middle Ages: Studies Presented to Henry Mayr-Harting*, ed. Gameson and Henrietta Leyser (Oxford: Oxford University Press, 2001), 45, n. 2.

[95] Lawrence Nees, "Reading Aldred's Colophon for the Lindisfarne Gospels," *Speculum* 78, no. 2 (2003): 341; Michelle Brown, "'A Good Woman's Son': Aspects of Aldred's Agenda in Glossing the Lindisfarne Gospels," in *The Old English Gloss to the Lindisfarne Gospels: Language, Author and Context*, ed. Julia Fernández Cuesta and Sara M. Pons-Sanz (Berlin: De Gruyter, 2016), 23–24.

[96] See, for example, Cuesta and Pons-Sanz, eds., *The Old English Gloss to the Lindisfarne Gospels*; E. G. Stanley, "The Lindisfarne Gospels: Aldred's Gloss," in *The Lindisfarne Gospels: New Perspectives*, ed. Richard Gameson (Leiden: Brill, 2017); Gameson, "Why Did Eadfrith Write the Lindisfarne Gospels?"; Nees, "Reading Aldred's Colophon"; W. J. P. Boyd, *Aldred's Marginalia: Explanatory Comments in the Lindisfarne Gospels* (Exeter: University of Exeter, 1975).

[97] Richard Gameson, *The Scribe Speaks? Colophons in Early English Manuscripts* (Cambridge: Department of Anglo-Saxon, Norse and Celtic, University of Cambridge, 2002), 38–39.

Saxon copy of Ovid survives.⁹⁸ If Aldred was indeed knowledgeable of this range of sources, his education, complete by the mid-tenth century, is remarkable for a cleric in a practically secular community.

Despite interest in Aldred's education and "the high culture of Aldred and his circle", a relatively recent article on Aldred's colophon asserts that "very few of the brothers [at Chester-le-Street] were educated in Latin", in light of the glossing of the Lindisfarne Gospels in English and the fact that there were few monks in the community.⁹⁹ But the supposition that the community was unlearned on the grounds that an ornate gospelbook was glossed in the vernacular and the Chester-le-Street community lacked monks in significant numbers is untenable. As has been shown by scholars such as Mechthild Gretsch, Old English was a viable and developing "medium for scholarly and religious discourse" in the late Anglo-Saxon period and its use should not be interpreted as an automatic indicator of Latin illiteracy.¹⁰⁰ The glossing of the Lindisfarne Gospels is no more an indicator of Latin illiteracy among the Chester-le-Street clerics than Æthelwold's Old English translation of the *Rule of Benedict* is for the monks at Winchester; on the contrary, Stanley has recently asserted that "Aldred assumes in his readers a learned understanding of the gospels".¹⁰¹ Indeed, the glossing of the Lindisfarne Gospels is instead a witness to the existence of significant scholarship, Latinity, and scribal ability in a community of secular clerics, particularly considering the lack of evidence for Aldred having taken monastic vows. Despite assumptions by a number of scholars that Aldred was a monk and claims of his association with the Benedictine reform, Aldred never identifies himself as a monk and there is little reason to believe that he was not a secular priest. Michelle Brown assumes that Aldred was a monk when he joined the community, but does not explain the reasoning behind this assumption aside from later suggesting that "explanatory glossing of certain passages evinces a concern with celibacy and simony".¹⁰² On the other hand,

---

[98] Francis L. Newton, Francis L. Newton, Jr., and Christopher R. J. Scheirer, "Domiciling the Evangelists in Anglo-Saxon England: A Fresh Reading of Aldred's Colophon in the 'Lindisfarne Gospels'," *Anglo-Saxon England* 41 (2012): 111–12. For Bede's possible knowledge of Ovid, see Michael Lapidge, *The Anglo-Saxon Library* (Oxford: Oxford University Press, 2005), 66, 115.

[99] Newton, Newton, and Scheirer, "Domiciling the Evangelists in Anglo-Saxon England," 110.

[100] Gretsch, "Winchester Vocabulary and Standard Old English," 87. Also see Helen Gittos, "The Audience for Old English Texts: Ælfric, Rhetoric and 'the Edification of the Simple'," *Anglo-Saxon England* 43 (2014).

[101] Stanley, "The Lindisfarne Gospels: Aldred's Gloss," 210. On this translation of the *Rule of Benedict*, see Mechthild Gretsch, "Æthelwold's Translation of the *Regula Sancti Benedicti* and Its Latin Exemplar," *Anglo-Saxon England* 3 (1974).

[102] Michelle Brown, "'A Good Woman's Son': Aspects of Aldred's Agenda,", 23, 32; Boyd, *Aldred's Marginalia*, 4.

Karen Jolly believes it probable that Aldred was a secular priest and other recent work has cast doubt on connections between Aldred and Southumbrian reform efforts.[103] With little more than the information proffered to us by Aldred's writings and glossing, it is difficult to make more general statements about the literacy of the tenth-century community of St Cuthbert. However, as the clerics at Chester-le-Street in the tenth century remembered their history and saw themselves in some sense as the heirs to the monks at Lindisfarne, there may have been an enduring academic tradition upheld by the clerics, who made an effort to preserve at least part of the libraries of Lindisfarne and Wearmouth-Jarrow.[104] In any case, there is no question that Aldred himself was highly literate and if Chester-le-Street could attract or sustain scholars of Aldred's caliber, and potentially train others under his tutelage, there may have been a higher standard of literacy in the clerical community than has previously been assumed.

Another manuscript glossed by at least one priest in the tenth century is the MacRegol Gospels (Oxford, Bodleian Library, Auct. D. 2. 19). Written in Ireland in the late eighth or early ninth century, the volume had come to England by the late tenth century when two men who identify themselves as Owun and Farmon provided Old English glosses for the Latin text of the gospels.[105] Though it is uncertain exactly how this manuscript ended up in the hands of members of the Anglo-Saxon clergy, B.'s *Life of St Dunstan* records that Dunstan read the books that Irish pilgrims brought with them when they came to see the relics of St Patrick.[106] It may be that trading, buying, and selling of books also took place on these pilgrimages and the MacRegol Gospels came to England via these channels.

The relevance of this book to the literate activities of Anglo-Saxon priests becomes clear in a reading of its two colophons. The first, appearing at f. 50v, reads "Far[mon] pbr. þas boc þus gleosede dimittet ei dominus omnia peccata sua si fieri potest apud deum".[107] This

---

[103] Karen Jolly, *The Community of St. Cuthbert in the Late Tenth Century: The Chester-le-Street Additions to Durham Cathedral Library A.IV.19* (Columbus, OH: Ohio State University Press, 2012), 69, n. 74; Philip Rusche, "The Glosses to the Lindisfarne Gospels and the Benedictine Reform: Was Aldred Trained in the Southumbrian Glossing Tradition?," in *The Old English Gloss to the Lindisfarne Gospels*, 63, 76–77.

[104] Gerald Bonner, "St Cuthbert at Chester-le-Street," in *St Cuthbert, His Cult and His Community to AD 1200*, ed. Gerald Bonner, Clare Stancliffe, and David Rollason (Woodbridge: Boydell Press, 1989), 395.

[105] Kenichi Tamoto, ed., *The Macregol Gospels or the Rushworth Gospels: Edition of the Latin Text with the Old English Interlinear Gloss Transcribed from Oxford Bodleian Library, MS Auctarium D. 2. 19* (Philadelphia: John Benjamins, 2013), xi, xxix.

[106] Winterbottom and Lapidge, *Early Lives of St Dunstan*, 18–21.

[107] "Farmon the priest glossed this book thus. If it is possible with God, let the Lord put away all his sins."

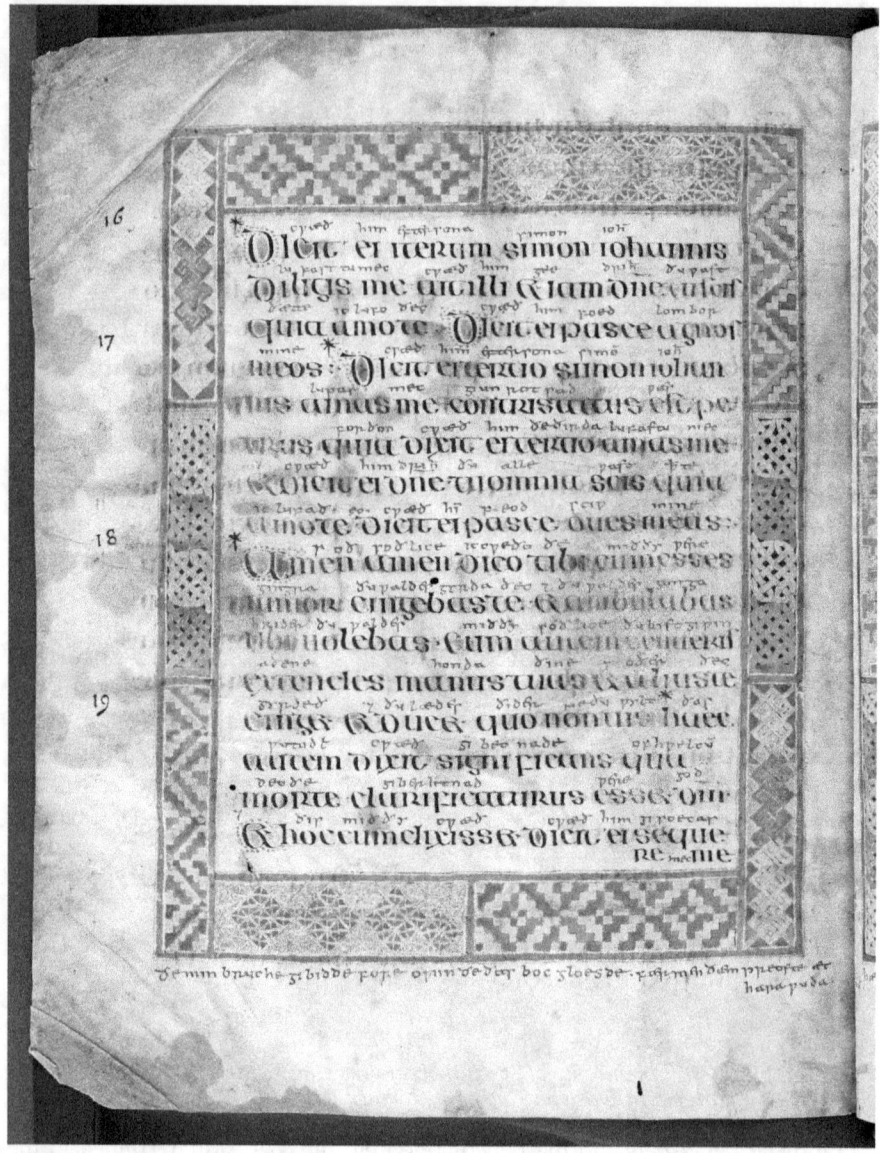

Plate 2: Oxford, Bodleian Library, Auct. D. 2. 19, f. 168v. A glossed page of the MacRegol Gospels, with part of Farmon's colophon visible at the bottom of the page.

unfortunately does not tell us much other than that a priest glossed this manuscript, though it is interesting that the inscription consists of mixed Latin and Old English. The second colophon provides slightly more information: "Ðe min bruche gibidde fore owun þe þas boc gloesde. Faermen ðaem preoste aet harawuda haefe nu boc awritne bruca mið willa symle mið soðum gileofa sibb is eghwaem leofost."[108] Most scholars have agreed that this Harewood most likely refers to the Harewood in Yorkshire, though alternate locations have been suggested.[109] Domesday Book notes neither a church nor a priest at Harewood, but the inconsistency of Domesday's church records is well known and the Yorkshire Harewood cannot be eliminated on this account.[110] In this case we are fortunately well served by other means of assessment. Physical evidence from Harewood is indicative of "burial, and presumably worship, on this site from the century before the Norman Conquest"; this evidence includes stone sculpture of tenth- and eleventh-century date as well as a small hoard of late Anglo-Saxon coins discovered close to the churchyard in 1895.[111] Lawrence Butler has suggested that documentary evidence concerning Harewood, including the considerable size of its parish in the later Middle Ages, "could suggest a community of priests before the Conquest of the type which twelfth-century reformers assimilated to the Augustinian pattern".[112] The lack of monastic activity north of the River Trent in the late Anglo-Saxon period reinforces the supposition that Harewood was the site of a secular minster.

The argument for the connection of the MacRegol Gospels to the Yorkshire Harewood is further strengthened by the dialect of the glosses. The glossators were at times sourcing their glosses from the Lindisfarne Gospels or a gospelbook containing an Old English gloss that shared a common source with the Lindisfarne Gospels, part of the differences between the glosses being evident in the use of regional spellings.[113] Owun's gloss is certainly in a Northumbrian

---

[108] "Whoever uses me, may he pray for Owun who glossed this book [and for] Faermon the priest at Harewood. Now have/hold the written book, use it with good intent and always with true faith. Peace is dearest to everyone." Gameson, *The Scribe Speaks?*, 39.

[109] Eric Stanley, "Karl Luick's 'Man schrieb wie man sprach' and English Historical Philology," in *Luick Revisited: Papers Read at the Luick-Symposium at Schloss Liechtenstein, 15.–18.9.1985*, ed. Dieter Kastovsky, Gero Bauer, and Jacek Fisiak (Tübingen: Gunter Narr, 1988), 321; Andrew Breeze, "The Provenance of the Rushworth Mercian Gloss," *Notes and Queries* 43, no. 4 (1996); Paul Bibire and Alan Ross, "The Differences between Lindisfarne and Rushworth Two," *Notes and Queries* 28, no. 2 (1981): 99. For Lichfield as an alternative location, see Richard Coates, "The Scriptorium of the Mercian Rushworth Gloss: A Bilingual Perspective," *Notes and Queries* 44, no. 4 (1997).

[110] Blair, *The Church in Anglo-Saxon Society*, 418; Blair, "Secular Minster Churches in Domesday Book," 121.

[111] Elizabeth Coatsworth, *Western Yorkshire*, vol. 8 of *Corpus of Anglo-Saxon Stone Sculpture*, ed. Rosemary Cramp (Oxford: Oxford University Press, 2008), 161–62; L. A. S. Butler, "All Saints Church, Harewood," *The Yorkshire Archaeological Journal* 58 (1986): 87, n. 15, 89.

[112] Butler, "All Saints Church, Harewood," 87.

[113] Gameson, *The Scribe Speaks?*, 29; Tamoto, *The Macregol Gospels*, cii; Tadashi Kotake, "Did Owun Really Copy from the Lindisfarne Gospels? Reconsideration

dialect, though one distinct from and more southerly than that of Aldred, as Owun seems to use Scandinavian loanwords only when relying on the Lindisfarne (or closely related) glosses. Farmon's gloss has been regarded as most probably east Mercian considering the apparent lack of Welsh features in the glossator's dialect, which is in contrast with the Welsh influence that would be expected if the glosses had been copied at the alternate Harewood in Herefordshire.[114]

It is plain that the evidence from the gloss to the MacRegol Gospels is contested and complex, but some reasoned suppositions can be made. Firstly, the Harewood referred to in the MacRegol Gospels can be most firmly associated with a location in West Yorkshire which was probably the site of a secular minster. Secondly, it seems probable that these two glossators were members of the secular clergy who were not only literate in Latin and Old English, but were also competent scribes. This, along with Aldred's apparent education in the north of England, may indicate the existence of a relatively robust educational tradition in secular churches in the north. The means by which this book came to be in the possession of Farmon and Owun, what their relationship was, and the whereabouts of the MacRegol Gospels from the eleventh to the seventeenth century, are unknown.[115] Despite the many questions surrounding the MacRegol Gospels, it is certainly an indication of the significant literate skills of Anglo-Saxon secular priests, and its use and association with Harewood are deserving of further consideration.

In addition to their potential roles as glossators, some priests and lower clerics participated in the production of manuscripts. Richard Gameson thinks it probable that secular clerics were responsible for a portion of the "visually disparate manuscripts" that have survived, particularly from the first half of the tenth century, prior to the effects of the Benedictine reform on English book production.[116] Certainly both secular and monastic cathedral chapters were important centers for book production. Hemming's Cartulary records a lease made in the 980s by Worcester Cathedral to a *preost* named Goding in return for writing books. The cathedral community apparently made a good investment in Goding's scribal abilities, as Hemming records that he wrote "many books", though no extant manuscripts have as yet been

---

of His Source Manuscript(s)," in *The Old English Gloss to the Lindisfarne Gospels*. Though a direct connection between the glosses of the MacRegol Gospels and the Lindisfarne Gospels has long been posited, Kotake has made a credible case for a less immediate relation between them.

[114] Stanley, "Karl Luick's 'Man schrieb wie man sprach'," 321–22; Breeze, "The Provenance of the Rushworth Mercian Gloss," 395.

[115] Tamoto, *The Macregol Gospels*, xxxi.

[116] Gameson, "Anglo-Saxon Scribes and Scriptoria," in *The Cambridge History of the Book in Britain*, 96–97.

attributed to him due to a lack of extant colophons or identification of his handwriting.[117] Winchester Cathedral seems to have actively produced books prior to Æthelwold's episcopacy and scribes there were most probably secular clerics.[118] Indeed, prior to the resurgence of English monasticism in the mid-tenth century, most scribes were probably members of the secular clergy, whether active in a religious or secular context. But even during and after the apogee of late Anglo-Saxon monastic life, secular clerics still played a noteworthy role in manuscript production. From the 1050s, the scriptorium at Exeter, made up of secular canons, was responsible for a significant amount of manuscript production, producing books equal in quality to those made by contemporary monasteries in "a distinctive script of a very high calibre".[119] Though some scholars have expressed skepticism, Elaine Drage has argued that the scribes at Exeter were the canons themselves, as Teresa Webber has demonstrated to be the case at Salisbury later in the eleventh century.[120] Additionally, there is evidence for some degree of manuscript production by clerics in secular minsters, which will be discussed in greater detail in the next chapter.

In addition to scribal activity among the secular clergy, there are also indications that some Anglo-Saxon clerics authored hagiographical texts. The *Life of St Dunstan* was written by an Anglo-Saxon secular cleric known to us only as B., who was at least a deacon and likely a priest. Far from being simply literate in Latin, B. was educated at Glastonbury, a member of Dunstan's retinue, a scholar on the Continent, and a practitioner of the hermeneutic style.[121] Additionally, Rosalind Love has suggested a possible connection between B. and

---

[117] Francesca Tinti, *Sustaining Belief: The Church of Worcester from c. 870 to c. 1100* (Farnham: Ashgate, 2010), 34; Richard Gameson, "Book Production and Decoration at Worcester in the Tenth and Eleventh Centuries," in *St Oswald of Worcester: Life and Influence*, ed. Nicholas Brooks and Catherine Cubitt (London: Leicester University Press, 1996), 198. It appears that Goding was a member of the cathedral community at Worcester. However, Eric John has taken a different view, asserting that "Hemming has no notion that Goding was a member of the community." John, *Orbis Britanniae and Other Studies* (Leicester: Leicester University Press, 1966), 246.

[118] Manuscripts probably produced at Winchester in the first half of the tenth century include the Junius Psalter (Oxford, Bodleian Library, Junius 27), the Lauderdale Orosius (London, British Library, Add. 47967), and the Parker Chronicle (Cambridge, Corpus Christi College 173).

[119] Gameson, "Anglo-Saxon Scribes and Scriptoria," 96; Elaine Treharne, "The Bishop's Book: Leofric's Homiliary and Eleventh-Century Exeter," in *Early Medieval Studies in Memory of Patrick Wormald*, ed. Stephen Baxter et al. (Farnham: Ashgate, 2009), 528.

[120] Elaine Drage, "Bishop Leofric and the Exeter Cathedral Chapter, 1050–1072: A Reassessment of the Manuscript Evidence" (DPhil thesis, University of Oxford, 1978); Teresa Webber, *Scribes and Scholars at Salisbury Cathedral, c.1075–c.1125* (Oxford: Clarendon Press, 1992), 28–30.

[121] For the status of Glastonbury in the early tenth century, see page 89.

the *Life and Miracles of St Eadburg*, indicating there may yet be more hagiographical texts penned by B. awaiting identification.[122] In addition, Stephen Baxter has suggested that the chaplain of Earl Leofric of Mercia may have been responsible for the composition of the eleventh-century *Vision of Leofric*, citing the liturgical interest of the writer and his familiarity with the makeup of the earl's retinue. Though he does not endorse Baxter's view of this text's authorship, Peter Stokes has noted that the opening line of the *Vision of Leofric* is a phrase found "almost exclusively at the opening of vernacular writs".[123] Earl Leofric's household priest may well have had experience in the production of documents of this kind and while this is no proof of authorship, the resemblance is suggestive. These examples, along with the *Life of St Wulfstan*, written by Coleman, Wulfstan's chaplain, may indicate a trend in the composition of hagiographical texts by household priests; it is certainly known that parish priests were involved in this sort of activity in the twelfth century.[124]

The *Life of St Cuthman* may also be evidence for the priestly production of hagiography, specifically at a secular minster. St Cuthman was born in Sussex in the late seventh century and is most remembered as the founder of St Andrew's, Steyning as well as for the primitive wheelbarrow he used to transport his disabled mother. John Blair has edited this particular *vita* and asserted that the content and vocabulary of the text suggest a date in the late eleventh century, possibly the 1080s. The text concludes with St Cuthman's construction of a wooden church at Steyning, Sussex, where the church and its surrounding features became strongly associated with the saint.[125] At the time of the *vita*'s composition, the minster was controlled by Fécamp Abbey in Normandy, but Blair contends that the content of the *Life of St Cuthman* was not a direct product of the monks of Fécamp, as the source includes a great deal of local history that was unlikely to interest Norman ecclesiastics. For example, "the author or his source knew a stave-church

---

[122] Lapidge has made an argument for much of this in Lapidge, "B. and the *Vita S. Dunstani*" and Stephenson has similarly identified the author's Latin as hermeneutic. See Rebecca Stephenson, "Ælfric of Eynsham and Hermeneutic Latin: *Meatim Sed et Rustica* Reconsidered," *The Journal of Medieval Latin* 16 (2006): 112; Rosalind Love, "Wars of the Word," *Cambridge Alumni Magazine* 73 (2014): 37.

[123] Stephen Baxter, *The Earls of Mercia: Lordship and Power in Late Anglo-Saxon England* (Oxford: Oxford University Press, 2007), 4, 154, n. 6; Peter Stokes, "The Vision of Leofric: Manuscript, Text and Context," *The Review of English Studies* 63 (2012): 545.

[124] C. S. Watkins, "Sin, Penance and Purgatory in the Anglo-Norman Realm: The Evidence of Visions and Ghost Stories," *Past and Present* 175, no. 1 (2002): 6, 12, 18–19.

[125] John Blair, "Saint Cuthman, Steyning and Bosham," *Sussex Archaeological Collections* 135 (1997): 173–74, 176–77; E. W. Holden, "New Evidence Relating to Bramber Bridge," *Sussex Archaeological Collections* 113 (1975): 111.

at Steyning" and was apparently familiar with the construction techniques of Anglo-Saxon wooden churches, such as the use of the vertical tongue-and-groove system. Indeed, there are significant similarities between the construction method ostensibly used by Cuthman and those used in the building of Anglo-Saxon timber churches, including the extant church at Greensted, Essex.[126] Furthermore, the hagiographical motifs in the text are strongly associated with Insular, rather than continental traditions, such as the "preoccupation with ferocious nature-miracles" and Cuthman's association with sheep.[127] It may not be possible to conclusively attribute the authorship of the *Life of St Cuthman* to a minster priest in the decades following the Conquest, but the author's local knowledge, familiarity with Insular hagiographical themes, and acquaintance with the architecture of minster churches point to a member of the secular clergy serving at Steyning.

Conclusions

From the above discussion of the evidence concerning priestly literacy in the late Anglo-Saxon period, a few broad conclusions can be drawn. Firstly, throughout the tenth and eleventh centuries, and particularly after the mid-tenth-century Benedictine reform, there were a variety of educational means available for the training of clerics. Some of these educational avenues, such as cathedral and monastic schools, may have been primarily available to wealthy and aristocratic students. But other types of educational opportunities were available to aspiring clerics, such as schools based in minsters, some of which may have been founded along with the *burhs* constructed via royal prerogative in the late ninth and early tenth centuries. It has been suggested that these minster schools may be what Alfred had in mind for the education of freeborn young men as well as those who intended to take clerical orders.[128] Additionally, there are potential indications of the practice of individual tutoring or the operation of local schools by priests, particularly for those intended for a clerical vocation. Furthermore, education for the performance of the liturgy was an integral part of clerical education at all levels, as it was for monastic education. This type of training, in which students would not only observe, but also participate in liturgical celebrations, prepared future clerics and those already in orders via practical training. As illustrated by an excerpt from *The Waltham Chronicle*, the importance of the celebration of the mass and Office for the clergy made training and participation in ser-

---

[126] Blair, "Saint Cuthman," 177, 179.
[127] Ibid., 177.
[128] Whitelock, *English Historical Documents*, 889.

vices a necessary part of clerical curricula.

Secondly, monastic indictments of clerical literacy must be understood and interpreted in context. English monks of the later tenth century and beyond were concerned to differentiate themselves from the secular clergy and did so rhetorically in a number of ways, including indicting the linguistic competency of priests. Monks and secular clerics were rivals for aristocratic patronage and status, making monastic disparagement of secular priests a potentially political strategy for Benedictine writers. In addition, the standards of Latin literacy that were expected of the clergy by monks may have far exceeded the linguistic proficiency needed for priests to perform their pastoral duties. I have argued that literacy for priests was primarily functional in nature and based on the need to perform the liturgy and provide pastoral care. Monastic criticisms may have accurately portrayed a proportion of the secular clergy, but such statements should be contextualized and measured against the available evidence for priestly literacy.

Thirdly, we can see that the divide between churches of varying status was permeable. Ælfric, in his mostly unknown early years, was educated by a local and, in Ælfric's view, fairly ignorant priest, but furthered his education at Æthelwold's Winchester, one of the intellectual centers of the Benedictine Reform. Æthelstan, the father of St Wulfstan, moved from the cathedral community at Worcester to a parish church in the same diocese, while Oda of Canterbury started his clerical education and career in a noble household before receiving episcopal appointments at Ramsbury and Canterbury. Though priestly literacy was largely determined by the education that an individual received, we should note that the individuals and institutions through which priests were educated were part of navigable ecclesiastical structures and networks, granting a degree of potential mobility and advancement.

Fourthly, the degree of Latin literacy on the part of the Anglo-Saxon clergy is on the whole difficult to determine. Much of the evidence against their literacy comes to us from monastic sources. A small but growing body of literature has attempted to parse and critically examine claims of clerical ignorance and ineptitude from these sources and has generally found that these passages show monastic writers attempting to unfavorably contrast reformed monastic principles with those of the secular church in order to define and differentiate themselves from the secular clergy.[129] While degrees of literacy must have varied, evidence such as the authorship of hagiographical works in both Latin and Old English, the production of charters and other docu-

---

[129] Hill, "Monastic Reform and the Secular Church," 111, 115–16; Stephenson, *The Politics of Language*; Stephenson, "Scapegoating the Secular Clergy".

mentation, and the glossing of gospelbooks by secular priests points to high levels of literacy among some clerics. Inferences of the liturgical competence of priests by even those who were otherwise skeptical of their literate abilities might indicate that it was assumed that priests would be, at minimum, functionally literate in Latin.

3

Demand and Supply: Production and Provision of Books for Priests

Books were expensive, labor-intensive commodities in the early medieval period. Their production required the availability of treated and prepared skins, ink, quills, and literate individuals who had received scribal training. Obtaining exemplars for the copying of a particular book would also have been a necessity and may at times have proven challenging, particularly for relatively small centers of book production as opposed to major scriptoria. In addition, copying books took a great deal of time on the part of a scribe, as a skilled copyist might write only seven pages per day, and some books were copied at a considerably slower rate.[1] In short, the production of books in the Middle Ages represented a significant investment of time and resources. Considering the great expense of obtaining books and the modest financial status of many early medieval priests, how were priests able to get access to the volumes they needed to carry out their pastoral duties? The nature of priestly ministry requires the availability of books, and a consideration of the production and provision of priestly books will help to illustrate the accessibility of pastoral texts to priests as well as wider relationships between priests, ecclesiastical authorities, and lay lords.

Issues of medieval book production

Before moving on to consider the production of books for priests in the late Anglo-Saxon period, an important issue to consider is how we define the term scriptorium. This term evokes images of monastic scribes hunched over writing desks, but the definition of what constitutes a scriptorium has been the subject of some disagreement. David Ganz has argued that the defining characteristic of a scriptorium is a "shared scribal discipline", particularly as an aspect of monastic discipline, and therefore that a scriptorium is not simply a group of scribes working under the same roof but "a means of training scribes

---

[1] David Ganz, "Book Production in the Carolingian Empire and the Spread of Caroline Minuscule," in *The New Cambridge Medieval History Volume 2: c.700–c.900*, ed. Rosamond McKitterick (Cambridge: Cambridge University Press, 1995), 791–92.

and of producing manuscripts in a homogeneous style".[2] Conversely, Richard Gameson has offered a more inclusive definition of a scriptorium as simply a place in which books were produced, though he also recognizes the more restrictive definition of a scriptorium as "an organised group of scribes, decorators and binders".[3] The more inclusive definition of a scriptorium is more helpful in thinking about diverse centers of book production, whereas Ganz's definition seems to be conceived specifically with monastic scriptoria in mind and with a view of scribal discipline as integrally related to monastic discipline. Additionally, Ganz's conception of a scriptorium would seemingly not encompass a book production center in which scribes who were trained in other localities and practiced varying scripts produced books. However, this is the precise circumstance in which a number of late Anglo-Saxon manuscripts seem to have been copied, including the *Beowulf* manuscript (London, British Library, Cotton Vitellius A. XV), which was written by two scribes with significantly distinct handwriting, as well as the several dozen manuscripts produced at Salisbury in the late eleventh and early twelfth centuries.[4]

Furthermore, if we only accept manuscripts of a homogenous style as those produced in a true scriptorium, we underestimate the losses that may prevent us from recognizing house styles now represented by only a few books or even a single book. The large number of unlocalized Anglo-Saxon manuscripts illustrates the limitations of our knowledge in reference to smaller centers that produced books in the tenth and eleventh centuries as well as those scriptoria whose existence might be concealed due to uneven patterns of manuscript survival. As Elaine Treharne has argued, the large numbers of ostensibly identifiable examples of handwriting from cathedrals and monasteries may at times obscure our view of other centers in which Anglo-Saxon manuscripts were produced and the networks through which they moved; I suggest later in this chapter that some of these other centers were secular minsters.[5] In light of these factors, taking a broader view of what might constitute a scriptorium may allow scholars to better contextualize the production of unlocalized manuscripts and, more

---

[2] Ibid., 791; Ganz, "The Preconditions for Caroline Minuscule," *Viator* 18 (1987): 28–29.

[3] Richard Gameson, "Anglo-Saxon Scribes and Scriptoria," in *The Cambridge History of the Book in Britain Volume 1: c.400–1100*, ed. Gameson (Cambridge: Cambridge University Press, 2011), 102–3.

[4] Andy Orchard, *A Critical Companion to Beowulf* (Cambridge: D. S. Brewer, 2001), 19–20; Teresa Webber, *Scribes and Scholars at Salisbury Cathedral, c.1075–c.1125* (Oxford: Clarendon Press, 1992), 9, 11.

[5] Elaine Treharne, "Scribal Connections in Late Anglo-Saxon England," in *Texts and Traditions of Medieval Pastoral Care: Essays in Honour of Bella Millett*, ed. Cate Gunn and Catherine Innes-Parker (York: York Medieval Press, 2009).

specifically, better inform us about the ways in which priests obtained the texts necessary for the provision of pastoral care.

A second issue is that of scribal training. The copying of books by hand is a laborious process to which medieval scribes brought skill, practice, and training. Though a scribe's innate talent for copying books is difficult for the historian to quantify, evidence for scribal training and the practice of these skills can be found in a significant number of early medieval books. In a scriptorium, scribes were probably trained by a master who would begin by teaching letterforms, syllables, and no doubt the practicalities of preparing a quill and ruling a page before copying. One such example of an English scribe in training can be found in the late seventh- or early eighth-century Durham Gospels (Durham, Cathedral Library, A. II. 17) and the pages from the contemporary Jarrow Luke bound with this copy of the gospels, where seven tenth-century marginal additions appear in an unpracticed and childish hand. The inscriptions are unambiguously that of a young student, and T. Julian Brown has suggested that the writer may have been an oblate or the child of one of the Durham clerics.[6] Some of the inscriptions imperfectly copy snippets of the gospel text, while others repeat short phrases in both English and Latin, such as "Boge messepreost god preost", "Aldred god biscop", and "in nomine domini". A number of Carolingian manuscripts show the efforts of somewhat more advanced trainee scribes. Ganz has noted a number of continental manuscripts in which inexperienced and often-poor scribes struggle with proper letter formation, rarely utilize ligatures, and frequently erase their mistakes. Passages in these manuscripts also show evidence of intervention and correction by a more experienced scribe, who is most probably identifiable with the master overseeing the training of a group of fledgling scribes.[7] As for Anglo-Saxon manuscripts, Karen Jolly has argued that we can see this pedagogical process at work in Durham, Cathedral Library, A. IV. 19, with no less a master than Aldred, the well-studied glossa-

---

[6] T. Julian Brown, "The Boge-Aldred-Mantat Inscriptions," in *The Durham Gospels, Together with Fragments of a Gospel Book in Uncial, Durham, Cathedral Library, MS A. II. 17*, ed. Christopher Verey, T. Julian Brown, and Elizabeth Coatsworth, Early English Manuscripts in Facsimile 20 (Copenhagen: Rosenkilde and Bagger, 1980), 51–52; Sarah Larratt Keefer, "Use of Manuscript Space for Design, Text and Image in Liturgical Books Owned by the Community of St Cuthbert," in *Signs on the Edge: Space, Text and Margin in Medieval Manuscripts*, ed. Keefer and Rolf H. Bremmer, Jr. (Paris: Peeters, 2007), 91–92.

[7] Ganz, "The Preconditions for Caroline Minuscule," 34–35. On the provision of exemplary scripts for learning and inexperienced scribes, also see Sidney Tibbetts, "*Praescriptiones*, Student Scribes and the Carolingian Scriptorium," in *La collaboration dans la production de l'écrit médiéval: Actes du XIIIe colloque du Comité international de paléographie latine*, ed. Herrad Spilling (Paris: École des chartes, 2003).

tor of the Lindisfarne Gospels.[8] A limited exemplary instruction on script may also be evident in London, Lambeth Palace Library, 489, a collection of mostly Ælfrician homilies copied at Exeter in the third quarter of the eleventh century, in which one scribe wrote to provide an example of an "Exeter-style" script for another scribe to imitate.[9] To mold competent scribes, this type of practical scribal training must have been common in English cathedrals and monasteries of the tenth and eleventh centuries.

A final issue, and indeed precondition, relating to book production is material resources, particularly ink, quills, and treated animal skins for parchment. Depending on the size and length of a given book, the need for skins could vary significantly: one estimate places the number of calf skins needed to produce the Codex Amiatinus at slightly over 500, while short, small-format books might require only five.[10] To make skins suitable for writing, the skin of a freshly slaughtered animal was soaked in lime, scraped, and dried under tension, often by a parchment maker, though there are indications that some medieval scribes prepared skins for writing themselves.[11] Whether or not a scribe had the knowledge to prepare parchment, nearly all scribes must have been able to prepare quill pens for their work. This involved choosing a suitable feather, typically from a goose, removing the barbs from the shaft of the feather, then shaping and cutting the nib to prepare it for writing. Likewise, ink preparation probably often fell to the scribe. The coloration of inks used in Anglo-Saxon manuscripts is often an indication of the composition of the ink, with oak gall and iron salts making up brown ink and black ink largely consisting of carbon from soot. Pigments for manuscript illumination and unusually colored inks were obtained from various natural sources such as certain types of shellfish, plants, insects, metals, and minerals.[12] Though most of the raw materials for producing books were plentiful in medieval Europe, their usage in bookmaking took training and experiential knowledge that, along with training in writing itself, was necessary for the production of manuscripts from the wealthiest monastic scriptorium to the local priest drafting a charter.

---

[8] Karen Jolly, "The Process of Glossing and Glossing as Process: Scholarship and Education in Durham, Cathedral Library, MS A.iv.19," in *The Old English Gloss to the Lindisfarne Gospels: Language, Author and Context*, ed. Julia Fernández Cuesta and Sara M. Pons-Sanz (Berlin: De Gruyter, 2016), 365–67.

[9] Takako Kato, "Exeter Scribes in Cambridge, University Library, MS Ii. 2. 11 + Exeter Book Folios 0, 1–7," *New Medieval Literatures* 13 (2011): 14.

[10] Rosamund McKitterick, *The Carolingians and the Written Word* (Cambridge: Cambridge University Press, 1989), 139–40.

[11] Ganz, "Book Production in the Carolingian Empire," 792.

[12] McKitterick, *The Carolingians and the Written Word*, 138, 141–46.

Scriptoria in cathedrals and monasteries

Of the surviving Anglo-Saxon manuscripts, many are liturgical books that have been associated with specific monasteries and cathedrals. It is thus relatively simple to identify some major centers that were responsible for the production of service books, notably Christ Church, Canterbury; Worcester; and Winchester, the communities of which all became monastic between 964 and the mid-eleventh century. This took place at Winchester through the expulsion of the secular clerics of the cathedral, while the changes in the makeup of the communities at Canterbury and Worcester seem to have been more gradual.[13] All of these cathedrals had a pre-monastic scribal tradition.[14] Most of the manuscripts written in scriptoria such as these in the decades after the Benedictine reform are not thought to have been produced for or used by the secular clergy and many of the surviving examples probably were not. However, considering the comparatively large number of secular clerics in late Anglo-Saxon England, it would be unusual if a considerable number of the books produced in major scriptoria were not intended for or used by priests, as suggested by Jonathan Wilcox in reference to the homilies of Ælfric.[15] It has been posited by other scholars that major centers of Anglo-Saxon book production copied liturgical manuscripts for smaller institutions and a small number of surviving manuscripts seem to conform to this pattern.[16] The Red Book

---

[13] Nicholas Brooks, *The Early History of the Church of Canterbury: Christ Church from 597 to 1066* (Leicester: Leicester University Press, 1984), 255–61; Julia Barrow, "Wulfstan and Worcester: Bishop and Clergy in the Early Eleventh Century," in *Wulfstan, Archbishop of York: The Proceedings of the Second Alcuin Conference*, ed. Matthew Townend (Turnhout: Brepols, 2004), 149–50.

[14] Michael Lapidge, "Latin Learning in Ninth-Century England," in *Anglo-Latin Literature, 600–899* (London: Hambledon Press, 1996), 434; Richard Gameson, "Book Production and Decoration at Worcester in the Tenth and Eleventh Centuries," in *St Oswald of Worcester: Life and Influence*, ed. Nicholas Brooks and Catherine Cubitt (London: Leicester University Press, 1996), 195–96. That books were produced at Winchester prior to the monastic reform is clear from manuscripts such as Oxford, Bodleian Library, Junius 27 and the books to which it is related by script and decoration.

[15] Olga Timofeeva, "Anglo-Latin Bilingualism before 1066: Prospects and Limitations," in *Interfaces between Language and Culture in Medieval England: A Festschrift for Matti Kilpiö*, ed. Alaric Hall et al. (Leiden: Brill, 2010), 14. Jonathan Wilcox, "Ælfric in Dorset and the Landscape of Pastoral Care," in *Pastoral Care in Anglo-Saxon England*, ed. Francesca Tinti (Woodbridge: Boydell Press, 2005), 60–61.

[16] Richard Gameson, "St Wulfstan, the Library of Worcester and the Spirituality of the Medieval Book," in *St Wulfstan and His World*, ed. Julia Barrow and Nicholas Brooks (Aldershot: Ashgate, 2005), 84–85; David Dumville, *Liturgy and the Ecclesiastical History of Late Anglo-Saxon England: Four Studies* (Woodbridge: Boydell Press, 1992), 141; Francesca Tinti, *Sustaining Belief: The*

of Darley (Cambridge, Corpus Christi College 422), a mid-eleventh-century missal produced at Winchester or Sherborne, seems to have been written for and seen use in a pastoral setting, judging from the liturgical contents of the manuscript and its well-used appearance.[17] At the time of the book's production, the cathedral communities of both Sherborne and Winchester were monastic, as were their bishops. Another example is Oxford, Bodleian Library, Laud Misc. 482, a book containing penitentials and rites for the sick and dying and, like the Red Book of Darley, a very pastorally oriented volume. It was produced in the mid-eleventh century at Worcester, where the cathedral community had been a mix of monks and clerics since the 970s but became wholly monastic at some point in the eleventh century, possibly during St Wulfstan's episcopate.[18] Neither of those books is much like the lavishly decorated volumes often associated with monastic scriptoria, but they may represent a common class of book produced by these centers.

Many of the scriptoria in cathedrals and monasteries were capable of producing high-status books, but not all the books they produced were of the highest quality. Many examples of books with script and materials of mediocre quality are available and many more "ordinary" books from these centers may not have survived precisely because they were not of great contemporary value.[19] Considering the cost of producing high-status books and the demand for service books that must have been generated by the building of large numbers of local churches, it is likely that liturgical volumes of average quality were the bread and butter of many Anglo-Saxon scribes and scriptoria.

Church of Worcester from c.870 to c.1100 (Farnham: Ashgate, 2010), 300; Brooks, *The Early History of the Church of Canterbury*, 273. Some local priests' books of the Carolingian period also seem to have been copied by scribes from major scriptoria. The scribe who copied most of Paris, Bibliothèque nationale de France, lat. 1603, a handbook of canon law from around the turn of the ninth century thought to be a Carolingian priest's book, appears to also have copied part of a book at the royal court at Aachen and was a brother at the Abbey of Saint Amand. Yitzhak Hen, "Knowledge of Canon Law among Rural Priests: The Evidence of Two Carolingian Manuscripts from around 800," *The Journal of Theological Studies* 50, no. 1 (1999): 130–31.

[17] For a discussion of the Red Book of Darley and the questions surrounding the context of its pastoral use, see chapter 5.

[18] Julia Barrow, "The Community of Worcester, 961–c. 1100," in Nicholas Brooks and Catherine Cubitt, *St Oswald of Worcester*, 98–99; Barrow, "Wulfstan and Worcester: Bishop and Clergy," 149–51. For more on the origin and provenance of this manuscript, see the relevant discussion in chapter 6.

[19] A prime example of this is London, British Library, Royal 1 D. III, a gospelbook described by Patrick McGurk as "scruffy, desultory and unfinished", though it may originally have had an ornate cover. McGurk, "Anglo-Saxon Gospel-Books, c. 900–1066," in Gameson, *The Cambridge History of the Book in Britain*, 445.

These books could be produced in a relatively short period of time with minimal decoration, and mass-books, lectionaries, and psalters of middling quality must have been available in significant numbers if minor churches were to be suitably equipped with service books.

Major scriptoria in England, many of which were monastic, might have produced manuscripts for minor churches and their priests for a number of reasons. Foremost among these was the production of books for their dependencies. If a cathedral or monastery had a functioning scriptorium, it is probable that at least some of the manuscripts needed by its dependent churches would have been produced there, and a significant number of minsters and local churches were under the control of reformed monastic institutions in the decades following the Benedictine reform.[20] When these churches were in need of books, the scriptorium of a controlling institution seems a likely place to turn, perhaps particularly for local churches on monastic estates.[21] Francesca Tinti has suggested that in the diocese of Worcester, monastic communities were concerned with the provision of pastoral care both on their estates and in minsters under their control and would have taken steps to facilitate its delivery, one facet of which was providing liturgical books.[22] One example of this is the church at Hawkesbury, which was probably a secular minster with a small clerical community and was controlled by Pershore Abbey in the eleventh century.[23] Before his monastic vows and ascension to the episcopate, St Wulfstan was a priest for some time at the church at Hawkesbury, to which he was appointed by Bishop Britheah, who may have been his brother.[24] His *vita* records reading at the common table as well as liturgical celebrations at Hawkesbury, implying that the church had a complement of books that exceeded those necessary for the performance of the liturgy; the availability of these books may have been a product of the

---

[20] John Blair, "Secular Minster Churches in Domesday Book," in *Domesday Book: A Reassessment*, ed. Peter H. Sawyer (London: Edward Arnold, 1985), 125–26; Barbara Yorke, *Wessex in the Early Middle Ages* (London: Leicester University Press, 1995), 236–38. For example, St John the Baptist at Clare, Suffolk was a secular minster under the control of Bury St Edmunds during the abbacy of Leofstan. Ann Williams, "Thegnly Piety and Ecclesiastical Patronage in the Late Old English Kingdom," in *Anglo-Norman Studies XXIV: Proceedings of the Battle Conference 2001*, ed. John Gillingham (Woodbridge: Boydell Press, 2002), 6.

[21] Richard Gameson has asserted that books written in reformed monasteries "may have been distributed to local churches throughout the south of England". Gameson, *The Role of Art in the Late Anglo-Saxon Church* (Oxford: Clarendon Press, 1995), 243.

[22] Tinti, *Sustaining Belief*, 119, 264.

[23] For more on Hawkesbury, see Michael Hare, "Wulfstan and the Church of Hawkesbury," in Barrow and Brooks, *St Wulfstan and His World*.

[24] Brooks, "Introduction: How Do We Know about St Wulfstan?," in Barrow and Brooks, *St Wulfstan and His World*, 20.

minster's relationship with Pershore Abbey.[25] Additionally, inventories of books from local churches in ninth-century Bavaria indicate that continental churches that were controlled by monasteries were often adequately supplied with a complement of basic liturgical books.[26] The significant number of monks who were ordained as priests in Anglo-Saxon England might also suggest a greater concern for the availability of pastoral texts, particularly in those reformed monastic institutions that had frequent pastoral interaction with laypeople. Recent work by Tinti and Christopher Riedel has shown that monastic cathedrals in urban centers were fertile fields for pastoral care offered by monks and the scriptoria in these sees may have been similarly active in the copying of pastoral texts.[27]

In addition to the provision of books for secular churches that were under their control, major scriptoria also produced work on commission. Recent scholarship has emphasized the work of the skilled Canterbury scribe Eadwig Basan, who not only produced books for use at Christ Church, Canterbury, but also a number of books commissioned by royalty, nobility, and other ecclesiastical institutions.[28] Though it is unlikely that he was involved in the production of manuscripts for local priests at the apogee of his career, other scribes in cathedrals and monasteries may have worked on commissioned manuscripts as Eadwig Basan did. It does seem that some Anglo-Saxon scribes specialized in the copying of liturgical books, such as a Peterborough scribe whose surviving work consists of six gospelbooks, two of which survive only as fragments, and a sacramentary.[29] A commission for the production of a book might come from various sources, but it is clear that Anglo-Saxon royalty and nobility used major scriptoria to produce books for their own purposes. In approximately 1020 and thereafter, Cnut and Emma commissioned manuscripts at a variety of such scriptoria to produce high-status books intended to be used as political capital or as patronage for monasteries and cathedral

---

[25] Gameson, "St Wulfstan, the Library of Worcester and the Spirituality of the Medieval Book," 88.

[26] Carl Hammer, "Country Churches, Clerical Inventories and the Carolingian Renaissance in Bavaria," *Church History* 49, no. 1 (1980).

[27] Francesca Tinti, "Benedictine Reform and Pastoral Care in Late Anglo-Saxon England," *Early Medieval Europe* 23, no. 2 (2015); Christopher Riedel, "Praising God Together: Monastic Reformers and Laypeople in Tenth-Century Winchester," *The Catholic Historical Review* 102, no. 2 (2016).

[28] See, for example, Susan Rankin, "An Early Eleventh-Century Missal Fragment Copied by Eadwig Basan: MS. Lat. Liturg. D. 3, fols. 4–5," *Bodleian Library Record* 18 (2004); Richard Gameson, "The Colophon of the Eadwig Gospels," *Anglo-Saxon England* 31 (2002); T. A. Heslop, "The Production of *de luxe* Manuscripts and the Patronage of King Cnut and Queen Emma," *Anglo-Saxon England* 19 (1990).

[29] Heslop, "The Production of *de luxe* Manuscripts," 176.

communities.³⁰ Anglo-Saxon aristocrats probably also used these scriptoria to supply recipients of their patronage, including secular churches and members of the secular clergy, with books.

Royal minsters, minor centers, and unlocalized manuscripts

Secular churches other than cathedrals have not generally been seen as centers of manuscript production, nor has the scribal ability of secular clerics been the subject of much consideration. In other words, there has been very little discussion of the possibility of manuscript production taking place outside Anglo-Saxon monasteries and cathedrals, which has served to limit our view of potential avenues of book production. Richard Pfaff has indeed remarked that "we do not associate with minster churches ... anything like a scriptorium".³¹ Despite this, it is clear that many priests were able to draft and copy texts. The role of priests in the production of charters and other legal documents in England and on the continent in the early medieval period has often been recognized, and at least some of the same scribes who wrote wills and charters of the tenth and eleventh centuries must also have had the ability to copy books.³² In the early eleventh century, Archbishop Wulfstan expected his clergy to have access to quills and parchment, indicating that priests were expected to be able to write and that the necessary materials for writing were available to them.³³ Furthermore, there is evidence that points to scribal activity in minor centers, particularly royal minsters of the tenth century and later secular minsters.

There are a number of examples of scribal activity at royal minsters from the first half of the tenth century. As has been mentioned in the preceding chapter, we find a single scribal hand practicing a relatively early form of English Square Minuscule that was responsible for both the writing of manumissions into a Cornish gospelbook, now Bern, Burgerbibliothek 671, and the will of Wulfgar, an English thegn. All of this writing was done between 920 and 940 and the book in which the manumissions were copied is strongly associated with the royal minster at Bedwyn by means of the content of these and other additions. Two other hands also added documents related to Bedwyn in

---

³⁰ Ibid., 179–80.
³¹ Richard Pfaff, *The Liturgy in Medieval England: A History* (Cambridge: Cambridge University Press, 2009), 64.
³² See chapter 2, note 89.
³³ Two versions of the *Canons of Edgar* require this of priests. See Dorothy Whitelock, Martin Brett, and Christopher N. L. Brooke, eds., *Councils and Synods, with Other Documents Relating to the English Church, AD 871–1204*, vol. 1 (Oxford: Clarendon Press, 1981), 316, n. 3.

the final folios of the gospelbook, which seems to indicate that multiple able scribes were at the minster in the early tenth century. Glastonbury, another royal minster of the early tenth century, was certainly producing manuscripts in the 930s and was probably also responsible for the production of charters in the church's favor, particularly those of the late ninth and early tenth centuries.[34] Additionally, according to B.'s *Life of St Dunstan*, it was at Glastonbury that the future archbishop was trained in writing and manuscript illumination, indicating that scribal activity was taking place at least in the 930s and probably significantly earlier.[35] Glastonbury's well-known connection to the early monastic movement in England might cause some to discount this evidence, but there is precious little evidence for monasticism at Glastonbury in the decades prior to Dunstan's abbacy and it seems that even during his tenure as abbot, the church housed both secular clerics and monks.[36]

In addition to evidence for scribal activity in royal minsters, there are further indications of scribal activity among priests in the reigns of Alfred and Edward the Elder. Simon Keynes has not only suggested that priests played a major role in the production of royal documents, but has also pointed out that Alfred seems to have had scribes copying books outside of the royal court, as is indicated by the king sending the Old English translation of Gregory's *Pastoral Care* "south and north to his scribes" to produce more copies.[37] Considering the general lack of monastic activity in England in the late ninth and early tenth centuries, it is likely that many of Alfred's scribes were priests and other secular clerics working in royal minsters, which, like those in Glastonbury and Bedwyn, were responsible to some degree for the production of books and documents.

---

[34] Michael Lapidge, "Schools, Learning and Literature in Tenth-Century England," in *Anglo-Latin Literature, 900–1066* (London: Hambledon Press, 1993), 22–23; Lesley Abrams, *Anglo-Saxon Glastonbury: Church and Endowment* (Woodbridge: Boydell Press, 1996), 7.

[35] Michael Lapidge and Michael Winterbottom, eds. and trans., *The Early Lives of St Dunstan* (Oxford: Clarendon Press, 2012), 40.

[36] Nicholas Brooks, "The Career of St Dunstan," in *St Dunstan: His Life, Times, and Cult*, ed. Nigel Ramsay, Margaret Sparks, and Tim Tatton-Brown (Woodbridge: Boydell Press, 1992), 12–13; Nicola Robertson, "Dunstan and Monastic Reform: Tenth-Century Fact or Twelfth-Century Fiction?," in *Anglo-Norman Studies XXVIII: Proceedings of the Battle Conference 2005*, ed. C. P. Lewis (Woodbridge: Boydell Press, 2006), 154–55. Brooks points out that some of the vignettes from B.'s *Life of St Dunstan* indicate the presence of both clerics and monks at Glastonbury and that when leaving Glastonbury, Æthelwold "took with him three *clerici*". Robertson has gone further in questioning the extent to which Glastonbury was monastic at all in the early tenth century as well as under the leadership of Dunstan.

[37] Simon Keynes, "Regenbald the Chancellor (sic)," in *Anglo-Norman Studies X: Proceedings of the Battle Conference 1987*, ed. R. Allen Brown (Woodbridge: Boydell Press, 1988), 188.

Later in the tenth century, further evidence for scribal activity in minsters emerges outside of royal foundations. Chapters 43 to 49 of the *Liber Eliensis* as it currently stands are drawn from an earlier text ostensibly written by a member of the pre-Benedictine clerical community at Ely. Janet Fairweather writes that the interpolated text is "of pre-Conquest date" and asserts that the text was probably written by a cleric who served at Ely and may have later joined the monastic community there.[38] The author of this section, named as Ælfhelm, relates a few healing miracles attributed to St Æthelthryth before going on to describe how some members of the former community were divinely punished for disrespecting the saint. One of the affected priests of the pre-monastic community was said to have been "trained in the scribal duties which belong to the church and its priesthood", providing further indication of the potential for scribal activity in secular centers.[39] Unlike Bedwyn, the community at Ely did not leave us with any surviving and identifiable writing associated with this scribe, but it speaks to the commonality of priests receiving scribal training that the writer of this section of the *Liber Eliensis*, who too was a secular cleric and probably later a monk at Ely in the tenth century, associates the priesthood with scribal activity.[40] Another example, discussed in greater detail in the previous chapter, comes from Harewood in West Yorkshire, which may have been the site of a minster community in the late tenth century.[41] Two scribes glossed the MacRegol Gospels (Oxford, Bodleian Library, Auct. D. 2. 19), drawing from the glosses to the Lindisfarne Gospels or a similarly glossed gospelbook, and one of these glossators is identified as Farmon, a priest at Harewood.

The fact that multiple minsters are associated with scribal activity in the tenth century, particularly in light of the poor survival of evidence from these institutions, suggests that some minsters, including those not under royal control, were capable of producing documents, booklets, and books. Though the production of charters and other documentary evidence does not necessarily imply the presence of a scriptorium, particularly at a small minster, it is clear that scribes were active in minsters and engaging in a variety of scribal activities, ranging from the production of documents to the copying of discrete volumes. The size and status of most of these minsters are largely unknown, but it is unlikely that they ranked alongside mid-eleventh-century Waltham or

---

[38] Janet Fairweather, trans., Liber Eliensis*: A History of the Isle of Ely from the Seventh Century to the Twelfth* (Woodbridge: Boydell Press, 2005), 77, n. 292.

[39] Ibid., 82.

[40] Certainly the criticism of the members of the secular community at Ely would be more understandable if the writer of this section had joined the Benedictines at Ely, as Fairweather suggests.

[41] See chapter 2 for a more detailed discussion. Lawrence Butler, "All Saints Church, Harewood," *The Yorkshire Archaeological Journal* 58 (1986): 87, 89.

Production and Provision of Books

Bosham in wealth or status. But if secular minsters that are not known for their wealth (or, like Harewood, are largely unknown) show evidence of scribal activity, then large and wealthy secular minsters, which must have possessed greater resources for book production than their humbler counterparts, could certainly have had scriptoria of their own.

If secular minsters were in some cases responsible for copying manuscripts, where are the books produced by these churches? The large proportion of unlocalized Anglo-Saxon manuscripts may suggest an answer. The production of a number of unlocalized Anglo-Saxon manuscripts has been associated with minor or provincial centers, often on account of the unusual or archaic nature of the decoration or scribal hand or the poor quality of the codex, such as the decorative additions to the Warsaw Lectionary (Warsaw, Biblioteka Narodowa, I. 3311) and the marginal texts of Corpus 41 (Cambridge, Corpus Christi College 41).[42] These distinctions may at times be justified, as most small, rural minsters no doubt had relatively meager resources and scribes with minimal training, when any were available at all, though even major scriptoria produced sub-par scribes.[43] On the other hand, some secular minster churches were exceedingly wealthy and were recipients of aristocratic patronage, and at least one eleventh-century minster had an erudite Lotharingian master who may have authored several works that do not survive.[44] Two examples of minsters that fit this description are Waltham Holy Cross, Essex and Bosham, Sussex, both of which do not seem to have lacked financial resources. Indeed, Emma Cownie has pointed out that the Domesday-era holdings of Bosham put it on roughly equal financial footing with monasteries like Peterborough and Ramsey, both of which had their own scriptorium.[45] In addition to the minsters that became wealthy through aristocratic patronage, large episcopal minsters, some of which seem to have acted as centers of diocesan administration, may also have been capable of book production on some level. This could have been the case for a

---

[42] Elżbieta Temple, *Anglo-Saxon Manuscripts, 900–1066* (London: Harvey Miller, 1976), 108; Christopher Hohler, review of *Cambridge, Corpus Christi College 41: The Loricas and the Missal*, by Raymond Grant, *Medium Aevum* 49 (1980): 275–76.

[43] Richard Gameson, "English Manuscript Art in the Late Eleventh Century: Canterbury and Its Context," in *Canterbury and the Norman Conquest: Churches, Saints and Scholars, 1066–1109*, ed. Richard Eales and Richard Sharpe (London: Hambledon Press, 1995), 112.

[44] Leslie Watkiss and Marjorie Chibnall, eds., *The Waltham Chronicle: An Account of the Discovery of Our Holy Cross at Montacute and Its Conveyance to Waltham* (Oxford: Clarendon Press, 1994), xxx; M. R. James, "Manuscripts from Essex Monastic Libraries," *Transactions of the Essex Archaeological Society*, n.s., 21 (1933): 42.

[45] Emma Cownie, *Religious Patronage in Anglo-Norman England, 1066–1135* (London and Woodbridge: The Royal Historical Society and Boydell Press, 1998), 28.

number of the minsters of the Archbishop of York, such as Beverley and Ripon, as well as some of the minsters in the similarly massive diocese of Dorchester.[46] Both wealthy minsters and minsters that acted as centers of administration frequently benefitted from large landed endowments and clerical communities of significant size, and thus may have had the personnel and the financial resources to produce books. Manuscripts that, in terms of quality, are on par with scribal products of Benedictine houses have been noted in relation to Exeter's scriptorium, which was built up in a relatively short period of time under the leadership of Bishop Leofric.[47] As Leofric was able to build up a scriptorium, minsters with well-trained and well-provisioned scribes may have been able to produce books with relatively high-quality script, decoration, and materials – qualities that would not lead most scholars to associate them with a secular church. However, some scribal products seem to be unambiguously associated with a minor church with minimal resources. The book now represented only by the four leaves of the Taunton Fragment (Taunton, Somerset County Record Office, DD\SAS\C1193/77) might well be the type of manuscript produced in a less well-provisioned church that lacked trained scribes, and the extensive use of marginal space by the priest who made additions to Corpus 41 could also indicate a shortage of institutional resources.[48]

The evidence for scribal activity in secular minsters is significant: we have multiple accounts of able scribes, surviving examples of their handwriting, and a large number of books and fragments which scholars have so far been unable to localize. Books produced in minsters, which might span a wide range in the quality of their script and materials, could thus make up a significant portion of the Anglo-Saxon manuscripts that remain unlocalized – a group that accounts for many manuscripts of the tenth and eleventh centuries, including the Exeter Book (Exeter, Cathedral Library 3501) and the *Beowulf* manuscript. As the evidence from the early tenth century concerns the royal minsters at Bedwyn and Glastonbury, it may be that royal minsters in particular were equipped to produce books, and Alfred's commis-

---

[46] Frank Barlow, *The English Church, 1000–1066: A History of the Later Anglo-Saxon Church*, 2nd ed. (London: Longman, 1979), 229; Dorothy Owen, "The Norman Cathedral at Lincoln," in *Anglo-Norman Studies VI: Proceedings of the Battle Conference 1983*, ed. R. Allen Brown (Woodbridge: Boydell Press, 1984), 191.

[47] Gameson, "Anglo-Saxon Scribes and Scriptoria," 96; Elaine Treharne, "The Bishop's Book: Leofric's Homiliary and Eleventh-Century Exeter," in *Early Medieval Studies in Memory of Patrick Wormald*, ed. Stephen Baxter et al. (Farnham: Ashgate, 2009), 530.

[48] Mechthild Gretsch, "The Taunton Fragment: A New Text from Anglo-Saxon England," *Anglo-Saxon England* 33 (2004): 145, 193, n. 121; Aidan Conti, "The Taunton Fragment and the Homiliary of Angers: Context for New Old English," *Review of English Studies* 60 (2008): 32–33.

sioning of multiple and geographically diverse royal institutions to copy the Old English translation of *Pastoral Care* may strengthen this supposition. Royal patronage of book and document production in minsters from the ninth century and later may have been a response to political upheaval and a lack of monastic scribal activity. During and after the monastic reforms of the tenth century, there is no doubt that scribal activity in these churches continued alongside that taking place at cathedrals and monasteries, though royal patronage of book production may have largely shifted to monastic centers and cathedral scriptoria. Of the Anglo-Saxon minsters that saw some level of scribal activity, whether royal or non-royal, many may not have met Ganz's criteria for what constitutes a scriptorium. Some however, particularly those with significant resources, were probably capable of producing their own books, and even less wealthy churches might have been capable of copying books and booklets for their own use and producing charters and other legal documents. Despite the likelihood of book production of a reasonable standard at some Anglo-Saxon minor churches, the localization of these volumes to more than a broad region has been hampered by the particularly low rate of manuscript survival outside monasteries and cathedrals and the resulting lack of comparative evidence upon which paleographical analysis relies.

Episcopal provision

Though it is rarely clear to us how a specific church or clergyman might have acquired books, bishops seem to have played a major role in their provision. A variety of early medieval sources indicate that bishops provided certain grades of clerics with particular books or booklets upon ordination, but evidence from the late Anglo-Saxon period points to a larger role for bishops in the provision of service books to their churches.[49] A scene from the *Life of St Wulfstan* provides direct evidence for the provision of books by a bishop to a church under his control. Wulfstan's *vita* records that he repaired the church at Westbury-on-Trym, gave it lands and tithes, and provided it with service books.[50] Westbury was the site of St Oswald's first monastic community, a foundation that eventually moved to Ramsey. The departure of the

---

[49] Roger Reynolds, "Ordinatio and the Priesthood in the Early Middle Ages and Its Visual Depiction," in *A Companion to Priesthood and Holy Orders in the Middle Ages*, ed. Greg Peters and C. Colt Anderson (Leiden: Brill, 2016), 51–52; Yitzhak Hen, "Priests and Books in the Merovingian Period," in *Men in the Middle: Local Priests in Early Medieval Europe*, ed. Steffen Patzold and Carine van Rhijn (Berlin: De Gruyter, 2016), 165–66.

[50] Michael Winterbottom and R. M. Thomson, eds. and trans., *William of Malmesbury: Saints' Lives* (Oxford: Oxford University Press, 2002), 120–23.

monks, probably in 965, apparently left the church at Westbury open to decay and attack, leaving only a single priest "who seldom celebrated the divine services" to staff the church.[51] When St Wulfstan refounded the church at Westbury-on-Trym a century later, this new foundation also seems to have been monastic, but this pattern of provision extended to endowment of secular churches as well. Gameson has written the following on Wulfstan's provision of books: "This is interesting evidence for what must have been a common pattern in the distribution of manuscripts: major centres providing minor ones with the volumes they needed for their day-to-day existence. Books were a necessity for a new church or community and it was incumbent upon a founder or reformer to supply them."[52] Perhaps the most prominent example of this in a secular church was occasioned by Bishop Leofric's relocation of the seat of his bishopric from Crediton to Exeter in 1050. At Exeter, Leofric found a woefully inadequate five service books in poor condition and in the course of his episcopate made significant efforts to build up a library both through collecting books and the founding of a scriptorium there. His efforts were remarkably successful: the inventory of Leofric's bequest to Exeter lists 59 volumes not already at Exeter, speaking to an energetic bishop's considerable ability to provide books.[53] In another similar though far less detailed case, Archbishop Cynesige of York (1051–1060) endowed the minster at Beverley, an episcopal minster and the center of the cult of John of Beverley, with books as part of a wider program that included the building of a new church tower, continued work on a refectory and dormitory, and gifts of bells to Beverley and other churches.[54] Ealdred of York (1060–1069) continued the endowment of archiepiscopal minsters and though books were not explicitly mentioned as part of what was provided, liturgical books and other volumes might well have been a part of the subsequent archbishop's patronage.[55] During his tenure as bishop of Winchester, Æthelwold also refounded and endowed a number of churches and monasteries, including Peterborough, Chertsey, and Thorney. His foundation of Thorney probably included books, as Wulfstan of Winchester notes that Æthelwold provided the

---

[51] Tinti, *Sustaining Belief*, 21, 206, 248–49.

[52] Gameson, "St Wulfstan, the Library of Worcester and the Spirituality of the Medieval Book," 84–85.

[53] Richard Gameson, "The Origin of the Exeter Book of Old English Poetry," *Anglo-Saxon England* 25 (1996). For an opposing view on the creation (or pre-existence) of the library at Exeter, see Patrick Conner, *Anglo-Saxon Exeter: A Tenth-Century Cultural History* (Woodbridge: Boydell Press, 1993).

[54] Janet M. Cooper, *The Last Four Anglo-Saxon Archbishops of York* (York: St. Anthony's Press, 1970), 22.

[55] Barlow, *The English Church, 1000–1066*, 89–90.

new monastery with "bonorum omnium possessione".[56] Furthermore, we know that the refoundation of Peterborough involved episcopal provision of books, because a list of the twenty-one books given to the monastery, which are mostly biblical or theological commentaries, has survived in a twelfth-century cartulary.[57] Though several of the extant narrative sources bearing witness to the provision of books by bishops concern monastic institutions, a similar pattern of episcopal provision of books is known at Exeter and Beverley and likely held true for other secular churches as well.

One of the major ways in which bishops would have provided texts to churches under their control was through the activity of their scriptoria or through episcopal scribes. The dissemination of the homilies of Ælfric is a prime example of use of a scriptorium under the control of a bishop for this purpose. Upon the completion of the First and Second Series of Ælfric's *Catholic Homilies*, both were sent to Archbishop Sigeric of Canterbury for his approval and ostensibly for the correction of any errors. Peter Clemoes has demonstrated that Canterbury subsequently acted as a center of distribution for the *Catholic Homilies*: we find the "Canterbury-distributed CH I" at Worcester and the West Midlands, Exeter and other parts of the southwest, East Anglia, areas north of the Thames, and other locales.[58] However, as Wilcox has pointed out, there are few surviving copies of the *Catholic Homilies* that appear to have been written for pastoral use by secular priests, though this is almost certainly the result of patterns of manuscript survival rather than an accurate representation of what was produced.[59] If Canterbury was producing and circulating these homiletic texts to other centers in the south of England, it is reasonable to assume that they were also providing them to the churches in their own diocese. The manuscript evidence for Canterbury's distribution of Ælfric's homilies is principally confined to large, relatively high-status copies, but their dissemination indicates the ability and willingness of bishops to produce and widely circulate pastoral texts and as a result, the practical role of cathedral scriptoria under the direction of a bishop in disseminating such texts.

---

[56] Michael Lapidge and Michael Winterbottom, eds. and trans., *Life of St Æthelwold* (Oxford: Clarendon Press, 1991), xlvii–l; H. R. Loyn, *The English Church, 940–1154* (New York: Pearson, 2000), 19–20.

[57] Michael Lapidge, "Surviving Booklists from Anglo-Saxon England," in *Learning and Literature in Anglo-Saxon England: Studies Presented to Peter Clemoes on the Occasion of His Sixty-Fifth Birthday*, ed. Lapidge and Helmut Gneuss (Cambridge: Cambridge University Press, 1985), 52–54.

[58] Peter Clemoes, ed., *Ælfric's Catholic Homilies: The First Series*, Early English Text Society Supplementary Series 17 (Oxford: Oxford University Press, 1997), 162–63.

[59] Jonathan Wilcox, "The Use of Ælfric's Homilies: MSS Oxford, Bodleian Library, Junius 85 and 86 in the Field," in *A Companion to Ælfric*, ed. Hugh Magennis and Mary Swan (Leiden: Brill, 2009), 350–51.

Another way in which bishops may have provided books to churches within their dioceses was lending. Several tenth- and eleventh-century lending lists from the continent record loans to diocesan clergy and it has been suggested that cathedrals such as Winchester and Sherborne may too have lent books to nearby churches.[60] Potential evidence for the lending of books to the English clergy has survived in the form of a booklist in Oxford, Bodleian Library, Auct. D. 2. 14, an Italian gospelbook of the sixth or seventh century which had come to England by the close of the seventh century.[61] The booklist in question was originally written into an eleventh-century service book that is now lost, but a single surviving leaf of this book was bound at an unknown date with the gospelbook in which it is now preserved.[62] The list of "xv bocas" consists mostly of service books, including two homiliaries. It also records several non-liturgical books, including a leechbook, what appears to be a chronicle, a book on grammar, and a book called "blake had boc", for which a number of interpretations have been suggested, including the possibility of a reference to a personal name. The list would at some point have numbered seventeen, but several erasures were made at or before the addition of the final tally. The books in the list are each assigned to one of four individuals, namely Salomon the priest, Wulfmær Cild, Sigar the priest, and Æilmer, and appear below the assigned names. After the booklist, a number of names were copied, including "Bealdwine abb.", identified as Baldwin, abbot of Bury St Edmund's during roughly the last third of the eleventh century.[63] Michael Lapidge hesitantly suggests that the books contained in the list might have been lent out and the list is a record of the monks within the cloister who had borrowed and returned the monastery's volumes, but he also notes that one weakness of this theory is the large number of liturgical books ostensibly lent to monks of Bury St Edmund's. Furthermore, it is not certain that the booklist originated

---

[60] Joyce Hill, "Ælfric: His Life and Works,"' in Magennis and Swan, *A Companion to Ælfric*, 55.

[61] David Ganz, "The Annotations in Oxford, Bodleian Library, Auct. D. II. 14," in *Belief and Culture in the Middle Ages: Studies Presented to Henry Mayr-Harting*, ed. Richard Gameson and Henrietta Leyser (Oxford: Oxford University Press, 2001), 35.

[62] Neil Ker, *Catalogue of Manuscripts Containing Anglo-Saxon* (Oxford: Clarendon Press, 1957), 350. The text on the opposite side of the leaf in question is the "Latin service *Ad introitum porte*". As Ker notes, this text is printed in Charles Wordsworth, Pontificale Ecclesiae S. Andreae: *The Pontifical Offices Used by David de Bernham, Bishop of S. Andrews* (Edinburgh: Pitsligo Press, 1885), 53.

[63] Lapidge, "Surviving Booklists," 74–76. "Þas bocas haueð Salomon preost þæt is þe codspel traht 7 þe martyrliua 7 þe 7 þe æglisce saltere 7 þe cranc 7 ðe tropere 7 Wulfmer cild þe atteleuaui 7 pistelari 7 þe 7 ðe imnere 7 ðe captelari 7 þe spel boc 7 Sigar preost þe lece boc 7 blake had boc 7 Æilmer ðe grete sater 7 ðe litle tropere forbeande 7 ðe donatum."

at Bury. The booklist itself was written using spelling Lapidge refers to as "chaotic" and in two poor hands dated by Neil Ker to the second quarter of the eleventh century.[64] The list of names associated with Bury was written at a later date by a third scribe and thus Baldwin's name cannot be connected to the list at the time of its composition. However, the most probable scenario is that the book originally containing the list was owned by Bury St Edmund's and did record loans made by the monastery as Lapidge suggests, but did so for loans of books made to those outside the cloister. This would make sense of the high proportion of liturgical books in the list, especially if the clerics borrowing books were serving churches controlled by or in close proximity to the monastery, and would also explain the need to record the loans in the first place.

Lending lists resembling this interpretation of the Bury list survive from both secular and monastic centers on the continent. The lending list from the monastery at Weissenburg, probably dating to the tenth century, records loans to those both in and outside the cloister. Basic liturgical books seem to have been commonly borrowed items: one Liudrih borrowed a set of vestments along with a psalter and a missal, and others frequently borrowed antiphoners, graduals, and psalters.[65] Another example comes from an Italian manuscript of the Abbey of San Salvatore at Monte Amiata, containing an eleventh-century lending list rendered in drypoint that provides brief notes on loans made to both individuals and ecclesiastical institutions. Michael Gorman has identified most of the borrowed books as biblical commentaries, though Gregory's *Dialogues* and a passional also appear.[66] Like the English list, some of the entries have been erased or struck through, possibly indicating that the books in question were noted as returned. Another eleventh-century Italian lending list from the cathedral at Verona similarly records several priests or groups of clerics borrowing books, all of which contain either portions of the biblical text or liturgical material: one entry reads "Clerici de Caprino habent psalterium sancti Hieronimi", while another records "Presbiter de sancta Cecilia libellum canticorum".[67]

---

[64] Ibid., 74, 76; Ker, *Catalogue of Manuscripts Containing Anglo-Saxon*, 350.
[65] McKitterick, *The Carolingians and the Written Word*, 264.
[66] Michael Gorman, "Manuscript Books at Monte Amiata in the Eleventh Century," *Scriptorium* 56 (2002): 243–46.
[67] Michael Gorman, "A List of Books Lent by the Cathedral Library in Verona in the Eleventh Century," *Scriptorium* 56 (2002): 321–23. "The priests at Caprino Veronese have a psalter in St Jerome's Vulgate translation." "A priest at Saint Cecilia has a book of prayers." Gorman translates "libellum canticorum" as "book of prayers", but he rightly notes that it may also be a reference to Song of Songs.

The "Salomon preost" of the Bury list may have been in a similar situation to that of Liudrih and the priests of the church at Caprino Veronese: all found it necessary to borrow a psalter, one of the most basic books for a cleric and one of a few books named by almost all of the prescriptive lists discussed in an earlier chapter. Though the context of these continental lending records is clearer than that of the Bury list, they all indicate that at times ecclesiastical institutions with significant bookholdings lent out books to lesser institutions and individuals who are often identified as clerics. This practice may have been especially prevalent in the provision of books to the dependencies of cathedrals and monasteries, as these lists may demonstrate. In some cases, loans of books may also have provided exemplars for the clerics of a church or a hired scribe for the copying of needed texts. The hazy origins of the Bury list and the lack of the original codex from which it came make it a difficult source to contextualize definitively, but the possibilities surrounding this list are wider than have been considered. If the way in which Anglo-Saxon bishops and abbots provided books for churches under their control was similar to that on the continent, lending may have been a useful if temporary way to provide smaller institutions with the books necessary for their operation or to provide exemplars for the copying of needed books.

As founders, reformers, or simply as endowers of existing churches, late Anglo-Saxon bishops did provide books to lesser churches under their control, whether they were secular churches or monasteries. The churches for which direct evidence of episcopal provision of books exists all seem to have been under the more or less direct control of those who were giving them books. This provision may have taken the form of endowment, as at Westbury-on-Trym and Beverley, or lending, as may have been the case for Bury. In light of the evidence, it is not unreasonable to suppose that monasteries and cathedrals, particularly those with active scriptoria and a strong episcopal commitment to pastoral care, would provide books for the churches under their control who had no books or whose books were no longer serviceable. We may then wonder if bishops did or were able to provide bibliographical resources for those churches which were in their diocese but were not under the control of the bishop or cathedral community. In all likelihood, this was strongly dependent on the wealth of the diocese in question, but if this sort of provision did take place, no record of it survives. Though extant accounts typically depict the provision of books as a direct action of the bishop, the business of providing books may not have been personally attended to by the bishop, but rather by a senior member of a cathedral or monastic community. In the later Middle Ages, possibly as early as the twelfth century, the business of providing books, emending and updating old books, and arranging for scribes to do the necessary work fell to the precentor of a community. In addition, we see grants of land being made from the later eleventh century onward to both secular and monastic churches to fund the production of new books and the repair and updating of old ones.[68] Funding for the production and updating of books no doubt came from similar sources in the late Anglo-Saxon period, as the later eleventh- and early twelfth-century practices of cathedrals and monasteries probably reflect earlier practice.

Aristocratic patronage

The patronage of lay lords was another common way in which churches obtained books. Though patronage of monastic institutions is better documented in both the historical record and modern scholarship, secular minsters and manorial churches were undoubtedly still major recipients of the patronage of Anglo-Saxon aristocracy and royalty. This patronage might take the form of gifts in life or the execution of a patron's bequests after death. The wills of the English nobility in the tenth and eleventh centuries show that in addition to grants of land to monasteries and cathedrals, patronage of secular minsters and their own manorial churches was common. For example, the will of Æthelgifu, dating to the second half of the tenth century, makes provision for St Alban's and several secular minsters, and the mid-tenth-century will of Ælfgar similarly provides for both secular and monastic foundations. The will of Æthelmær, drafted between 971 and the early 980s, gifted money to both minster churches and reformed monasteries, making no distinction between these institutions.[69] In addition to the textual evidence, evidence from inscriptions indicates that lay lords were responsible for the foundation or refoundation of a number of local churches, which would have invariably included the provision of books as a necessary part of any foundation.[70] Some lay

---

[68] Richard Sharpe, "The Medieval Librarian," in *The Cambridge History of Libraries in Britain and Ireland Volume 1: To 1640*, ed. Elisabeth Leedham-Green and Teresa Webber (Cambridge: Cambridge University Press, 2006), 219–21; Michael Gullick, "Professional Scribes in Eleventh- and Twelfth-Century England," *English Manuscript Studies* 7 (1998): 1–4, 7. Also see Teresa Webber, "Cantor, Sacrist or Prior? The Provision of Books in Anglo-Norman England," in *Medieval Cantors and Their Craft: Music, Liturgy and the Shaping of History, 800–1500*, eds. Katie Bugyis, A. B. Kraebel, and Margot Fassler (York: York Medieval Press, 2017).

[69] Julia Crick, ed., *Charters of St Albans* (Oxford: Published for the British Academy by Oxford University Press, 2007), 96; Dorothy Whitelock, ed. and trans., *Anglo-Saxon Wills* (Cambridge: Cambridge University Press, 1930), 6–9; Cownie, *Religious Patronage in Anglo-Norman England*, 17.

[70] Elisabeth Okasha, *Handlist of Anglo-Saxon Non-runic Inscriptions* (Cambridge: Cambridge University Press, 1971), 47, 64, 131; Philip Rahtz and Lorna Watts, "Three Ages of Conversion at Kirkdale, North Yorkshire," in *The Cross Goes North: Processes of Conversion in Northern Europe, AD 300–1300*, ed. Martin Carver

aristocrats took interest in certain foundations to which they showed particular liberality. Earl Leofric and Godiva were generous benefactors of the clerical community at Stow, which they refounded in 1054 and where they requested that the Divine Office be celebrated as it was at St Paul's in London.[71] Books are not specifically mentioned in their patronage of Stow, but celebration of the Divine Office in a full form in addition to the performance of various masses would have required a significant number of books, which were probably provided by the couple endowing the church. And Leofric and Godiva's patronage was not exclusive to either secular or monastic churches: we are told that they founded and thereafter enriched a monastery at Coventry, supported the reformed monastery at Evesham, and gave to several secular minsters in addition to Stow, such as the communities of priests at Much Wenlock and St Werburgh's, Chester.[72] Even King Edgar, well known for his support of reformed monasticism, was a benefactor of multiple secular churches.[73]

Clearly, lay landowners showed generosity to secular churches as they did to monasteries and this manifested itself both in supporting existing churches and founding new ones. Lay men and women who founded or refounded a church would have been responsible for its endowment and it must have been common for them to provide these churches with books as part of a range of necessary items including land and liturgical vessels.[74] A straightforward example of a refounded church receiving books through aristocratic patronage is Harold Godwinson's lavish endowment of the secular minster community

---

(York: York Medieval Press, 2003), 306. An inscription from a late tenth- or eleventh-century sundial at the church at Aldbrough reads, "Ulf ordered the church to be erected for himself and Gunwaru's soul", and the famous Kirkdale dial records that the church there was "completely ruined and collapsed" and subsequently "built anew from the ground", funded by Orm Gamalson, a wealthy Yorkshire thegn of probable Scandinavian heritage. A tenth-century inscription found at St Mary's, Castlegate in York seems to follow a similar pattern.

[71] S 1478.
[72] *The Chronicle of John of Worcester*, vol. 2, *The Annals from 450 to 1066*, ed. R. R. Darlington and P. McGurk, trans. Jennifer Bray and McGurk (Oxford: Clarendon Press, 1995), 583; John Hunt, "Piety, Prestige or Politics? The House of Leofric and the Foundation and Patronage of Coventry Priory," in *Coventry's First Cathedral: The Cathedral and Priory of St Mary, Papers from the 1993 Anniversary Symposium*, ed. George Demidowicz (Stamford: Paul Watkins, 1994), 102–4.
[73] Cownie, *Religious Patronage in Anglo-Norman England*, 15.
[74] Gameson, "St Wulfstan, the Library of Worcester and the Spirituality of the Medieval Book," 84–85; Catherine Cubitt, "Individual and Collective Sinning in Tenth- and Eleventh-Century England: Penance, Piety and the Law," in *Religion und Politik im Mittelalter: Deutschland und England im Vergleich*, ed. Ludger Körntgen and Dominik Waßenhoven (Berlin: De Gruyter, 2013), 52; Wendy Davies, *Small Worlds: The Village Community in Early Medieval Brittany* (Berkeley: University of California Press, 1988), 27.

at Waltham. This is attested in the twelfth-century house history that specifically records Harold's endowment of Waltham with eight gospelbooks in addition to other treasures.[75] A confirmation of the accuracy of this account may be provided by a Dissolution-era inventory from the church that lists three pre-Conquest gospelbooks that were ornamented with silver and depictions of Christ and other New Testament characters.[76] In addition to this, William the Conqueror was said to have carried off "four codices ornamented with gold, silver and jewels", which, due to their removal in the eleventh century, obviously cannot be identified with the volumes recorded in the later inventory.[77] From the significant collection of high-status volumes, we can safely assume that Waltham had other books, including books for the education of the boys in its school and those necessary for the performance of mass and the Divine Office. The rich endowment of books that Waltham received from Harold shows that aristocratic provision of books was one of a number of ways to express piety and display wealth, which motivated aristocrats to supply such books. Accordingly, other aristocrats who provided land, commissioned art, or funded repairs for a church may also have provided books.

Books were not always provided directly, however. In the later eleventh century, Abbot Paul of St Alban's specifically allocated the revenue from a particular estate belonging to the monastic community as well as a monetary gift from a knight for the production of books. Redon Abbey in Brittany also earmarked income from specific estates for certain purposes, such as maintenance of the poor and lighting of the church.[78] Cathedrals, secular minsters, and other monasteries might have similarly diverted revenue from their estates and aristocratic gifts when significant expenditure on books became necessary. The provision of land, ecclesiastical furniture, books, and other items by lay lords to secular minsters was no doubt a pattern to which much of the patronage of the tenth and eleventh centuries conformed and one which churches utilized in one form or another to ensure the availability of the books they needed.

The provision of books as a form of aristocratic patronage likely benefitted not only minster churches, but also local churches under the control of the nobility. Certainly the large number of local churches

---

[75] Watkiss and Chibnall, *The Waltham Chronicle*, 33.
[76] Nicholas Rogers, "The Waltham Abbey Relic-List," in *England in the Eleventh Century: Proceedings of the 1990 Harlaxton Symposium*, ed. Carola Hicks (Stamford: Paul Watkins, 1992), 161.
[77] Ibid., 163; David Dumville, "Anglo-Saxon Books: Treasure in Norman Hands?," in *Anglo-Norman Studies XVI: Proceedings of the Battle Conference 1993*, ed. Marjorie Chibnall (Woodbridge: Boydell Press, 1994), 85, 94. William II was also said to have preyed on the books and artwork of Waltham.
[78] Gullick, "Professional Scribes," 7; Davies, *Small Worlds*, 53.

built in England in the tenth and eleventh centuries were not only a boon to the builder, but also to the scribe and bookseller, as manorial churches, like any active church, required at least a few books to fulfill their liturgical and pastoral function. Manorial churches were built in close proximity to lordly residences and were a fundamental part of what constituted a thegnly estate, making them important to the way a lord's piety and wealth were displayed.[79] The provision of service books, vestments, and other items necessary for the performance of the liturgy is thus another potential form of conspicuous consumption on the part of lay patrons. One example of this comes from a mid-eleventh-century will that records the bequest of what appears to be the appurtenances of a chapel.[80] Wulf, the testator of the will, left a "chalice, dish and mass-book, and the thickest dorsal" to St Alban's, items that may have been used in his own manorial church for the performance of mass by a resident priest. The testimony of this will may be further evidence that priests' books and other items necessary for liturgical observance were often provided by lay lords, who in the case of Wulf saw fit to dispose of these items as he pleased after his death. This accords with Catherine Cubitt's suggestion that the "accoutrements, liturgical vessels, vestments and books" utilized in local churches were the property of, and were most probably provided by, the lay landowner and patron.[81]

Contemporary accounts of how and where books were obtained by Anglo-Saxon aristocrats to be provided as a form of patronage are essentially nonexistent, but accounts of the ways in which these individuals had books produced for other purposes may shed some light on how books were procured for manorial churches and other ecclesiastical recipients of patronage. Judith of Flanders, wife of Earl Tostig, commissioned four books which we have evidence for, all of which are copies of the gospels. These books appear to have been commissioned and produced as a group, as indicated by the style, script, and readings preserved in these four volumes.[82] It has been suggested that "one or more Anglo-Saxon scribe-artists appear to have worked

---

[79] A. Williams, "A Bell-House and a Burh-geat: Lordly Residences in England before the Norman Conquest," in *Medieval Knighthood IV: Papers from the Fifth Strawberry Hill Conference, 1990*, ed. Christopher Harper-Bill and Ruth Harvey (Woodbridge: Boydell Press, 1992), 230–33; Gameson, "Anglo-Saxon Scribes and Scriptoria," 119.

[80] S 1532. Wulf (or Ulf) is not given a title in his will and some uncertainty exists as to his lay status. Linda Tollerton, *Wills and Will-Making in Anglo-Saxon England* (York: York Medieval Press, 2011), 214.

[81] Cubitt, "Ælfric's Lay Patrons," in Magennis and Swan, *A Companion to Ælfric*, 187.

[82] Patrick McGurk and Jane Rosenthal, "The Anglo-Saxon Gospelbooks of Judith, Countess of Flanders: Their Text, Make-Up and Function," *Anglo-Saxon England* 24 (1995): 255.

in the household of Judith of Flanders" and were in part occupied with writing books for use in her private chapel. Mary Dockray-Miller has recently proposed that one of these scribe-artists may have been Judith's household priest.[83] In addition to the employment of professional scribes, Anglo-Saxon nobles also had manuscripts produced by major scriptoria, such as the gospelbook London, British Library, Royal 1 D. III, that was ostensibly produced for Godgifu, sister to Edward the Confessor, at Canterbury in the mid-eleventh century.[84] On a larger scale, the abovementioned group of gospelbooks commissioned by Cnut and Emma seems to have been written by "a small group of expert scribes who were apparently working in different centres but under central direction", primarily at Peterborough, Canterbury, and Winchester.[85] This suggests a well-organized system for the production of manuscripts which were in large part intended for ecclesiastical institutions. Additionally, these examples show that Anglo-Saxon royalty and nobility had the resources and connections to commission books from major monastic and cathedral scriptoria and what were probably professional scribes working outside ecclesiastical scriptoria, as in the case of Judith of Flanders. The Anglo-Saxon aristocracy was deeply invested in the patronage of both secular and monastic religious communities, and the connections that these individuals utilized to procure books for themselves and the monastic foundations they supported are doubtless the same that they would have used to obtain a missal for their chaplain or a bejeweled gospelbook for a favored minster.

Individual purchase and the early medieval book trade

Though much of the evidence for the commissioning and purchase of manuscripts involves ecclesiastical authorities and laypersons of high status, bishops and nobility were not the only ones capable of purchasing books. Rather, it was financial ability and not necessarily social position that enabled individuals to commission books or to purchase secondhand volumes. Though many local priests of the late Anglo-Saxon period were probably unable to afford commissioned books of their own, the financial position and accordingly the purchasing

---

[83] Gameson, "Anglo-Saxon Scribes and Scriptoria," 98; McGurk and Rosenthal, "The Anglo-Saxon Gospelbooks of Judith," 274–75; Mary Dockray-Miller, *The Books and the Life of Judith of Flanders* (Farnham, Surrey: Ashgate, 2015), 29–30.

[84] McGurk, "Anglo-Saxon Gospel-Books, *c.* 900–1066," in Gameson, *The Cambridge History of the Book in Britain*, 445.

[85] Lapidge, "Artistic and Literary Patronage in Anglo-Saxon England," in *Anglo-Latin Literature, 600–899*, 158; Heslop, "The Production of *de luxe* Manuscripts," 181–82.

power of priests varied enormously. Royal priests, many of whom had significant landholdings in eleventh-century England, would certainly have had the resources to obtain books for themselves or their churches. Though it is not clear who commissioned or purchased the book, Paris, Bibliothèque nationale de France, lat. 8092 contains an eleventh-century note that reads "domino suo, N., dei gracia Regis capellano", indicating that a royal priest was the end user of this book, a predominately Latin "collection of religious verse".[86] Eadmer the priest, who held Hurstmonceaux (Herstmonceux), Sussex, controlled what was essentially "a small thegn's estate", complete with a church, meadow and woodland, thirty villagers, and a dozen cottars.[87] Though Eadmer's status is unusual, a broader view of Domesday records shows that in some regions, a sizeable minority of priests were of notably higher status than a manorial tenant, potentially enabling these priests to purchase books secondhand or commission books of lower quality for their own use.[88] Little indication of the early medieval book trade and its customers has survived, but twelfth-century sources show English priests who had substantial personal libraries, liturgical and otherwise, and some Anglo-Saxon priests may too have had significant personal collections of books.[89]

Priests who purchased books likely did so in one of two ways. A book could be commissioned by a buyer and subsequently produced by a scribe or scriptorium, as with many of the aristocratic examples mentioned above, or a book could be purchased secondhand.[90] The books that have survived that we can associate with commissioning are high-status, expensive productions that were probably out of the reach of most priests. For example, a colophon from a psalter produced in the late eleventh century informs the reader that "Ðeos Boc wæs geal gewriten on feower Wyken 7 kostede þreo 7 fifti syllinges."[91]

---

[86] "[T]o his lord, n[ame], by the grace of God chaplain of the king." Gameson, "Anglo-Saxon Scribes and Scriptoria," 98; Michael Lapidge, "Some Old English Sedulius Glosses from BN Lat. 8092," *Anglia* 100 (1982): 2, n. 5. This book was probably produced in England in the second quarter of the eleventh century, but the note mentioned dates to the late eleventh century. Lapidge suggests that this book might have belonged to "Nigel *medicus*", a member of the household of William I. Gameson sees the note as evidence that the book may have been copied by a royal priest.

[87] Susan Wood, *The Proprietary Church in the Medieval West* (Oxford: Oxford University Press, 2006), 676.

[88] Barrow, "Wulfstan and Worcester: Bishop and Clergy," 145–46.

[89] Hugh M. Thomas, *The Secular Clergy in England, 1066–1216* (Oxford: Oxford University Press, 2014), 246–65.

[90] It has also been suggested that some books could have been produced without a specific commission on the basis of "anticipation of need". Dumville, *Liturgy and the Ecclesiastical History of Late Anglo-Saxon England*, 141.

[91] "This whole book was written in four weeks and cost fifty-three shillings." Helmut Gneuss, "More Old English from Manuscripts," in *Intertexts: Studies*

Fifty-three shillings was a substantial sum. Though we have no indication for whom or by whom the psalter was originally written, this, combined with significant textual evidence, indicates that manuscripts could be and were commissioned and purchased, though a minority of English priests in the tenth and eleventh centuries would have had the means to commission a psalter like this for themselves. Nonetheless, less ornate mass-books may have been efficiently and inexpensively produced on commission, particularly if they were sparsely decorated and did not contain masses for weekdays, as is the case in some extant manuscripts. For example, the Stowe Missal (Dublin, Royal Irish Academy, D. II. 3) was probably relatively inexpensive to produce, and it has been estimated that the scribal work of the book could have been completed in a week to ten days, making books such as this cheaper and thus more accessible for early medieval priests of meager or middling wealth.[92]

The production of books on commission is relatively well known, though we may not fully understand the way in which the commissioning of a book might take place. Only one explicit account of the commissioning of a manuscript is extant from Anglo-Saxon England, found in the *Colloquy* of Ælfric Bata, an eleventh-century schoolmaster who probably taught at Canterbury.[93] As this was a text intended for instruction in vocabulary and grammar, its primary purpose was didactic rather than documentary, and therefore we should approach the evidence it offers with caution. But despite its status as a school text, it is instructive to reproduce the hypothetical process of commissioning a manuscript:

> Customer: You, scribe, good and handsome lad, I ask you humbly.
>   Write me an exemplar on a roll or sheet, or on a parchment or tablet.
> Scribe: If you're willing to pay me.
> Customer: First write me a psalter or hymnal, or an epistolary or troper, or a missal or a good itinerary or capitulary, well composed and laid out, properly written and corrected, and I'll give you good pay. Or I'll buy all those things from you right now – I'll give you their price

---

in *Anglo-Saxon Culture Presented to Paul E. Szarmach*, ed. Virginia Blanton and Helene Scheck (Tempe: Arizona Center for Medieval and Renaissance Studies, 2008), 418–19. The book in which this note was written is unfortunately now lost, but extensive notes on the manuscript were made prior to the book's destruction, preserving this colophon.

[92] Hohler, review of *Cambridge, Corpus Christi College 41*, 276; Sven Meeder, "The Early Irish Stowe Missal's Destination and Function," *Early Medieval Europe* 13, no. 2 (2005): 182. One example of a relatively humble mass-book lacking masses for weekdays is Oxford, Corpus Christi College 282. Hohler also suggests that the mass-book available to the marginal scribe of Cambridge, Corpus Christi College 41 lacked masses for weekdays.

[93] Scott Gwara, ed., *Anglo-Saxon Conversations: The Colloquies of Ælfric Bata*, trans. David W. Porter (Woodbridge: Boydell Press, 1997), 3.

in gold or silver, or in horses or mares, or oxen, sheep, swine, goats, clothing, wine, honey, grain or beans.

Scribe: Nothing would suit me more than for you to give me coins, since one who has coins or silver can get everything he wants.

Customer: Now you're a sharp one.

Scribe: You're much craftier than I, who am a simple little fellow.

Customer: Stop that kind of talk. Let's speak better! How many coins must I give you for one missal?

Scribe: If you want to have it, you must give me two pounds of pure silver. And if you don't want it, somebody else will. This is an expensive thing and somebody else should buy it more dearly than you.

Customer: Even if someone else wants to be so foolish, I don't. I want to be careful and buy your book at the right price – at the price my friends will tell me it's worth. That's a fair price.

Scribe: But how much will you give me?

Customer: I don't want to give quite that much …

Scribe: What do you want then? How many coins will you pay, or how many mancuses?

Customer: Believe me, I don't dare give you more or buy it more dearly. Take this if you please. It's not worth more. I'll pay you twelve mancuses and count them into your hand. What else can I do? I'll do only what you want.

Scribe: Count the coins here and now so I can tell if they're valuable and whether they're pure silver.[94]

Few medieval customers of scribes would have had such an obvious interest in a vocabulary exercise as this fictitious client, but despite the didactic purpose of this text, it is a useful starting point for considering how manuscripts were commissioned. Though monks were ostensibly not allowed to have personal property, it seems from this account that monastic scribes, probably at times independent of the scribal projects of the monastery, did "write large numbers of books, sell them, and earn lots of money for themselves". Earnwig, St Wulfstan's tutor at Peterborough Abbey, produced sumptuous liturgical manuscripts to curry favor with the king and queen and may have written books on commission as well.[95] It may even be that particular scribes specialized in producing liturgical books, as it appears Eadwig Basan and an anonymous scribe from Peterborough did.[96] The scribe common to all of the gospelbooks of Judith of Flanders may also have been one such scribe, as he often laid out the text of the gospels "in paragraphs corresponding to Eusebian or chapter divisions", which might indicate

---

[94] Ibid., 135, 137.

[95] Ibid., 137; Gameson, "St Wulfstan, the Library of Worcester and the Spirituality of the Medieval Book," 81, 83.

[96] Heslop, "The Production of *de luxe* Manuscripts," 176.

some experience in copying books for the liturgy.[97] Though much of the commissioning activity for which we have evidence was undertaken for the production of high-status books, there is little reason that this pattern could not have been repeated at lower levels for the production of less ornate volumes. Indeed, the copying of a small, plain mass-book or lectionary completed by a single scribe, monastic or otherwise, within a few weeks and at the fringe of the "official" work of a given scriptorium, would be very unlikely to leave written evidence of the process by which it was commissioned.

The buying and selling of used books in the early Middle Ages is less well attested than commissioning and it is difficult to assess how common the practice may have been. However, there are certainly indications that secondhand books could readily change hands. In addition to receiving the products of the Exeter scriptorium, Bishop Leofric's library at Exeter benefitted from volumes produced elsewhere that do not seem to have been originally produced for Exeter; some of these may have been purchased secondhand. The clearest example of this may be Cambridge, Corpus Christi College 41, which was produced in an unknown center in the mid-eleventh century and received voluminous marginal additions, but bears an Exeter *ex libris* inscription. Moreover, Charlemagne's books were sold after his death and the proceeds distributed to the poor, and elsewhere in the Carolingian Empire, between 835 and 842, a Reichenau monk named Regimbert paid eight *denarii* for a book that contained the laws of the Lombards and the passion of Servulus.[98] These examples clearly imply the existence of a market for secondhand books in the early medieval period and records of book theft may further suggest this. The account of an eleventh-century incident from continental Europe indicates that a psalter stolen from a monastery was sold at some distance from the site of the theft to avoid detection or recognition of the book's origin. The book was subsequently sold to a noblewoman who purchased it to help her son learn the Psalms.[99] The theft of two books from Worcester Cathedral was also said to have taken place shortly after St Wulfstan's death and though both volumes were reportedly recovered, the theft of early medieval books from churches implies that thieves knew that

---

[97] McGurk and Rosenthal, "The Anglo-Saxon Gospelbooks of Judith," 281. Gameson similarly suggests that the production of liturgical books for the secular clergy may have been a large part of the work of some Anglo-Saxon scribes. See Gameson, "English Manuscript Art in the Late Eleventh Century," 100.

[98] McKitterick, *The Carolingians and the Written Word*, 136–37.

[99] A. L. P. de Robaulx de Soumoy, trans., *Chronique de l'Abbaye de St-Hubert dite Cantatorium* (Brussels: Méline, Cans et Compagnie, 1847), 54–55.

the books had significant value and that a market existed for the purchase of such books secondhand.[100]

Additionally, some priests may have obtained secondhand books from other clerics by purchasing them or receiving them as gifts. Certainly the fathers of many late Anglo-Saxon priests had been priests themselves and service books and other texts may have been passed down from father to son, as in some cases from continental Europe. A ninth-century Bavarian priest named Egino arranged for ten books, including two mass-books, a lectionary, a penitential, and the *Dialogues* of Gregory the Great, to be passed on in benefice to his son Egino. Similarly, the bishop of Regensburg in the later ninth century gifted no fewer than eighteen books, which had been received from a priest, to his nephew, who, predictably, was in orders.[101] A further case from the late Middle Ages shows a priest who bequeathed seven of his books to a young man expected to enter the priesthood, and early medieval priests might have made arrangements similar to these in order to transfer the ownership of their books after death.[102]

The buying and selling of books is on the whole poorly attested in this period, but priests and other secular clerics, as one of the primary groups using books, may have had some involvement in the processes of commissioning a book or purchasing one secondhand. Early medieval priests were certainly active in the buying and selling of real estate and seem to have frequently served as witnesses of local transactions; the book trade might have been another market in which clerics were active.[103] Most instances of book provision through episcopal endowment and aristocratic patronage indicate an ecclesiastical institution as the recipient of the volumes, but the purchase of books through commissioning or secondhand markets is more likely to directly involve priests, as obtaining books in this way was probably more often for the benefit of a priest's personal bookholdings rather than those of a particular church, and an awareness of this distinction is important in considering a priest's agency or involvement in obtaining of books as

---

[100] Winterbottom and Thomson, eds. and trans., *William of Malmesbury: Saints' Lives*, 148–51.

[101] Thomas Kohl, "*Presbyter in parochia sua*: Local Priests and Their Churches in Early Medieval Bavaria," in *Men in the Middle*, ed. Patzold and van Rhijn, 63, n. 60.

[102] Barry Windeatt, "1412–1534: Texts," in *The Cambridge Companion to Medieval English Mysticism*, ed. Samuel Fanous and Vincent Gillespie (Cambridge: Cambridge University Press, 2011), 209.

[103] Fairweather, *Liber Eliensis*, 116, 131; Felix Liebermann, ed., *Die Gesetze der Angelsachsen*, vol. 1, *Text und Übersetzung* (Halle: Max Niemeyer, 1903), 156; Miriam Czock, "Practices of Property and the Salvation of One's Soul: Priests as Men in the Middle in the Wissembourg Material," in *Men in the Middle*, ed. Patzold and van Rhijn; Davies, *Small Worlds*, 81, 87–88, 92, 94–95, 98–99, 100–102.

part of the literate minority. Though we have almost no knowledge of the personal book collections of secular priests before the Conquest, the relative frequency with which twelfth-century priests collected books hints that late Anglo-Saxon priests also had an interest in purchasing and collecting books.[104] The ability of a priest to commission a book or purchase a secondhand one would have depended on the financial status of a given priest, which could vary greatly, but the evidence reviewed from the tenth and eleventh centuries indicates that if financial resources were available, books, whether liturgical, pastoral or otherwise, could be had.

Conclusions

We will never know all the ways in which medieval priests obtained their books, but clear avenues existed through which priests and the clerical communities to which many of them belonged received their books. Books for priests were produced in the major cathedral and monastic scriptoria of the late Anglo-Saxon period, as well as in a variety of smaller centers of book production, some of which were probably secular minsters. This may be particularly true of royal minsters during Alfred's reign and through much of the first half of the tenth century, though scribal activity in some secular minsters, particularly those with the resources to support a scriptorium, carried on throughout the late Anglo-Saxon period. It is likely that contemporary expectations of the provision of books were placed on the founders of churches, whether they were bishops, abbots, or lay aristocrats. Books were also provided to churches as part of a range of patronal activities common to the endowment of both secular and monastic churches that included the provision of art, sculpture, and grants of land. In addition, the significant variation that existed in the financial status of priests, when considered in light of what is known about the early medieval book trade, indicates that some wealthier priests could have afforded to buy their own liturgical books and other books for private reading, as priests did in the twelfth century and later. Direct evidence concerning how priests and their churches obtained books is rare, but the secular priests of Anglo-Saxon England must have been part and parcel of the channels through which books were produced and distributed. The fact that these channels existed and that secular churches were part of them is a strong indication that books were routinely accessible to priests.

---

[104] See Thomas, *The Secular Clergy in England*, chapter 11. Thomas also argues that Anglo-Norman secular clergy "fostered ... the rise of a professional book trade." Ibid., 247.

4

Preaching and Homiletic Books for Priests

Old English homilies are a witness to a precocious and widespread tradition of vernacular preaching in Anglo-Saxon England, one in which secular priests played a primary role. Homilies form a great deal of the corpus of Old English prose: more than ten percent of the manuscripts listed in Neil Ker's *Catalogue of Manuscripts Containing Anglo-Saxon* contain Old English homilies.[1] Some aspects of these manuscripts have seen significant study in the last century, but their pastoral use and potential connections with the secular clergy have received less attention. As Tracey-Anne Cooper has pointed out, there is significant difficulty in using homilies as windows into pastoral care, due to our ignorance of how episcopal and elite aspirations for pastoral care translated into reality and the uncertainty surrounding how and to what extent homilies were performed for lay audiences.[2] Nonetheless, English priests of the tenth and eleventh centuries were heirs to a long tradition of preaching, as is shown by episcopal prescriptions and the early, fragmentary manuscript record, and priests' books provide a perhaps undervalued means of approach in understanding the uses of and contexts for Anglo-Saxon homilies.

The preceding chapters have addressed the contextual factors of studying priests' books, such as literacy and the practical availability of books to priests. This chapter is the first of three that will examine specific manuscripts in greater detail. I do not attempt an exhaustive analysis of these manuscripts here; they will instead be considered specifically with relevance to their use by secular clerics in pastoral care. The initial sections of this chapter will concern themselves with the contextualization and use of Anglo-Saxon homilies, while the final section will consider three relevant manuscripts, namely the Taunton Fragment (Taunton, Somerset County Record Office, DD\

---

[1] Jonathan Wilcox, "Ælfric in Dorset and the Landscape of Pastoral Care," in *Pastoral Care in Late Anglo-Saxon England*, ed. Francesca Tinti (Woodbridge: Boydell Press, 2005), 53, n. 3. Manuscripts containing Ælfric's *Catholic Homilies* comprise just over ten percent of Ker's corpus and the addition of manuscripts containing anonymous homilies without any pieces by Ælfric would increase this figure.

[2] T. Cooper, "Lay Piety, Confessional Directives and the Compiler's Method in Late Anglo-Saxon England," *Haskins Society Journal* 16 (2006): 47–48.

SAS/C1193/); Oxford, Bodleian Library, Junius 85 and 86; and the Blickling Homilies (Princeton, New Jersey, Princeton University Library, Scheide Collection 71).

The homiletic tradition in Anglo-Saxon England

From a very early stage in the history of the Anglo-Saxon church, priests were involved in preaching to the laity. Bede records that one of the main duties of a priest in the seventh century was to preach to the laity and the Council of *Clofesho* in 747 enjoined priests to preach in addition to baptizing, teaching, and visiting the sick.[3] It has been shown that religious communities in England in the seventh and eighth centuries were both "numerous and influential", providing a framework within which the pastoral care described in contemporary sources may have been provided.[4] Early prescriptions for preaching are accompanied by some contemporary manuscript evidence for Latin homiliaries, including Boulogne-sur-Mer, Bibliotheque municipale, 106; Edinburgh, National Library of Scotland, Advocates 18. 7. 8; Esztergom, Archiepiscopal Library, s.n.; Karlsruhe, Badische Landesbibliothek, Aug. perg. 221; London, British Library, Cotton Titus C. XV, f. 1; and Rome, Vatican City, Biblioteca Apostolica Vaticana, Pal. lat. 259.[5] All these manuscripts are fragmentary and all contain homilies by Gregory the Great, simultaneously limiting the scope of the evidence and showing the strong influence of Gregory's homilies on the Anglo-Saxon preaching tradition.[6] Due to their English origin, the homilies of Bede were probably also available in the eighth century

---

[3] Bertram Colgrave and R. A. B. Mynors, eds., *Bede's Ecclesiastical History of the English People* (Oxford: Clarendon Press, 1969), 310; Arthur West Haddan and William Stubbs, eds., *Councils and Ecclesiastical Documents Relating to Great Britain and Ireland*, vol. 3, *English Church during the Anglo-Saxon Period: A.D. 595–1066* (Oxford: Clarendon Press, 1871), 365.

[4] Thomas Pickles, "Church Organization and Pastoral Care," in *A Companion to the Early Middle Ages: Britain and Ireland c.500–c.1000*, ed. Pauline Stafford (Oxford: Wiley-Blackwell, 2009), 169; John Blair, *The Church in Anglo-Saxon Society* (Oxford: Oxford University Press, 2005), 161–65.

[5] Helmut Gneuss and Michael Lapidge, *Anglo-Saxon Manuscripts: A Bibliographical Handlist of Manuscripts and Manuscript Fragments Written or Owned in England up to 1100* (Toronto: University of Toronto Press, 2015), 200–201, 305, 572, 589, 598, 659.

[6] Though the origin of most of these manuscripts is firmly English, the Esztergom and Vatican fragments could have originated in Anglo-Saxon centers on the continent rather than England itself. See Thomas Hall, "The Early English Manuscripts of Gregory the Great's *Homiliae in Evangelia* and *Homiliae in Hiezechihelem*: A Preliminary Survey," in *Rome and the North: The Early Reception of Gregory the Great in Germanic Europe*, ed. Rolf H. Bremmer, Jr., Kees Dekker, and David Johnson (Paris: Peeters, 2001).

and may have been used as a basis for vernacular preaching the laity.[7] One of the letters of Boniface implies that the homilies of Bede were available in York in the first half of the eighth century and, considering York's status as an intellectual center at that time, the library there may well have contained a significant number of texts for preaching.[8] The homilies of Gregory and Bede probably acted as complementary sources for preachers, as they overlap in only one pericope; in the ninth century and later, they circulated together in the homiliary of Paul the Deacon.[9]

Direct evidence for preaching and the use of homilies in ninth-century England is rare and documentary records in general are relatively sparse. The difficulties of the evidence have incited scholarly debate concerning continuity in Anglo-Saxon *monasteria* in light of Viking raids and occupation, with recent studies arguing for a significant degree of continuity in ecclesiastical institutions and the strongly regional nature of substantial discontinuity.[10] Despite the paucity of source material for homilies in the ninth century, Donald Scragg has recently uncovered significant new evidence. An Old English "scribble" on f. 9r of Oxford, Bodleian Library, Digby 63 has been shown to be the beginning of an Old English homily copied prior to the Latin text that is now most clearly visible. Other contents of Digby 63 allow Scragg to date and localize this homiletic snippet to, at the latest, the second half of the ninth century in Northumbria.[11] Though the copyist stopped short after two lines of text, this shows that at least one Old English homily was available for copying in the ninth century, pushing the date of the earliest written vernacular homilies in England back by roughly a century. Furthermore, the homily was probably available in Northumbria, moving us outside the typical channels of survival for Anglo-Saxon manuscripts. Scragg's close study of this snippet

---

[7] Alan Thacker, "Monks, Preaching and Pastoral Care in Early Anglo-Saxon England," in *Pastoral Care before the Parish*, ed. John Blair and Richard Sharpe (Leicester: Leicester University Press, 1992), 141–42.

[8] Ephraim Emerton, trans., *The Letters of Saint Boniface* (New York: Columbia University Press, 1940), 146.

[9] The lack of overlap may well have been intentional, as Bede "is indebted to Gregory the Great for his basic approach to the Gospel text in his homilies". They may have been conceived as a supplement to Gregory's homilies. Lawrence Martin, "Bede and Preaching," in *The Cambridge Companion to Bede*, ed. Scott DeGregorio (Cambridge: Cambridge University Press, 2010), 162, 166.

[10] Julia Barrow, "Survival and Mutation: Ecclesiastical Institutions in the Danelaw in the Ninth and Tenth Centuries," in *Cultures in Contact: Scandinavian Settlement in England in the Ninth and Tenth Centuries*, ed. Dawn M. Hadley and Julian D. Richards (Turnhout: Brepols, 2000); Dawn M. Hadley, "Conquest, Colonization and the Church: Ecclesiastical Organization in the Danelaw," *Historical Research* 69 (1996).

[11] Donald Scragg, "A Ninth-Century Old English Homily from Northumbria," *Anglo-Saxon England* 45 (2016).

supports the assertions of scholars who proposed that vernacular homilies that appeared in the manuscript record in the tenth century went back to ninth-century antecedents and provides a tangible, if limited, link between the earliest evidence for Anglo-Saxon homilies and the flowering of English vernacular preaching in the tenth and eleventh centuries.

In addition to this new discovery, there is considerable indirect evidence for the availability of Latin homiliaries in ninth-century England, and much of this evidence comes from source studies. The Old English martyrologist, probably writing in the first half of the ninth century, seems to have had access to a collection of Gregory's homilies and at least one other liturgically arranged homiliary that contained works by Augustine, Caesarius of Arles, and Petrus Chrysologus, as well as several anonymous Latin homilies.[12] Alfred and his circle were similarly influenced by preaching texts. The Old English translation of Augustine's *Soliloquia* uses Gregory's fortieth gospel homily as a source and the Old English Orosius draws from one of Gregory's homilies and a homily by Hrabanus Maurus.[13] A notable exception to the general lack of extant homiletic manuscripts from this period is Cambridge, Corpus Christi College 69, a manuscript copied in southern England at the end of the eighth or the beginning of the ninth century, consisting of the final twenty homilies of Gregory's *Homiliae in evangelia*, surviving mostly intact. Raymond Étaix has noted the manuscript's often-poor readings and unusual spellings, but the intact survival of such a manuscript, which may originally have had a companion volume containing the remainder of Gregory's gospel homilies, is an important, physical witness to the continued copying and circulation of preaching texts in England.[14]

The Anglo-Saxon homiletic tradition was also influenced by early medieval homilies from the continent, such as the new collections of

---

[12] James Cross, "On the Library of the Old English Martyrologist," in *Learning and Literature in Anglo-Saxon England: Studies Presented to Peter Clemoes on the Occasion of His Sixty-Fifth Birthday*, ed. Michael Lapidge and Helmut Gneuss (Cambridge: Cambridge University Press, 1985), 232–33, 237. On the date of the *Old English Martyrology*, see Christine Rauer, ed. and trans., *The Old English Martyrology: Edition, Translation, and Commentary* (Cambridge: D.S. Brewer, 2013), 1–3.

[13] Rohini Jayatilaka, "King Alfred and His Circle," in *The Cambridge History of the Book in Britain Volume 1: c.400–1100*, ed. Richard Gameson (Cambridge: Cambridge University Press, 2011), 672; Fontes Anglo-Saxonici Project, "Source Summary for Anglo-Saxon Text: Orosius, History against the Pagans," *Fontes Anglo-Saxonici: World Wide Web Register*, accessed February 10, 2018, http://fontes.english.ox.ac.uk/data/content/astexts/src_summary.asp?refer=C%2EB%2E9%2E2.

[14] Raymond Étaix, ed., *Homiliae in evangelia*, Corpus Christianorum Series Latina 141 (Turnhout: Brepols, 1999), xxxvii.

homilies composed and compiled in the Carolingian empire in the ninth century, including those by Hrabanus Maurus, Haimo of Auxerre, and the homiliary of Saint-Père de Chartres. Some of these homiliaries were composed for reading in the Night Office while others were better suited for devotional reading, but many were written either specifically for the laity or were adaptable to a variety of audiences. For example, the homiliary of Paul the Deacon (compiled by Paul, but consisting primarily of patristic homilies) was commissioned by Charlemagne and primarily intended for reading in the Night Office, but Carolingian preachers made use of it in preaching to the laity, as did Anglo-Saxon homilists.[15] Moreover, the composition of these new homiliaries in Francia was contemporaneous with conciliar decrees and episcopal legislation in the Carolingian Empire instructing priests to preach to laypeople. The *Admonitio Generalis*, promulgated in 789, and the Council of Arles in 813 both made clear the right and duty of priests to preach in local churches, and multiple sets of episcopal statutes from this period similarly call for priests to preach to the laity or to own books of homilies containing preaching texts for the liturgical year.[16] Scholars have directly connected ecclesiastical legislation with the development of new preaching texts, with Mary Clayton writing that these collections "are presumably the results of the well-documented Carolingian attempts to ensure adequate preaching throughout the empire".[17] Carolingian compilations of patristic homilies and wholly new preaching texts were later imported into England, certainly in the course of the Benedictine reform of the tenth century, and may have come to England as early as the reign of Alfred, as is suggested by the use of a Hrabanus Maurus homily as a source for the Old English Orosius.[18] Anglo-Saxon homilists of the tenth

---

[15] Mary Clayton, "Homiliaries and Preaching in Anglo-Saxon England," *Peritia* 4 (1985): 210, 216–17. For a discussion of the use of homilies in the early medieval Divine Office, see Jesse D. Billett, "*Sermones ad diem pertinentes*: Sermons and Homilies in the Liturgy of the Divine Office," in *Sermo doctorum: Compilers, Preachers, and Their Audiences in the Early Medieval West*, ed. Maximilian Diesenberger, Yitzhak Hen, and Marianne Pollheimer (Turnhout: Brepols, 2013).

[16] *Capitularia regum Francorum*, pt. 1, ed. Alfred Boretius, *Monumenta Germaniae Historica* (Hanover: Hahnsche Buchhandlung, 1883), 61; *Concilia aevi Karolini*, vol. 2, pt. 1, ed. Albert Werminghoff, *Monumenta Germaniae Historica* (Hanover, 1906), 251; *Capitula episcoporum*, pt. 1, ed. Peter Brommer, *Monumenta Germaniae Historica* (Hanover: Hahnsche Buchhandlung, 1984), 47, 211.

[17] Clayton, "Homiliaries and Preaching," 214. See also Rosamond McKitterick, *The Frankish Church and the Carolingian Reforms, 789–895* (London: Royal Historical Society, 1977), 113.

[18] Mechthild Gretsch, "Cambridge, Corpus Christi College 57: A Witness to the Early Stages of the Benedictine Reform in England?," *Anglo-Saxon England* 32 (2003): 137–39; Fontes Anglo-Saxonici Project, "Source Summary for Anglo-Saxon Text: Orosius, History against the Pagans".

and eleventh centuries, including Ælfric and authors of anonymous homilies, drew heavily and adapted freely from Carolingian homiletic collections composed in the eighth and ninth centuries, and their use is apparent in the earliest English homiletic books in the vernacular.

It is in the tenth century that we first see homiletic books in Old English. Both anonymous and overtly Benedictine-influenced homilies came at a time when there were more churches and more priests than ever before in England as local churches were being built in large numbers, both through aristocratic foundation and in response to the more pedestrian needs of those in villages. Concurrently, secular minsters remained active in the provision of pastoral care and were attractive foundations for royal and aristocratic patronage, while after the mid-tenth century, some monasteries were also active in ministry to laypeople.[19] Episcopal legislation of the late tenth and early eleventh centuries required priests to preach to the people on Sundays and feast days, and these prescriptions coincide with the appearance of vernacular preaching texts.[20] The Blickling and Vercelli manuscripts and the tradition they represent are early evidence of a demand for vernacular preaching texts as local churches became increasingly common and bishops emphasized preaching. Despite voluminous bibliography on both books, neither has been firmly localized. Additionally, the homilies contained within these codices are anonymous and by various authors, though some groups of homilies have been attributed to a single author.[21] The production of the Vercelli codex was dated by Ker to the second half of the tenth century, but this has been more recently revised to a date in "the middle of the second half of the tenth century", while the Blickling book has generally been dated to the end of the tenth or beginning of the eleventh century, though internal evidence from Blickling XI has been taken by some as an indication of a date in the 970s.[22]

---

[19] John Blair, introduction to *Minsters and Parish Churches: The Local Church in Transition, 950–1200*, ed. Blair (Oxford: Oxford University Committee for Archaeology, 1988), 7–9.

[20] Dorothy Whitelock, Martin Brett, and Christopher N. L. Brooke, eds., *Councils and Synods, with Other Documents Relating to the English Church, AD 871–1204*, vol. 1 (Oxford: Clarendon Press, 1981), 208, 294, 331.

[21] Charles D. Wright, "Old English Homilies and Latin Sources," in *The Old English Homily: Precedent, Practice, and Appropriation*, ed. Aaron Kleist (Turnhout: Brepols, 2007), 32–34. Examples of this include Vercelli XI–XIII and Vercelli XIX–XXI.

[22] Donald G. Scragg, ed., *The Vercelli Homilies and Related Texts*, Early English Text Society Original Series 300 (Oxford: Oxford University Press, 1992), xxiii–xxiv; Samantha Zacher and Andy Orchard, introduction to *New Readings in the Vercelli Book*, ed. Zacher and Orchard (Toronto: University of Toronto Press, 2009), 3; Jonathan Wilcox, "The Blickling Homilies Revisited: Knowable and Probable Uses of Princeton University Library, MS Scheide 71," in *The Genesis of Books: Studies in the Scribal Culture of Medieval England in Honour of A. N. Doane*,

Though we can approximately date the copying of anonymous homilies, it has proven more difficult to date the composition of the homilies themselves. Some have argued for dates as early as the mid-ninth century for the Blickling Homilies, while the editor of the Vercelli homilies, who had remained open to the possibility of their composition in the late ninth century, has now shown that an Old English homiletic snippet in Digby 63 is dateable to the ninth century, confirming the validity of previous suppositions.[23] Like the Blickling and Vercelli codices, many manuscripts of the eleventh century are mixed collections of anonymous homilies, often including versions of texts contained in Blickling and/or Vercelli, and those by authors known to us by name, predominately Ælfric. The sources of these anonymous homilies are diverse, but most common are the writings of Caesarius of Arles, the homilies of Gregory the Great, pseudo-Augustinian homilies, and, predictably, a range of Old and New Testament books.[24] Recent studies have also been able to identify the sources of some anonymous homilies as the Saint-Père homiliary and the Homiliary of Angers, which was only identified in an English manuscript in 2004.[25] Unfortunately, source studies have rarely enabled us to date anonymous homilies more closely as the sources tend to be of early date; the latest of these sources is Theodulf I, a Carolingian episcopal statute from the early ninth century and a source for Vercelli III.[26]

Referring to a tradition of anonymous Old English homilies may at first seem a misnomer, as there is much to lead one to the conclusion that these works are heterogenous, such as various and unknown authorship as well as indeterminate dates and locations of composition. While much is unclear about these texts, there are strands that

---

    ed. Matthew T. Hussey and John D. Niles (Turnhout: Brepols, 2011), 99–100; Rowland Collins, *Anglo-Saxon Vernacular Manuscripts in America* (New York: Pierpont Morgan Library, 1976), 52–53.

[23] Scragg, *The Vercelli Homilies*, xxxix; Scragg, "A Ninth-Century Old English Homily," 42–45. For scholarly suggestions of early dates for the Blickling Homilies, see Rudolf Vleeskruyer, *The Life of St. Chad: An Old English Homily* (Amsterdam: North-Holland, 1953); Marcia Dalbey, "Structure and Style in the Blickling Homilies for the Temporale" (PhD thesis, University of Illinois, 1968).

[24] This was derived from an examination of the sources of Old English anonymous homilies as provided in Fontes Anglo-Saxonici Project, "Titles by Anglo-Saxon Author: ANON (OE)," *Fontes Anglo-Saxonici: World Wide Web Register*, accessed February 10, 2018, http://fontes.english.ox.ac.uk/data/content/astexts/title_list.asp?TextAuthor=ANON+%28OE%29&pagesize=All&submit1=Submit+Query.

[25] This identification of the homiliary behind Oxford, Bodleian Library, Bodley 343 and the Taunton Fragment was made by Aidan Conti. For the Saint-Père homiliary, see James E. Cross, *Cambridge, Pembroke College MS 25: A Carolingian Sermonary Used by Anglo-Saxon Preachers* (London: King's College, 1987).

[26] Hans Sauer, *Theodulfi Capitula in England: Die altenglischen Übersetzungen, zusammen mit dem lateinischen Text* (Munich: Wilhelm Fink, 1978), 278–80.

lend a certain thematic and pragmatic unity to the corpus of anonymous homilies. A few of the major points of coherence within this corpus are a major emphasis on eschatology, hell, and judgement; the inveterate tendency to borrow and rework material from sources at hand, including other homilies, rather than composing a wholly new work; and a reliance on rhetorical conventions stemming from oral and traditional sources.[27] There are of course exceptions and variations within this tradition, but it was broadly within this context that the Blickling and Vercelli books, and lost manuscripts like them, were produced.

Approximately two decades after the production of the Vercelli book, Ælfric, the most prolific and well-known homilist of the Anglo-Saxon period, produced two sets of liturgically arranged homilies, the First and Second Series of his *Catholic Homilies*. The manuscript evidence shows the immense popularity of these works: the First Series of the *Catholic Homilies* survives in thirty-four manuscripts and the transmission history of these manuscripts attests to the existence of at least fifty others that have been lost.[28] By comparison, the homilies of Wulfstan, Archbishop of York survive in nineteen manuscripts, many of which are copies of his "commonplace book" from his own dioceses of Worcester and York, though his homilies were also copied at Canterbury, Winchester, and Exeter.[29] Ælfric's work has been seen, with some justification, as a departure from the Anglo-Saxon homiletic tradition as seen in the anonymous homilies of the tenth century. Ælfric even attempts to distance himself from this tradition, condemning the "great error in many English books", which has been understood to refer to works in the vernacular homiletic tradition.[30] The homilies of

---

[27] On anonymous Anglo-Saxon homilies, see, for example, Donald G. Scragg, "The Corpus of Vernacular Homilies and Prose Saints' Lives," in *Old English Prose: Basic Readings*, ed. Paul E. Szarmach and Deborah A. Oosterhouse (London: Garland, 2000); Scragg, *Dating and Style in Old English Composite Homilies* (Cambridge: University of Cambridge, Department of Anglo-Saxon, Norse and Celtic, 1998); Mary Swan, "*Men ða leofestan*: Genre, the Canon, and the Old English Homiletic Tradition," in *The Christian Tradition in Anglo-Saxon England: Approaches to Current Scholarship and Teaching*, ed. Paul Cavill (Woodbridge: D. S. Brewer, 2004); Malcolm Godden, "Ælfric and the Vernacular Prose Tradition," in *The Old English Homily and Its Backgrounds*, ed. Paul Szarmach and Bernard Huppé (Albany: State University of New York Press, 1978).

[28] Peter Clemoes, ed., *Ælfric's Catholic Homilies: The First Series*, Early English Text Society Supplementary Series 17 (Oxford: Oxford University Press, 1997), 162.

[29] Jonathan Wilcox, "The Dissemination of Wulfstan's Homilies: The Wulfstan Tradition in Eleventh-Century Vernacular Preaching," in *England in the Eleventh Century: Proceedings of the 1990 Harlaxton Symposium*, ed. Carola Hicks (Stamford: Paul Watkins, 1992), 201–3.

[30] Clemoes, *Ælfric's Catholic Homilies*, 174; Scragg, *Dating and Style in Old English Composite Homilies*, 2; Godden, "Ælfric and the Vernacular Prose Tradition," 99–100.

Wulfstan, Archbishop of York have also generally been separated out from anonymous compositions and inevitably compared to the work of Ælfric as the only other homilist whose name and career are known, though Wulfstan's rhetorical style has been recognized as drawing more inspiration from the anonymous homiletic tradition.[31]

Despite the care Ælfric took to separate himself from the material disseminated in anonymous homilies, he was still in many ways informed by and a part of the tradition witnessed in earlier homilies. Though Ælfric imagines his homilies both correcting "deceptive errors" and filling a need for preaching texts in local churches, the act of composing and disseminating collections of vernacular homilies presupposes that preaching to the laity is common and widespread.[32] And while the sources of Ælfric's homilies are often more diverse than those of the anonymous homilies, a significant number of his sources match those most commonly used by anonymous composers, most notably the homilies of Gregory the Great, homilies and commentary by Bede (particularly his *Commentary on Luke*), Augustinian and pseudo-Augustinian homilies, and the sermons of Caesarius of Arles.[33] Many of these homiletic sources came down to the anonymous composers and Ælfric through the homiliary of Paul the Deacon, which in its original form transmits more than 200 homilies by patristic and early medieval writers. Ælfric's dependence on Paul the Deacon was established by Cyril Smetana more than half a century ago, but due to significant variability in the recensions of Paul's homiliary, the exact contents of the tenth-century Anglo-Saxon copies of Paul the Deacon are unknown.[34] English manuscripts containing Paul's homiliary are relatively common in the late eleventh century, but their contents have been reorganized, adapted, and expanded from the original and their relationship to English copies of the late tenth century is unclear.[35]

---

[31] Andy Orchard, "Crying Wolf: Oral Style and the *Sermones Lupi*," *Anglo-Saxon England* 21 (1992): 249; Scragg, *Dating and Style in Old English Composite Homilies*, 7.

[32] Jonathan Wilcox, ed., *Ælfric's Prefaces* (Durham: Durham Medieval Texts, 1994), 127–28.

[33] Malcolm Godden, "Ælfric's Library," in Gameson, *The Cambridge History of the Book in Britain*, 681. For specific sources of Ælfric's homilies and those of the anonymous collections, see the Fontes Anglo-Saxonici database.

[34] Cyril Smetana, "Ælfric and the Early Medieval Homiliary," *Traditio* 15 (1959). Malcolm Godden points out that "Ælfric used a number of texts that appear in later versions but not in the original and it is likely, therefore, that he was using an expanded and revised version, but its precise contents cannot be known." Godden, *Ælfric's Catholic Homilies: Introduction, Commentary and Glossary*, Early English Text Society Supplementary Series 18 (Oxford: Oxford University Press, 2000), xli.

[35] For example, Durham, Cathedral Library, B. II. 2 and Lincoln, Cathedral Library 158, are both partial, late eleventh-century copies of Paul the Deacon's homiliary. Clayton, "Homiliaries and Preaching," 219.

Archbishop Wulfstan's homiletic sources may too have included Paul the Deacon's homiliary, but in general his sources diverge from both Ælfric and the anonymous tradition. Wulfstan tended to rely on a number of Carolingian sources, some of Ælfric's homilies, and reworkings of his own writings for source material, though his rhetorical devices are often similar to those of some anonymous homilies.[36] Ælfric's divergence from the source material of the anonymous tradition comes in the form of repeated references to works by Haimo of Auxerre and Smaragdus. He also acknowledged several of his major intellectual debts in his preface to the First Series, though some of his named sources serve more as indicators of orthodox tradition than citation of sources.[37]

In his composition and dissemination of the *Catholic Homilies*, we can see the effect of Benedictine ideology and source material, but Ælfric remained very much a part of the vernacular homiletic tradition. The writers and compilers of anonymous homilies have often been associated with a "copy and paste" method of homiletic composition and Ælfric did similarly. However, his "copy and paste" method is not so much concerned with his source material, but rather with the ideology and rhetoric employed. Ælfric retained the sources stretching back to the earliest homiletic manuscripts in England, primarily as transmitted by Paul the Deacon, and also retained much of the additional source material of the anonymous homilies. But Ælfric took care to excise those texts that he considered unorthodox, notably the *Visio Pauli*, which he condemns strongly in a Rogationtide homily from the Second Series. On the other hand, other apocryphal texts, such as the *Passio Apostolorum Petri et Pauli*, were used by both Ælfric and Wulfstan in addition to their use by anonymous homilists; Aideen O'Leary has shown that much of Ælfric's objection to apocryphal material in his works is specific and based on prior concerns expressed by patristic authorities about the veracity of certain texts.[38]

---

[36] Gareth Mann, "The Development of Wulfstan's Alcuin Manuscript," in *Wulfstan, Archbishop of York: The Proceedings of the Second Alcuin Conference*, ed. Matthew Townend (Turnhout: Brepols, 2004), 274–75; Richard Dance, "Sound, Fury, and Signifiers; or Wulfstan's Language," in Townend, *Wulfstan, Archbishop of York*, 50, 60. Dance calls Wulfstan's style "traditional" and "formulaic" and compares his vocabulary with that of the Vercelli and Blickling homilies, though the lexical correspondence is inconclusive.

[37] Clemoes, *Ælfric's Catholic Homilies*, 173; Joyce Hill, "Reform and Resistance: Preaching Styles in Late Anglo-Saxon England," in *De l'homélie au sermon: Histoire de la prédication médiévale*, ed. Jacqueline Hamesse and Xavier Hermand (Louvain-la-Neuve: Université catholique de Louvain, 1993), 34–38.

[38] Aideen O'Leary, "An Orthodox Old English Homiliary? Ælfric's Views on the Apocryphal Acts of the Apostles," *Neuphilologische Mitteilungen* 100, no. 1 (1999); Godden, "Ælfric and the Vernacular Prose Tradition," 100–102; Joyce

Additionally, material not witnessed in the anonymous homilies that is linked to the bibliographical importations of the Benedictine reform was included in an effort to provide priests with orthodox preaching materials. This effort was successful in the sense that Ælfric's homilies saw wide circulation within a short time of their composition. But rather than being marginalized by Ælfric's writings, the tradition of anonymous homilies was integrated with them both by the circulation of Ælfrician and anonymous pieces in the same manuscripts as well as the adaptation of material from Ælfric for use in anonymous composite homilies. This practice was proscribed in the Latin preface to the First Series of the *Catholic Homilies*, but we already see the absorption of Ælfrician material into composite homilies by the early eleventh century, generally avoiding the "systematic exegesis" and "complex theology" of Ælfric and instead borrowing narrative passages and material on "basic practical topics".[39] Preachers probably found these sections unhelpfully deep and discursive when their main purpose was inculcating basic Christian principles and the need to prepare for God's imminent judgement. For example, an anonymous homily for Easter Sunday found in Cambridge, Corpus Christi College 162 (dated xi^{in}) borrows significantly from a Second Series Easter homily, sourcing more than 30 of the homily's 180 lines from Ælfric's material. Eschewing "Ælfric's sophisticated and carefully modulated discussion of the nature of the Eucharist", the homilist instead adapts part of the narrative of the Last Supper and two illustrations.[40]

The adaptation and reuse of Ælfric's homilies was not limited to anonymous composers. Even while Ælfric was living, Archbishop Wulfstan consistently altered and reworked the homilies of his contemporary, and Wulfstan's homilies were themselves imitated, reused, and reframed by anonymous homilists.[41] These processes of reworking and adaptation continued after the deaths of both Ælfric and Wulfstan, whose material saw use in one form or another into

---

Tally Lionarons, "Another Old English Text of the *Passio Petri et Pauli*," *Notes and Queries* 45, no. 1 (1998).

[39] Hill, "Reform and Resistance," 40–41; Clemoes, *Ælfric's Catholic Homilies*, 174. For a full treatment of borrowings from Ælfric, see Mary Swan, "Ælfric as Source: The Exploitation of Ælfric's *Catholic Homilies* from the Late Tenth to Twelfth Centuries" (PhD thesis, University of Leeds, 1993), http://etheses.whiterose.ac.uk/1949/1/uk_bl_ethos_394542.pdf.

[40] Clare Lees, "Theme and Echo in an Anonymous Old English Homily for Easter," *Traditio* 42 (1986): 115–16, 139–40.

[41] Malcolm Godden, "The Relations of Wulfstan and Ælfric: A Reassessment," in Townend, *Wulfstan, Archbishop of York*, 362–70; Orchard, "Crying Wolf," 256–57. At least three extant anonymous homilies incorporate sections of Wulfstan's homilies verbatim.

the thirteenth century.[42] Despite the stark division made between the named and anonymous homilists, the English homiletic tradition was more homogenous than has been imagined, particularly in light of the use of a great deal of common source material and the processes of editing, rewriting, and adaptation that circulating homilies underwent. As users and performers of late Anglo-Saxon homilies, many secular clerics were undoubtedly active participants in these processes.

Preaching and the uses of homilies

Examining the form of the homiletic tradition leads us to explore Old English homilies in use, space, and place. Different collections of homilies could and did serve varying purposes, including use in the Night Office, as devotional reading, and in preaching to the laity as a form of pastoral care.[43] But how and in what contexts did Anglo-Saxon secular clerics use homilies?

The performance of a homily was most typically envisioned in a liturgical context, as was formally codified at the Council of Trent in the sixteenth century, but its origins are much earlier: Justin Martyr describes in the mid-second century how an exhortation to the congregation was given after the reading of Scripture.[44] Preaching was seen as an episcopal function in Late Antiquity, but the right and duty of priests to preach was established prior to the conversion of Anglo-Saxons. English priests had been expected to preach to the laity from an early stage of Anglo-Saxon Christianity, and several homiletic books and fragments show the availability of preaching texts in these formative centuries, as is discussed earlier in this chapter. Written homiletic texts are essential evidence for early English preaching, but oral performances of these texts may sometimes have depended on memory rather than the written word. Mary Swan has argued that some manuscript copies of Ælfric's homilies could bear witness to "memorized, orally-delivered versions" of these texts and Loredana Teresi has identified an anonymous Old English homily that appears in two twelfth-century manuscripts as "compiled through memory".[45] These cases are clearly exceptional; we do not generally expect

---

[42] Mary Swan, "Preaching past the Conquest: Lambeth Palace 487 and Cotton Vespasian A. XXII," in Kleist, *The Old English Homily*.

[43] Clayton, "Homiliaries and Preaching," 211–14.

[44] Leslie W. Barnard, trans., *St Justin Martyr: The First and Second Apologies* (New York: Paulist Press, 1997), 71.

[45] Mary Swan, "Memorialised Readings: Manuscript Evidence for Old English Homily Composition," in *Anglo-Saxon Manuscripts and Their Heritage*, ed. Phillip Pulsiano and Elaine Treharne (Aldershot: Ashgate, 1998), 211; Loredana

memories or oral performances a thousand years distant to leave detectable remains. These records do however point to the potential for the memorization of preaching texts for oral performance, a process which could have mitigated a priest's need for the written text itself.

Within the mass, the homily would have been preached after the reading of the gospel, but there has been some suggestion that the homily "disappeared" from the mass in the Middle Ages.[46] However, prescriptive texts from the Anglo-Saxon period indicate that the primary expectation was for priests to preach within the context of the mass. Ælfric's Old English pastoral letter for Bishop Wulfsige III, written between 992 and 1002, stipulates that priests are to "tell to the people on Sundays and festivals the meaning of the gospel in English", implying that preaching was to take place along with the liturgical services for these days. Dorothy Whitelock has in fact given the translation "festivals" for the term "mæssedagum", the liturgical association of which is obvious.[47] Ælfric's first Old English letter for Wulfstan is less liturgically specific, but still states that "[t]he masspriest must preach to men the true faith and tell them homilies".[48] Milton Gatch at least partially rejects preaching within the context of the mass, arguing instead that vernacular preaching occurred within the context of the Prone and that this vernacular office was "not ... integral to the Mass". He however presents no positive evidence for the practice, citing only "language implying the separability of Mass and preaching".[49] Thomas Amos, considering the liturgical context of Carolingian preaching, finds no evidence for a "vernacular preaching office" outside the mass and earlier precedents show the ubiquity of preaching within the mass, probably after the reading of the gospel. One anonymous Carolingian statute clearly sets out the intended liturgical context for preaching:

> We order that each of you in the church assigned to you, on two or three Sundays or feast days of the saints shall strive to teach the people subject

---

Teresi, "Mnemonic Transmission of Old English Texts in the Post-Conquest Period," in *Rewriting Old English in the Twelfth Century*, ed. Mary Swan and Elaine Treharne (Cambridge: Cambridge University Press, 2000), 99.

[46] John Harper, *The Forms and Orders of Western Liturgy from the Tenth to the Eighteenth Century: A Historical Introduction and Guide for Students and Musicians* (Oxford: Clarendon Press, 1991), 113.

[47] "Se mæssepreost sceal secgan Sunnandagum 7 mæssedagum þæs godspelles angyt on englisc þam folce." Whitelock, Brett, and Brooke, *Councils and Synods*, 208.

[48] "Se mæssepreost sceal mannum bodian þone soþan geleafan 7 hym larspel secgan." Ibid., 294.

[49] Milton Gatch, *Preaching and Theology in Anglo-Saxon England: Ælfric and Wulfstan* (Toronto: University of Toronto Press, 1977), 36–39.

to you the healthful doctrine from the Holy Scripture after the Gospel has been read, and that you order the people so that no one shall leave the church before the blessing, that is, "Benedicamus domino" or "ite, missa est", is spoken by the priest or deacon.[50]

As the Anglo-Saxon evidence implies similar practices, there appears to be little reason to doubt the continuity of this practice into the tenth and eleventh centuries. The homily may also have followed the recitation of the Creed in this period, providing an opportunity for catechetical instruction that was not ignored by Anglo-Saxon homilists.[51]

Internal evidence is also an indication that Anglo-Saxon homilies were designed for performance within the mass. The beginning of one of Ælfric's First Series homilies refers to "this gospel which we have now heard from the mouth of the deacon" and similarly, after summarizing the gospel reading, Blickling II refers to the congregation hearing "þis halige godspel beforan us rædan".[52] Additionally, as the gospel preceding the homily was in Latin, most laypeople would have been unable to understand its content. Many Old English homilies therefore provide approximate translations or summaries of the pericope within their texts prior to the exhortatory portion of the homily. In Ælfric's First Series homily "Sermo de Natale Domini", he provides a fairly close translation of Luke 2:1–20 to facilitate understanding of the passage for those listening. Similarly, the first 27 lines of Blickling II are almost wholly concerned with giving a vernacular synopsis of Luke 18:31–43.[53] Indications such as these, as well as evidence from early medieval prescriptive texts, seem to point most clearly towards the use of Anglo-Saxon homilies within the mass.

Though the primary context for Anglo-Saxon preaching was within the mass, there are other potential contexts and audiences for homiletic

---

[50] "Praecimus vobis ut unusquisque vestrum super duas vel tres ebdomadas diebus dominicis seu festivitatibus sanctorum populum sibi subiectum doctrinas salutiferis ex sacra scriptura sumptis in illis, ut nullus de ecclesia exeat, antequam a presbitero sive diacono laus, id est 'Benedicamus domino' aut 'ite, missa est' pronuntietur." Thomas Amos, "Preaching and the Sermon in the Carolingian World," in *De Ore Domini: Preacher and Word in the Middle Ages*, ed. Amos, Eugene Green, and Beverly Kienzle (Kalamazoo: Medieval Institute Publications, 1989), 49–50, 58.

[51] Karl Young, *The Drama of the Medieval Church* (Oxford: Clarendon Press, 1933), 1:28; Clemoes, *Ælfric's Catholic Homilies*, 335–44; Dorothy Bethurum, ed., *The Homilies of Wulfstan* (Oxford: Clarendon Press, 1957), VII, VIIa; Helen Foxhall Forbes, *Heaven and Earth in Anglo-Saxon England* (Farnham: Ashgate, 2013), 41–42.

[52] Wilcox, "Ælfric in Dorset," 53–54; Richard Morris, ed., *The Blickling Homilies: With a Translation and Index of Words Together with the Blickling Glosses*, Early English Text Society Original Series 58, 63, and 73 (London: Oxford University Press, 1967), 15.

[53] Morris, *The Blickling Homilies*, 15.

performance. For example, a chaplain might find an audience for homilies in the household he served. There are a significant number of chaplains who served in aristocratic Anglo-Saxon households in the tenth and eleventh centuries, tasked with providing pastoral care for the household and possibly a manorial church, among other duties.[54] Aside from preaching in the context of the mass, these priests may have had occasion to read out homilies to those within their household, as Jonathan Wilcox has suggested may have been the case in Ealdorman Æthelweard's household.[55] In a context such as this, those listening to texts being read could be a diverse group, consisting of the nobleman and his immediate and possibly extended family, a number of retainers, servants, and their wives and children. The types of literacy practiced within the aristocratic household, as discussed in an earlier chapter, and the commissioning and procurement of texts like Ælfric's *Lives of Saints* by a noble household imply that homilies might be used in this way.[56]

Preaching outside the liturgy might also occur in a more public setting, such as in meetings of a local guild.[57] All four of the surviving sets of Anglo-Saxon guild statutes show a connection with a local minster and it seems that a priest or priests were chosen by the lay members of the guild to perform services for them at their meetings and to commemorate the dead. In the case of the Exeter guild, the priest was to "sing two masses at each meeting, one for the living friends, the other for the departed".[58] These may have been private masses however, involving only the members of a given religious community, and thus may not have typically acted as opportunities for preaching to the laity.[59] On the other hand, the multiple yearly meetings held by

---

[54] For more information on household priests, see pages 24–25.
[55] Jonathan Wilcox, "The Audience of Ælfric's *Lives of Saints* and the Face of Cotton Caligula A. XIV, fols. 93–130," in *Beatus vir: Studies in Early English and Norse Manuscripts in Memory of Phillip Pulsiano*, ed. A. N. Doane and Kirsten Wolf (Tempe: Arizona Center for Medieval and Renaissance Studies, 2006), 241–42, 249.
[56] Æthelweard and his son Æthelmær commissioned the production of this work, as is noted by Ælfric in the Latin and Old English prefaces. Walter W. Skeat, ed., *Ælfric's* Lives of Saints*: Being a Set of Sermons on Saints' Days Formerly Observed by the English Church*, vol. 1, Early English Text Society Original Series 76 and 82 (London: Oxford University Press, 1966), 4.
[57] Patrick Conner, "Parish Guilds and the Production of Old English Literature in the Public Sphere," in *Intertexts: Studies in Anglo-Saxon Culture Presented to Paul E. Szarmach*, ed. Virginia Blanton and Helene Scheck (Tempe: Arizona Center for Medieval and Renaissance Studies, 2008), 266–67.
[58] *English Historical Documents*, ed. David C. Douglas, vol. 1, *c. 500–1042*, ed. Dorothy Whitelock, 2nd ed. (London: Eyre Methuen, 1979), 604–7. For the appointment of a priest by the guild members, see Gervase Rosser, "The Anglo-Saxon Gilds," in Blair, *Minsters and Parish Churches*, 32.
[59] Cyrille Vogel, *Medieval Liturgy: An Introduction to the Sources*, ed. and trans.

parish guilds on days with liturgical and spiritual significance may have been another context for preaching, though possibly one better suited to a sermon for a general occasion than a homily explicating a set passage of Scripture.[60] Though some guilds of this period seem to have been predominately aristocratic, such as the Thegns' Guild of Cambridge, others indicate guild membership for the lower classes, particularly toward the end of the eleventh century, implying potential audiences of men and women "whose status would appear to run from freeman to ealdorman" in guild meetings.[61]

Annotations and evidence for use

In some cases, annotations and marginal notes in homiletic manuscripts aid us in understanding how these texts were used by allowing us to see indications of a performative function. Kathryn Powell's examination of marginal annotations in Cambridge, Corpus Christi College 162 affords us a view of a preacher active in the early eleventh century who used homilies by Ælfric and anonymous composers and made changes and additions to the contents of the manuscript. Powell shows the particular relevance of the preacher's notes and expansions of the text in light of the intensifying Viking raids of 1006–1007 and 1009–1012, demonstrating the way in which this preacher had adapted his text to capitalize on these political events for the purpose of Lenten exhortation.[62] Though this preacher seems to have been active at Canterbury, possibly St Augustine's, his process of addition and adaptation must have been a common one for secular priests in the late Anglo-Saxon period. More basic interpolations appear in an Ælfric homily for the first Sunday in Lent in the unlocalized Oxford, Bodleian Library, Junius 85 and 86, discussed in detail later in this chapter, in which the copyist inserted biblical quotations in Latin where only Old English is found in the authorial text. Wilcox takes this as an indication of "a pride in some ability at Latin", as the quotations appear in none of the most closely related manuscripts. Additionally, at least one annotation in the same homily, a vertical line making clear the separation of two words, is the kind of note we might expect to see in a homily which a preacher had read and mentally prepared prior to preaching.[63] Though

---

William George Storey, Niels Rasmussen, and John Brooks-Leonard (Washington, DC: Pastoral Press, 1986), 156–58.
[60] Conner, "Parish Guilds and the Production of Old English Literature," 267.
[61] Ibid., 268; Rosser, "Anglo-Saxon Gilds," 31.
[62] Kathryn Powell, "Viking Invasions and Marginal Annotations in Cambridge, Corpus Christi College 162," *Anglo-Saxon England* 37 (2008).
[63] Jonathan Wilcox, "The Use of Ælfric's Homilies: MSS Oxford, Bodleian Library, Junius 85 and 86 in the Field," in *A Companion to Ælfric*, ed. Hugh Magennis

John Chadbon is unsure of the use of Junius 85 and 86 in preaching, he notes what appear to be contemporary additions to Homily 4 intended "to improve the deliverability of the text".[64] Furthermore, ff. 10–18 of Oxford, Bodleian Library, Auct. F. 4. 32, written in England in the later eleventh century, were originally an independently circulating homiletic booklet containing a vernacular homily on the Invention of the Cross and relevant annotations. Within the text of the homily, there are more than forty corrections and annotations, some of which are the work of the original scribe, but at least two other hands are evident. The first hand aside from the main scribe added "prefixes, pronouns, and a single instance of a verb phrase", whereas the second post-scribal annotator added significantly more material, consisting of words and short phrases as well as the emendation of certain regional linguistic features.[65] Textual emendations such as these, particularly when they indicate performative changes in the text rather than simple correction of scribal errors, can provide us with additional evidence for the pastoral use of a homily or homiletic collection. For example, notes of this kind may help to show the pastoral priorities of individual preachers and, if the annotations or additions pertain to oral performance as some of the above examples do, they can point to the practical use of a given book in a pastoral setting. Due to the differing habits of individual readers and preachers, not all texts used in preaching will show evidence of usage through annotation. Despite this, evidence from notes in the text, where available, can more clearly point to a preaching text's use and thus aid in uncovering its context.

Homiletic composition and circulation

Scholars of Anglo-Saxon homilies took great pains in the last century to establish the ways in which homilies were transmitted as written texts. These studies often concerned themselves with defining common sources, now mostly lost, for homiletic collections, examining the ways in which interpolations within texts have been diffused, and

---

and Mary Swan (Leiden: Brill, 2009), 364–65. Paul Szarmach notes this sort of annotation in several homilies in Pembroke College 25, using them as evidence for the "positive response" the texts received. Szarmach, "Pembroke College 25, Arts. 93–95," in Via Crucis: *Essays on Early Medieval Sources and Ideas in Memory of J. E. Cross*, ed. Thomas N. Hall, Thomas D. Hill, and C. D. Wright (Morgantown: West Virginia University Press, 2002), 304.

[64] John Chadbon, "Oxford, Bodleian Library, MSS Junius 85 and 86: An Edition of a Witness to the Old English Homiletic Tradition" (PhD thesis, University of Leeds, 1993), 90.

[65] Mary-Catherine Bodden, ed. and trans., *The Old English Finding of the True Cross* (Cambridge: D. S. Brewer, 1987), 8–10.

tracing linguistic variations and regional forms in Old English homilies. While these studies are very valuable, the practical realities of homiletic composition and circulation can get lost in the knots of manuscript sigla and the intricacies of philological analysis. Conversely, examining the ways that preaching texts moved among the secular clergy forces us to consider these realities, if hypothetically at times. Homiletic books are included in some of the prescriptive lists of books for priests that have been surveyed in an earlier chapter, but due to their absence from many of the tenth- and eleventh-century lists, they do not feature in what I have referred to as the "core of priestly texts" gleaned from a collation of these lists. But there is significant manuscript evidence for priestly utilization of homiletic books and evidence from prescriptive sources, including the preface to Ælfric's *Catholic Homilies*, indicates the expectation and necessity of preaching by secular priests.[66] In order to have access to these texts, it is probable that secular clerics were active at many levels in the composition and distribution of preaching texts.

It is a truism that circulation of a text first requires its composition. In the cases of Ælfric, Wulfstan, and a number of continental homilists, we are able to identity these composers by name, but the identities of other homilists of the Anglo-Saxon period remain unknown and likely unknowable. Though their names are irrecoverable, by contextualizing the period in which they were active, we can assemble some information about their status and position. Donald Scragg has argued that the composer of Vercelli XIX, XX, and XXI and an Ascension Day homily in Corpus 162 was active at Canterbury from the 960s to the 980s, but makes no further suggestion about the homilist's identity.[67] As Nicholas Brooks has shown, there is no explicit indication that monks were a part of the Canterbury cathedral community in the period in question nor is there evidence for a wholly monastic community until roughly half a century after Scragg's proposed date, despite a series of monastic archbishops.[68] It is possible that this homilist was based at St Augustine's, which seems to have remained monastic throughout the Anglo-Saxon period, but the centrality of Christ Church in the circulation of preaching texts in the late tenth and eleventh centuries points to the cathedral community as the more likely location

---

[66] In this preface, Ælfric imagines his homilies "recited ... in their entirety in church by the ministers of God" to a lay audience. Wilcox, *Ælfric's Prefaces*, 127.

[67] Donald Scragg, "An Old English Homilist of Archbishop Dunstan's Day," in *Words, Texts and Manuscripts: Studies in Anglo-Saxon Culture Presented to Helmut Gneuss on the Occasion of His Sixty-Fifth Birthday*, ed. Michael Korhammer, Karl Reichl, and Hans Sauer (Cambridge: D.S. Brewer, 1992), 191–92.

[68] Nicholas Brooks, *The Early History of the Church of Canterbury: Christ Church from 597 to 1066* (Leicester: Leicester University Press, 1984), 255–56.

for the homilist's activities.[69] If this is the case, then the composer of these Vercelli homilies and one further anonymous text may have been a secular member of the Canterbury cathedral community in the second half of the tenth century. Similarly, Charles Wright has argued that Vercelli XI–XIII were the work of a secular cleric who carefully adapted his source material to his audience, which Wright argues was also composed of secular clergy, though these homilies are also suitable for a lay audience. Internal evidence from this group of homilies may go so far as to point to a clerical author using homilies as a vehicle for criticism of "state-sponsored expulsions and confiscations of the Benedictine Reform movement".[70] Additionally, arguments for early dating of the homilies in the Blickling and Vercelli books, as mentioned above, propose ninth-century dates for the composition of some of these texts, dates that are newly supported by Scragg's recent study of Digby 63. A ninth-century date, and indeed a date up to the mid-tenth century, would essentially preclude monastic authorship of these texts due to the almost complete lack of monasteries in England in this period.[71] If these early homilies were not being written by monks, we can plausibly conclude that those composing these texts were the clergy of English minsters and cathedrals. Thus secular clerics certainly would have played a major role in the composition and circulation of vernacular homilies from an early date and likely continued in similar roles from the later tenth century onward.

Though we often have little information on the composers of Old English homilies, the circulation of some homiletic materials is relatively clear due to the large number of surviving and well-studied manuscripts. For the homilies of Ælfric and, to a lesser extent, Wulfstan, there is a manuscript tradition that serves to provide us with some information on the original form of their compositions, and this record has been strengthened by the identification of the handwriting of both Ælfric and Wulfstan, showing the corrections and emendations they made in their homilies over time.[72] The way

---

[69] Clemoes, *Ælfric's Catholic Homilies*, 161–63; Wilcox, "Ælfric in Dorset," 61; Brooks, *The Early History of the Church of Canterbury*, 281–82.

[70] C. D. Wright, "Vercelli Homilies XI–XIII and the Anglo-Saxon Benedictine Reform: Tailored Sources and Implied Audiences," in *Preacher, Sermon and Audience in the Middle Ages*, ed. Carolyn Muessig (Leiden: Brill, 2002), 207, 224–26.

[71] An exception to this would be Athelney, founded by King Alfred in the late ninth century.

[72] Neil Ker, "The Handwriting of Archbishop Wulfstan in His Books," in *Books, Collectors and Libraries: Studies in the Medieval Heritage*, ed. Andrew Watson (London: Hambledon Press, 1985); Peter Clemoes, "History of the Manuscript and Punctuation (from Ælfric's First Series of Catholic Homilies – British Library, Royal 7. C. XII, fols. 4–218)," in *Anglo-Saxon Manuscripts: Basic Readings*, ed. Mary P. Richards (New York: Routledge, 1994), 345–46.

in which Ælfric's homilies were distributed can also be examined to some extent geographically. Some of the earliest copies were written at Cerne Abbey, but the main distribution center for his preaching texts was Canterbury, where Ælfric sent both the First and Second Series, dedicating them to Sigeric, Archbishop of Canterbury from 990 to 994. From Canterbury, the *Catholic Homilies* were at minimum distributed throughout southern England and the Midlands, with much of the circulation of the extant copies of Ælfric's homilies taking place in monasteries and cathedrals, institutions which commonly provided priests and dependent churches with books.[73] The utility of Ælfric's homilies as well as their popularity may also suggest that they achieved a greater degree of low-level circulation than is evident in the manuscript record.

Less is known about the way in which anonymous homilies traveled, but some had a great deal of currency over two centuries or more. For example, Blickling IX/Vercelli X is, as part of these two early codices, one of the earliest extant Old English homilies. Nine copies of this homily have survived in various forms and recensions, varying in date from the second half of the tenth century to the second half of the twelfth century, indicating the potential demand for and popularity of certain anonymous homilies.[74] But the textual history of most anonymous homilies is largely obscured; many were designed to be preached in pastoral contexts, which were mostly outside the major ecclesiastical centers through which most manuscripts have survived. This has caused difficulty in tracing the use and movement of homiletic texts outside the major scriptoria of the period. However, much of the circulation of anonymous homilies, and later the homilies of Ælfric and Wulfstan, may have taken place at a local level and was potentially facilitated by what could be termed "horizontal circulation". This term is used here to denote the transmission of texts across institutions and between individuals as opposed to the top-down provision of texts by a cathedral or monastery. For example, the priest of a local church might travel to a nearby minster or other ecclesiastical institution to copy or borrow homilies or liturgical texts, and it is this type of circulation that we might surmise from the homiletic additions to the margins of Cambridge, Corpus Christi College 41. Old English homilies are a major feature of the marginal additions to this manuscript, occupying the margins of more than fifty pages. Thomas Bredehoft has convincingly argued that this copying took place in multiple stages, according to when the scribe was able to access different texts, and almost all

---

[73] Clemoes, *Ælfric's Catholic Homilies*, 162–63.
[74] Donald Scragg, "The Corpus of Vernacular Homilies and Prose Saints' Lives," 79–81; Paul Szarmach, "The Vercelli Prose and Anglo-Saxon Literary History," in Zacher and Orchard, *New Readings in the Vercelli Book*, 36–37.

of the homilies in the book were copied in Bredehoft's Stage 3, along with excerpts from the *Old English Martyrology*, a vernacular charm, and passages from *Solomon and Saturn*.[75] We are unaware of the context in which the marginal scribe had access to these texts and others for copying; it may have been carried out in multiple trips to a cathedral, but could equally have been a priest copying texts from the books of other nearby churches. Despite this uncertainty, Corpus 41 illustrates an often-obscured way in which homiletic texts may have been disseminated: not from major scriptoria, but organically and unevenly through local institutions whose primary function was providing pastoral care. As has been more generally discussed in the preceding chapter, major ecclesiastical centers, such as cathedrals and monasteries, and minor secular churches both had the potential to act as centers of scribal activity, and thus as centers of textual transmission for the secular clergy.

Another way in which homiletic texts circulated is through transmission in independently circulating unbound booklets. All of the extant homiletic texts from Anglo-Saxon England have been preserved in codices, whether as an integral text, a later addition, or a fragment used in binding. However, in an important article, Pamela Robinson clearly identifies a number of booklets that show evidence of independent circulation, each having survived by later binding into a codex.[76] For example, Oxford, Bodleian Library, Hatton 115, ff. 140r–147r contains a version of Vercelli IX and wear is apparent on the outer pages of what constituted the booklet. Additionally, the text of the homily has been annotated in both Latin and Old English by later users, one of whom is the Tremulous Hand, but at least one other reader made annotations and emendations in an earlier script.[77] The most notable of these is the addition of an alternate ending to the homily at f. 146r, which indicates that the user of the booklet changed and adapted the form of the homily to better suit a particular oral performance. Folios 10–18 of Oxford, Bodleian Library, Auct. F. 4. 32, which contain an anonymous homily for the Invention of the Cross, is another unambiguous example of a homiletic booklet: it displays soiling on the outer pages of the booklet and a vertical crease running through all the

---

[75] Thomas A. Bredehoft, "Filling the Margins of CCCC 41: Textual Space and a Developing Archive," *Review of English Studies* 57 (2006): 730–31. This manuscript and its liturgical contents will be discussed in more detail in chapter 5.

[76] Pamela Robinson, "Self-Contained Units in Composite Manuscripts of the Anglo-Saxon Period," *Anglo-Saxon England* 7 (1978). Since the publication of Robinson's study several decades ago, more independently circulating booklets have been proposed and further arguments made for Robinson's preliminary suggestions. See Wilcox, "The Use of Ælfric's Homilies," 356–59; M. J. Toswell, "The Codicology of Anglo-Saxon Homiletic Manuscripts, Especially the Blickling Homilies," in Kleist, *The Old English Homily*, 219–21.

[77] Scragg, "The Corpus of Vernacular Homilies and Prose Saints' Lives," 96.

folios, suggesting that the booklet was folded for easier storage during travel. Though few clear examples such as these have survived, the relative infrequency of booklets compared to extant homiletic codices may well misrepresent the frequency of this method of circulation. As has been previously discussed, manuscripts used in minsters and local churches were unlikely to survive considering the general lack of continuity in these foundations and the wear and damage caused by constant use. These considerations apply to booklets as well, particularly as their more impermanent fabric would have deteriorated more quickly and may have led future generations to see little value in small, unbound gatherings such as these. One can imagine, as is so vividly told by John Bale's preface to John Leland's *New Year's Gift*, the pages of a low-status and apparently valueless homiletic booklet being used in place of a boot brush or as a fire starter.[78] Despite the losses that have taken place, the booklets that have survived point to a means of transmitting homilies that was inexpensive, portable, and within the financial reach of many institutions that provided pastoral care, including rural and impoverished local churches.

Homilies in their manuscript context

Studying the surviving manuscripts which are likely to have been used in a pastoral setting may allow us to recover some information about the practice of pastoral care as expressed through preaching. The second half of this chapter presents three case studies of Anglo-Saxon homiletic books which were plausibly used by the secular clergy: the Taunton Fragment, Junius 85 and 86, and the Blickling book. Through these books and others, we can see specific examples of the content of preaching texts, learn something about the textual milieu within which homilies circulated, and see how preachers adapted and constructed texts for oral delivery.

The Taunton Fragment (SHC DD\SAS/C1193/77)[79]

The Taunton Fragment consists of four leaves of what at one time was an eleventh-century copy of the Homiliary of Angers, remarkably containing a bilingual version of this homiliary in alternating

---

[78] C. E. Wright, "The Dispersal of the Libraries in the Sixteenth Century," in *The English Library before 1700: Studies in Its History*, ed. Francis Wormald and C. E. Wright (London: University of London, Athlone Press, 1958), 153.

[79] Most scholars refer to this fragment with the shelf mark "Taunton, Somerset County Record Office, DD/SAS C/1193/77". However, per the request of the Somerset Archives, I refer to the fragment in the format they have provided.

Latin and Old English. As it stands, the fragment contains homilies for the fifth to the eighth Sundays after Pentecost, comprising items 29–31 and item 33 of the Homiliary of Angers as reconstructed by Étaix. Most of the homilies are significantly incomplete due to the loss of leaves, though similar Latin versions of three of the four homilies can be found in the twelfth-century Oxford, Bodleian Library, Bodley 343.[80] Despite being in the possession of the Somerset Archaeological and Natural History Society since at least 1883, the fragment was unknown to Anglo-Saxonists until 1995 and was not the subject of any published scholarly work until 2004.[81] Mechthild Gretsch's article on the fragment, the first to appear, provides commentary and an edition of the text of the extant folios. Unable to identify a source for the homilies, Gretsch proposes that the text represents "the remnants of a homiliary which was composed by some continental cleric … and then copied by an English scribe", probably written and intended for use outside "mainstream intellectual centres".[82] Two years later, Helmut Gneuss noted the similarity of the fragment's text to the homiliary found in ff. 11–39 of Bodley 343 and briefly remarked on Aidan Conti's identification of this section of Bodley 343 with the Homiliary of Angers.[83] Conti's subsequent article on the Taunton Fragment firmly identifies it with the Homiliary of Angers and, while he convincingly disproves much of Gretsch's argument in relation to the composition of the text, Conti does find common ground with Gretsch in his proposition that the Taunton Fragment "circulated and … [was] transmitted predominately outside the better equipped intellectual centres of eleventh-century England".[84]

The Homiliary of Angers (subsequently HA) is a collection of homilies composed for preaching to the laity and is analogous to several other collections of early medieval homilies from the continent used for instruction and exhortation, such as the homiliary of Hrabanus

---

[80] Raymond Étaix, "L'homéliaire carolingien d'Angers," *Revue bénédictine* 104, no. 1 (1994): 153–54; Aidan Conti, "Preaching Scripture and Apocrypha: A Previously Unidentified Carolingian Homiliary in an Old English Manuscript, Oxford, Bodleian Library, MS Bodley 343" (PhD thesis, University of Toronto, 2004), 352–53. Conti notes that though Étaix designated the homilies that appear in Taunton as those for the fourth through the seventh Sundays following Pentecost, they are here (and in Gretsch's and Conti's articles) designated as those for the fifth through eighth Sundays following Pentecost, as this reflects "the system that came to dominate throughout Europe, and had reached widespread use in the eleventh century". Conti, "The Taunton Fragment and the Homiliary of Angers: Context for New Old English," *Review of English Studies* 60 (2008): 4.

[81] Mechthild Gretsch. "The Taunton Fragment: A New Text from Anglo-Saxon England," *Anglo-Saxon England* 33 (2004): 145–46.

[82] Ibid., 191.

[83] Helmut Gneuss, "The Homiliary of the Taunton Fragments," *Notes and Queries* 52, no. 4 (2005).

[84] Conti, "The Taunton Fragment and the Homiliary of Angers," 1–2, 32–33.

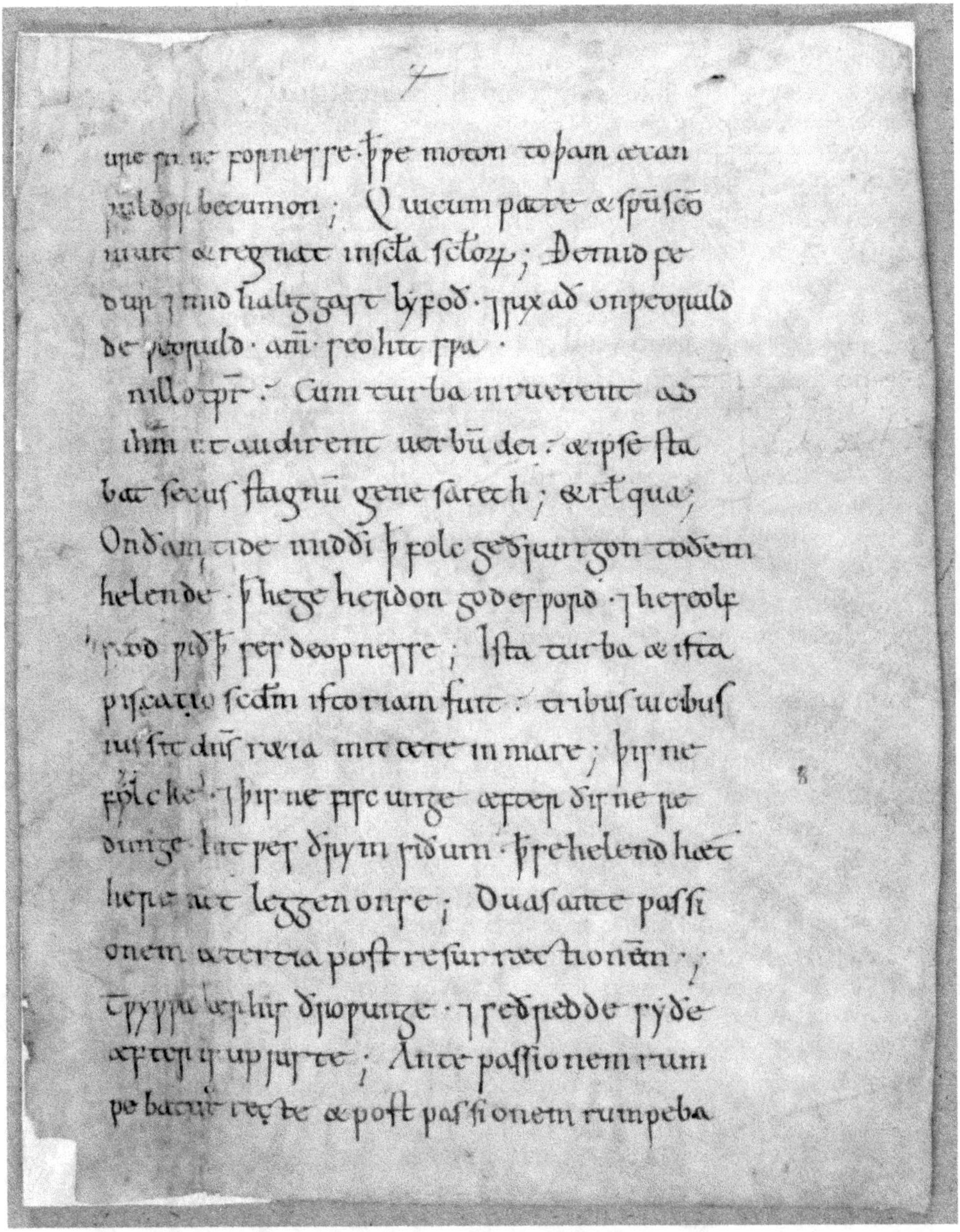

Plate 3: The Taunton Fragment, SHC DD\SAS/C1193/77, p. 7. The conclusion of a homily for the fifth Sunday after Pentecost and the first fifteen lines of a homily for the sixth Sunday after Pentecost.

Maurus and that of Saint-Père de Chartres.[85] HA is found in manuscripts across Europe from the tenth to the thirteenth century and the earliest-known witness was copied in England roughly a century before the Taunton Fragment.[86] Unlike other collections of homilies more suitable for reading verbatim, the individual texts of HA are typically shorter, providing a "rapide glose de l'évangile du jour" along with rudimentary exegesis presented in a straightforward rhetorical style that has led scholars to believe that they generally functioned as a series of sermon outlines.[87] This, combined with the linguistic simplicity of the homilies, seems to have made it attractive for preachers to adapt and reuse HA as a framework for vernacular preaching, a supposition that is reinforced by Conti's argument that HA is likely to have circulated in unbound booklets in the eleventh and twelfth centuries. Furthermore, the homilies presented have internal indications of their intended users and audience: one homily "puts the exposition in the mouth of a *sacerdos* addressing those entrusted to his care", while another specifically exhorts those with wives and earthly possessions.[88] In short, the texts transmitted in HA are brief, accessible outlines for homilies which seem to have been intended for use by the secular clergy for preaching to the laity.

Having established a probable pastoral context for HA, it should be noted that at least two factors make it unlikely that the complete codex from which the surviving leaves originated was used in its immediate form for reading aloud to a lay audience. Firstly, the text in Taunton appears in alternating Latin and Old English. Reading the text as it stands would probably produce a halting oral performance as the preacher scanned the page for only the Old English lines. Additionally, though we cannot be certain of the precise interpolation of HA that appears in this particular fragment and are therefore unaware of the length of each homily as it originally stood, many of the texts as they appear in other manuscripts are fairly short when compared with most vernacular homilies. With these considerations in mind, the bilingual version of HA, unattested elsewhere, would most likely have been used as an aid and an outline for the composition of vernacular sermons, as it was used in Spain from c. 1200 until the close of the Middle Ages.[89] Use of HA in this fashion would not have required a high level of Latin

---

[85] Ibid., 5.
[86] Winfried Rudolf, "The Homiliary of Angers in Tenth-Century England," *Anglo-Saxon England* 39 (2010).
[87] Étaix, "L'homéliaire carolingien d'Angers," 177; Conti, "The Taunton Fragment and the Homiliary of Angers," 5.
[88] Conti, "The Taunton Fragment and the Homiliary of Angers," 5–6, 13–14.
[89] Manuel Ambrosio Sánchez Sánchez, "Vernacular Preaching in Spanish, Portuguese and Catalan," in *The Sermon*, ed. Beverly Mayne Kienzle, Typologie des Sources du Moyen Âge Occidental 81–83 (Turnhout: Brepols, 2000), 797–98;

literacy from a prospective preacher. The Latin is idiosyncratic but relatively simple and accessible, and clearly a line-by-line Old English translation would have further simplified its use. An examination of the way in which HA is transmitted in Old English homilies will not only show that this homiliary was intended as an aid to medieval preachers, but that it in fact was used as such in late Anglo-Saxon England.

Stephen Pelle has recently shown that HA was used in Anglo-Saxon England as a source and outline for vernacular homilies, and a similar pattern of use is evident in other parts of Europe later in the medieval period.[90] A version of HA 22, most likely in Old English, was used in the composition or reworking of the homilies in Cambridge, Corpus Christi College 162 and the version of Vercelli IX recorded in the Hatton 115 booklet.[91] Neither of these homiletic texts draws on HA or its Latin-Old English version as its main source, but the borrowings in both are clear and constitute several lines of each homily. Slight evidence may also indicate that the homilist of Blickling VI knew HA 55 or a homily that drew on it, as Blickling VI records an apocryphal tradition attested only in HA and one of the homilies in London, Lambeth Palace Library 487.[92] If the source of these borrowings is an Old English translation of HA, most probably represented by the Taunton Fragment, then the date of Corpus 162 would place the *terminus ante quem* of the translation of HA in the early eleventh century. Though it cannot be proven at this point that Corpus 162 drew from a pre-existing Old English translation, and that that translation is represented by the Taunton Fragment, it is an economical hypothesis. More significant dependence on HA can be seen in the early Middle English Lambeth Homily I, the author of which relied heavily on HA 55, but freely added his own material and excised passages as he saw fit.[93] Pelle argues that this homily "is more representative of the everyday use to which the Homiliary of Angers was likely put than are more literal vernacular translations of the collection, such as the Taunton Fragment".[94] The dating of the composition of this homily remains unsure, but a pre-Conquest date has not been rejected and Celia Sisam

---

Stephen Pelle, "Source Studies in the Lambeth Homilies," *Journal of English and Germanic Philology* 113, no. 1 (2014): 38–39.

[90] Sánchez Sánchez, "Vernacular Preaching in Spanish, Portuguese, and Catalan," 797–98.
[91] Stephen Pelle, "The Seven Pains of Hell: The Latin Source of an Old English Homiletic Motif," *Review of English Studies* 62 (2010): 169–70. The inclusion of material from HA 22 into Vercelli IX is an interpolation and does not appear in the Vercelli book itself.
[92] Pelle, "Source Studies in the Lambeth Homilies," 42.
[93] Ibid., 37, 39–42.
[94] Ibid., 47.

argues in an important article that the group of homilies containing Lambeth I "certainly go[es] back to Old English".[95]

Though the Taunton Fragment itself – and the codex in which it originated – was probably not directly used in preaching to the laity, it represents a collection that saw use as a significant source for Old English sermons and would have been an invaluable pastoral resource for Anglo-Saxon priests. The homiliary represented by the current fragment would have allowed a preacher with a limited command of Latin to easily draft or mentally prepare homiletic performances using the short and rudimentary exegetical content of HA as a malleable framework. Its content is eminently suitable for preparing and augmenting texts for preaching within the mass, and potential use in this vein may reinforce earlier suggestions that secular priests were involved in the composition and adaptation of vernacular homilies. Furthermore, the universal conclusion that the Taunton Fragment originated in a provincial center, combined with indications of the circulation of HA in booklets, would suggest that this manuscript and other Anglo-Saxon copies of HA are strong candidates for texts used in a pastoral setting. Studies of both the Taunton Fragment and the Homiliary of Angers are still in their early stages and there is no doubt that more correspondence between this uniquely bilingual homiliary and other Old English homilies has yet to be uncovered.

Oxford, Bodleian Library, Junius 85 and 86

This manuscript, copied in the mid-eleventh century, is a small, low-status homiletic collection originally produced as one volume, but now bound in two; I refer to it in the singular below in light of the medieval form of the book. The manuscript was written by two or three scribes on parchment of generally poor quality and irregular size.[96] Decoration is minimal, consisting primarily of a few embellished initials and two stints of crude borders. Six homilies survive, most of them fragmentary, and the manuscript seems to be missing at least one quire and therefore probably contained more preaching texts

---

[95] Celia Sisam, "The Scribal Tradition of the Lambeth Homilies," *Review of English Studies* 2 (1951): 110.

[96] The scribal work of Junius 85 and 86 has been the subject of some disagreement. Some of the text of the manuscript has been retouched, to some extent obscuring a clear view of its paleographical features. Neil Ker thought the manuscript the work of two scribes, Antonette Healey noted two hands and thought the presence of a third indeterminable, and John Chadbon has argued that it was a third scribe who wrote fols. 35–41. Ker, *Catalogue of Manuscripts Containing Anglo-Saxon* (Oxford: Clarendon Press, 1957), 411; Healey, *The Old English Vision of St. Paul* (Cambridge, MA: Mediaeval Academy of America, 1978), 8; Chadbon, "Oxford, Bodleian Library, MSS Junius 85 and 86," 47–48.

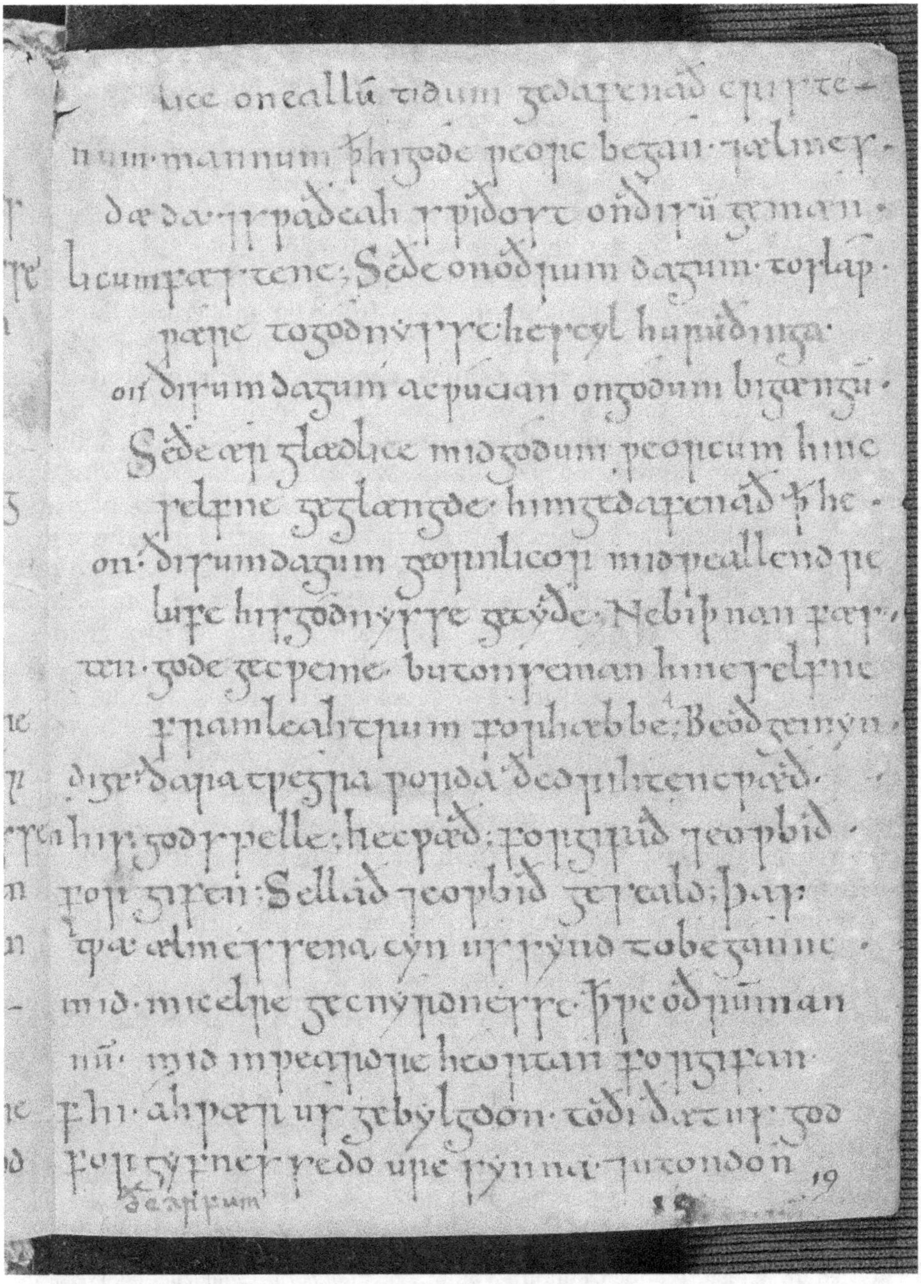

Plate 4: Oxford, Bodleian Library, Junius 85, f. 19r. Part of Ælfric's Second Series homily for the First Sunday in Lent and one page of Wilcox's proposed booklet.

at the time of its copying. The manuscript's endleaf was originally a fragment of the Old English *Consolation of Philosophy*, but was lost at some point between 1886 and 1937.[97] The first, penultimate, and final homilies of Junius 85 and 86 are shared with the Blickling book, the second is unique to this manuscript aside from a section occurring in a composite homily, the third is from the Second Series of Ælfric's *Catholic Homilies*, and the fourth homily is unattested elsewhere and will be discussed in due course.[98]

Scragg has argued that the scribes of Junius 85 and 86 had access to a tenth-century homiletic collection similar to Blickling and Vercelli, but, as with those earlier and more well-studied manuscripts, linguistic and paleographical analyses have not established a firm place of origin for its exemplar. Some of the source material for the scribes of Junius 85 and 86 may have been significantly earlier than the copy of the book itself, as the homily unique to this manuscript contains a relatively large number of *ie* spellings, which are associated with an earlier stage in the development of Old English.[99] In addition to its homiletic content, the manuscript contains four charms in Latin with rubrics and directions for use in Old English following directly after the second homily. Nothing is known of the location of the manuscript's production nor do we have any information on the provenance of the manuscript prior to the seventeenth century, at which time it was given to Franciscus Junius, a seventeenth-century scholar and manuscript collector, by his nephew Isaac Vossius.[100] Drawing on previous work by Robinson, Wilcox has recently proposed that ff. 18–24 were produced as a booklet designed for independent circulation and were later bound into the codex, citing the change in scribal hand, the difference in layout and rubrication, and a moderate amount of soiling on the first page of the quire as indications of their original purpose.[101]

Though Junius 85 and 86 had previously been little noted as a candidate for a priestly book, Wilcox has made a convincing case for understanding it as a book for a local priest or a minster priest "whose preaching centered on basic eschatological issues, who

---

[97] Falconer Madan, H. H. E. Craster, and N. Denholm-Young, *A Summary Catalogue of Western Manuscripts in the Bodleian Library at Oxford* ..., vol. 2, pt. 2 (Oxford: Clarendon Press, 1937), 983.

[98] The first homily, which is fragmentary, is a version of Blickling IX and Vercelli X, and the final homily is Blickling XVII and Vercelli XVIII. Scragg, "The Corpus of Vernacular Homilies and Prose Saints' Lives," 84–85.

[99] Ibid., 86; Chadbon, "Oxford, Bodleian Library, MSS Junius 85 and 86," 89.

[100] Madan, Craster, and Denholm-Young, *A Summary Catalogue of Western Manuscripts*, 983. Chadbon suggests the possibility that the manuscript traveled to France in the later Middle Ages in light of several marginal notes in French, but many English manuscripts contain French annotations. Chadbon, "Oxford, Bodleian Library, MSS Junius 85 and 86," 37–39.

[101] Wilcox, "The Use of Ælfric's Homilies," 356–57.

Table 2. Contents of Oxford, Bodleian Library, Junius 85 and 86

Junius 85	
f. 2r	Fragment of an Anonymous Homily for Tuesday in Rogationtide (Blickling IX, Vercelli X)
ff. 2–17	Anonymous Homily: *Men ða leofestan we gelornodon on godcundum gewritum*
f. 17	Charms
ff. 18–24	Ælfric, Second Series: First Sunday in Lent (proposed booklet)
ff. 25–35	Anonymous Homily: *Geherað nu men þa leofestan hu us godes bec*[a]
Junius 86	
ff. 36–40	Anonymous Homily: *Geherað nu men þa leofestan hu us godes bec* (cont.)
ff. 40–61	Anonymous Homily: *Geherað nu men þa leofestan hwæt her sægþ* (Blickling IV)
ff. 62–81	Anonymous Homily on St Martin (Blickling XVII, Vercelli XVIII)[b]

[a] Owen Roberson, "Oxford, Bodleian Library, Junius 85," in *The Production and Use of English Manuscripts 1060 to 1220*, ed. Orietta Da Rold et al. (Leicester: University of Leicester, 2010–), accessed February 11, 2018, http://www.le.ac.uk/english/em1060to1220/mss/EM.Ox.Juni.85.htm.

[b] Roberson, "Oxford, Bodleian Library, Junius 86," in Da Rold et al., *The Production and Use of English Manuscripts*, accessed February 11, 2018, http://www.le.ac.uk/english/em1060to1220/mss/EM.Ox.Juni.86.htm.

was probably less scholarly than Ælfric's injunctions anticipate, yet who was functionally – indeed, proudly – literate in Latin as well as English, and who was deeply involved in the basics of life in his community".[102] Wilcox's analysis of this priest's pastoral concerns and Latinity are based on the selection of the homilies in Junius 85 and 86 and the unique interpolations in the manuscript, such as the inclusion of Latin biblical quotations in place of the solely vernacular quotations provided in the original Ælfrician version of the homily.[103] As the collection is brief, perhaps somewhat shorter than it once was, it is worthwhile to list the contents of the manuscript.

The fragment beginning the collection is a popular homily in Anglo-Saxon homiletic books, appearing in various forms in close to ten manuscripts, and as a Rogationtide homily, it is concerned with judgement and repentance.[104] Much of the rest of the book follows a similar theme. The second homily weaves the *Visio Pauli* into an Address of the Soul

---

[102] Ibid., 361–62.
[103] Ibid., 364–65.
[104] For the closest textual affiliations of the fragmentary version in this manuscript, see Paul Szarmach, "MS Junius 85 F. 2r and Napier 49," *English Language Notes* 14, no. 4 (1977).

to the Body homily and the fourth, a Lenten homily now split between Junius 85 and 86, further addresses this theme. Ælfric's homily and the penultimate anonymous homily in the collection are too composed for delivery during Lent, and the collection ends with a homily on the life of St Martin. Wilcox has described the codex as possessing "a clear thematic coherence centring around consideration of death and judgement and the fate of the body and soul", and the "eschatological thrust" of the parallels drawn between Lent and the present world and Easter and life after death correspond with the common themes of Anglo-Saxon Lenten preaching.[105] The collection also shows some interest in such spiritual duties as almsgiving and confession, themes that would have been emphasized by medieval preachers.

We are also able to witness through this book the creation of a composite homily. The homily that occupies ff. 25–40, unlike all the other surviving homiletic texts in this manuscript, is wholly unique to Junius 85 and 86. Chadbon cautiously suggests the possibility that this text could be a composite homily, writing that "such a suspicion cannot be easily dispelled or confirmed".[106] Despite this, the evidence for a unique composite homily composed by the scribes of this manuscript is stronger than Chadbon supposes. Much of his reasoning rests on the linguistic evidence of Homily 3. The piece transmits a relatively large number of *ie* spellings, such as in the pronoun "hiera", which are typically features of Old English prior to Late West Saxon.[107] Of the homilies in Junius 85 and 86, this text is the only one in which *ie* spellings appear. Chadbon understands the appearance of these spellings as an indication that the homily was copied from a single exemplar, casting doubt on its identification as a composite homily. However, the three scribes of Junius 85 and 86 all contributed to this piece in a way that bears further analysis.

Scribe A contributed the majority of the homily, ff. 25–33, as well as the majority of the *ie* spellings; Scribe B contributed f. 34 and no *ie* spellings; and Scribe C wrote the remaining five folios with the inclusion of only four *ie* spellings, of which there are none past line 244.[108] Significantly, scribal stints and the occurrence of *ie* spellings correlate with the sources drawn upon by the homilist or homilists.

---

[105] Wilcox, "The Use of Ælfric's Homilies," 360; M. Bradford Bedingfield, *The Dramatic Liturgy of Anglo-Saxon England* (Woodbridge: Boydell Press, 2002), 78. On the themes of Anglo-Saxon Lenten preaching, see Dalbey, "Themes and Techniques in the Blickling Lenten Homilies," in Szarmach and Huppé, *The Old English Homily and Its Backgrounds*; Robert Upchurch, "Catechetic Homiletics: Ælfric's Preaching and Teaching during Lent," in Magennis and Swan, *A Companion to Ælfric*.

[106] Chadbon, "Oxford, Bodleian Library, MSS Junius 85 and 86," 62.

[107] Alastair Campbell, *Old English Grammar* (Oxford: Clarendon Press, 1959), 128.

[108] Chadbon, "Oxford, Bodleian Library, MSS Junius 85 and 86," 89.

For example, no *ie* spellings occur in Scribe B's stint, which consists of the final portion of the Three Utterances section, discussed by Mary Wack and Charles Wright, and a brief prayer-like passage.[109] Chadbon dismisses the lack of *ie* spellings here, noting that only two words in Scribe B's stint could have utilized these spellings, both of which appear in the prayer-like passage, but he fails to fully appreciate the implications. The presence of *ie* spellings in most of the Three Utterances section and their absence in much of the rest of the homily would seem to indicate that the translation of this section was made at an earlier date than the composition of the prayer-like passage or the pseudo-Augustinian excerpt that follows line 257. Scribe B's lack of spelling features common to the remainder of the homily in lines 199–207 could indicate either his use of a different source material or insertion of his own transitional material, which forms an effective bridge between the Three Utterances material and the concluding section of the homily. Furthermore, Scribe C, writing ff. 35–40 of Homily 3, uses *ie* spellings only in the coherent section directly following Scribe B's prayer-like transition. The section immediately following is drawn from a pseudo-Augustinian homily identified by James Cross as a source for Homily 3, but it and the approximately twenty lines that follow it contain none of the distinctive spellings of the earlier sections, despite the common use of the pronoun form "hyra", elsewhere written as "hiera". In sum, the argument for the creation of a composite homily uniquely preserved in Junius 85 and 86 is not certain, but the correspondence of scribal stints with changes in the homily's source material and the distribution of *ie* spellings indicate that there may be more merit to this suggestion than has previously been thought.

Though we cannot firmly place the location of the production or use of Junius 85 and 86, it represents a type of manuscript that must have been more common than patterns of survival would lead us to believe: a portable, low-status collection of homilies concerned with themes of judgement, repentance, and the spiritual duties of believers. The visual evidence of the manuscript's utilitarian appearance, the internal evidence from the homilies chosen for inclusion in this particular book, and the ways in which its content has been adapted imply use by a priest or priests serving in a minor church. As Wilcox has argued, the manuscript provides a probable context for pastoral provision through preaching at a church of this kind, particularly for the season of Lent. The evidence from Chadbon's Homily 3 may also show how the scribes of the manuscript, possibly preachers themselves, may

---

[109] Mary F. Wack and Charles D. Wright, "A New Latin Source for the Old English 'Three Utterances' Exemplum," *Anglo-Saxon England* 20 (1991).

have constructed a composite homily from earlier homiletic source material to create a new Lenten homily.

The Blickling Homilies (Princeton, New Jersey, Princeton University Library, Scheide Collection 71)

The Blickling book, briefly discussed earlier in this chapter, is one of the two earliest collections of vernacular homilies in Old English and was probably copied towards the end of the tenth century, though a date in the 970s has been suggested by some.[110] The collection is, according to Scragg's fundamental article, most probably original and the product of two scribal hands. Scragg writes that "the scribes took care to put together a book which followed a preconceived design ... and they perhaps took individual items from different sources, rather than blocks of items."[111] Unlike the Vercelli book with which it is often compared, Blickling's Old English contents are purely homiletic, consisting of eighteen pieces arranged according to the liturgical year. The location of its production is unknown and the suggestions as to its geographical origin are diverse, though it was certainly in Lincoln in the early fourteenth century, as it was intermittently used by the city government of Lincoln for recordkeeping from the beginning of the fourteenth century until at least 1623.[112] Like the manuscripts discussed above, the Blickling codex has several incomplete sections of the surviving texts and multiple quires may have been lost since the book's production.

The textual relationships of the Blickling homilies are relatively limited. Blickling IX is the only homily from the collection habitually found in other manuscripts, while many of the homilies in Blickling that appear elsewhere do so with significant variations, and eight of the seventeen surviving texts do not appear in any other manuscript.[113] But one manuscript with a potentially close connection is Cambridge, Corpus Christi College 198. Building on a previous argument by Rudolph Willard, Mary Swan has made a detailed case

---

[110] Wilcox, "The Blickling Homilies Revisited," 99–100; Collins, *Anglo-Saxon Vernacular Manuscripts in America*, 52–53.

[111] Scragg, "The Homilies of the Blickling Manuscript," in Lapidge and Gneuss, *Learning and Literature in Anglo-Saxon England*, 302, 315.

[112] Rudolph Willard, ed., *The Blickling Homilies (The John H. Scheide Library, Titusville, Pennsylvania)*, Early English Manuscripts in Facsimile 10 (Copenhagen: Rosenkilde and Bagger, 1960), 41–42, 47–65. Willard exhaustively notes these entries in his facsimile edition of this volume. Additionally, four leaves containing gospel pericopes were also bound into the book at approximately the same time it came into use by the city of Lincoln to enable its use as a book upon which to swear oaths.

[113] Scragg, "The Corpus of Vernacular Homilies and Prose Saints' Lives," 83.

for the close association of Blickling and Corpus 198, asserting the possibility that the latter "was made in an institution very directly connected to, if not identical with, the one which housed the Blickling manuscript in the first half of the eleventh century".[114] Both manuscripts have significant Anglian dialectal features and localization to the East Midlands has been suggested on linguistic grounds.[115] Wilcox has gone further in arguing that the Blickling homilies were produced in Lincoln, an Anglo-Saxon town with a relatively large population, significant economic resources, and probably considerably more than the five churches recorded in Domesday, as Lincoln had thirty-two churches within the town in the early twelfth century.[116] Additionally, from the mid-tenth century until 1011, Lincoln was a diocesan seat, providing a plausible date and location for the book's production. The content and associations of the Blickling book are congruent with what we would expect to see in a book intended for preaching to the laity, and if Wilcox's argument in reference to Lincoln is tenable, the supposition that the book was intended for use by the secular clergy can be strengthened. No monastic foundations are known in Lincoln in the late Anglo-Saxon period, and while Lincoln Cathedral is a candidate for the production of the Blickling homilies, other ecclesiastical institutions in the immediate vicinity of Lincoln may also have had the resources to produce such a book.

Though some, particularly Gatch, have questioned the use of the Blickling Homilies in a pastoral context, recent scholarship has pointed to the use of this particular codex in preaching to the laity.[117] Wilcox has argued that the book was both produced and potentially used in Lincoln, concluding that "any priest operating in Lincoln – or anywhere else that English was spoken and understood – could have picked up this book and fruitfully performed its wisdom".[118] M. J. Toswell, examining the codicology of Blickling, contends that "[t]he writing ... is large enough to be easily read aloud, and the manuscript pointing and the use of accents to mark long vowels not otherwise immediately recognizable also suggest oral delivery."[119] Internal evidence from the Blickling homilies further suggests that this book was meant to be used for preaching in the mass. As has been noted

---

[114] Mary Swan, "Cambridge, Corpus Christi College 198 and the Blickling Manuscript," *Leeds Studies in English* 37 (2006): 96.
[115] Wilcox, "The Blickling Homilies Revisited," 103.
[116] Francis Hill, *Medieval Lincoln* (Cambridge: Cambridge University Press, 1948), 74; Peter H. Sawyer, *Anglo-Saxon Lincolnshire* (Lincoln: Committee for the Society for Lincolnshire History and Archaeology, 1998), 185.
[117] Milton Gatch, "The Unknowable Audience of the Blickling Homilies," *Anglo-Saxon England* 18 (1989).
[118] Wilcox, "The Blickling Homilies Revisited," 115.
[119] Toswell, "The Codicology of Anglo-Saxon Homiletic Manuscripts," 221.

earlier in this chapter, the book is arranged according to the church year with a number of internal indications that the homilies were meant to be read following the gospel reading. Many of the texts show concern for penitential practices, including fasting and almsgiving, the latter of which would be more appropriate for laypersons than for an audience of monks who could not own property.[120] Furthermore, the closest textual associations of this manuscript do little to recommend a monastic context for its production or use. Though Blickling transmits a relatively large number of unique pieces, what does appear elsewhere does so primarily in Junius 85 and 86 and the second section of Corpus 198. An argument has been made above for the suitability of Junius 85 and 86 for use by secular priests, and despite indications of a later Worcester provenance, Corpus 198 has few firm associations other than with the Blickling codex.

A great deal of scholarship has addressed the Blickling codex over the last century and this chapter does not approach this book intending to redefine scholarly views concerning it. Rather, it seeks to show that it is plausibly a book intended for preaching to the laity and for use by a pastorally active Anglo-Saxon priest or community of secular clerics. The readily apparent historical importance of this book and the voluminous bibliography on it have at times hindered a straightforward approach to the book and its intended purpose, but Wilcox's reassessment of the book and the evidence it presents is important in understanding the "knowable and probable uses" of the Blickling Homilies.[121]

Conclusions

Anglo-Saxon preachers, many of whom were secular priests, were part of a tradition of English preaching that stretched back to the early years of Anglo-Saxon Christianity. Like their tenth- and eleventh-century successors, early Anglo-Saxon priests were expected to preach to the laity, and the limited but significant evidence from manuscripts, source studies of extant texts, and documentary evidence for this practice indicates the availability of homiletic texts prior to the tenth century. However, it was not until after the boom of local churches in the tenth century that we can observe the copying and circulation

---

[120] For example, Blickling II exhorts its audience to atone "mid fæstenum, ond mid gebedum, ond mid ælmes-weorcum, ond mid soþre hreowe". Additionally, Wilcox notes that Blickling X is explicitly directed at a broad and apparently secular audience. See Morris, *The Blickling Homilies*, 25; Wilcox, "The Blickling Homilies Revisited," 108–9.

[121] Wilcox, "The Blickling Homilies Revisited," 97.

of vernacular preaching texts on an appreciable scale. The earliest examples of Old English homilies are invariably anonymous, but it is Ælfric's massively successful forays into the provision of homilies for preaching to the laity that best illustrate the need for texts of this kind that existed in the tenth and eleventh centuries. The homilies of named authors, namely Ælfric and Archbishop Wulfstan, and anonymous composers were consistently used, reused, and adapted by preachers in processes that can be glimpsed through the manuscript record.

Though the circulation of homilies and homiletic collections is often obscured by large gaps in the manuscript record, particularly for manuscripts that may have been used by secular priests, analysis of what does survive combined with work done on the sources of Anglo-Saxon homilies serves to illustrate the ways in which these texts traveled. Homiletic books and other books intended to meet pastoral needs might be provided by a controlling bishop or institution, and the spread of preaching texts between minor churches may also have facilitated the distribution of preaching texts through what I have termed horizontal circulation. Extant and independently circulating homiletic booklets, the existence and utility of which have been increasingly recognized by scholars, are a further indication of how preaching texts may have circulated among minor churches. Additionally, it has been seen that Anglo-Saxon priests probably acted as composers and adapters of vernacular homilies: Wright has suggested that a secular cleric composed three of the homilies that appear in the Vercelli book and Scragg's Canterbury homilist may have been a secular cleric. The dearth of monastic institutions in the first half of the tenth century further suggests the activity of the Anglo-Saxon secular clergy in composing homiletic texts and this did not stop with the renewal of Benedictine monasticism. Manuscript evidence supports this contention, as the bilingual Homiliary of Angers contained in the eleventh-century Taunton Fragment, formerly a low-status manuscript from a minor center, can be convincingly seen as a resource for sermon preparation, and a homily from Junius 85 and 86, also a low-status and unlocalized manuscript, has left indications that suggest the construction of a composite homily. The sum of this evidence illustrates the important role of secular clerics in the processes of composition, adaptation, and reworking that characterize the homiletic tradition of the late Anglo-Saxon period.

5

Performing the Liturgy: Priests' Books for the Mass and Office

In the early-eleventh-century *Canons of Edgar*, Archbishop Wulfstan informed his diocesan clergy that they should never celebrate mass without a mass-book and that the open book should be in front of the priest during the service so that he could avoid making mistakes.[1] This text indeed provides a great deal of direction to the secular clergy on the "dos and don'ts" of the celebration of mass: no animals are to be allowed in the church, correct vestments are to be worn, and the chalice for the Eucharistic wine is to be made of metal rather than wood or bone.[2] Wulfstan's concern here is for the proper celebration of mass, but the archbishop clearly believed that the priests under his authority had access to mass-books and that they should use them rather than relying on memory. Liturgical books are most frequently mentioned in prescriptive lists of books for priests, but some scholars have been cautious in accepting that these books were actually available to the early medieval clergy. This is in large part due to the loss of untold numbers of Anglo-Saxon manuscripts, but the evidence that does survive and the centrality of mass to a priest's duties and to pastoral care suggest that the books for the performance of the mass, and potentially the Divine Office, were accessible. Evidence further suggests that secular minsters in particular celebrated the Divine Office, which played a more prominent role in lay religious life than has previously been recognized. Furthermore, the form of the mass-books available from the end of the tenth century and later can inform us of the changing way in which pastoral care was delivered. The shift away from the sacramentary and towards the missal, this chapter argues, reflects the change from the minster to the local church as the primary provider of pastoral care in late Anglo-Saxon England.

However, the records of liturgical books for priests present a number of challenges. Foremost among these is the overwhelming number of

---

[1] Dorothy Whitelock, Martin Brett, and Christopher N. L. Brooke, eds., *Councils and Synods, with Other Documents Relating to the English Church, AD 871–1204*, vol. 1 (Oxford: Clarendon Press, 1981), 324–25. "7 riht is þæt preost ærre ne mæssige butan bec; ac beo se canon him ætforan eagum. Beseo to, gyf he wylle, þæ læs þe him misse."
[2] Ibid., 323, 325, 327–28.

liturgical manuscripts that have been assigned to monastic or episcopal use. The few manuscripts that are thought to have been used by Anglo-Saxon secular priests have received some scholarly attention, but the small size of this group contributes to the difficulty of a study of priests' books in this period. However, the general paucity of manuscript evidence for priests' books seems unrepresentative of the conditions on the ground in the light of sources describing the liturgical life of minor Anglo-Saxon churches, which will be discussed below. The often complex and extensive liturgy performed in these churches, particularly minster churches, would have required a reasonable complement of liturgical books not unlike those seen in the booklist from Sherburn-in-Elmet, discussed later in this chapter, and some churches may have had significantly more than Sherburn. The books used in small, local churches present an even knottier problem. To function properly, these churches would at the very least have needed a mass-book that included the appropriate readings from Scripture and the proper and ordinary mass chants. Both archaeological and textual evidence point to the proliferation of local churches in the thousands in England in the tenth and eleventh centuries, with Domesday's notoriously incomplete records attesting to the existence of more than two thousand – so where are the books used in these churches?[3] Most of them have of course been lost or destroyed, but a witness to the large number of mass-books that must have been used in local churches might be visible in the mass-book fragments of the period. Despite the perennial issue of difficult or inadequate source material and the prescriptive nature of liturgical texts, studying liturgical books in context and with the aid of other types of evidence where available can reveal a great deal about pastoral care and the liturgical resources for Anglo-Saxon priests of the tenth and eleventh centuries.

A further challenge is understanding the role that memorization played in the use and transmission of important texts, especially within the liturgy. Memorization was an important part of early medieval life for both the literate and illiterate: all Christians were to memorize the Pater Noster and Creed and a variety of narrative sources emphasize the role of memorization in ecclesiastical life, the commonality of the memorization of the Psalms by clerics and monks being especially well-known.[4] Archbishop Wulfstan's directive to the clergy of his diocese to "never celebrate mass without the book" and to look at the open book to avoid making mistakes implies that some

---

[3] John Blair, *The Church in Anglo-Saxon Society* (Oxford: Oxford University Press, 2005), 369, 418–21.
[4] Gail Ivy Berlin, "Memorization in Anglo-Saxon England: Some Case Studies," in *Oral Tradition in the Middle Ages*, ed. W. F. H. Nicolaisen (Binghamton, NY: Center for Medieval and Early Renaissance Studies, 1995), 100–104.

priests were able to and did in fact celebrate mass from memory, as Sidonius Apollinaris did centuries earlier.[5] Some preachers may also have memorized homiletic texts, or at least their general outlines, for later recitation. Clearly the memorization of homilies or mass liturgy would have reduced a priest's need for books, or at least one's reliance on a particular text. However, as Gail Berlin has pointed out, those performing acts of memorization "made use of or had access to writing as a first step in the formation of memory".[6] An individual who was able to celebrate mass without a mass-book was able to do so as a result of intense familiarity with the texts of the mass over an extended period of time through reading, recitation, and listening. Similarly, monks and secular clerics who memorized the Psalms learned them through what was probably a combination of rote memorization of the written text and liturgical experience.[7] There is also a distinction to be made between the ordinary and proper portions of the mass. Priests may have commonly memorized the unchanging ordinary of the mass and some votive masses, but proper prayers, lessons, and chants varied from one liturgical occasion to the other, substantially complicating the task of memorizing the mass liturgy, not to mention the readings from scripture that accompanied each occasion. So while liturgical texts for priests could be and were memorized, this should not be seen as a complete substitute for the availability of written texts, considering their importance as a part of the creation of memory and the wide variety of texts that would have to be memorized in order to do without books.

Liturgical texts for priests

An earlier chapter has discussed and collated several influential lists of books that priests were expected to own. What I have referred to as the core of priestly texts populating these lists are predominately liturgical in nature and broadly consist of a mass-book, a lectionary, a psalter, a minimal number of books for the Office, a book of occasional offices, a penitential, and a computus. I will now discuss the use of the books relating to the liturgy of the mass and Office, focusing mainly on the mass-book, lectionary, psalter, and books for the Office.

---

[5] Whitelock, Brett, and Brooke, *Councils and Synods*, 324–25; *Scriptores rerum Merovingicarum*, vol. 1, pt. 1, ed. Bruno Krusch and Wilhelm Levison, *Monumenta Germaniae Historica* (Hanover: Hahnsche Buchhandlung, 1951), 67.
[6] Berlin, "Memorization in Anglo-Saxon England," 113.
[7] Ibid., 100–101.

Mass-books

As the primary duty of priests was to celebrate the mass, a mass-book, whether a sacramentary or a missal, was an important part of a priest's toolkit.[8] Sacramentaries contain only the texts necessary for the priest himself to celebrate mass, and thus do not contain readings or chants, which in larger churches would have been performed by participants other than the celebrant.[9] On the other hand, missals (or plenary missals) contain texts derived from the sacramentary, lectionary, and gradual and enable the celebration of mass from a single book, making the missal a desirable book for local, single-priest churches. Between the ninth century and the early twelfth century, there was a gradual move away from sacramentaries and towards missals, reflecting changes in the way priests participated in the mass. The development of the missal was advantageous in several ways, not least of which was the relative ease of using one volume in place of several. Cyrille Vogel argues that the development of the plenary missal also reflects "a new way of regarding the mass" in which the priest is "the sole *actor* in this liturgical process".[10] In short, rather than acting as one participant in the corporate celebration of mass, the priest became the only necessary figure for the celebration of mass. Though plenary missals had been available in Italy as early as the eighth century, the move away from the sacramentary in northern Europe is not evident until the ninth and tenth centuries. In England, where manuscript evidence for the plenary missal does not appear until the end of the tenth century, this development coincided with a massive increase in the number of local churches, many of which were likely staffed by only one priest who may not have had the assistance of clerics in lower orders.[11]

Since having access to a missal or a sacramentary was essential for a priest in any church, one would expect a large number of mass-books to have been produced, thus increasing the chances that such manuscripts would survive. While some have survived, most of these mass-books are relatively high-status volumes, several of which demonstrably belonged to bishops, while others originated in

---

[8] This was certainly the view of early medieval bishops as expressed in a variety of prescriptive booklists. See page 36.

[9] Cyrille Vogel, *Medieval Liturgy: An Introduction to the Sources*, ed. and trans. William George Storey, Niels Rasmussen, and John Brooks-Leonard (Washington, DC: Pastoral Press, 1986), 64.

[10] Ibid., 105.

[11] Ælfric implies that this may be the case by suggesting that priests without assistants train boys to help them perform the liturgy. Bernhard Fehr, ed., *Die Hirtenbriefe Ælfrics in altenglischer und lateinischer Fassung* (Hamburg: Henri Grand, 1914), 174–76.

monasteries and monastic cathedrals.[12] Relatively few manuscripts that can be attributed to priestly use have survived and only one intact mass-book, the Red Book of Darley (Cambridge, Corpus Christi College 422), a complex and disputed manuscript, can be plausibly ascribed to a pastoral context. Nonetheless, a large number of English missal and sacramentary fragments from the tenth and eleventh centuries have survived and may be an important witness to the mass-books used by secular priests.[13]

Graduals

The gradual contains the proper chants sung in the mass and is the counterpart to the Office antiphoner; these volumes were sometimes combined to include the chants for both the mass and the Office.[14] The gradual goes by various names in Anglo-Saxon sources: Ælfric uses the term *gradale*, other sources refer to it as *ad te leuaui* – the first words of the introit for the first Sunday in Advent – and some simply use the term *antiphonarius* or *antiphonarium*, which may refer either to the mass antiphoner or the Office antiphoner. These chant texts, which in some cases contained musical notation for the chants, were necessary for the performance of mass and were thus incorporated into Anglo-Saxon missals of the eleventh century, as can be seen in a fragment from one of Bishop Leofric's *fulle mæssebec* from Exeter and in the Red Book of Darley.[15]

---

[12] For example, the Missal of the New Minster (Le Havre, Bibliothèque municipale 330), the Winchcombe Sacramentary (Orléans, Médiathèque 127), and Worcester, Cathedral Library, F. 173 were all produced in and associated with monastic contexts. Others, such as the Leofric Missal (Oxford, Bodleian Library, Bodley 579), the Giso Sacramentary (London, British Library, Cotton Vitellius A. XVIII), and the Sacramentary of Robert of Jumièges (Rouen, Bibliothèque municipale, 274, Y.6) all have episcopal associations, and some are associated with both monasteries and bishops. See Helmut Gneuss and Michael Lapidge, *Anglo-Saxon Manuscripts: A Bibliographical Handlist of Manuscripts and Manuscript Fragments Written or Owned in England up to 1100* (Toronto: University of Toronto Press, 2014), 323–24, 456–58, 547, 602, 624, 666–67.

[13] Helmut Gneuss, "Liturgical Books in Anglo-Saxon England and Their Old English Terminology," in *Learning and Literature in Anglo-Saxon England: Studies Presented to Peter Clemoes on the Occasion of His Sixty-Fifth Birthday*, ed. Michael Lapidge and Gneuss (Cambridge: Cambridge University Press, 1985), 101–2. A number of additions can now be made to the list of fragments compiled by Gneuss. See Introduction, note 39.

[14] Eric Palazzo, *A History of Liturgical Books from the Beginning to the Thirteenth Century* (Collegeville, MN: Liturgical Press, 1998), 69–70.

[15] A fragment from this Exeter missal can be seen in Christopher de Hamel, *A History of Illuminated Manuscripts* (London: Phaidon Press, 1986), 204.

Lectionaries

In the Roman Rite, there were only two readings from scripture in the mass: one from the epistolary and one from the gospels. To facilitate these readings, several types of lectionaries were produced. An epistolary mostly contained readings from the epistles of the New Testament, but some lessons in place of the epistle were drawn from Acts, Revelation, or the Old Testament; a gospel lectionary contained the set readings from the gospels; and a full lectionary (or mass lectionary) contained both the epistle and gospel readings.[16] In addition, a plenary missal would also contain the first and second readings for mass, which tend to be written out in full. The gospel lections could too be read from a book containing the full text of the four gospels, which survive in much greater numbers than lectionaries. Two systems were used in making gospelbooks suitable for liturgical reading. Marginal annotations could be added to the manuscript which would point out the readings for a particular day, or a "gospel list" (*capitulare euangeliorum*) could be included with the text of the gospels, listing pericopes in the order of the liturgical year along with the days on which they were to be read out.[17]

Unfortunately, the tenth- and eleventh-century examples of Anglo-Saxon lectionaries are often fragmentary and many of those that have survived intact or mostly intact cannot be firmly associated with use in a secular church. Additionally, only fragments of mass lectionaries, which contain the readings for both the gospel and the epistle, are extant and no trace of Anglo-Saxon manuscript evidence for an epistolary survives, though several booklists make reference to them.[18] However, as Helmut Gneuss points out, the disparate number of gospelbooks and lectionaries does not necessarily indicate a lack of lectionaries in the Anglo-Saxon period, but may instead suggest that many gospelbooks owe their survival to the manuscripts' rich decoration and the immutability of the text of the gospels, whereas lectionaries could more easily become outdated and warrant recycling.[19]

---

[16] Ursula Lenker, "The West Saxon Gospels and the Gospel-Lectionary in Anglo-Saxon England: Manuscript Evidence and Liturgical Practice," *Anglo-Saxon England* 28 (1999): 154. Also see Lenker, *Die Westsächsische Evangelienversion und die Perikopenordnungen im Angelsächsischen England* (Munich: Wilhelm Fink, 1997).

[17] Gneuss, "Liturgical Books in Anglo-Saxon England," 106.

[18] Rebecca Rushforth, "The Prodigal Fragment: Cambridge, Gonville and Caius College 734/782a," *Anglo-Saxon England* 30 (2001): 143; Gneuss, "Liturgical Books in Anglo-Saxon England," 107–8, 110; Lenker, "The West Saxon Gospels and the Gospel-Lectionary," 158–59.

[19] Gneuss, "Liturgical Books in Anglo-Saxon England," 107.

Psalters

The psalter played a vital role in the liturgical celebrations of the medieval church. The Psalms were used in both the mass and Office, typically truncated in the former and forming the basis for the latter. In the Office, the psalter would be recited in its entirety in the course of a week in both the Benedictine and secular *cursus*, though the secular and monastic systems recited different texts for various offices and inserted divisions into psalters according to their particular *cursus*.[20] In addition to the texts of the Psalms, psalters designed for liturgical performance typically contained other texts, such as a calendar containing the dates of saints' feasts and festivals, litanies, and canticles. Psalters are well represented in the corpus of Anglo-Saxon manuscripts, with more than twenty-five surviving codices and a number of fragments, and, like the books previously discussed, they are found in almost every prescriptive list of books for priests.[21] Both the *Psalterium Romanum* and the *Psalterium Gallicanum* are represented in surviving Anglo-Saxon manuscripts, with the earlier manuscripts tending to be those of the *Romanum*, as the *Gallicanum* was imported during the course of the Benedictine reform, though some later *Romanum* manuscripts do exist.[22] Although Anglo-Saxon psalters survive in relatively large numbers, few can be directly associated with use in a secular church.

Books for the Office

The celebration of the Divine Office required a variable number of books. While some books could be bound together, a few basic texts usually comprised the Office books that would have been used by secular clerics. These are the Office antiphoner, collectar, hymnal, and breviary, in addition to the psalter.

The Office antiphoner contains the chants for the celebration of the Divine Office. Antiphoners feature significantly in Anglo-Saxon booklists, including the booklist from Sherburn-in-Elmet and the record of Leofric's donation to Exeter, while Ælfric's second Latin letter for Wulfstan mentions a *nocturnale*, an antiphoner for the Night Office. These books are rare in the manuscript record and no complete examples survive from the Anglo-Saxon period. Some antiphoner fragments have survived, several of which are firmly pre-

---

[20] John Harper, *The Forms and Orders of Western Liturgy from the Tenth to the Eighteenth Century: A Historical Introduction and Guide for Students and Musicians* (Oxford: Clarendon Press, 1991), 69–70.
[21] Gneuss, "Liturgical Books in Anglo-Saxon England," 115–16.
[22] Ibid., 114.

Conquest, and most of these fragments now reside in Scandinavian libraries.[23]

Early medieval collectars included "prayers, chapters, versicles and responses, preces and benedictions".[24] These books would have been read at every hour of the Office apart from Nocturns, making their relative rarity conspicuous. Their general absence may be explained by their combination with other books and their close reliance on the sacramentary; churches lacking a collectar may have used a sacramentary to read out the collects for the daily offices, as was presumably the case in the ninth century and earlier. However, collectars have survived from the secular communities at Durham and Exeter and both the provenance and liturgical contents of these volumes indicate the suitability of their texts for the celebration of secular Office liturgy, though the Durham Collectar was probably not used directly in this context.[25]

Hymns also formed a significant part of the Office and were sung at each of the canonical hours. In the earlier decades of the tenth century, the typical hymns for the Office were relatively few in number, approximately twenty, but in the later tenth century, a continental hymnal consisting of over a hundred compositions was imported into England. Most of the surviving hymnals are monastic, and the importation of the larger continental hymnal was doubtless connected with the Benedictine Reform of the tenth century, though these hymns also appear in secular contexts.[26] The Leofric Collectar contains hymns and both Leofric's donation list and the Sherburn list contain hymnals, though the volumes from these booklists have not survived.[27]

The breviary is to the Divine Office what the missal is to the mass: it combines all the texts necessary for the celebration of the Office into a single volume. Gneuss has written that there were no English breviaries prior to the twelfth century, only indications of the

---

[23] Ibid., 118.
[24] Harper, *The Forms and Orders of Western Liturgy*, 62.
[25] Alicia Corrêa, "Daily Office Books: Collectars and Breviaries," in *The Liturgical Books of Anglo-Saxon England*, ed. Richard Pfaff (Kalamazoo: Medieval Institute Publications, 1995), 47, 49, 51. For more on the volumes from Durham and Exeter, see Jesse D. Billett, "The Divine Office and the Secular Clergy in Later Anglo-Saxon England," in *England and the Continent in the Tenth Century: Studies in Honour of Wilhelm Levison (1876–1947)*, ed. Conrad Leyser, David Rollason, and Hannah Williams (Turnhout: Brepols, 2010).
[26] Gneuss, "Liturgical Books in Anglo-Saxon England," 118. For detailed studies on Anglo-Saxon hymns and hymnals, see Inge B. Milfull, *The Hymns of the Anglo-Saxon Church: A Study and Edition of the "Durham Hymnal"* (Cambridge: Cambridge University Press, 1996); Gneuss, *Hymnar und Hymnen im englischen Mittelalter* (Tübingen: Max Niemeyer, 1968).
[27] Lapidge, "Surviving Booklists from Anglo-Saxon England," in Lapidge and Gneuss, *Learning and Literature in Anglo-Saxon England*, 56, 65.

incremental development of this type of book.[28] However, fragments of two manuscripts show that this is not the case. Both London, British Library, Royal 17 C. XVII, ff. 2–3 and 163–166 and the Muchelney Breviary fragment (London, British Library, Add. 56488, ff. i, 1–6) are the remains of Anglo-Saxon breviaries preserved in the bindings of later manuscripts. Both fragments are monastic in origin, but they are indicative of the existence of this type of book in the late Anglo-Saxon period and the influence of secular Office liturgy on that of English monasteries.[29]

After this discussion of these classes of liturgical books, it should be expressly noted that the separation of liturgical texts neatly by category into independent volumes is by no means a certainty. The combining of multiple types of texts into one book or booklet was an economical practice and a common feature of the books of early medieval priests, as is noted in Yitzhak Hen's augmentation of Rasmussen's framework.[30] For example, the Red Book of Darley contains "full breviary services for Common of Saints, Holy Week and Easter", texts properly constituting a missal, and computistical material. Both the Durham Collectar (Durham, Cathedral Library, A. IV. 19) and the Leofric Collectar (London, British Library, Harley 2961) also contain material additional to a "pure" collectar, such as hymns and hymn incipits.[31]

The mass and Office in secular foundations

Much of the attention directed towards the study of medieval liturgy has focused on monastic liturgy, which is often better represented in surviving manuscripts and is explicated in English sources such as the *Regularis Concordia*. But as has been discussed in previous chapters,

---

[28] Gneuss, "Liturgical Books in Anglo-Saxon England," 110–12.
[29] The first of these is discussed at length and edited in Jesse Billett, *The Divine Office in Anglo-Saxon England, 597–c.1000* (London and Woodbridge: Henry Bradshaw Society and Boydell Press, 2014), 252–300, 356–73. I am grateful to Jesse Billett for his comments on this and other liturgical matters, as well as allowing me access to material on the Muchelney fragment prior to publication.
[30] Niels Rasmussen, "Célébration épiscopale et célébration presbytérale: Un essai de typologie," in *Segni e riti nella Chiesa altomedievale occidentale*, vol. 33, no. 2 of *Settimane di studio del Centro italiano di sull'alto medioevo* (Spoleto: Presso la sede del Centro, 1987); Yitzhak Hen, "Knowledge of Canon Law among Rural Priests: The Evidence of Two Carolingian Manuscripts from around 800," *The Journal of Theological Studies* 50, no. 1 (1999): 129. This framework and my caveats for its use are discussed in the Introduction.
[31] Gneuss, "Liturgical Books in Anglo-Saxon England," 111. The computistical material in the Red Book of Darley can be found at pages 27–49 of the manuscript.

secular clerics in England in the tenth and eleventh centuries formed a much larger group than did monks, and the saying of mass by secular priests was probably the most common form of pastoral care in the late Anglo-Saxon period. Thus, in order to better understand pastoral care and the religious landscape of Anglo-Saxon England, we must consider the role of the liturgy – as seen through priests' books – in secular churches.

The mass

The texts performed in a given mass fall into one of two categories: the ordinary of the mass or the proper of the mass. The ordinary represents the liturgical material of the mass that is unchanged regardless of the occasion, while the proper is variable and could consist of prayers, lessons, and sung portions of the mass that were appropriate to a particular day. Additionally, the structure of the mass is two-fold. The first part of the service is known as the fore-mass and consists of sung readings and prayers. The latter part of this first section also contains the readings from the gospel and the epistolary. The rituals of the second part of the mass are concerned with the administration of the Eucharist.[32] Communion itself is preceded by the offertory, the secret, Eucharistic prayers, the recitation of the *Pater Noster*, and the typically sung *Agnus Dei*. The sacrament was then followed by a proper post-communion prayer and the sung *Ite missa est*.

Performing these various parts of the mass required the use of several different liturgical books. To present a view of how particular books functioned in liturgical performance, I have here tabulated the books needed in each section of the mass.

From this we can see essentially three types of texts utilized within the mass: the prayers and canon contained in the sacramentary, the readings found in a lectionary or a gospelbook, and the "lyrical component" of the mass (i.e., the proper and ordinary chants).[33] Additionally, the table shows these texts in their forms prior to the development of the missal, which combined all of these texts and does not appear in the manuscript record in England until the late tenth century.

MASS IN ANGLO-SAXON CATHEDRALS

Despite the relatively plentiful source material for Anglo-Saxon cathedrals, examining these churches in a study of priests' books presents

---

[32] Andrew Hughes, *Medieval Manuscripts for Mass and Office: A Guide to Their Organization and Terminology* (Toronto: University of Toronto Press, 1982), 82–87.

[33] Ibid., 65–67.

Table 3. The structure of the mass with the liturgical books needed for each section[a]

Order of the mass	Book(s) needed
Introit (antiphon and psalm verses)	Gradual
Kyrie eleison	
Gloria in excelsis[b]	
First oration: Collect	Sacramentary
Reading of the epistle	Epistolary or lectionary
Gradual response and alleluia[c]	Gradual[d]
Reading of the gospel	Gospelbook or lectionary
Offertory (antiphon)	Gradual
Second oration: Secret	Sacramentary
Preface	Sacramentary
Sanctus and Benedictus	Sacramentary and gradual
Canon of the mass	Sacramentary
Pater Noster	
Agnus Dei	
Communion (antiphon)	Gradual
Postcommunion	Sacramentary

[a] Adapted from Palazzo, *A History of Liturgical Books*, 19–20, 67.

[b] Palazzo lists some of the ordinary mass chants as being contained in the gradual, but this is not generally the case for early medieval books.

[c] Sequences could also be "sung on a number of greater feasts effectively as an extension of the Alleluia". Harper, *The Forms and Orders of Western Liturgy*, 117.

[d] Some early medieval sources refer to the use here of the *cantatorium*, a book for a soloist that contained "the chants intercalated between the readings at the beginning of the Mass ... with sometimes the verses of the offertory". Palazzo, *A History of Liturgical Books*, 74–75. For these books, see Michel Huglo, "The Cantatorium: From Charlemagne to the Fourteenth Century," in *The Study of Medieval Chant: Paths and Bridges, East and West, in Honor of Kenneth Levy*, ed. Peter Jeffery (Woodbridge: Boydell Press, 2001).

significant issues. The first of these is that many of the liturgical books surviving from the most well-attested Anglo-Saxon cathedrals are monastic. Winchester, for example, was one of the most influential liturgical centers of the Anglo-Saxon period, but the surviving Winchester mass-books cannot be directly related to the liturgical celebrations of the secular clerics at Winchester due to the relatively late dates of the books' production or importation.[34] The secular clerics

[34] Michael Lapidge and Michael Winterbottom, eds. and trans., *Life of St Æthelwold* (Oxford: Clarendon Press, 1991), lxiii–lxv; Francis Wormald, "Fragments of a Tenth-Century Sacramentary from the Binding of the Winton Domesday," in *Winchester and the Early Middle Ages: An Edition and Discussion of Winton*

at Winchester in both the Old and New Minsters were expelled in 964, meaning that we cannot associate any liturgical manuscripts produced later than the mid-tenth century with the pre-monastic cathedral community. The prolific centers of Christ Church, Canterbury and Worcester also see a similar lack of surviving mass-books that can be firmly associated with secular priests. Furthermore, very few books of any kind have survived from the cathedrals that remained secular in the Anglo-Saxon period, such as Hereford, Lichfield, and London.

The second issue is that of bishops' books. The books that do survive from secular cathedrals can generally be associated with bishops, rather than the priests of the secular community. One example of this is the Giso Sacramentary (London, British Library, Cotton Vitellius A. XVIII), typically connected with Giso of Wells. This association has been challenged by some scholars, but even if the book has nothing to do with Giso, the contents of the book are clearly episcopal in nature.[35] A complex witness to the celebration of the Mass at Exeter, to which Leofric moved the seat of his diocese in 1050 and where he built up a significant library, survives in the Leofric Missal.[36] This late ninth or early tenth-century mass-book is in fact a combined sacramentary rather than a missal, may have been originally intended for Plegmund, Archbishop of Canterbury, and was housed at Christ Church, where it

---

Domesday, ed. Martin Biddle (Oxford: Clarendon Press, 1976). The earliest from the period in question is the fragmentary sacramentary that survived in the binding of the Winton Domesday and is now catalogued as London, Society of Antiquaries 154. This manuscript is not an Anglo-Saxon product, despite its association with Winchester, but was probably written in Brittany in the tenth century and imported in the course of the Benedictine reform. Other mass-books associated with Winchester include the Missal of the New Minster (Le Havre, Bibliothèque municipale 330), probably written in the 1070s, and the fragmentary Oslo, Riksarkivet, Lat. fragm. 206 + 209, nos. 1–4 + 239, nos. 6–7. The latter has been assigned a date of xi *in.* by David Dumville, but Corrêa has questioned the manuscript's Winchester origin and argued for a date in the third quarter of the eleventh century. See David Dumville, *Liturgy and the Ecclesiastical History of Late Anglo-Saxon England: Four Studies* (Woodbridge: Boydell Press, 1992), 68; Alicia Corrêa, "A Mass for St Birinus in an Anglo-Saxon Missal from the Scandinavian Mission-Field," in *Myth, Rulership, Church and Charters: Essays in Honour of Nicholas Brooks*, ed. Julia Barrow and Andrew Wareham (Aldershot: Ashgate, 2008), 170, 182.

[35] Pfaff, "Massbooks," in Pfaff, *The Liturgical Books of Anglo-Saxon England*, 19–20.

[36] A great deal of work has been done on the library of Exeter and Leofric's acquisition of books. For divergent views on the library and its origins, see Richard Gameson, "The Origin of the Exeter Book of Old English Poetry," *Anglo-Saxon England* 25 (1996) and Patrick Conner, *Anglo-Saxon Exeter: A Tenth-Century Cultural History* (Woodbridge: Boydell Press, 1993). Also see Elaine Treharne, "Producing a Library in Late Anglo-Saxon England: Exeter, 1050–1072," *The Review of English Studies* 54, no. 112 (2003) and Joyce Hill, "Leofric of Exeter and the Practical Politics of Book Collecting," in *Imagining the Book*, ed. Stephen Kelly and John J. Thompson (Turnhout: Brepols, 2005).

received significant additions termed by its modern editors "Leofric B". The third portion of the mass-book is "Leofric C", which was added at Exeter in the mid-eleventh century by a large number of scribes, roughly a dozen, one of whom was probably the bishop himself.[37] Leofric instituted a rule for the canons at Exeter, probably the *Rule of Chrodegang* due to the bishop's continental background, and the *Rule* provides copious instructions to the canons for the performance of mass.[38] But one of the issues with recovering the liturgical practices of the Exeter community is that Bodley 579 is unambiguously a bishop's book: Leofric A was written for a bishop and one of the Exeter additions is specifically a proper mass intended to be said by the bishop of Exeter, and was most likely composed there.[39] Leofric's donation lists records *ii fulle mæssebec*, however. The second mass-book, a missal dating to the mid-eleventh century, was broken up at some point and now survives in fragments that have been dispersed across several libraries and have not been the subject of much scholarly attention.[40] We do know a few things concerning this now-fragmentary missal, however: it was written by Exeter scribes, it drew on the Leofric Missal, and it was fully neumed.[41] This largely unstudied book may have been intended for the presbyteral liturgy at Exeter.

It is certain that secular priests were involved in the celebration of the mass in Anglo-Saxon cathedrals in the tenth and eleventh centuries. Unfortunately, the lack of evidence for priests' books and the very limited narrative evidence concerning liturgical practice by priests from these centers in large part precludes meaningful analysis. But evidence of direct priestly involvement in liturgy and pastoral care comes into somewhat sharper focus in the secular minsters and local churches of the late Anglo-Saxon period.

---

[37] Nicholas Orchard, ed., *The Leofric Missal I: Introduction, Collation Table and Index* (London: The Henry Bradshaw Society, 2002), 209–12.

[38] A bilingual copy of the Rule surviving as Cambridge, Corpus Christi College 191 bears an Exeter *ex libris* inscription and may well be identifiable with the "Regula canonicorum" of Leofric's donation list. For the textual history of the *Rule of Chrodegang*, especially in England, see Brigitte Langefeld, ed. and trans., *The Old English Version of the Enlarged Rule of Chrodegang* (Frankfurt: Peter Lang, 2003).

[39] Orchard, ed., *The Leofric Missal I*, 219.

[40] London, British Library, Additional 62104; London, British Library, Harley 5977 no. 59; London, Westminster Abbey, MS 36, nos. 17–19; Lincoln, Cathedral Library, V.5.11; Oxford, Bodleian Library, MS lat. lit. e.38. Gneuss and Lapidge, *Anglo-Saxon Manuscripts: A Bibliographical Handlist*, 419.

[41] Susan Rankin, "From Memory to Record: Musical Notations in Manuscripts from Exeter," *Anglo-Saxon England* 13 (1984): 102.

Mass in Minor Churches

In his definitive work on the mass, Josef Jungmann wrote: "In the titular churches of the city and in the country towns of the vicinity, which as a rule had only one presbyter and one or the other extra cleric ... the Mass was the Mass of a simple priest, not that of a bishop."[42] Though Jungmann's statement concerns the celebration of mass in Italy in the eighth century, it is also true of most churches in England in the late Anglo-Saxon period. The books of bishops and their cathedrals are more prominent in the manuscript record than books for local churches and secular minsters, but there is important evidence that will help to elucidate the bookholdings and liturgical life of Anglo-Saxon minor churches.

Though more than a dozen booklists survive from Anglo-Saxon England, the only record of the books held by a non-monastic church other than a cathedral is contained in the inventory from Sherburn-in-Elmet. Sherburn had been an estate of the archbishops of York since the later tenth century and though evidence before the tenth century is slim, there are indications that the minster at Sherburn was a mother church.[43] The record of these books is part of a mid-eleventh-century inventory of the furnishings and possessions of the church which was copied into the York Gospels (York Minster, Minster Library, Add. 1), a high-status manuscript produced at Canterbury around the turn of the eleventh century. The inventory occurs among several additions to the final folios of the gospels dating mostly to the early 1020s, though the inventory itself has been dated to the mid-eleventh century. These additions include homilies, prayers, and tenurial records for archiepiscopal estates at Sherburn-in-Elmet, Ripon, and Otley. Christopher Norton makes a sound argument for the storage of the York Gospels at Sherburn for several decades of the eleventh century, an arrangement that he suggests preserved the book despite the fire that consumed the cathedral in 1069.[44] If this is the case, the inventory was likely copied into the gospelbook during its residence there.

The booklist, noted and printed by Michael Lapidge, though with little accompanying discussion, consists of service books and other

---

[42] Josef Jungmann, *The Mass of the Roman Rite: Its Origins and Development*, trans. Francis A. Brunner (New York: Benziger, 1951), 1:75.
[43] Dawn M. Hadley, *The Northern Danelaw: Its Social Structure, c. 800–1100* (London: Leicester University Press, 2000), 276. One indication is the considerable size of its later medieval parish.
[44] York Minster, Minster Library, Add. 1, f. 161r; Christopher Norton, "York Minster in the Time of Wulfstan," in *Wulfstan, Archbishop of York: The Proceedings of the Second Alcuin Conference*, ed. Matthew Townend (Turnhout: Brepols, 2004), 214–15.

items belonging to the church, such as bells and vestments. The portion of the list concerned with books is as follows: "twa Cristes bec ... 7 .i. aspiciens 7 .i. adteleuaui 7 .ii. pistolbec 7 .i. mæsse-boc 7 .i. ymener 7 .i. salter".[45] This list is not unlike the collection of texts that Ælfric envisioned for priests in terms of books for the mass and Office. Sarah Hamilton notes in this list a lack of "a manual for pastoral rites" and suggests that the occasional offices may have been contained in other books, such as sacramentaries or penitentials, as in the Red Book of Darley or Oxford, Bodleian Library, Laud Misc. 482.[46] While this is wholly plausible, the context of the list may raise an alternative possibility. The booklist from Sherburn-in-Elmet is found amongst miscellaneous items written in the final folios of the York Gospels, including surveys of the archbishops' landholdings. Considering that these records "are demonstrably associated with the Archbishops of York", and that the York Gospels may have been stored at Sherburn for some time in the eleventh century, it may be that the list is simply a record of the books for the altar, possibly provided and tacitly owned by the archbishops of York. Provision of books to churches under episcopal control has been discussed previously and is exemplified by Archbishop Cynesige's (1051–1060) endowment of Beverley with books around the same time as the compilation of this list.[47] The above-noted lack of a manual in the Sherburn booklist may simply be due to the fact that it was not a book for the altar. If this is the case, it would not have been likely that the list would include any books personally owned by the clerics who staffed the church, which might include one or more books of occasional offices, or as Gneuss suggests, a small booklet containing the necessary rites.[48]

---

[45] "Two gospel-books, an antiphonary, a gradual, two books of the epistles, a mass-book, a hymnal, and a psalter." Lapidge, "Surviving Booklists," 56–57.

[46] Sarah Hamilton, "Rites of Passage and Pastoral Care," in *A Social History of England, 900–1200*, ed. Julia Crick and Elisabeth van Houts (Cambridge: Cambridge University Press, 2011), 294.

[47] Norton, "York Minster in the Time of Wulfstan," 214; Janet M. Cooper, *The Last Four Anglo-Saxon Archbishops of York* (York: St Anthony's Press, 1970), 22.

[48] Gneuss, "Liturgical Books in Anglo-Saxon England," 134; Richard Pfaff, "Liturgical Books," in *The Cambridge History of the Book in Britain Volume 1: c.400–1100*, ed. Richard Gameson (Cambridge: Cambridge University Press, 2011), 451. The mid-eleventh-century inventory from Bury St Edmunds is a contemporary example of the separate consideration of books for the altar and liturgical books held by individuals. Carl Hammer came to a similar conclusion about clerical inventories from early medieval Bavaria: "Another explanation for the absence of items in church inventories is that they might be considered the personal possessions of the priest." Teresa Webber, "Books and Their Use across the Conquest," in *Bury St Edmunds and the Norman Conquest*, ed. Tom Licence (Woodbridge: Boydell Press, 2014), 165–66; Carl Hammer, "Country Churches, Clerical Inventories and the Carolingian Renaissance in Bavaria," *Church History* 49, no. 1 (1980): 10.

More importantly, this list is a witness to the liturgical practices of the church in Sherburn. When compared to Table 3 above, the list reveals that the church was well provisioned for the celebration of mass with the availability of a mass-book, a gradual, two lectionaries, and two gospelbooks. Additionally, the clerics at Sherburn-in-Elmet generally had the books needed to celebrate the Office. We might however point to the absence of a collectar, which is perhaps unsurprising as it does not appear in Ælfric's lists and could be bound with other books for the Office, and a homiliary, used in conjunction with scripture to provide readings for Nocturns.[49] While this evidence may not be as full as one might wish considering the lack of narrative evidence for actual practice at Sherburn, it does give an indication of the service books available in what was probably a well-provisioned late Anglo-Saxon church and can be taken as an indication of the regular performance of liturgical services.

Some of the most explicit evidence for liturgical observance in a minster comes from Holy Trinity, Twynham, now in Dorset, but historically considered part of Hampshire. There is no direct evidence for the existence of the church prior to the Domesday survey, but it seems that it existed at least from the ninth century and possibly earlier, as the plan for the *burh* of Twynham as recorded in the Burghal Hidage "only makes sense on the assumption that the church and its cemetery were there before the *burh* was established".[50] The workings of the church become unusually clear for the decades following the Conquest by means of an internal history of the church, probably written shortly after 1146 by an elderly canon. Patrick Hase suggests that the author of the history may be identifiable with either Ailmer or Almetus, two elderly priests who had served at the church in the late eleventh century and were familiar with life at the minster. Despite the political changes after 1066, the church seems to have been continuing a vibrant and essentially Anglo-Saxon tradition in the late eleventh century.[51] A passage from the history provides a great deal of information concerning the liturgical services of the church:

---

[49] Gneuss, "Liturgical Books in Anglo-Saxon England," 112.
[50] P. H. Hase, "The Mother Churches of Hampshire," in *Minsters and Parish Churches: The Local Church in Transition, 950–1200*, ed. John Blair (Oxford: Oxford University Committee for Archaeology, 1988), 51.
[51] Ibid., 51–52. Hase notes that the church "seems to have continued to function as it did before 1066". Additionally, the account given here notes that the Twynham canons did not know Godric as a dean and were not even familiar with the term. The imposition of deans in English churches seems to have been a Norman practice. David Knowles, *The Monastic Order in England: A History of Its Development from the Times of St Dunstan to the Fourth Lateran Council 940–1216*, 2nd ed. (Cambridge: Cambridge University Press, 1963), 428.

> At the time when William Rufus reigned in England there was a certain clerk named Godric in this church of Twynham – a man famous for his life and honesty. In accordance with their custom Godric every day celebrated the night hours and those of the whole day, from dawn to dusk, together with the 24 canons of the church. Now at that time, his clerks treated this Godric not as dean, for they did not even understand that term, but as leader and chief.
>
> It was the ecclesiastical custom of those canons that this Godric, the leader of the canons should receive as his own the offerings of the Morrow Mass and of the High Mass, no matter who gave them, without anyone else sharing in them. Other offerings, however, that is to say those made before Mass, or between Masses, and those offered at Vespers, were shared out equally between the canons. The lands near the church, that is, Hurn, Burton and Preston, were treated in the same way, the income from them being distributed by division. Furthermore, any canon celebrating a Mass received all the offerings of that Mass without anyone sharing in them, that is to say, an offering made after he was vested in his cope.[52]

This account is a fascinating look into the liturgical life of canons in an English minster in the later eleventh century. We can see that multiple daily masses were said, seemingly by multiple priests, and observe the way in which the offerings given at these masses were parceled out. The canons, of which there were twenty-four, celebrated Morrow Mass and High Mass daily with the leader of the canons, named as Godric, presiding. Morrow Mass took place in the morning after either Prime or Terce and High Mass took place later in the day and was more elaborate. The account explicitly mentions the saying of mass at least twice a day, but the history also notes that "any canon celebrating a Mass received all the offerings of that Mass without anyone sharing in them", implying that additional masses would have been said by priests other than Godric.[53] A similar state of affairs likely existed in other well-staffed minsters. Like Twynham, the minster at Dover, refounded by Earl Godwine, housed twenty-four canons at the time of the Conquest, each canon holding a sulung of land.[54] Considering the large staff and its wealthy benefactor, the liturgical life of the minster at Dover may have been similar to that at Twynham. Other collegiate churches like Waltham Holy Cross and Stow in Lincolnshire seem

---

[52] Hase, "The Mother Churches of Hampshire," 59. The Latin text and another translation of this history can be found in Blair, *The Church in Anglo-Saxon Society*, 515–17.
[53] Hase, "The Mother Churches of Hampshire," 59.
[54] Ann Williams, "Thegnly Piety and Ecclesiastical Patronage in the Late Old English Kingdom," in *Anglo-Norman Studies XXIV: Proceedings of the Battle Conference 2001*, ed. John Gillingham (Woodbridge: Boydell Press, 2002), 8.

to have fully observed the liturgy of the mass and Office, financially enabled by wealthy patrons, and at least six other secular minsters of the late eleventh century supported clerical communities of a dozen or more canons.[55] Like Stow, Leominster and Wenlock were secular minsters that, according to John of Worcester, had too been endowed by Leofric of Mercia and his wife, and liturgical observances similar to that of Twynham may also have taken place at these foundations.[56]

Much more uncertain is the saying of mass in "field churches" and proprietary churches, which seem to have been generally staffed by a single priest. Mass was certainly celebrated within the walls of these small churches – this was unquestionably their *raison d'être* – but the frequency and form of liturgical celebrations at this level are difficult to tease out and we typically know more about architectural trends and tenurial patterns than about liturgical trends.[57] Though the number of local churches saw exponential growth in this period, direct references to mass in these churches are rare, but we can infer certain characteristics and developments from the extant sources. As from the earliest days of the Church, Sunday was the primary day designated for the gathering of the wider Christian community, and mass on Sunday morning would probably have been the most important liturgical event of a given week. In addition to this, public masses were celebrated on the feast days of noteworthy saints and during the main festivals of the liturgical year, typically at around nine o'clock in the morning.[58] In the *Canons of Edgar*, Archbishop Wulfstan instructs his priests to preach to the people every Sunday, but shortly thereafter notes that most of the people can be expected to come to the church at Easter, Rogationtide, and midsummer, though this could be more in reference to minster churches rather than the more convenient local church. Major liturgical celebrations may particularly have drawn churchgoers to minsters, as some local churches, many of which were dependent chapels of minsters, may not have had the personnel to observe them properly and the minsters too benefitted from offerings given at these feasts. There is evidence that priests from local churches would process to the minster from their churches along with their flock on important saints'

---

[55] Emma Cownie, *Religious Patronage in Anglo-Norman England, 1066–1135* (London and Woodbridge: The Royal Historical Society and Boydell Press, 1998), 28, n. 122.

[56] *The Chronicle of John of Worcester*, vol. 2, *The Annals from 450 to 1066*, ed. R. R. Darlington and Patrick McGurk, trans. Jennifer Bray and McGurk (Oxford: Clarendon Press, 1995), 583.

[57] Blair, *The Church in Anglo-Saxon Society*, 371–425; Helen Gittos, *Liturgy, Architecture, and Sacred Places in Anglo-Saxon England* (Oxford: Oxford University Press, 2013), 179–82.

[58] Jungmann, *The Mass of the Roman Rite*, 245–47.

days, Christmas, Easter, and Palm Sunday.[59] In addition, a unique source, the later eleventh-century *Vision of Leofric*, shows how a pious nobleman might have used his manorial church for the celebration of mass. The text records that the Earl of Mercia "would have two masses each day, if not more, and all his services one after the other before he went out".[60] Though the account lacks specific details, it is important that the author notes that these masses took place "before he went out" (*ær he ut eode*), probably early in the morning. These services would presumably have taken place in a manorial church or a private chapel, one of the "marks of thegnly status" according to *Geþyncðo*, an early eleventh-century text on status and hierarchy.[61]

The Office in secular foundations

The Office consists primarily of the recitation of the psalms, readings, and prayers and was practiced by both monks and secular clerics as a form of "sung, corporate prayer".[62] This practice took place in seven periods throughout the day, namely the Night Office (later called Matins), Lauds, Terce, Prime, Sext, None, Vespers, and Compline. Though the Office would seem to consist of eight rather than seven offices, early medieval churchmen, including Ælfric, seem to have regarded the combination of the Night Office and Lauds as a single office.[63] Both monastic and secular churches celebrated the Office, but there were distinctions between the monastic and secular Office. These differences can be witnessed in the surviving manuscripts by the number of lessons and responsories included in Office texts for Sundays and important feast days: those intended for the secular Office contain nine lessons and responsories and those for the Benedictine Office twelve. Prior to the early ninth century however, "[i]t is impossible to speak of a 'monastic Office' as distinct from a 'secular Office'",

---

[59] Whitelock, Brett, and Brooke, *Councils and Synods*, 331–32; Gittos, *Liturgy, Architecture, and Sacred Places*, 139; Helen Foxhall Forbes, *Heaven and Earth in Anglo-Saxon England: Theology and Society in an Age of Faith* (Farnham: Ashgate, 2013), 52–53.

[60] "Ða wæs his gewuna þæt he wolde ælce dæge habban twa mæssan butan hit ma wære, 7 ealle his tida togædere ær he ut eode." Peter Stokes, "The Vision of Leofric: Manuscript, Text and Context," *The Review of English Studies* 63 (2012): 549.

[61] Ann Williams, "A Bell-House and a Burh-geat: Lordly Residences in England before the Norman Conquest," in *Medieval Knighthood IV: Papers from the Fifth Strawberry Hill Conference, 1990*, ed. Christopher Harper-Bill and Ruth Harvey (Woodbridge: Boydell Press, 1992), 226; *English Historical Documents*, ed. David C. Douglas, vol. 1, *c. 500–1042*, ed. Dorothy Whitelock (London: Eyre Methuen, 1979), 468.

[62] Harper, *The Forms and Orders of Western Liturgy*, 76.

[63] Billett, *The Divine Office in Anglo-Saxon England*, 32–33; Whitelock, Brett, and Brooke, *Councils and Synods*, 2.

as the Roman *cursus*, the form later used solely by clerics, was used by both groups up until the Aachen councils of 816–817.[64]

As far as manuscripts and relevant references to the Office are indications, the study of which has been significantly advanced by Jesse Billett's monograph, the form of the Office celebrated in England until the mid-tenth century was the Roman Office, also known as the secular *cursus*. Prior to a strict interpretation of the *Rule of Benedict* decided upon at the early ninth-century Aachen councils, there was no distinction between the celebration of the monastic and secular forms of the Office. Even in the areas where monastic adherence to the form of the Office described in the *Rule* was mandated by church councils, the implementation of this new liturgical form was inconsistent.[65] In England on the other hand, episcopal legislation in the form of the Council of *Clofesho* in 747 required the celebration of the Office according to the practices of the Roman church, and the F version of the Anglo-Saxon Chronicle depicts monks and secular clerics at Canterbury celebrating the Office together, apparently in the same form, after a plague wiped out much of the ostensibly monastic community in 870. Billett has argued for the continuity of the performance of the Office in England, in many cases supported by royal patronage, through the ninth and into the tenth century "within the stable framework of the Roman *cursus*" and despite the multi-faceted disruptions of the era.[66] The monastic reforms of the mid-tenth century however seem to have aligned the monastic form of the Office in England with that mandated by the Carolingian reforms of the early ninth century, adopting the Benedictine *cursus* in place of the Roman.

Though its monastic and secular forms were identical in Western Europe until at least the early ninth century and in England until the mid-tenth, the celebration of the Divine Office is most often associated with monks. There are various reasons for this association, two of which readily present themselves. Firstly, the secular clergy had a clearly pastoral function, with a focus on ministry to the laity. This may have meant that the secular Office would be celebrated mostly in cathedrals and other well-staffed churches that had enough clerics to perform the full round of offices and still carry out their pastoral duties. Monks, while their role in pastoral care has been debated, would certainly have had a lesser role in the spiritual care of laypeople than

---

[64] Billett, *The Divine Office in Anglo-Saxon England*, 62–64.
[65] Ibid., 72–73, 75.
[66] Arthur West Haddan and William Stubbs, eds., *Councils and Ecclesiastical Documents Relating to Great Britain and Ireland*, vol. 3, *English Church during the Anglo-Saxon Period: A.D. 595–1066* (Oxford: Clarendon Press, 1871), 367; Billett, *The Divine Office in Anglo-Saxon England*, 89–90, 148.

most secular priests.[67] Secondly, monks took care to depict themselves as those primarily celebrating the Divine Office and some texts portray clerics as lazy and incompetent in the performance of the Office. A confirmation charter of Edgar in favor of the Old Minster gives one of the rationales for the expulsion of the secular clerics in 964 as their failure to observe the Office, though to what degree this reflects reality is unknown.[68] A potential reason for the strong association of monks with the observance of the Office may be medieval concern for the efficacy of prayers. This was certainly a concern for medieval royalty and nobility, particularly those who were commemorated as benefactors of religious houses, and communities of celibate monks who celebrated the hours had a strong claim to efficacious prayer.[69]

Despite the general association of monks with the Office, evidence for the performance of the Divine Office in secular churches is less scarce than the general lack of scholarly attention to it would lead one to believe. Manuscript evidence comes to us in the form of Oxford, Bodleian Library, Junius 27, a psalter probably copied at Winchester in the first half of the tenth century, probably in the 920s. Not only does this book predate the expulsion of the secular clerics, but the division of the psalter also suggests its use in the celebration of the Roman form of the Office.[70] Additionally, the booklist from Sherburn-in-Elmet contains an Office antiphoner, a psalter, and a hymnal, all necessary for the celebration of the Office, and the list of donations made by Leofric to the church at Exeter also contains a significant number of books for the Office, including three psalters, two hymnals, an antiphoner for

---

[67] A proportion of early medieval monks were certainly involved in pastoral care, as has been pointed out by several scholars, but it seems that most of these were involved in missionary work or churches under the direct control of monastic institutions. See Giles Constable, "Monasteries, Rural Churches and the *Cura Animarum* in the Early Middle Ages," in *Cristianizzazione ed organizzazione ecclesiastica delle campagne nell'alto medioevo: Espansione e resistenze*, vol. 28, no. 1 of *Settimane di studio del Centro italiano di studi sull'alto medioevo* (Spoleto: Presso la sede del Centro, 1982); Thomas Amos, "Monks and Pastoral Care in the Early Middle Ages," in *Religion, Culture, and Society in the Early Middle Ages: Studies in Honor of Richard E. Sullivan*, ed. Thomas F. X. Noble and John Contreni (Kalamazoo: Medieval Institute Publications, 1987); Alan Thacker, "Monks, Preaching and Pastoral Care in Early Anglo-Saxon England," in *Pastoral Care before the Parish*, ed. John Blair and Richard Sharpe (Leicester: Leicester University Press, 1992).

[68] Alexander R. Rumble, *Property and Piety in Early Medieval Winchester: Documents Relating to the Topography of the Anglo-Saxon and Norman City and Its Minsters* (Oxford: Clarendon Press, 2002), 131.

[69] Susan Boynton, "The Bible and the Liturgy," in *The Practice of the Bible in the Middle Ages: Production, Reception, and Performance in Western Christianity*, ed. Boynton and Diane Reilly (New York: Columbia University Press, 2011), 17–18.

[70] Billett, *The Divine Office in Anglo-Saxon England*, 141–42.

the Night Office, and a surviving collectar (London, British Library, Harley 2961).[71]

However, narrative evidence for the celebration of the Office comes to us not from a cathedral, but from minster churches. The passage from the history of Holy Trinity, Twynham, discussed earlier in this chapter in regard to the mass, refers to how the canons "every day celebrated the night hours and those of the whole day, from dawn to dusk" and also makes reference to offerings given at Vespers, indicating that laypeople were in attendance at this service.[72] The church was obviously well staffed, apparently supporting several times more canons than were found in most minster churches and indeed had more canons than some contemporary cathedrals.[73] Though not as explicit as the evidence from Twynham, *The Waltham Chronicle* also seems to indicate that the Office was consistently performed at Waltham. The author states that in the time of Harold, "there was no church in the kingdom that approached Waltham in its fine performance of ecclesiastical offices".[74] Though vague and possibly formulaic, this statement was probably intended to indicate that the Divine Office was fully celebrated at Waltham at least after its refounding by Harold. A negative miracle story purported to have taken place during the childhood of the author of the *Chronicle*, apparently in the early twelfth century, also records the performance of the Divine Office there. In the story, the Waltham canons, including the young chronicler, were gathered for Vespers during one Saturday in Eastertide and a laywoman came to the altar as if to present a monetary offering, though her intentions were less than pious. As part of the backdrop of this story, it is recorded that the canons sang *Ad cenam agni prouidi*, a hymn that was indeed intended to be sung at Vespers during Eastertide.[75] Though the story is clearly late, it confirms that the clerics at Waltham continued to perform the Office in the twelfth century and that lay attendance and offerings at Vespers were not uncommon. Like Twynham, Waltham was a well-staffed and wealthy minster that certainly seems to have had the resources to celebrate the Divine Office both in Harold's time and in the decades after the Conquest. Just as churches often acted as

---

[71] Lapdige, "Surviving Booklists," 56, 65.
[72] Hase, "The Mother Churches of Hampshire," 59.
[73] John Blair, "Secular Minster Churches in Domesday Book," in *Domesday Book: A Reassessment*, ed. Peter H. Sawyer (London: Edward Arnold, 1985), 114; Frank Barlow, *The English Church, 1000–1066: A History of the Later Anglo-Saxon Church*, 2nd ed. (London: Longman, 1979), 241–42.
[74] "[Q]uod non esset secunda huic in regno ecclesia, in tam decenti amministratione ecclesiasticorum officiorum." Leslie Watkiss and Marjorie Chibnall, eds., *The Waltham Chronicle: An Account of the Discovery of Our Holy Cross at Montacute and Its Conveyance to Waltham* (Oxford: Clarendon Press, 1994), 30–33.
[75] Ibid., 67, 69.

a measure of status in this period, the Divine Office may too have been a measure of wealth and prestige in churches founded by noblemen. Leofric of Mercia and his wife Godiva are known to have established Stow in Lincolnshire, requesting that the Office be celebrated there as it was in St Paul's Cathedral in London.[76] For Harold, who considerably enriched Waltham, it is probable that he provided for the church at a level which would have enabled the celebration of the full round of canonical hours as both an act of piety and an indicator of wealth.

The role of the Divine Office is not typically seen in a pastoral light and is more often associated with the internal liturgical celebrations of a given church. Additionally, as an act of worship that is most often associated with cloistered monks, its relevance to the laity might seem negligible. Several streams of evidence indicate that this is not so. Firstly, the Office seems to have functioned penitentially in some ways for laypeople. Some continental texts refer to lay attendance at the Office during the Lenten season and the constant prescription of psalm-singing in Anglo-Saxon penitentials might indicate that those penitents for whom psalm-singing was prescribed could have attended the observance of the Office at a nearby church.[77] A penitential text in Cambridge, Corpus Christi College 190 requires that those unable to fast should "sing fifty psalms in the right order in church or in some private place" and the *Old English Penitential* found in Laud Misc. 482 prescribes psalm-singing in place of fasting for a number of food-related sins.[78] Secondly, narrative evidence also seems to suggest lay participation in the Office. The vignette from *The Waltham Chronicle* depicts a laywoman presenting an offering at Vespers on a Saturday in Eastertide and the history from Twynham refers to the distribution of offerings given at Vespers, seemingly indicating that it was not uncommon for laypersons to attend this evening office, occurring around 6 pm, in secular minsters. Furthermore, the aristocratic laity showed considerable interest in the Divine Office. As Leofric and Godiva specifically requested that the Office be celebrated at Stow as it was at St Paul's in London, others of the nobility may also have emphasized the performance of the Office in churches that received

---

[76] S 1478.
[77] For the continental material, *Capitula episcoporum*, pt. 1, ed. Peter Brommer, *Monumenta Germaniae Historica* (Hanover: Hahnsche Buchhandlung, 1984), 137; Jacques-Paul Migne, ed., *Burchardi vormatiensis episcopi opera omnia …*, Patrologia Latina 140 (Paris: Garnier, 1880), 962.
[78] *Old English Introduction*, ed. Allen J. Frantzen, "Corpus 190 (S) 369," in *Anglo-Saxon Penitentials: A Cultural Database*, accessed February 13, 2018, http://www.anglo-saxon.net/penance/index.php?p=TOEI190_369; *Old English Penitential*, ed. Frantzen, "Laud Misc. 482 (Y) 18a," in *Anglo-Saxon Penitentials*, accessed February 13, 2018, http://www.anglo-saxon.net/penance/index.php?p=TOEP482_18a.

their patronage. Leofric was accustomed to having "all his services [OE *tida*] one after the other before he went out" and King Alfred had a handbook that contained the Psalms, the offices for the day hours, and a selection of prayers.[79]

Surviving liturgical manuscripts for priests

Liturgical manuscripts intended for everyday use have a notoriously poor rate of survival. Workaday books were often used until they were worn out or fell behind contemporary liturgical trends, after which they were discarded or recycled for use in binding, as palimpsests, or in other ways that have not left detectable remains.[80] The rate of survival for priestly manuscripts in particular has not been favorable due to the nature of sacerdotal ministry. Most priests' books were probably not high status nor well cared for: they were meant to be used, carried around, and read from daily. Additionally, single-priest churches and minsters, where the majority of secular priests would have engaged in pastoral ministry, have generally not been conduits for manuscript survival. This, combined with history's general unkindness to Anglo-Saxon manuscripts, has resulted in an often-profound lack of extant books for the mass and Office that were used by priests in the field. Despite the loss of hundreds or thousands of liturgical manuscripts belonging to minor churches in the Anglo-Saxon period, a small number of these books have survived and can significantly contribute to the understanding of priests' books and their use in pastoral care.

The Red Book of Darley (Cambridge, Corpus Christi College 422)

The Red Book of Darley primarily consists of a missal dating to the middle of the eleventh century. The Easter tables that have been copied into the manuscript begin at 1061 and continue to 1098, probably indicating a date of copying around 1060. It had been combined with an early eleventh-century copy of *Solomon and Saturn* by the twelfth century, and the poem now occupies the first twenty-six pages of the manuscript as it stands today. Most scholars have suggested that the missal was produced at the New Minster, Winchester, possibly for use at Sherborne. These associations, along with some of the content

---

[79] Stokes, "The Vision of Leofric," 549; Simon Keynes and Michael Lapidge, trans., *Alfred the Great: Asser's* Life of King Alfred *and Other Contemporary Sources* (London: Penguin Books, 1983), 99–100.
[80] Richard Gameson, *The Earliest Books of Canterbury Cathedral: Manuscripts and Fragments to c. 1200* (London: Bibliographical Society and the British Library, 2008), 35.

of the book, including masses "which ... bespeak a monastic, indeed Winchester, content", would seem to suggest a monastic context for its production.[81] Some of the masses in this manuscript are presented in the form normally transmitted in a sacramentary (i.e., only the prayers to be said by the celebrant are given in full), while others are presented as is typical for a missal, with all the texts needed given in full. The gospel and epistle readings are inconsistently given in full, with some gospel readings in full and only the incipit for the epistle and others vice versa.[82] The manuscript also contains a significant number of liturgical texts for the performance of occasional offices such as baptism, anointing of the sick, confession and communion for the dying, and burial services. For certain offices, such as baptism, feminine pronoun variants have been added between the lines, implying use in parochial ministry. In addition to these offices, there are rites for various ordeals, exorcisms, and the blessing of ashes, water, and salt.[83] The last major portion of the book consists of material for the Divine Office, some of which is now earlier in sequence than in the book's original form due to the incorrect placement of a quire at some later stage. The offices that are given are relatively limited as far as completeness in relation to the liturgical calendar – they cover only the Office of the Dead, Common of Saints, the second half of Holy Week, and Easter. These offices also provide what is perhaps the strongest evidence for the monastic associations of this book's production: the Office material transmitted in the Red Book of Darley conforms to the monastic rather than secular *cursus*.

Despite this, the book's early associations with monastic cathedrals do not seem to accord with the later history of the volume. A sixteenth-century inscription on the last page of the book reads "The rede boke of darleye in the peake in darbyshire", providing us with some information about the book's provenance and indicating that the book had traveled a significant distance north by the later Middle Ages.[84] Earlier evidence may too suggest that it was being used in Derbyshire in the early twelfth century, as the Anglo-Saxon church at Darley was dedicated to St Helen and a mass for this saint was added to the manuscript in the twelfth century.[85] It may also be significant that the

---

[81] Pfaff, "Massbooks," 21–33; Richard Pfaff, *The Liturgy in Medieval England: A History* (Cambridge: Cambridge University Press, 2009), 94–95.

[82] Helen Gittos, "Is There Any Evidence for the Liturgy of Parish Churches in Late Anglo-Saxon England? The Red Book of Darley and the Status of Old English," in *Pastoral Care in Late Anglo-Saxon England*, ed. Francesca Tinti (Woodbridge: Boydell Press, 2005), 69.

[83] Mildred Budny, *Insular, Anglo-Saxon, and Early Anglo-Norman Manuscript Art at Corpus Christi College, Cambridge: An Illustrated Catalogue* (Kalamazoo: Medieval Institute Publications, 1997), 645.

[84] Cambridge, Corpus Christi College 422, page 586.

[85] Budny, *Insular, Anglo-Saxon, and Early Anglo-Norman Manuscript Art*, 648.

church at Darley came into the possession of Lincoln Cathedral before 1105 where the book may have been "refurbished" before it came to the place of its later medieval provenance.[86] But the material added in the early twelfth century is still problematic for this book's use in a secular context. Richard Pfaff has shown that these additions that reference St Helen do not indicate a secular context for the use of the Red Book of Darley, as "the lessons at matins in the two sanctorale offices of that same final quire [containing the masses for St Helen] are in number four for Alexander, Eventius, and Theodolus, and eight for the Invention of the Cross – both feasts fall on May 3rd – thus adding up to a feast of twelve lessons", meaning that these texts follow the monastic *cursus* for the Office.[87]

Considering the contents and supposed origins of the Red Book of Darley, it is unsurprising that this manuscript has posed something of a quandary to scholars. The script and the contents of the calendar, as well as the monastic form of its Office material, point to its creation within a monastic scriptorium for a monastic user or users. Though some books used by priests certainly had monastic origins, this book is challenging not due to its origins, but in light of the texts it contains. If the manuscript was used by a monk, how did the book end up being used at St Helen's in Darley Dale, Derbyshire by the twelfth century? The "monk-missionary" that Pfaff presents as a problematic hypothesis for the origin of this manuscript seems untenable in light of the prevailing religious conditions in England in the mid-eleventh century. However, the assertion that the evidence for its association with St Helen's in Derbyshire is coincidental and that the book was not used parochially would too strain the limits of credulity. The dedication of the medieval church in Darley Dale to St Helen, the sixteenth-century note that associates the manuscript with Darley, and the addition of liturgical material for St Helen, not to mention the suitability of the manuscript for parochial use, seem too great a body of evidence to ascribe to happenstance.

The Red Book of Darley is in many ways the type of book we could expect an Anglo-Saxon priest to own. The book is intensely pastoral, containing texts for the mass and Office, occasional offices, and charms, all of which could have been used in ministry by a priest. Though the manuscript appears to be the kind of book that would be used by a secular priest, and it seems to have been used in a parochial context, its liturgical contents are monastic and it is too problematic to associate it with use by the secular clergy. Due to the difficulties of the evidence, the Red Book of Darley cannot be firmly placed as a book

---

[86] Gittos, "Is There Any Evidence for the Liturgy of Parish Churches," 68.
[87] Pfaff, *The Liturgy in Medieval England*, 95.

for a secular priest, though a similar, secularly oriented volume would have been eminently suitable for a local priest of the late Anglo-Saxon period.

Cambridge, Corpus Christi College 41

This manuscript has been of significant interest to both scholars of English liturgy and those studying the text of Bede's *Historia ecclesiastica*. The main text of the manuscript consists of the Old English Bede, and this recension of the text has been used extensively in the various editions of Bede's *Ecclesiastical History* as well as in the compilation of the Parkerian Old English dictionary.[88] The manuscript has more recently seen significant scholarly attention in light of its copious liturgical marginalia, consisting of masses, offices, prayers, antiphons, and hymns, as well as homilies, poems, and charms. The Bedan text was written by two scribes whose hands "are rather rough" and the marginal materials are "probably all in one unusual angular hand" of the first half or middle of the eleventh century.[89] The location of its production and later use are unknown, though both Mildred Budny and Sarah Keefer have asserted that the manuscript likely originated in "a provincial scriptorium of not great size".[90] It was also probably at a center of this kind that liturgical material was copied into this manuscript. The marginal texts were added by a single individual at several stages, probably as exemplars became available to him. Later in the eleventh century, the manuscript was acquired by Bishop Leofric at Exeter, as is shown by an *ex libris* inscription, and it may have seen further additions while at Exeter. Though the manuscript itself was almost certainly never directly used for the celebration of mass or the Office, it is an important witness to the sort of texts that were available to priests in the late Anglo-Saxon period, particularly texts for the performance of the liturgy.

Thomas Bredehoft has argued that the marginal additions to Corpus 41 were copied in four stages, of which the liturgical material comprised Stages 2 and 4, indicating that the marginal scribe had copied charms into the manuscript before the mass and Office texts and that most of the martyrological and homiletic texts were added between the two stints of liturgical copying.[91] There is no clear delineation of the

---

[88] Sharon M. Rowley, ed., *The Old English Version of Bede's* Historia Ecclesiastica (Cambridge: D. S. Brewer, 2011), 23–24.

[89] Neil R. Ker, *Catalogue of Manuscripts Containing Anglo-Saxon* (Oxford: Clarendon Press, 1957), 45.

[90] Sarah Keefer, "Margin as Archive: The Liturgical Marginalia of a Manuscript of the Old English Bede," *Traditio* 51 (1996): 147; Budny, *Insular, Anglo-Saxon, and Early Anglo-Norman Manuscript Art*, 508.

[91] Homiletic texts received significant interest from the marginal scribe: more

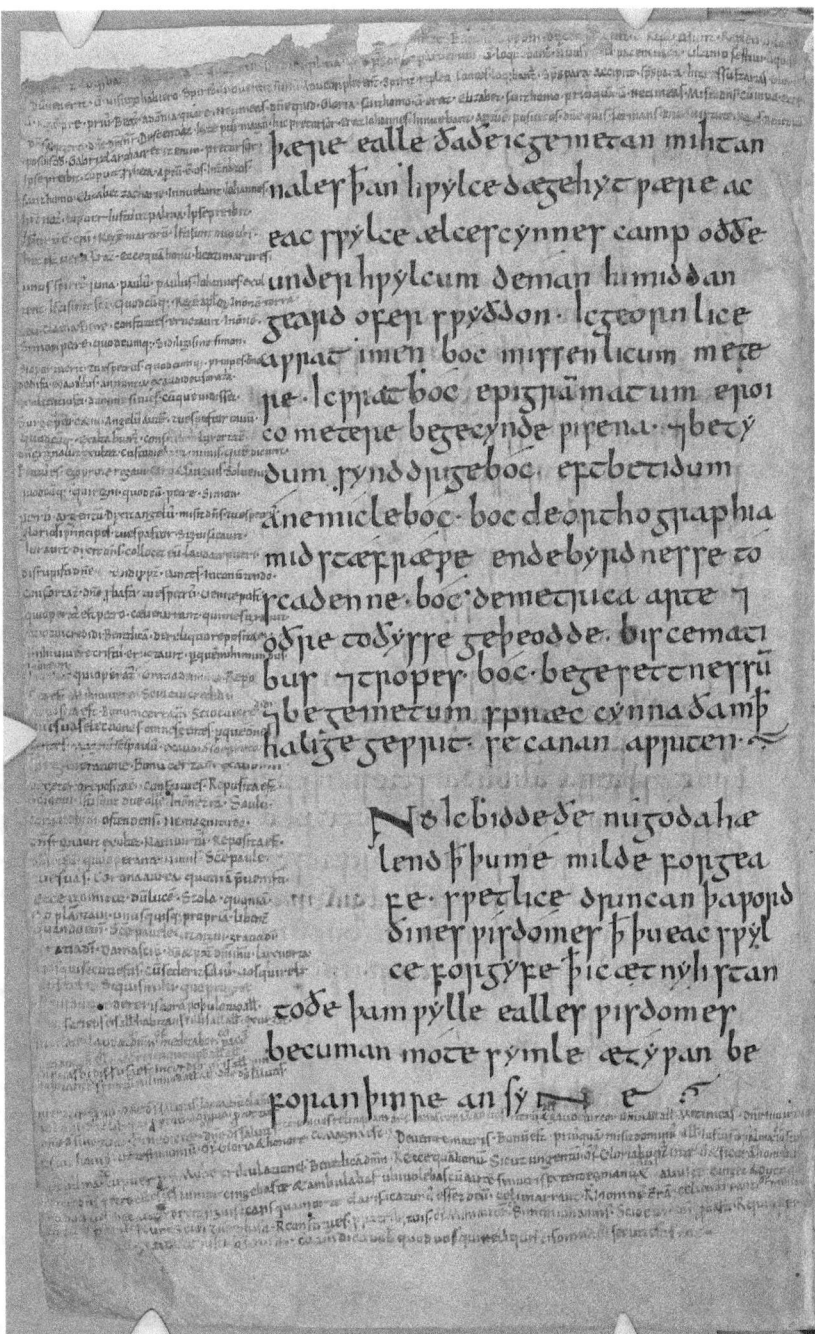

Plate 5: Cambridge, Corpus Christi College 41, p. 482. A page from the Old English Bede with marginalia containing the incipits of Office chants for Pentecost and several saints' feasts.

type of liturgical texts copied in particular stages. Stage 2 as identified by Bredehoft contains material for both the mass and Office, though it should be noted that almost all of the Office chants discussed by Billett were copied in Stage 2.[92] The second phase of liturgical copying (Stage 4) is similar, with both types of texts copied, though masses predominate. As texts were copied in stages, with multiple types of texts – liturgical and otherwise – being copied in one period, it would seem that the scribe traveled to another center, a cathedral, minster church, or even a local church, that had multiple books from which to copy, as is implied by the copying of texts from multiple types of liturgical books in a single stint. That this center was secular is implied by the presence of nine rather than twelve responsories in the material for the Office, indicating that these texts follow the secular *cursus*. Christopher Hohler imagines these marginal additions to be those of a priest who "was being told to bring his liturgical books up to date by a reforming bishop of Wells" and asserts that this cleric likely had a missal, one which lacked the masses for weekdays, and "an office-book-cum-manual" not unlike the Durham Collectar.[93] In short, the priest in question was attempting to augment the books that he owned using Corpus 41 as a medium of transmission. Hohler's suggestions are reasonable considering the liturgical content of the margins, though his suggestion of Wells as the secular center in question is speculative. Keefer has suggested that the manuscript functioned more as an archive for a variety of texts, with the intention of "reorganization and recopying into a volume where they would form at least part of the main liturgical text".[94] Hohler's and Keefer's arguments are not wholly contradictory, though perhaps the latter places too much emphasis on the liturgical compendium-making of the eleventh century rather than the simple supplementation or creation of already well-defined types of liturgical books. What these appraisals of Corpus 41 point to is a window into what kinds of texts eleventh-century secular priests needed or were interested in obtaining.

Firstly, the marginal scribe of this manuscript was concerned to augment his sacramentary, which is evidenced by his copying of masses in both Stage 2 and Stage 4. The scribe's copying of several pages of ferial masses may in particular point to a lack of masses for weekdays, as is the case for the twelfth-century Irish missal Oxford,

---

than fifty pages of margins contain Old English homilies, possibly to augment a book of homilies or to copy into a booklet. Thomas A. Bredehoft, "Filling the Margins of CCCC 41: Textual Space and a Developing Archive," *Review of English Studies* 57 (2006): 730–31.

[92] Ibid., 729–31; Billett, "The Divine Office and the Secular Clergy," 454.

[93] Christopher Hohler, review of *Cambridge, Corpus Christi College 41: The Loricas and the Missal*, by Raymond Grant, *Medium Ævum* 49 (1980): 275–76.

[94] Keefer, "Margin as Archive," 151.

Corpus Christi College 282. Additionally, Corpus 41 seems to have been added to from more than one sacramentary; some masses for the same day were copied twice and Hohler points out that in these overlapping texts "one mass is usually more 'Gelasian' than the other", indicating that at least two mass-books were used as exemplars.[95] Secondly, the marginal scribe seems to have had access to and been well acquainted with an Office antiphoner. Corpus 41 contains more chants for the secular Office than any other pre-Conquest English manuscript, and the large number of chants for a variety of occasions probably indicates that the marginal scribe was copying from an Office antiphoner rather than a composite volume. Like the mass texts added to Corpus 41, the addition of these chants probably indicates particular gaps in the Office antiphoner of the marginal scribe. Billett has asserted that evidence from Corpus 41, along with the Durham Collectar, "impl[ies] the availability in England in the tenth century of Office chant books containing the 'Gregorian' repertory first codified in Frankish Gaul under the Carolingians" and that this material for the secular Office was introduced and potentially circulated outside the influence of the Benedictine reformers.[96] The familiarity of the scribe with Office liturgy is indicated by his significant and erratic abbreviation of the texts he was copying and the fact that it was sufficient to copy only the incipits of the chants to enable him to use them later.[97] This implies that these sorts of texts were habitually used in the liturgical services of the church in which this cleric was serving or had served. Furthermore, the copyist was familiar with musical notation and utilized Breton neumes where notation is provided.[98]

Despite the improbability of the direct use of this manuscript in the liturgy, Corpus 41 is a valuable witness not only to the repertoire of liturgical texts, particularly Office chants, available to the secular clergy in the late Anglo-Saxon period, but also to the complement of liturgical books to which the marginal scribe had access, namely multiple mass-books, probably sacramentaries, at least one Office antiphoner, a book of homilies, and more. These texts were most probably copied to supplement the texts at hand in the scribe's church and, if so, it seems likely that the church in question had, at minimum, a basic mass-book, possibly lacking masses for weekdays, an antiphoner, and a homiliary. In addition, the extensive material for the Office in this book is striking and indicative of more than just an archival interest in Office chants. Bearing in mind the scribe's familiarity with these sorts of texts and the evidence for the celebration of the Divine Office in

---

[95] Hohler, review of *Cambridge, Corpus Christi College 41*, 276.
[96] Billett, *The Divine Office in Anglo-Saxon England*, 225, 234.
[97] Keefer, "Margin as Archive," 148.
[98] See, for example, page 475 of this manuscript.

minster churches, Corpus 41 is a further indication of the significance of the Divine Office and its performance by the Anglo-Saxon secular clergy in minor churches.

The Warsaw Lectionary (Warsaw, Biblioteka Narodowa, I. 3311)

Warsaw, Biblioteka Narodowa, I. 3311, also known as the Warsaw Lectionary, has until recently been neglected in studies of Anglo-Saxon liturgical books.[99] The book has long resided outside the typical geographical purview of those studying Anglo-Saxon manuscripts, but recent digitization by the National Library of Poland has made it accessible to the scholarly community.[100] Those scholars who have previously made mention of this manuscript have generally discounted its use in the liturgy due to the canonical, rather than liturgical, order of the gospel readings in the first section of the book, and most have concluded that the Warsaw Lectionary had a private, devotional function.[101] In light of a detailed analysis of the manuscript and its contents however, I propose that its liturgical function should be reconsidered.

The Warsaw Lectionary is a small, portable book measuring 155 × 99 mm. It presently consists of 151 folios and was written around the year 1000 in a somewhat inconsistent form of Style I Anglo-Caroline Minuscule. The text of this manuscript contains selections from the four gospels and is made up of two sections. Unusually, the passages are presented in canonical order from ff. 1–110 and given in liturgical order from ff. 111–151, where the book ends imperfectly at Luke 6:45. Lenker has noted this division of the book, contending that the first section "could not be employed in the mass in this form" due to the order of the gospels and the fact that the liturgical occasion for each reading is not given at the beginning of the passage.[102] The canonical order of the book's first section also seems to have led Richard

---

[99] For a more detailed treatment of this book, see Gerald P. Dyson, "Liturgy or Private Devotion? Reappraising Warsaw, Biblioteka Narodowa, I. 3311," *Anglo-Saxon England* 45 (2016). Portions of this article have been reprinted here. Copyright © Cambridge University Press. Reprinted with permission of Cambridge University Press.

[100] The facsimile can be found at http://polona.pl/item/14637590/0/.

[101] Lenker, "The West Saxon Gospels and the Gospel-Lectionary," 155; Richard Gameson, "The Gospels of Margaret of Scotland and the Literacy of an Early Medieval Queen," in *Women and the Book: Assessing the Visual Evidence*, ed. Lesley Smith and Jane Taylor (London: The British Library and University of Toronto Press, 1996), 149. By canonical order, I mean the order in which these books are given in a gospelbook or pandect, namely Matthew, Mark, Luke and John.

[102] Lenker, "The West Saxon Gospels and the Gospel-Lectionary," 155, 177. Lenker assigns a date of s. x^2 to the second section while dating the first s. x/xi, but it will be shown that it is not possible for the second section of this book to predate the first.

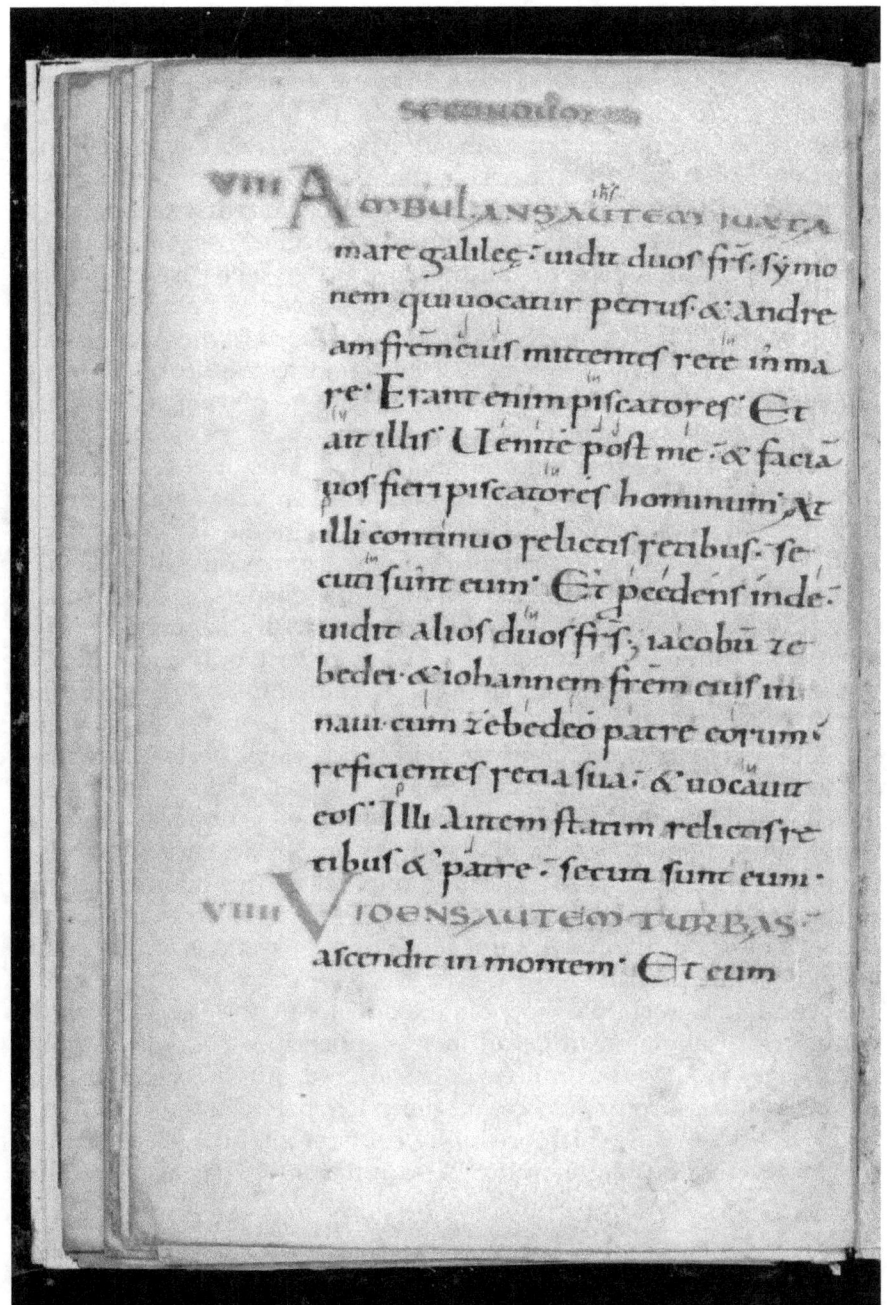

Plate 6: Warsaw, Biblioteka Narodowa, I. 3311, f. 17v. Neumes added to Matthew 4:18–22, pericope for the feast of St Andrew.

Gameson to assume that it was not used in the liturgy, but rather as a book for "private use by an individual reader", though he identified the manuscript, presumably ff. 111–151, as potentially "written for use in parish churches" in an earlier publication.[103]

Academic literature concerning the Warsaw Lectionary has thus generally concluded that the first part of this manuscript was not used liturgically. Despite this, the canonical order of the first section of the book is not necessarily an impediment to liturgical use. Gospelbooks, which present their contents in canonical order, were used to supply readings for the mass for many centuries. Indeed, gospelbooks continued to be used for this purpose through to the end of the Anglo-Saxon period.[104] Perhaps the more robust objection to the liturgical use of the manuscript's first section is that there are no markings to indicate which passages should be read on a given day.[105] In gospelbooks, these cues are provided either via marginal annotations or gospel lists that note the pericopes in the order of the liturgical year and the proper liturgical occasion for each reading. Late Anglo-Saxon gospelbooks tend to favor the use of gospel lists for this purpose and these aids are most commonly located at the end of the gospels.[106] As this manuscript ends imperfectly, it could have originally contained such a system. Additionally, before the beginning of each gospel, the incipits of the readings are listed, which may have aided in finding the proper lection. Clerics may too in some cases have known by heart which pericopes were to be used for certain liturgical days, particularly those for the major feasts of the year, and it is precisely these readings that are contained in the first section of the Warsaw Lectionary. Therefore neither the canonical order of the readings nor the absence of marginal annotations is a definitive indication of whether this manuscript was utilized in the mass. Rather, the evidence proffered in the following analysis indicates that the liturgical use of both sections of this manuscript is highly probable.

Several things should be pointed out about the contents of the manuscript (tabulated in detail in the appendix). Firstly, a number of passages are now incomplete or disordered. A folio originally containing readings from Matthew has been lost between the current ff. 8 and 9. Another leaf, which originally contained John 17:8–11 and the first two verses of the following Passion narrative, has also been lost

---

[103] Gameson, "The Gospels of Margaret of Scotland," 149; Gameson, *The Role of Art in the Late Anglo-Saxon Church* (Oxford: Clarendon Press, 1995), 243.

[104] Gneuss, "Liturgical Books in Anglo-Saxon England," 108–9. Gneuss lists twenty-three English gospelbooks marked for liturgical use dating from the eighth to the twelfth centuries.

[105] This is in contrast to the second section, which contains marginal annotations indicating the appropriate liturgical day for a given passage.

[106] Gneuss, "Liturgical Books in Anglo-Saxon England," 106–9.

after f. 97. As decorated pages begin the Passion readings from both Matthew and Luke, this folio from John may have been excised for its decoration.[107] Additionally, Lenker has stated that the beginning of the liturgically ordered second section of the book is fragmentary because it does not contain the readings for the Vigil of Christmas and Christmas itself.[108] However, the readings for both of these occasions are included in the first section of the book, making it unlikely that the second section originally began with these lections. In addition to these losses, parts of Matthew and Mark are now disordered due to the incorrect placement of a quire. Quire 2, containing the final pericope from Matthew and the first few pericopes from Mark, was originally situated after f. 39, but now bifurcates the early readings from Matthew.

Another notable characteristic revealed by a tabulation of its contents is that most of the pericopes for major feasts of the church are found in the canonically ordered first section, including those for Christmas, Holy Week, Easter, and Pentecost. In addition to these readings for the major events of the *temporale*, the first section also contains all the pericopes for saints' days. In contrast, the second section of the book most typically contains readings for Sundays falling between the major liturgical occasions of the year, including readings for Lent, the Sundays after Epiphany and twenty-six Sundays after Pentecost; however, this section lacks the readings for Pentecost, Epiphany, Holy Week, and Easter. A closer examination of the pericopes in both sections shows them to be complementary, with the second section of the book supplementing the pericopes found in the first. For example, the second section begins with the readings for the week following Christmas and the weeks following Epiphany, but it is the first section of the book that contains the readings for Christmas and Epiphany themselves. Lections for Advent are similarly split: the first and second Sundays in Advent are included in the canonically ordered section, while the readings for the third and fourth Sundays appear toward the end of the liturgically ordered section. A similar pattern is evident in the Lenten gospel pericopes. The readings for Ash Wednesday and the second to the fifth Sundays in Lent are contained in the book's latter section, but the readings for the first Sunday in Lent and Palm Sunday are conspicuously absent. Continuing the complementary pattern, these lections appear in the first section of the book. Furthermore, after supplying the reading for the second Sunday after Easter, f. 125v contains a marginal note explicitly instructing the user of the manuscript to refer back to the Gospel of John for the readings

---

[107] The surviving decoration preceding Passion narratives can be found at ff. 28r and 69r.
[108] Lenker, *Die Westsächsische Evangelienversion*, 472.

for the next two Sundays, which are supplied in the first section at ff. 96v–97r and 95v–96v. The remainder of f. 125v goes on to supply the reading for the fifth Sunday after Easter.[109] This marginal note is in the same contemporary hand and in the same position as other marginal annotations in the second section of the book informing the user of the appropriate occasion for each reading. From the complementary pattern evident here and even a marginal note instructing the manuscript's user to refer back to the first section, it is clear that the second section of this book was bound and used in conjunction with the pericopes from the canonically ordered section in the Anglo-Saxon period. Moreover, it is evident the second section was written based on the pericopes available in the first.[110] This indicates that if the second section of the manuscript was intended for liturgical use, as Gameson seems to suggest and as I argue here, it can be shown by extension that the entire book was used liturgically.

What may be less obvious than the complementary pattern identified here is the rationale for the production of the book's first section, which lacks many passages needed to celebrate mass for the whole of the liturgical year. However, the beginning of the manuscript may indicate that the reason for the production of this book was simple necessity. The text of f. 1v reads, "In christi nomine incipit pars sanctorum evangeliorum qvedam hoc in libello causa necessitatis descripta".[111] Though it is not outside the realm of possibility that an aristocratic layperson might commission a manuscript like the first section of this book for private use, it is unlikely that the production of such a book would be considered a necessity. Additionally, the limited readings supplied in the first section would probably rule out its production for a monastery, cathedral community, or even a larger secular minster, as the daily liturgical celebrations of these institutions would almost certainly call for a gospel lectionary that included more than just the readings for the most important liturgical days.[112] Instead, the most plausible context for its production might be to fill a need for a lectionary in a small clerical community or for a priest whose primary role

---

[109] The note in question reads, "Dominicum II et III require in sancto Iohanne" (Look for the second and third Sundays in St John).

[110] This is partially shown by the almost complete lack of overlapping pericopes. To the best of my knowledge, Matthew 3:13–17, now lost from the first section, is the only passage originally shared by both parts of the book.

[111] "In the name of Christ here begins a certain part of the holy gospels copied into this little book on account of need." From the abbreviated text on f. 1v, it is not immediately clear if the Latin should be rendered as "sanctorum evangeliorum" or "sancti evangelii". However, as the book contains readings from multiple gospels, it has been understood as plural in the above translation.

[112] For example, mass was celebrated at least twice a day in the later eleventh century at Holy Trinity Twynham, a relatively large secular minster. Hase, "The Mother Churches of Hampshire," 59.

was to conduct services for the main liturgical events of the year. The lections for the *temporale* suggest a concern to include the pericopes for the most important liturgical days, with relatively few readings for weekdays and the Sundays between feast days. For a priest or small community concerned primarily with the delivery of pastoral care, the availability of readings for mass on the most important liturgical days of the year, when laypeople were most likely to be present, was crucial. The fact that the complementary second section of the book almost exclusively contains readings for Sundays also implies a parochial context for its use. Any sizeable religious community would have had daily liturgical celebrations requiring a broader range of gospel readings than those presented in this volume, but a small church whose principal liturgical event was mass on Sunday would have found the Warsaw Lectionary well suited to its needs.

Furthermore, the canonical order of the gospel readings in the first section of this book is not indicative of its use in private reading, but may instead reflect the source from which the readings were copied. The order of this first section might suggest that the book was not copied from a lectionary, but rather from a gospelbook that indicated the appropriate readings for a given occasion and naturally presented these readings in canonical rather than liturgical order. The Warsaw Lectionary is the earliest example of an Anglo-Saxon gospel lectionary produced in what was potentially for England a developmental period for this type of liturgical book; thus a gospelbook marked for liturgical use was probably more readily available to a scribe than a liturgically ordered lectionary, which might explain the canonical order of the book's first section.

Further evidence of the liturgical use of this manuscript is apparent from the previously unknown musical notation and performance directions in the form of *litterae significativae* that appear in the book's first section.[113] The neumed portions of the manuscript are found at ff. 17v and 38r, the former containing the pericope for the feast of St Andrew, Matthew 4:18–22, and the latter Matthew 27:46, a small portion of the reading for Palm Sunday and one of Christ's last utterances on the cross.

The notation that appears in the Warsaw Lectionary is consistent with the neumatic forms typically found in Anglo-Saxon manuscripts of the early eleventh century, which conforms to the northern French forms adopted at Winchester rather than the Breton neumes used at Canterbury. A closer examination of the neumes in these two passages also suggests their addition by separate scribes. The neumes added to

---

[113] To the best of my knowledge, the musical material in the Warsaw Lectionary was noted for the first time in Dyson, "Liturgy or Private Devotion?," 279–83.

Matthew 27:46 are in ink of the same color as that of the gospel text and the ascending strokes tend to be very straight, whereas the notation added to Matthew 4:18–22 was written in a lighter, brown ink and its vertical strokes often exhibit a slight curvature. Additionally, the oriscus at f. 17v is almost without a descending stroke, whereas the oriscus at f. 38r exhibits a pronounced descender. Considering these differences, the neumes were almost certainly written by two different scribes, though it is impossible to know if either of these individuals can be identified with the scribe of the main text. It may be that the notation for Matthew 27:46 was copied from the same exemplar as the gospel text and was added by either the scribe himself or by a music scribe at the same center. The color of the ink and the divergent forms of the neumes for the feast of St Andrew might indicate that this was added elsewhere at a different time, possibly by an Anglo-Saxon cleric or a group of clerics who used the book.

As mentioned previously, the lection containing Matthew 27:46 gives an account of the Passion and was intended for mass on Palm Sunday. The Passion narratives from the gospels were sung according to a recitation tone that was distinct from the standard tone for gospel pericopes.[114] Additionally, there is variation within the recitation tone for Passion narratives in accordance with their content, with "the narrative and all indirect speech ... sung on a central reciting note, the words of Christ a 5th lower, and other direct speech a 4th higher".[115] To indicate when each tone is to be used, *litterae significativae* also appear in the Passion narratives in this manuscript and will be discussed in due course. As Hiley has pointed out, some of the words of Jesus in the Passion narratives were frequently neumed, indicating to the cleric chanting the gospel that he should deviate from the recitation tone for the Passion narratives and perform the words of Christ within a particular verse in a more elaborate way. Though other phrases spoken by Jesus in the Passion could be neumed, Matthew 27:46 frequently received musical notation in contemporary manuscripts, including the Red Book of Darley and the late tenth- or early eleventh-century missal fragment contained in Bodley 386.[116]

While neumed passages for the Passion were common in the tenth and eleventh centuries, a pericope for the feast of St Andrew with musical notation is significantly less so. As opposed to the neumes

---

[114] David Hiley, *Western Plainchant: A Handbook* (Oxford: Clarendon Press, 1993), 56; M. Huglo and J. W. McKinnon, "Gospel (i)," Grove Music Online, http://www.oxfordmusiconline.com/subscriber/article/grove/music/11500.

[115] Huglo and McKinnon, "Gospel (i)".

[116] Hiley, *Western Plainchant*, 56; Huglo and McKinnon, "Gospel (i)"; Mark Alan Singer, "Evidence for an Early English Plenary Missal: The Flyleaves of MS Bodley 386," *Manuscripta* 57, no. 1 (2013).

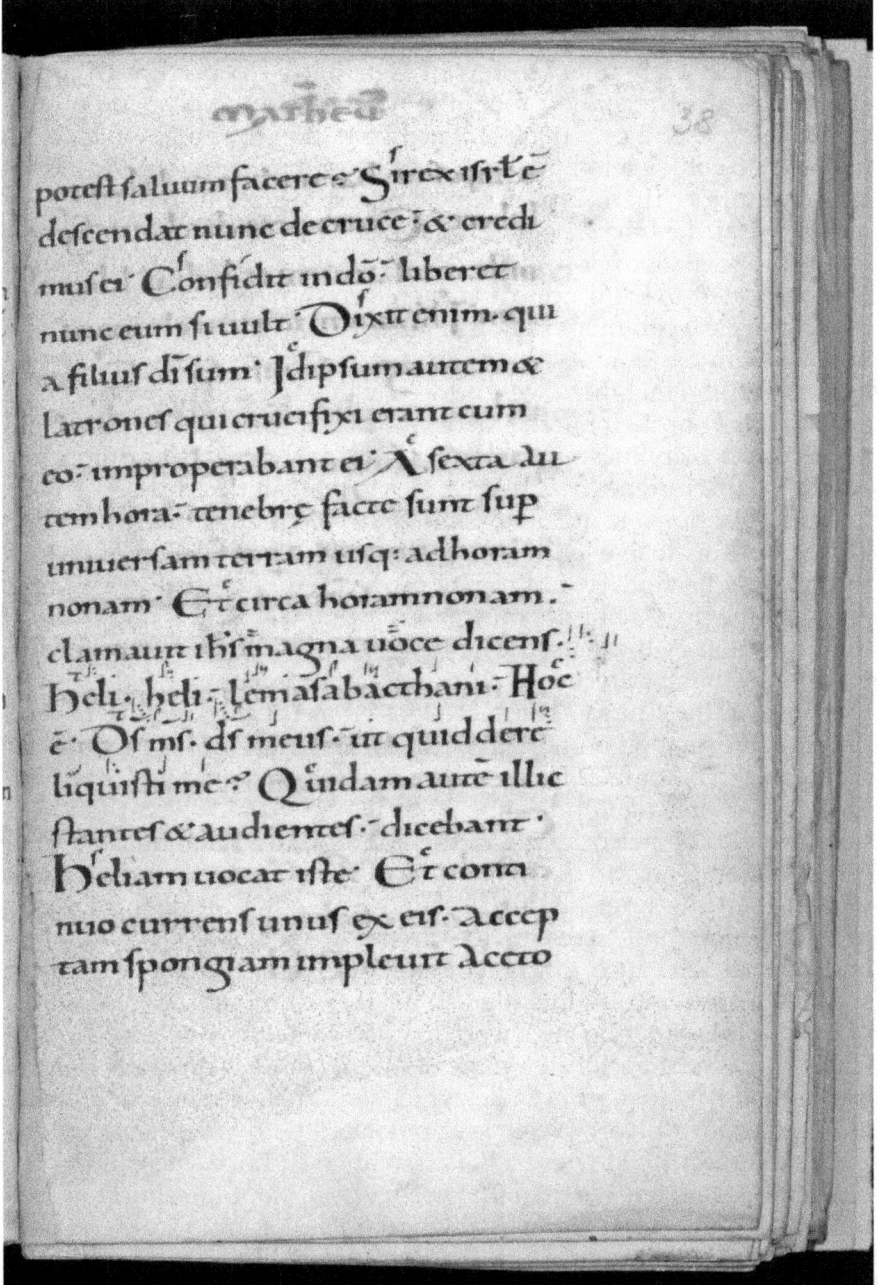

Plate 7: Warsaw, Biblioteka Narodowa, I. 3311, f. 38r. Neumes added to Matthew 27:46, part of the reading for Palm Sunday.

for the Passion, the notation that has been added to Matthew 4:18–22 appears only above certain syllables and is relatively sparse and significantly less elaborate. On top of signalling a departure from the standard gospel recitation tone, the neumes here appear to be indicating the cadence of a non-standard recitation formula, which does not seem to conform to the standard tone used in books of the modern Roman liturgy. The use of a non-standard recitation tone here may indicate that the church where this book was used had a particular interest in the cult of St Andrew. It is indeed possible that this church was dedicated to St Andrew and therefore showed a specific interest in the liturgical commemoration of his feast day. The addition of these neumes with a different ink and by a different hand may strengthen the supposition that these were added by the users of the book and are an intimation of the church's dedication. If this is the case, there are numerous possibilities for its localization, as a significant number of Anglo-Saxon churches bear dedications to this saint, such as Greensted in Essex, Bishopstone in Sussex, and Wroxeter, among many others.[117] This is not conclusive evidence of a location of production or use for the Warsaw Lectionary, but it may prove useful in future attempts to establish the provenance of this manuscript.

In addition to the presence of neumes in the Warsaw Lectionary, there are other performance directions that demonstrate the use of this book in the liturgy. These are known as *litterae significativae* and provide information on how to perform the text. Various sections are marked with *c* (for *celeriter*), some with *s* (for *sursum*), and some with *t* (for *tenere* or *tarde*), indicating both the speed at which these sections were to be performed and the appropriate recitation tone for a given section. The *litterae significativae* in this book are found far more widely than the brief neumed sections, covering all of the Passion from Matthew and much of the Passion from Luke. This notation has internal relevance to the telling of the Passion, as the narrative sections were typically intended to be performed *celeriter*, the words of the disciples and the Jews were marked *sursum*, while the words of Christ were to be performed more slowly or more elaborately. Part of the Passion narrative from Luke, which would have been read at mass on Wednesday of Holy Week, is also notated with *litterae significativae* in this manuscript. However, the annotation in Luke's account of the Passion is less extensive than that in Matthew, stopping short towards the end of Luke 22. It is unclear why the Passion from Luke was not fully notated, but the presence of *litterae significativae*, combined with

---

[117] Lawrence Butler, "Church Dedication and the Cults of Anglo-Saxon Saints in England," in *The Anglo-Saxon Church: Papers on History, Architecture, and Archaeology in Honour of Dr H. M. Taylor*, ed. Butler and Richard Morris (London: Council for British Archaeology, 1986), 44.

Priests' Books for the Mass and Office

the neumatic notation from Matthew, points to the liturgical use of this book within the mass.

This reappraisal of Warsaw, Biblioteka Narodowa, I. 3311 has shown that both sections of this manuscript were used in the liturgy. This is demonstrated through the congruence of the readings in the first section of the book with the main liturgical festivals of the year, the complementary pattern evident from the tabulation of the pericopes from both parts of the manuscript and the musical notation and performance directions throughout the book. Furthermore, the presence of musical notation at f. 17v may offer some indication that this manuscript was used at a church dedicated to St Andrew. The readings contained in the Warsaw Lectionary focus on Sundays and the primary liturgical events of the year, suggesting that the book was intended for a secular priest or small clerical community whose primary purpose was the provision of pastoral care. The relatively limited range of readings contained in this book is unlikely to have been suitable for the more extensive liturgical celebrations that took place in monasteries, cathedrals, and even larger secular minsters. Indeed, this is the type of book that we might expect a small Anglo-Saxon clerical community or parochially oriented priest to own – a small, portable, and modestly decorated book that provides the pericopes needed for the performance of the mass.

The Junius Psalter (Oxford, Bodleian Library, Junius 27)

This manuscript, briefly mentioned earlier in this chapter, is a *Psalterium Romanum* typically associated with Winchester and probably copied in the 920s.[118] Like a number of other well-known Anglo-Saxon psalters, the Junius Psalter contains a continuous Old English gloss of the Latin text that conforms to the A-type gloss found in the Vespasian Psalter (London, British Library, Cotton Vespasian A. I). The scribe responsible for the bulk of the Latin text, and possibly the gloss as well, may have been the scribe of a portion of the Parker Chronicle (Cambridge, Corpus Christi College 173) and the Lauderdale Orosius (London, British Library, Add. 47967), manuscripts that were at least produced in the same scriptorium, an association that points to a Winchester origin

---

[118] The date and localization of this manuscript largely rest on arguments made by Malcolm Parkes and Francis Wormald. Parkes, "The Palaeography of the Parker Manuscript of the Chronicle, Laws and Sedulius, and Historiography at Winchester in the Late Ninth and Tenth Centuries," in *Scribes, Scripts, and Readers: Studies in the Communication, Presentation, and Dissemination of Medieval Texts* (London: Hambledon Press, 1991), 158–60; F. Wormald, "The 'Winchester School' before St. Æthelwold," in *Collected Writings I: Studies in Medieval Art from the Sixth to the Twelfth Centuries*, ed. J. J. G. Alexander, T. J. Brown, and Joan Gibbs (London: Harvey Miller, 1988), 76–78.

for the psalter.[119] The paleographical and art historical associations of this manuscript probably indicate its production at Winchester during the episcopate of Frithestan (909–931), which Mechthild Gretsch has suggested may have relevance for the later use of the manuscript by Æthelwold.[120]

The text of the Psalms is used in both the mass and Office and despite the scholarly attention that Junius 27 has received due to its early date, gloss, and association with Winchester, the liturgical function of this book remained largely unexplored until its brief mention by Billett in reference to the performance of the Office by the Anglo-Saxon secular clergy. As both Billett and Gretsch have pointed out, the psalms in this book are divided liturgically according to the secular *cursus*, "with the first psalm sung at the Night Office on each day of the week given special decoration".[121] The divisions apparent in the Junius Psalter in fact imply a continuation of the celebration of an archaic form of the Roman Office stretching back to the early days of Anglo-Saxon Christianity, as is indicated by the witness of two early English psalters.[122] The psalm text is further divided into three sets of fifty, at Psalms 1, 51, and 101. Additionally, the calendar of this manuscript, while relatively brief, is liturgically oriented, unlike the calendar that was added to the Æthelstan Psalter (London, British Library, Cotton Galba A. XVIII). Much of the material in the calendar in Junius 27 was in fact adapted from this earlier psalter and calendar: all of the twenty-eight entries recorded in verse are drawn from the calendar recorded in the Æthelstan Psalter and 87 of 98 prose entries agree with those of its primary source.[123] In addition, the source material from the Æthelstan Psalter was adapted by those responsible for the production of Junius 27 to fit their immediate needs.[124] A calendar like the Metrical Calendar of Hampson, the calendar found in the Æthelstan Psalter, is impractical for liturgical use, and thus it was necessary to bring in more practical, liturgically oriented material and pare the calendar down. As a result, the calendar of the Junius Psalter

---

[119] Mechthild Gretsch, "The Junius Psalter Gloss: Its Historical and Cultural Context," *Anglo-Saxon England* 29 (2000): 89, 99.

[120] Mechthild Gretsch, *The Intellectual Foundations of the English Benedictine Reform* (Cambridge: Cambridge University Press, 1999), 328–30.

[121] Billett, "The Divine Office and the Secular Clergy," 442; Gretsch, "The Junius Psalter Gloss," 116. On the divisions of psalters, particularly those for the secular Office, see Hughes, *Medieval Manuscripts for Mass and Office*, 50–52; Phillip Pulsiano, "Psalters," in Pfaff, *The Liturgical Books of Anglo-Saxon England*, 72–73.

[122] Billett, *The Divine Office in Anglo-Saxon England*, 141–42.

[123] Gretsch, "The Junius Psalter Gloss," 108.

[124] For an in-depth study of this calendar, see Dumville, *Liturgy and the Ecclesiastical History of Late Anglo-Saxon England*, 1–38. Dumville posits a Canterbury origin for the Junius Psalter, a conclusion that does not seem to be generally accepted.

is far more suitable for liturgical use than its main source. Overall, the form and contents of the Junius Psalter make a strong case for its liturgical use, and the division of the psalms particularly points to its potential for use in the celebration of the Divine Office. Additionally, the strong association of this manuscript with pre-reform Winchester, prior to the expulsion of the secular clerics serving the Old and New Minsters, suggests its production and use by the secular clergy of Winchester.

From an art historical perspective, the decoration of the Junius Psalter was influential, inspiring decoration in the Bosworth Psalter (London, British Library, Add. 37517) and other manuscripts. But intriguingly, despite its Winchester connections, the Junius Psalter seems to have exerted little to no influence on manuscripts produced at Winchester in the episcopate of Æthelwold, beginning approximately thirty years after the production of the book. In addition, the "Saxonization" of the A-type gloss copied into Junius 27 seems not to have influenced the Royal Psalter (London, British Library, Royal 2. B. V), another psalter carrying the same Vespasian-based gloss that was produced at Winchester during Æthelwold's tenure. Furthermore, examples of manuscript art from monastic Winchester, such as the Benedictional of St Æthelwold (London, British Library, Add. 49598) and the foundation charter of the New Minster, do not incorporate design elements from the Junius Psalter that were influential in other manuscripts.[125] Two immediate possibilities present themselves: either Æthelwold wished to suppress the contents of this book or the book was no longer at one of the main ecclesiastical centers of Winchester. Gretsch endorses the former supposition on the grounds that the clerical establishment at Winchester, including Frithestan, who was likely responsible in some sense for the production of the Junius Psalter, was at odds with King Æthelstan in the early years of his reign. Æthelwold spent his early career in the king's household however, leading Gretsch to suggest that the book was deliberately suppressed because of Æthelwold's association of the Junius Psalter with the clerical opposition to Æthelstan.[126] Though this is possible, there is a simpler hypothesis that might both explain this book's lack of influence at Winchester and Dumville's argument for a Canterbury origin.

It seems clear that this psalter was written with thought to its use in the secular Office. Considering the emphasis placed on the celebration

---

[125] For a list of manuscripts influenced by the type of art appearing in Junius 27, see F. Wormald, "Decorated Initials in English Manuscripts from A.D. 900 to 1100," in Alexander, Brown, and Gibbs, *Collected Writings I: Studies in Medieval Art*, 72–75.

[126] Gretsch, *The Intellectual Foundations*, 328–31.

of the monastic Office by the Benedictine reformers in England, it could be that this psalter would have been considered unsuitable for practical reasons, as the Benedictine *cursus* for the Office utilized psalm divisions significantly different from those of the secular *cursus*. Later in the tenth century, the type of decoration utilized in Junius 27 seems to have influenced book production at Canterbury and it could be that Æthelwold sold or gifted this book to Canterbury, the community of which was not wholly monastic until the 1020s or later.[127] It is of course difficult to point decisively to the influence of the Junius Psalter on Canterbury manuscripts, but considering the popularity of this kind of decoration in Canterbury manuscripts and what would appear to be the book's absence from Winchester, Canterbury stands out as a possibility.[128] Dispersal of the service books used by the secular clerics at Winchester by Æthelwold might too explain the lack of surviving liturgical manuscripts from either the Old or New Minster prior to 964. Though not impossible, Gretsch's theory relies heavily on speculation concerning Æthelwold's personal relationships prior to his episcopacy; using the witness of the Junius Psalter itself to elucidate the reasoning behind its lack of influence at post-reform Winchester may place our analysis on firmer footing.

The Junius Psalter is a unique manuscript and potentially the only liturgical book of the pre-reform clerics at Winchester to have survived. It is unlikely to have been the book of a local priest, as some of the other books in this chapter may be, but the divisions of the psalm text imply that this manuscript was intended for liturgical use and the creation of the calendar by abbreviating and adapting its voluminous source further suggests that this is a manuscript for practical use in the liturgy of the Divine Office. Additionally, I have argued that this manuscript exerted little to no influence at Winchester during and after Æthelwold's episcopate because this book and the other liturgical books not suitable for monastic use were dispersed by the bishop; this psalter in particular may have gone to Canterbury. Though the Junius Psalter is now an isolated example of a liturgically oriented psalter for the secular clergy, and seemingly the lone surviving example of the books of the secular clerics at Winchester, it is nonetheless evidence for a tradition of performance of the secular Office in the first half of the tenth century.

---

[127] Nicholas Brooks, *The Early History of the Church of Canterbury: Christ Church from 597 to 1066* (Leicester: Leicester University Press, 1984), 255–56.
[128] See note 125.

Manuscript fragments

In an examination of the liturgical books used by priests in late Anglo-Saxon England, fragments constitute a significant body of evidence. Most common among these are fragments of missals, with dozens of extant examples.[129] Due to the mutability of liturgical trends, outdated mass-books were often used in the binding of later manuscripts, with Anglo-Saxon missal fragments being used in the bindings of manuscripts produced from the High Middle Ages to the early modern period. We can learn a great deal from these fragments and at the very least they serve to indicate that liturgical books, and fragments of mass-books in particular, were more numerous than a review of the manuscripts that have survived more or less intact would lead one to believe. It has been proposed that at least one Anglo-Saxon missal fragment was used and potentially produced by a priest and the now-scattered missal fragments from Exeter were probably also intended for priests in the cathedral community, leaving little doubt that concerted study of the body of Anglo-Saxon fragments would yield indications of use by secular priests.[130]

But the survival of this expanding group of missal fragments can tell us more about trends in Anglo-Saxon priests' books than can a single example. The move away from the sacramentary and towards the missal, which had started in Italy in the eighth century, came at a time in which liturgical responsibilities within the celebration of mass increasingly fell to priests.[131] More telling however is the architectural and documentary evidence that accompanies the change in English mass-books. These changes in the ecclesiastical landscape are attested in the Wulfstan-composed lawcodes VIII Æthelred and I Cnut, both of which demarcate the "chief minster", a "minster of the middle class", a smaller minster, and a field church, as well as the monetary penalties to be paid for violating the sanctuary of each category.[132] Excavations have revealed small churches which were first built in wood, beginning roughly in the mid-tenth century, many of which were later expanded and rebuilt in stone, representing the

---

[129] Susan Rankin, "An Early Eleventh-Century Missal Fragment Copied by Eadwig Basan: MS. Lat. Liturg. D. 3, Fols. 4–5," *Bodleian Library Record* 18 (2004): 238.

[130] Singer, "Evidence for an Early English Plenary Missal," *passim*. Susan Rankin, "From Memory to Record: Musical Notations in Manuscripts from Exeter," *Anglo-Saxon England* 13 (1984): 102.

[131] Vogel, *Medieval Liturgy*, 105.

[132] Whitelock, *English Historical Documents*, 449. I Cnut incorporated a great deal of material from VIII Æthelred, including the section containing the penalties for breach of church sanctuary.

lower tiers of the legal classification of churches.[133] Both the size and the limited financial resources of such foundations likely mean that they were typically staffed by a single priest tasked with the saying of mass, performance of occasional offices, and other forms of pastoral care. For these priests, a missal would have been supremely practical and convenient, combining multiple discrete volumes into one and significantly simplifying the saying of mass by a single individual. Therefore, the concurrence of the multiplication of local churches with the proliferation of missals by the end of the tenth century and into the eleventh may be an indication that these books were at least in part produced to meet demand in these churches. While many of the surviving fragments may never be associated with parochial use, the production of missals in such numbers indicates a trend that may have been related to the need for practical mass-books for the local clergy.

Conclusions

Several of the secular minster churches discussed in this chapter must have had significant bibliographical resources to allow them to function as they did. Large, well-staffed minsters like Twynham and Waltham were probably celebrating at least two masses per day, the full round of the Divine Office, and must too have been in some way involved in pastoral care to the laity. This sort of observance would have required a large number of liturgical texts such as mass-books, chant books, psalters, and books for liturgical readings. In light of this evidence, scholars have perhaps underestimated the availability of books in and to minsters. The often-generous endowment of minsters by Anglo-Saxon royalty and nobility reinforces the plausibility of this supposition, as does the book list from Sherburn-in-Elmet. But even minster churches for which no record of aristocratic patronage has survived cast doubt on the pessimism expressed towards the bookholdings of secular churches. The marginal scribe of Corpus 41, who probably served at a secular minster or even a smaller church, had access to a significant number of liturgical texts for copying and clearly had experiential knowledge of chant texts for the Office and musical notation. These indicators should prompt reevaluation of scholarly views on the availability of liturgical books to secular priests and thus their ability to provide pastoral care and perform the liturgy.

In addition, this chapter has examined surprisingly strong evidence for the celebration of the Divine Office in minor churches. Well-staffed

---

[133] Gittos, *Liturgy, Architecture, and Sacred Places*, 179–80.

and generously endowed minsters like those at Waltham, Twynham, and Stow seem to have observed the full round of the daily offices, and other evidence, such as the large number of Office chants in Corpus 41, would seem to indicate that smaller and less wealthy Anglo-Saxon secular churches also celebrated the Divine Office. This gives credence to prescriptive texts like Ælfric's pastoral letters and the *Canons of Edgar* which call for the celebration of the Office by all priests.[134] Additionally, laypersons seem to have taken a greater interest in the Divine Office than has previously been recognized. The nobility certainly showed interest in the celebration of the Office, as Leofric and Godiva endowed Stow and enjoined the observance of the canonical hours, and Alfred's handbook contained office texts for the day hours in addition to the Psalms. Additionally, attendance at Vespers by the non-elite laity appears to be indicated at both Waltham and Twynham, and this may have been common in churches where the Office was regularly celebrated. Attendance at Vespers seems to have been common and expected in England in the later Middle Ages, an observance that may have its roots in the Anglo-Saxon period.[135]

With regard to manuscripts, it has been shown that the Warsaw Lectionary, contrary to previous thought, was suitable for liturgical use in light of an analysis of its readings and the presence of musical notation and performance indicators. Additionally, the book almost exclusively presents readings for Sundays and the major liturgical feasts of the year, making it likely that it was utilized by a small clerical community or a single priest rather than by a community with more elaborate liturgical needs. On the other hand, the Red Book of Darley is a complex and at times frustrating volume that cannot be placed with certainty in a secular context due to its liturgical texts with monastic associations. We can however see that the Red Book of Darley is a type of book that would be very useful to a secular priest, containing all the texts needed in a portable format, and similar, unambiguously secular books of this kind may have existed. Junius 27 is a psalter certainly designed for the celebration of the secular *cursus* of the Divine Office and may have been used for this purpose by the pre-reform canons at Winchester. It may be the only Winchester liturgical manuscript surviving from prior to Æthelwold's tenure as bishop and as such is a valuable witness to liturgical activities at Winchester prior to the 960s, after which Æthelwold may have dispersed the books used by the secular clerics. Corpus 41, while the main text is not liturgical, is another important witness to the mass and Office texts that were available to a secular cleric in England in the mid-eleventh century,

---

[134] Whitelock, Brett, and Brooke, *Councils and Synods*, 206, 329.
[135] Eamon Duffy, *The Stripping of the Altars: Traditional Religion in England, c.1400–c.1580* (New Haven: Yale University Press, 1992), 11.

informing us about the bibliographical resources of the church in which he served and the libraries to which he had access. Particularly striking is the large number of Office chants, the most of any Anglo-Saxon manuscript, and the scribe's familiarity with the content of these chants as well as musical notation.

6

Locating Penitentials, Manuals, and *Computi*

Around 800, a small booklet containing the *Penitential of Egbert* was copied out in an Anglo-Saxon hand practicing Insular minuscule either in England or at Lorsch, an Anglo-Saxon monastic foundation in the modern German state of Hesse. Shortly after the date of its copying, this booklet was supplemented with further penitential material, and the original penitential plus these additions constitute what is now Vatican, Pal. lat. 554. At just thirteen folios, including the additions, and measuring 250 × 185 mm, this brief collection would have been portable and inexpensive to produce, taking a scribe only a few days to copy it.[1] Despite their obvious utility, booklets like this one from the Vatican are rare: only a few Anglo-Saxon booklets of any kind survive and this is the only penitential booklet with English connections of which I am aware. Nonetheless, the Vatican booklet is illustrative of the way in which short texts may often have been efficiently and cheaply produced for priestly use.

Unlike missals, lectionaries, or collections of homilies, the types of priestly texts discussed in this chapter do not stand alone in surviving Anglo-Saxon manuscripts. Instead, most of the examples that survive are bound with other books and no surviving late Anglo-Saxon manuscript contains penitentials, computistical material, or liturgical texts for occasional offices alone. Thus penitentials, manuals, and *computi* have been grouped here in one chapter – not due to a similarity of content, but rather to a similarity of context. As these types of texts were often relatively short, they could easily be combined with other volumes, as are our surviving examples, or they could be used in booklet or loose-leaf form, a state in which their chances of survival are slim to none. One can imagine the ease with which a few folios with no protective binding could be lost, and continental sources from the

---

[1] Reinhold Haggenmüller, *Die Überlieferung der Beda und Egbert zugeschriebenen Bußbücher* (Frankfurt: Peter Lang, 1991), 108; David Ganz, "Book Production in the Carolingian Empire and the Spread of Caroline Minuscule," in *The New Cambridge Medieval History Volume 2: c.700–c.900*, ed. Rosamond McKitterick (Cambridge: Cambridge University Press, 1995), 792. Ganz estimates that a "skilled scribe" could copy approximately seven pages of twenty-five lines per day.

twelfth-century express concerns about the vulnerability of *libelli* to theft, destruction, or wear.[2] We are also faced with the problem of how representative these rites are, especially when considering regional differences, poor survival rates, and questions concerning their oral performance. As Carol Symes has pointed out, written liturgical texts are essentially prescriptive in nature and it is often difficult to know precisely how these texts were used in worship.[3]

Despite potential uncertainty about the ways in which these fragile collections might have been used and transmitted, the material that they contain was vital to the duties of a priest. The manual in particular contained rites fundamental to life in the Christian community, such as baptism and spiritual care for those near death. Penitentials facilitated the practice of private penance, a pastoral duty that bishops were keen to emphasize in the late Anglo-Saxon period.[4] The computus allowed the priest to calculate the date of Easter and other moveable feasts, and correct computation was vital to the medieval church in maintaining Christian unity and liturgical uniformity. Since these texts have always survived in volumes containing other material, an examination of the manuscripts in which they are contained, along with some of the texts themselves, will help to contextualize their use.

The penitential tradition of Anglo-Saxon England

Despite the objections of some scholars in regard to its actual use in pastoral care, the penitential is found in all but one of the prescriptive booklists discussed in chapter 1, where I have argued that it was one of the books that formed the core of expected priestly texts.[5] The earliest penitentials seem to have been introduced to the English through Irish missionaries at least by the seventh century. The extent to which these texts were used in the early Anglo-Saxon church is unknown, but the apparent export of English penitentials to the Continent through the missionary efforts of the eighth century, including those purportedly

---

[2] Carol Symes, "Liturgical Texts and Performance Practices," in *Understanding Medieval Liturgy: Essays in Interpretation*, ed. Helen Gittos and Sarah Hamilton (Farnham: Ashgate, 2015), 245–46.

[3] Ibid., 239–41.

[4] Dorothy Whitelock, Martin Brett, and Christopher N. L. Brooke, eds., *Councils and Synods, with Other Documents Relating to the English Church, AD 871–1204*, vol. 1 (Oxford: Clarendon Press, 1981), 213–15, 295, 335, 454.

[5] For skepticism concerning lay confession in the early Middle Ages and the use of penitentials in pastoral care, see Alexander Murray, "Confession before 1215," *Transactions of the Royal Historical Society*, 6th ser., 3 (1993); Franz Kerff, "Libri paenitentiales und kirchliche Strafgerichtsbarkeit bis zum Decretum Gratiani. Ein Diskussionsvorschlag," *Zeitschrift der Savigny-Stiftung für Rechtsgeschichte. Kanonistische Abteilung* 75 (1989).

associated with well-known Anglo-Saxon churchmen, suggests not only familiarity with these types of texts, but also that the practices imported by the Irish were put into action in the English church.[6] In the reforms of the Carolingian period, the penitentials imported to continental Europe by Anglo-Saxon missionaries were utilized and adapted while new penitentials were also composed, such as the penitential written by Halitgar, Bishop of Cambrai, and the *Liber poenitentium* of Hrabanus Maurus. Allen Frantzen has argued that in the course of the tenth century, penitential texts, some of which were composed in England centuries earlier, were reintroduced to the Anglo-Saxon church.[7] Though this certainly took place in the mid-tenth century under reforming monastic bishops, the importation of penitentials from the continent may have taken place earlier than the manuscript evidence would suggest. The laws of Alfred, composed c. 890, require that an oath-breaker "compensate that surety-breaking as justice directs, and that pledge-breaking as his confessor prescribes".[8] Æthelstan's Grately code, probably dating to the late 920s, similarly requires a confessor to inform his bishop whether an oath-breaker has accepted the penance prescribed for him; II Edmund also refers to ecclesiastical penalties involving confession for particular breaches of the law.[9] This would imply not only that private penance was already being practiced in the late ninth and early tenth centuries, but also that texts for the assignment of penance were available. Indeed, Catherine Cubitt has argued that the connections between penance and law in this early period indicate that "the discipline of penance was deeply embedded in the regulation of Anglo-Saxon society", an impossible state of affairs without the availability of texts with which to assign penance.[10] It is unclear how these texts came to prominence in the late ninth and early tenth centuries, but the continental scholars brought to England under the auspices of Alfred and his successors provide a plausible, if conjectural, means of transmission for penitentials.[11]

---

[6] For the history of these early texts, see Allen J. Frantzen, "The Tradition of Penitentials in Anglo-Saxon England," *Anglo-Saxon England* 11 (1982): 27–35.

[7] Frantzen, *The Literature of Penance in Anglo-Saxon England* (New Brunswick, NJ: Rutgers University Press, 1983), 122–23.

[8] "Gif þær ðonne oþer mennisc borg sie, bete þone borgbryce swa him ryht wisie, 7 ðone wedbryce swa him his scrift scrife." Todd Preston, *King Alfred's Book of Laws: A Study of the* Domboc *and Its Influence on English Identity, with a Complete Translation* (Jefferson, NC: McFarland, 2012), 119.

[9] *English Historical Documents*, ed. David C. Douglas, vol. 1, *c. 500–1042*, ed. Dorothy Whitelock (London: Eyre Methuen, 1979), 422, 428. Catherine Cubitt also utilizes these examples; see note 10.

[10] Catherine Cubitt, "Individual and Collective Sinning in Tenth- and Eleventh-Century England: Penance, Piety and the Law," in *Religion und Politik im Mittelalter: Deutschland und England im Vergleich*, ed. Ludger Körntgen and Dominik Waßenhoven (Berlin: De Gruyter, 2013), 57–58.

[11] Frantzen, *Literature of Penance*, 127–28.

Regardless of the means of transmission, penitentials were again absorbed into English ecclesiastical culture and by the second half of the tenth century and possibly earlier, new English penitentials had been composed, this time in the vernacular.[12] These new penitentials come into focus in the manuscripts known as "commonplace books", and we find most of the late Anglo-Saxon manuscript evidence for penitentials in this type of volume. In addition to penitentials, these manuscripts typically contain collections of canon law, the writings of the Fathers, texts from Carolingian writers and reformers, and preaching texts. Manuscripts of this kind connected with Archbishop Wulfstan, approximately ten of which survive, frequently contain penitentials and it has been asserted that he certainly knew and may have even been the author of the Old English penitential termed by Fowler the *Late Old English Handbook for the Use of a Confessor* (hereafter *Old English Handbook*).[13] After the early eleventh century, there is little evidence for the composition of new penitentials in England, but these texts were certainly still being copied. Oxford, Bodleian Library, Laud Misc. 482 was copied at Worcester in the mid-eleventh century and contains two vernacular penitentials, while the fragmentary Cambridge, University Library, Add. 3206, a product of the second quarter of the eleventh century, transmits much of the *Old English Handbook*. The first manuscript certainly had a pastoral function while the unfortunately fragmentary state of the second forestalls a firm determination of its purpose. In addition to this, some of the "commonplace book" manuscripts transmitting vernacular penitential texts were copied up until the third quarter of the eleventh century.[14] The sum of this manuscript evidence certainly indicates continuing interest in and likely practical use of penitentials up to the end of the eleventh century, though there may have been a shift in pastoral priorities after the Conquest under some non-native bishops.[15]

---

[12] Frantzen, "Tradition of Penitentials," 40–42.

[13] Hans Sauer, "The Transmission and Structure of Archbishop Wulfstan's 'Commonplace Book'," in *Old English Prose: Basic Readings*, ed. Paul Szarmach and Deborah Oosterhouse (New York: Garland, 2000), 340–43; Melanie Heyworth, "The 'Late Old English Handbook for the Use of a Confessor': Authorship and Connections," *Notes and Queries* 54, no. 3 (2007).

[14] Sauer, "Transmission and Structure," 341. Cambridge, Corpus Christi College 265 and Oxford, Bodleian Library, Junius 121, both of which contain significant penitential material, have been dated s. xi med. (possibly $xi^{3/4}$) and s. $xi^{3/4}$ respectively.

[15] Sarah Hamilton, "Rites of Passage and Pastoral Care," in *A Social History of England, 900–1200*, ed. Julia Crick and Elisabeth van Houts (Cambridge: Cambridge University Press, 2011), 306–7.

The assignment of penance and its practice

A large number of penitentials saw use in the early medieval period and most of them are simple sources which are relatively uniform in their structure and guidance to the priest utilizing them. They typically give instruction and explanation to the confessor at the beginning, with many from the late eighth century onward providing an *ordo* for confession, and from there simply consist of lists of sins and their corresponding penances.[16] It is important to note the presence or absence of confession *ordines* prior to the tariff lists central to most penitentials, as a copy of a penitential lacking an *ordo* might have been less likely to see pastoral use.[17] Additionally, the introductory matter of a penitential often gives some guidance for the confessor in the assignment of penance and exhorts the priest to take into account mitigating factors such as age and health in his judgement. The *Old English Handbook* reminds the confessor that "you must never pass judgment in the same way on the powerful and the lowly, the free and the enslaved, the old and the young, the well and the sickly, the humble and the proud; the strong and the weak, those in orders and lay people".[18] The *Penitential of Halitgar*, a translation of which makes up the majority of the *Old English Penitential*, similarly advises confessors to consider a penitent's financial and personal status when commuting fasts and exhorts them to be particularly lenient with slaves.[19] Though priests were to tailor their judgements to each individual, the actual

---

[16] Sarah Hamilton, *The Practice of Penance, 900–1050* (Woodbridge: Boydell Press, 2001), 44. I do not address public penance in this volume for two reasons. Firstly, though rites for public penance do appear in some Anglo-Saxon liturgical books, the practice seems to have been relatively uncommon in the late Anglo-Saxon period; as M. Bradford Bedingfield has pointed out, the Anglo-Saxon penitential system was "heavily dominated by private penance". Secondly, priests seem not to have been involved in overseeing public penance, as the most serious sins would be referred to the bishop for judgement and the reconciliation of penitents and excommunicates was an episcopal duty in this period. Bedingfield, "Public Penance in Anglo-Saxon England," *Anglo-Saxon England* 31 (2002): 224, 229; Hamilton, "Remedies for 'Great Transgressions': Penance and Excommunication in Late Anglo-Saxon England," in *Pastoral Care in Late Anglo-Saxon England*, ed. Francesca Tinti (Woodbridge: Boydell Press, 2005), 92.

[17] Hamilton, *The Practice of Penance*, 44.

[18] "[G]eþengc ðu. þæt þu ne scealt næfre gelice deman. þam rícan & þam héanan. þam freon & þam þeowan · þam ealdan & þam geongan · þam halan · & þam unhalan. þam eadmodan & þam ofermodan. þam strangan & þam unmagan. þam gehadodum & þam læwedum." I have reproduced this text as translated and transcribed by Frantzen. *Old English Handbook*, ed. Frantzen, "Corpus 201 (D) 115," in *Anglo-Saxon Penitentials: A Cultural Database*, accessed February 15, 2018, http://anglo-saxon.net/penance/index.php?p=TOEH201_115.

[19] John T. McNeill and Helena M. Gamer, eds. and trans., *Medieval Handbooks of*

penances recommended in penitentials form a fairly static group of observances. Fasting is the most commonly prescribed penance, followed closely by almsgiving and psalm-singing. The length and severity of penance could vary considerably: fairly minor sins might involve saying a hundred psalms, while the penances recommended for the most serious sins are fasts of ten years or more. It is important to note however, that fasting did not entail complete abstinence from food, but rather consisted of fasting on certain days of the week, fasting more strictly during Lent and other periods of ritual fasting, and avoidance of high-status food items.[20]

In addition to the role of penance as a facet of pastoral care, recent scholarship has emphasized the practical role that penance and penitential language played in early medieval society and particularly in the politics of the early medieval period. Louis the Pious was famously removed from power through a penitential ceremony that was pregnant with political meaning, but Carolingian Francia was not the only stage on which penitential drama took place.[21] Despite their focus on the royalty and nobility of early medieval Europe, political uses of penance provide some insight into the way in which penance may have actually taken place as opposed to its prescription in penitential texts. For example, some of the charters of Æthelred the Unready utilize penitential vocabulary in his admission of wrongdoing in the early years of his reign. One of these in particular records a grant of privileges to Abingdon made at Pentecost in 993, capitalizing on the penitential character of one of the great feasts of the liturgical year, and the penitential theme of Æthelred's reign was furthered via the kingdom-wide fast instituted through royal legislation in 1009.[22] The political use of penitential practices in the latter case is unmistakeable: a mandatory fast was instituted, processions were to be held, and priests and reeves were to hold the people accountable for their observance of the fast. Practices of this kind were not confined to the highest levels of medieval government, however. An individual example of this political function of penitential acts can be seen in the case of a nobleman named Ælfwold, who made a very public display of his remorse for

---

Penance: A Translation of the Principal Libri Poenitentiales *and Selections from Related Documents* (New York: Columbia University Press, 1965), 299.

[20] Frantzen, *Literature of Penance*, 16; Frantzen, *Food, Eating and Identity in Early Medieval England* (Woodbridge: Boydell Press, 2014), 232.

[21] Mayke de Jong, "Power and Humility in Carolingian Society: The Public Penance of Louis the Pious," *Early Medieval Europe* 1, no. 1 (1992).

[22] See Catherine Cubitt, "The Politics of Remorse: Penance and Royal Piety in the Reign of Æthelred the Unready," *Historical Research* 85 (2012); De Jong, "Power and Humility in Carolingian Society"; Simon Keynes, "An Abbot, an Archbishop, and the Viking Raids of 1006–7 and 1009–12," *Anglo-Saxon England* 36 (2007).

ordering the murder of another aristocrat, ostensibly because the aristocrat was intent on despoiling the lands of Peterborough. Traveling to Winchester and walking barefoot through the city to meet with Æthelwold, Ælfwold was met by a procession of the bishop and his clergy, and the account utilizes some vocabulary similar to penitential *ordines* from contemporary pontificals.[23] This intersection of politics and penance shows the degree to which penance was ingrained in the culture of the late Anglo-Saxon period. Kings and the nobility were of course influenced by the clerical element present in their entourages, but these displays of penance would not have been undertaken if they were not understood as a type of religious and political language that had external meaning for its intended audience and often had internal meaning for the penitent.

Penitential books and their use

Like books for the celebration of the mass and Office, penitentials were mutable texts that were prone to going out of fashion and, at times, suppression by ecclesiastical authorities. In 829, Carolingian bishops ordered that *libelli* containing erroneous penitential texts were to be burned, and more than two centuries later, Peter Damian wrote in the *Liber gomorrhianus* that the *Penitential of Egbert* consisted of "diabolical figments instituted to deceive the souls of the simple with cunning devices".[24] Despite the opposition to certain penitentials deemed unfit for use, these texts were seen as necessary in prescriptive lists in both Carolingian episcopal capitula and Anglo-Saxon sources.

As fairly short texts, penitentials are most often preserved in manuscripts that contain other sorts of material. Penitential texts could be bound with or written into liturgical books, though English examples from the tenth and eleventh centuries are limited. Rob Meens has identified four such continental manuscripts, one of which is bound with a sacramentary and martyrology, while another contains various liturgical texts related to penance in addition to the *Paenitentiale Vallicellianum I*.[25] Furthermore, penitentials that were bound with collections of canon law on the continent seem to have been significantly more likely to survive than purely pastoral volumes, a phenomenon

---

[23] Michael Lapidge, ed. and trans., *Byrhtferth of Ramsey: The Lives of St Oswald and St Ecgwine* (Oxford: Clarendon Press, 2009), 129–32.

[24] Hamilton, *The Practice of Penance*, 6; Frantzen, *Literature of Penance*, 148.

[25] Rob Meens, "The Frequency and Nature of Early Medieval Penance," in *Handling Sin: Confession in the Middle Ages*, ed. Peter Biller and A. J. Minnis (York: York Medieval Press, 1998), 43. The manuscripts in question are Berlin, Deutsche Staadtsbibliothek, Phillips 1667 and Rome, Bibliotecha Vallicelliana, E 15.

that has likely distorted our view of their distribution.[26] A similar trend is apparent for England, where penitentials are for the most part preserved in commonplace books such as Oxford, Bodleian Library, Junius 121 and Cambridge, Corpus Christi College 190 and 201. Junius 121, produced at Worcester with a great deal of material associated with Archbishop Wulfstan, contains several penitentials in addition to homilies, pastoral letters, and catechetical texts. Corpus 190, the English section of which was produced at Exeter, contains multiple penitentials along with liturgical material and a collection of canon law; this is almost certainly the "scriftboc on englisc" found in the record of Bishop Leofric's donations to Exeter.[27]

Anglo-Saxon England clearly had a strong tradition of producing penitential texts, while law codes and narrative sources indicate that this tradition translated into practice in Anglo-Saxon society. Bishops of the tenth and eleventh centuries took care to emphasize the importance of confession and penance to priestly ministry and prescriptive booklists for priests almost universally include a penitential. Though most of the copies of penitentials in later Anglo-Saxon manuscripts are in the miscellanies known as commonplace books, it is likely that these texts were made available to priests in other ways, including in small, unbound booklets that have not survived the vagaries of time. However, most copies of penitentials that potentially saw pastoral use have survived through inclusion into bound collections.

Manuals and the performance of occasional offices

Some of the most crucial rites of pastoral care fall under the category of occasional offices and were therefore ostensibly contained within the book known in the early Middle Ages as a *manuale*. Early prescriptive booklists, such as those in the *Enlarged Rule of Chrodegang* and the *Penitential of Egbert*, do not refer to a *manuale*, but rather a *baptisterium* or its Old English equivalent *fulluhtian*. This book may have contained more services than only those for baptism, but the lack of early manuscript witnesses leaves us with no more than this slight linguistic evidence. Certainly by the late tenth or very early eleventh century, English sources refer to a single book containing occasional offices as the *manuale*.[28] Sarah Hamilton has asserted that the *manuale* as a

---

[26] Ibid., 46.
[27] Michael Lapidge, "Surviving Booklists from Anglo-Saxon England," in *Learning and Literature in Anglo-Saxon England: Studies Presented to Peter Clemoes on the Occasion of His Sixty-Fifth Birthday*, ed. Lapidge and Helmut Gneuss (Cambridge: Cambridge University Press, 1985), 65, 67.
[28] Some liturgists refer to this book as a *rituale*, though the more common term for

Locating Penitentials, Manuals, and Computi

distinct liturgical book "emerged out of a post-Carolingian episcopal context" which, similarly to the ninth century, emphasized the importance of pastoral care for the laity.[29] But like the other types of priestly texts discussed in this chapter, the manuscripts that survive, both in England and on the continent, are typically not discrete, self-contained volumes. Most of the Anglo-Saxon manuscript evidence is incorporated into other types of liturgical books, such as pontificals, benedictionals, mass-books, and at least one book containing a penitential. It may be that this characteristic of the bibliographical record is a result of the circulation of rites for occasional offices in unbound booklets of one or two quires that have not survived in the manuscript record, not unlike that of the penitentials.[30] Rites for occasional offices are found in liturgical books from both monastic and secular contexts, though as monks were not involved in pastoral care to the same extent as most secular priests, monastic liturgical books are less likely to contain offices for baptism. For example, the Winchcombe Sacramentary (Orléans, Bibliothèque municipale 127) and the Winchester sacramentary fragment (London, Society of Antiquaries 154) contain no baptismal offices, but do contain those for the sick and dying.[31]

Significance and necessity of occasional offices

Despite the fragility of manuals outside bound liturgical collections, the rites that they contain could hardly have been more central to the life and death of the medieval Christian. The three rites that figure most prominently in these books are baptism, confession, and rites for the sick and dying.[32] Infant baptism was a nearly universal practice in the tenth and eleventh centuries in England, and this is reflected in the manuscripts of the period. The English manuscripts containing baptismal *ordines*, typically derived from the Supplemented Hadrianum,

---

these books in Anglo-Saxon England seems to have been *manuale*, used by Ælfric in the early eleventh century. Sarah Hamilton, "The *Rituale*: The Evolution of a New Liturgical Book," in *The Church and the Book*, ed. R. N. Swanson (Woodbridge: Boydell Press, 2004). See also Helen Gittos and Sarah Hamilton, eds., *Understanding Medieval Liturgy: Essays in Interpretation* (Farnham: Ashgate, 2015), which focuses on the evidence offered by rites.

[29] Hamilton, "The *Rituale*," 81.
[30] Ibid., 100; Helmut Gneuss, "Liturgical Books in Anglo-Saxon England and Their Old English Terminology," in *Learning and Literature in Anglo-Saxon England*, 134.
[31] Sarah Larratt Keefer, "Manuals," in *The Liturgical Books of Anglo-Saxon England*, ed. Richard Pfaff (Kalamazoo: Medieval Institute Publications, 1995), 105–6.
[32] Though nuptial masses and blessings are found in some Anglo-Saxon liturgical books, the Anglo-Saxon marriage ceremony itself does not seem to have taken place inside the church or necessarily involved a priest. Keefer, "Manuals," 103.

tend to assume infant baptism and the Red Book of Darley's vernacular liturgical directions for the officiating priest contain copious references to the "cild" being baptized.[33] Medieval Christians believed that the baptism of infants was necessary for the salvation of the child's soul if he or she was to die suddenly, and this view prompted attempts to ensure that baptism took place as soon as possible. Archbishop Wulfstan's *Canons of Edgar*, a text written for the clergy of the diocese of York and known at Worcester, stipulates that priests must let parents know that a baby should be baptized within a week of his or her birth.[34] This requirement was to be taken seriously: the *Scrift boc* prescribes a three-year fast for parents whose child died unbaptized and a priest who failed to baptize a sick child brought to him for such a purpose was to be defrocked.[35] Most of these baptisms probably took place in cathedrals or minster churches, as with the famous example of St Wulfstan baptizing children from across the diocese in the city of Worcester.[36] Furthermore, a number of Anglo-Saxon minsters in the eleventh century were still making annual payments to their bishop in return for chrism, the sanctified oil used for baptism and unction, which suggests the existence of a system of baptismal provision that was certainly in place by the late Anglo-Saxon period and probably much earlier.[37] If the presence of fonts is any indication of where baptismal rites were performed, it seems that local churches did not typically baptize for most of the late Anglo-Saxon period, though fonts begin to appear outside minsters and cathedrals in the late eleventh and early twelfth centuries, and the Red Book of Darley, probably produced in the early 1060s, contains a blessing for a baptismal font.[38]

---

[33] Ibid., 102; Cambridge, Corpus Christi College 422, pp. 389–92. See also Sally Crawford, "Baptism and Infant Burial in Anglo-Saxon England," in *Medieval Life Cycles: Continuity and Change*, ed. Isabelle Cochelin and Karen Smyth (Turnhout: Brepols, 2013).

[34] Whitelock, Brett, and Brooke, *Councils and Synods*, 319.

[35] *Scriftboc*, ed. Frantzen, "Junius 121 (X) 89b," in *Anglo-Saxon Penitentials*, accessed February 15, 2018, http://anglo-saxon.net/penance/index.php?p=TSBOC121_89b.

[36] Michael Winterbottom and R. M. Thomson, eds. and trans., *William of Malmesbury: Saints' Lives* (Oxford: Oxford University Press, 2002), 32–35.

[37] Sarah Foot, *Monastic Life in Anglo-Saxon England, c. 600–900* (Cambridge: Cambridge University Press, 2006), 299; David C. Douglas, *The Domesday Monachorum of Christ Church, Canterbury* (London: Royal Historical Society, 1944), 6, 77–78. Hugh the Chanter describes these payments as being "ex antiqua consuetudine" and Douglas suggests that the practice in the diocese of Canterbury "may well have derived from earlier custom". For a discussion of the parochial rights of lesser churches in Worcester specifically, see Nigel Baker and Richard Holt, *Urban Growth and the Medieval Church: Gloucester and Worcester* (Aldershot: Ashgate, 2004), 241–42.

[38] John Blair, *The Church in Anglo-Saxon Society* (Oxford: Oxford University Press, 2005), 459–62; Helen Gittos, "Is There Any Evidence for the Liturgy of Parish

A variety of rituals accompanied the act of confession and the administration of communion to a sick or dying individual in his or her home, rites often presented together in the *manuale*. As Martin Dudley has pointed out, these rites consisted of five primary elements: the visitation of the home by a priest (possibly accompanied by other clerics), confession by the infirm individual, the anointment of certain parts of the body by the priest, the administration of communion, and finally the watch with the individual and, if he or she was to die, the "commendation of the departing soul", after which the body was removed from the home and prepared for burial.[39] Rites following this general pattern are found in a number of manuscripts, and particular attention is paid to caring for the sick and dying in Oxford, Bodleian Library, Laud Misc. 482, which includes penitentials and material peripheral to lay confession, along with *ordines* for the visitation of the sick and dying, performance of mass in the home of the sick, and burial. From the witness of liturgical books, the type of care and commemoration received by the dying and dead in religious communities was often more intensive and elaborate than that for laypeople in local churches, a factor that may have prompted wealthy aristocrats to join monastic houses at the end of their lives.[40] For others, commemoration after death and care for the body likely encouraged membership in guilds, all the Anglo-Saxon examples of which were concerned with the commemoration of guild brothers. The surviving guild statutes are particularly concerned with funeral rites, masses, and the repatriation of the remains of deceased guild members. Guilds like those at Bedwyn and Abbotsbury were organized around a local minster, and the funeral rites and masses for the dead would have been conducted by the clerics of the minster, providing another possible context for the use of rites for the dead and dying.[41]

It is important here to note that many of the surviving manuscripts containing pastoral rites include a significant amount of Old English. Both the Red Book of Darley and Laud Misc. 482 have a great deal of Old English rubrication intended to guide the presiding cleric through the rite, sometimes in explicit detail. The vernacular is also used in the "scripts" for the celebrant and the lay participants in these rites, such as when the godparents of a child to be baptized are asked various

---

Churches in Late Anglo-Saxon England? The Red Book of Darley and the Status of Old English," in *Pastoral Care in Late Anglo-Saxon England*, 72.

[39] Martin Dudley, "Sacramental Liturgies in the Middle Ages," in *The Liturgy of the Medieval Church*, 2nd ed., ed. Thomas Heffernan and E. Ann Matter (Kalamazoo: Medieval Institute Publications, 2005), 213.

[40] Hamilton, "Rites of Passage and Pastoral Care," 300, 302.

[41] Gervase Rosser, "The Anglo-Saxon Gilds," in *Minsters and Parish Churches: The Local Church in Transition, 950–1200*, ed. John Blair (Oxford: Oxford University Committee for Archaeology, 1988), 31.

questions meant to be answered with formulaic responses.⁴² Gittos has observed that rather than reflecting the supposed ignorance of secular clerics, "[t]he extant manuscripts do not suggest that Old English was always employed specifically because a certain priest would not be able to decipher the Latin", and indeed, the *ordines* for baptism, confession, and unction would at times have been unusable for a priest who was not able to use the Latin vocabulary of the liturgy, particularly when written out in a heavily abbreviated form. The appearance of Old English in pastoral rites (and penitentials) may in part reflect the need for the priest to make himself and the liturgical process understood by the lay individuals participating therein, particularly in instances "when comprehension was vital for the well-being of the soul".⁴³ It should be noted however that vernacular liturgical instructions appear in some high-status liturgical books and are not confined to the administration of low-level pastoral care, though they may have been more common in this context.⁴⁴ The production of liturgical books with vernacular instructions and "scripts" for both clergy and laity may have simplified the performance of these rites for clerics and in some cases facilitated informed lay participation in the liturgy, particularly occasional offices.

Computus and its use

The term computus in the early Middle Ages carried three meanings: the computation of the date of Easter, a set of computistical texts, and the older and more generic sense of "computing, counting or reckoning", but the term eventually became associated almost wholly with the study and use of the ecclesiastical calendar.⁴⁵ The rationale for the necessity of computus for priests essentially lay in the tension that existed between the solar and lunar calendrical basis for the moveable feasts of the liturgical year. The date of Easter is a prime example of this difficulty and one that famously provoked a sharp disagreement in early Anglo-Saxon England. The death and resurrection of Christ were

---

⁴² Bryan D. Spinks, *Early and Medieval Rituals and Theologies of Baptism: From the New Testament to the Council of Trent* (Aldershot: Ashgate, 2006), 127–28.

⁴³ Gittos, "Is There Any Evidence for the Liturgy of Parish Churches," 80–81.

⁴⁴ A notable example of this is the Sacramentary of Robert of Jumièges (Rouen, Bibliothèque municipale, 274, Y.6).

⁴⁵ Charles Williams Jones, *Bedae Opera De Temporibus* (Cambridge, MA: Mediaeval Academy of America, 1943), 75; Wesley Stevens, "Cycles of Time: Calendrical and Astronomical Reckonings in Early Science," in *Cycles of Time and Scientific Learning in Medieval Europe* (Aldershot: Variorum, 1995), 28–29; Arno Borst, *The Ordering of Time: From the Ancient Computus to the Modern Computer* (Chicago: University of Chicago Press, 1993), 19–20, 29.

linked to two dates: the celebration of Passover, a date in the Jewish (lunar) calendar and three days after this (counting inclusively), the resurrection of Jesus on a Sunday. With Passover occurring on a fixed calendrical day that could fall on any day of the week, along with the differences of the Jewish calendar and the solar calendar used by medieval Christians, this created significant tension in reckoning the date of Easter. Historically, this tension between the calendars was dealt with in one of two general ways: fixing the date of celebration to the appropriate date in the Jewish calendar or fixing the date of Easter to Sunday and determining the appropriate Sunday by astronomical means. Early Christians almost certainly observed the former, but by the fourth century the latter method won out, though controversy surrounding the way in which the date of Easter should be calculated continues to the present day.[46] Not all feasts were moveable, however. Liturgical events such as Christmas and saints' feasts were held on a fixed day in the Roman calendar, eliminating the need for calculation and reconciliation of lunar and solar calendrical systems.

In the early medieval West, the computus formed an integral part of the ideal priestly curriculum after the *Admonitio Generalis* decreed that all clerics should be taught computus.[47] Byrhtferth of Ramsey indicates that priests would be examined on their computistical knowledge, presumably prior to their ordination, and the text termed by Dorothy Whitelock *On the Examination of Candidates for Ordination* seems to confirm this, as it instructs the bishop or his representative to determine "how he [the candidate for ordination] can divide the course of the year by computation".[48] Wesley Stevens has emphasized computistical education in English monastic schools and cathedral schools and it is not difficult to imagine instruction in computus at some level in schools at secular minsters.[49]

Despite the inclusion of computus into nearly every prescriptive list of books for priests, the contents of a given computus could vary widely. Charles Williams Jones points out that *computi* could consist of "extracts or complete tracts, often either anonymous or attributed to the wrong author, Easter-tables, a yearly calendar, lists of calculations, accessory tables for help in calculation, computistical verses

---

[46] "'Gift of Unity': Will Pope Francis Change the Date of Easter?," *National Catholic Register*, June 19, 2015, accessed January 19, 2018, http://www.ncregister.com/daily-news/gift-of-unity-will-pope-francis-change-the-date-of-easter/.

[47] *Capitularia regum Francorum*, pt. 1, ed. Alfred Boretius, *Monumenta Germaniae Historica* (Hanover: Hahnsche Buchhandlung, 1883), 60.

[48] Peter S. Baker and Michael Lapidge, eds. and trans., *Byrhtferth's Enchiridion*, Early English Text Society Supplementary Series 15 (Oxford: Oxford University Press, 1995), 42–43; Whitelock, Brett, and Brooke, *Councils and Synods*, 425.

[49] See Wesley Stevens, "Sidereal Time in Anglo-Saxon England," in *Cycles of Time and Scientific Learning*. For clerical education in minsters, see chapter 2.

for memorizing, dialogues for school catechism, and multiplication tables".[50] The computus used by Bede contained a calendar, Easter tables, lunar and solar "letter tables", various *argumenta*, and tracts authored by Dionysius Exiguus. But the computus for the priest whose primary role was the provision of pastoral care did not have to be an academic and theoretical collection, as some *computi* certainly were. The primary concern of the computus, the calculation of the date of Easter, makes its aim essentially problem-based while providing a theologically significant "technique of patterning time into repeating cycles".[51] Accordingly, many of the *computi* circulating in late Anglo-Saxon England were eminently practical. Two of the *computi* compiled in the second half of the tenth century in England, unlike some other contemporary collections, contain little theoretical material and few *argumenta*, and at least one of the major "families" of English computistical manuscripts required essentially no knowledge of mathematics on the part of its user.[52] A computus like this would probably have allowed most priests to calculate the date of Easter independently without simply relying on lists of Easter dates. A text that may further indicate the need for simple computistical texts is Ælfric's *De temporibus anni*, which, though not a computus, is a distillation of the basics of computus, natural science, and cosmology. Its most recent editor has suggested that the audience of this work may have been the secular clergy and Ælfric's clear prose and accessible explanations would certainly have aided clerics in learning the rudiments of practical computus.[53]

Prescriptive and documentary evidence for computistical books

Bishops recognized the need for priests to not only be aware of and observe the right events on the right days, but also to be able to calculate the days of the moveable feasts for themselves. Some dates, such as that of Easter, needed to be known well in advance, as the time in which Lent was to be observed was contingent upon this date. *Computi* are prescribed for priests in both Anglo-Saxon and Carolingian sources and evidence previously discussed suggests that English priests were examined on their computistical knowledge in the course of their ordination. The fact that priests were examined on this topic implies that

---

[50] C. W. Jones, *Bedae Opera De Temporibus*, 75–76.
[51] Faith Wallis, trans., *Bede: The Reckoning of Time* (Liverpool: Liverpool University Press, 1999), xx–xxi.
[52] Baker and Lapidge, *Byrhtferth's* Enchiridion, xlvi–xlix.
[53] Martin Blake, ed. and trans., *Ælfric's De Temporibus Anni* (Cambridge: D. S. Brewer, 2009), 1, 39–40, 45–46.

they had access to this kind of material, but other evidence also points to knowledge of computus among the secular clergy. The *Enchiridion* composed by Byrhtferth of Ramsey notably indicates not only a possible clerical audience for the written text, but also imagines these clerics, who are often at the receiving end of unflattering exhortations, being educated in computus in a classroom along with monks. This form of computistical instruction may go back to the days of Bede, as Faith Wallis has argued from the witness of Bede's *De temporibus ratione*.[54] Additionally, an Anglo-Saxon booklist copied into a tenth-century manuscript of Isidore's *De natura rerum* provides further evidence of the availability of computistical texts to priests. Though the books included in this list belonged to an individual named Æthelstan, who Michael Lapidge has suggested was a grammarian, one of the final books in the list is a computus (OE *gerim*) and the list specifies that this book was previously owned by a priest named Ælfwold. We have no further information on Æthelstan or Ælfwold, nor does the list specify the contents of this computus, but this does show that these texts were available to priests even before the "ruthless editing" of earlier computistical texts into the practical *computi* that emerged in the later tenth century.[55]

Computistical material in Anglo-Saxon manuscripts

Computi, like the other types of priestly texts discussed in this chapter, rarely survive in discrete volumes, but rather are bound with other types of texts. This may indicate that they tended to be copied into or compiled with certain types of manuscripts or they simply may not have survived other methods of transmission. We find computistical material copied into various types of manuscripts, though predictably many of these are liturgical. A computus occupying approximately eighteen pages is found in the Red Book of Darley. The computus transmitted in the Red Book of Darley is associated with both the Leofric-Tiberius computus and the Winchester computus, two practical collections of computistical texts probably composed in the second half of the tenth century. Though Leofric-Tiberius is a fairly practical computus, the slightly later Winchester computus is a condensed, stripped-down version of Leofric-Tiberius. The manuscript record attests to the popularity of these collections: thirteen Anglo-Saxon manuscripts, many of them liturgical, contain at least a few features of

---

[54] Wallis, *The Reckoning of Time*, xxxi–xxxiv.
[55] Lapidge, *The Anglo-Saxon Library* (Oxford: Oxford University Press, 2005), 133–34. See the discussion of the Leofric-Tiberius computus in P. Baker and Lapidge, *Byrhtferth's* Enchiridion, xlv–xlviii.

Table 4. The contents of the Winchester computus[a]

Ratio calculandi de duodecim mensibus
Tables of ferial regulars, concurrents, lunar regulars, and epacts
Calendar with golden numbers, lunar letters, and dominical letters
Lunar table
Table showing the age of the moon on the first of the month through the decennovenal cycle
Table showing the *feria* on the first of the month in a twenty-eight-year cycle
Zodiac table
Table of terms for Septuagesima, Quadragesima, Easter, and Rogationtide
Argumentum quo inueniatur aduentus Domini
Terminus secunde lune initii
Terminus quartadecime lune paschalis
Sentences on terms beginning with "post"
Horalogium horarum incipit
De epacta et de concurrenti ratio
Ieiunia legitima quattuor sunt in quattuor anni temporibus
Easter table (with information such as the year, date of Easter, time from Christmas to Quadragesima, lunar cycle, and the age of the moon on Easter day)

[a] Adapted from Baker and Lapidge, *Byrhtferth's* Enchiridion, xlix–li. Table 4 represents the general contents of the Winchester computus, but it should be noted that the texts included and the order in which they were included often vary from manuscript to manuscript. P. Baker, "Textual Boundaries in Anglo-Saxon Works on Time (and in Some Old English Poems)," in *Studies in English Language and Literature: "Doubt Wisely", Papers in Honour of E. G. Stanley*, ed. M. J. Toswell and Elizabeth Tyler (London: Routledge, 1996), 451–52.

the Leofric-Tiberius or Winchester computus.[56] The table above briefly summarizes the contents of the Winchester computus, the more practical and developed of these two collections.

The texts transmitted in the Winchester computus constitute a fairly basic collection of texts that would likely have been useful to most priests, particularly those living and working further from centers of diocesan administration. The usefulness and practicality of this form of the computus was obviously recognized as it was the source for most Anglo-Saxon *computi* over the next century, though it saw evolution in later recensions.[57] Additionally, if bishops were providing

---

[56] Baker and Lapidge, *Byrhtferth's* Enchiridion, xlv, xlviii–xlix.
[57] Ibid., lii.

priests with books containing computistical texts, as has been argued more generally in chapter 3, then it is likely that the Winchester computus saw use by secular priests from the late tenth century onward in bishoprics that had access to this utilitarian set of texts.

Manuscript evidence

The manuscripts discussed below are examples of the phenomenon that has been noted throughout this chapter, namely the combination of penitential material, rites for occasional offices, and computus into volumes containing other types of texts. The latter part of this chapter will practically demonstrate this by examining three Anglo-Saxon manuscripts in detail. Two of these, the Red Book of Darley and Laud Misc. 482, have previously been discussed at some length in published scholarship and are recognized as valuable witnesses to the types of texts circulating in manuscripts intended for use in pastoral care. The other manuscript discussed here, London, British Library, Cotton Vespasian D. XV has been the subject of little concerted study and I will argue below that the most probable context for the use of this book is by an Anglo-Saxon priest or community of clerics in the tenth and eleventh centuries.

Oxford, Bodleian Library, Laud Misc. 482

This is a small, though unusually tall, mid-eleventh-century book containing penitential texts (the *Old English Handbook* and *Old English Penitential*) and material for offices for the sick and dying. It has generally been recognized as a book for pastoral use.[58] Old English is prominent in this book as it contains multiple Old English penitential texts and a significant number of vernacular rubrics and directions within the liturgy for the sick and dying. One hand wrote the main text with two others providing notations. The main hand has Worcester connections and the manuscript was certainly at Worcester in the later Middle Ages, as it was annotated by the Tremulous Hand in the early thirteenth century.[59] There are two clearly divided sections of this book.

---

[58] Francesca Tinti, *Sustaining Belief: The Church of Worcester from c.870 to c.1100* (Farnham: Ashgate, 2010), 305; Tinti, "Looking for Local Priests in Anglo-Saxon England," in *Men in the Middle: Local Priests in Early Medieval Europe*, ed. Steffen Patzold and Carine van Rhijn (Berlin: De Gruyter, 2016), 159; Catherine Cubitt, "Bishops, Priests and Penance in Late Saxon England," *Early Medieval Europe* 14, no. 1 (2006), 57–58.

[59] Victoria Thompson, *Dying and Death in Later Anglo-Saxon England* (Woodbridge: Boydell Press, 2004), 68, 82; Thompson, "The Pastoral Contract in Late Anglo-Saxon England: Priest and Parishioner in Oxford, Bodleian Library, MS Laud

The first section, making up approximately two-thirds of the book, almost exclusively contains penitential texts and is clearly marked out from the second section, which is comprised of offices for the sick and dying, by the "FINITUM EST" that appears on f. 43v, after which a blank folio separates the two segments.[60] This discussion of the manuscript will move sequentially, beginning with the initial penitential section of the book, then moving on to the offices for the sick and dying.

The first forty or so folios of this manuscript concern themselves almost wholly with the administration of penance, containing two penitentials (ff. 1–19 and 30–40) among a number of shorter penitential texts and a brief computistical note on the Ember Days. The first penitential is the *Old English Penitential*, a fairly free translation of the penitential of Halitgar of Cambrai with a number of additions from other sources. This penitential is split into four books, with the first giving theological and practical guidance to the confessor, the second and third books containing lists of sins and corresponding penances, and the final book, among other material, providing guidance on the commutation of penance.[61] The second penitential is that rubricated *Scrift boc* in the version found in Corpus 190, though such a title is not found in this manuscript.[62] Additionally, the version of the *Scrift boc* included in Laud Misc. 482 is shorter than that found in both Corpus 190 and Junius 121, primarily omitting chapters concerning the liturgy as well as several on marriage and sexual conduct.[63] This manuscript also contains a brief extract from the *Old English Handbook* (f. 28), but does not transmit this text in full. Both penitentials that appear in full in this book, namely the *Scrift boc* and *Old English Penitential*, are found in other eleventh-century manuscripts, but other copies of these texts are generally found in commonplace books, particularly those associated with Archbishop Wulfstan. The contents of Laud Misc. 482, combined with its potential for use in the field, make this manuscript an extremely valuable witness to the pastoral application of vernacular penitential texts.

Miscellaneous 482," in *Pastoral Care in Late Anglo-Saxon England*, ed. Tinti, 106–7.

[60] A useful chart of the manuscript's contents appears in Thompson, *Dying and Death*, 68.

[61] Different recensions of this penitential contain varying material in the final book, though all seem to draw on the *Scrift boc* to some extent. For a brief but detailed discussion of this final material, see Frantzen, "Description of the OE Penitential & Indices," in *Anglo-Saxon Penitentials*, accessed February 15, 2018, http://anglo-saxon.net/penance/index.php?p=txhdoep.

[62] Here I follow the designations used by Frantzen, who has simplified the terminology used by previous generations of scholars.

[63] Frantzen, "Description of the Scriftboc & Indices," in *Anglo-Saxon Penitentials*, accessed February 15, 2018, http://anglo-saxon.net/penance/index.php?p=txhdsbc.

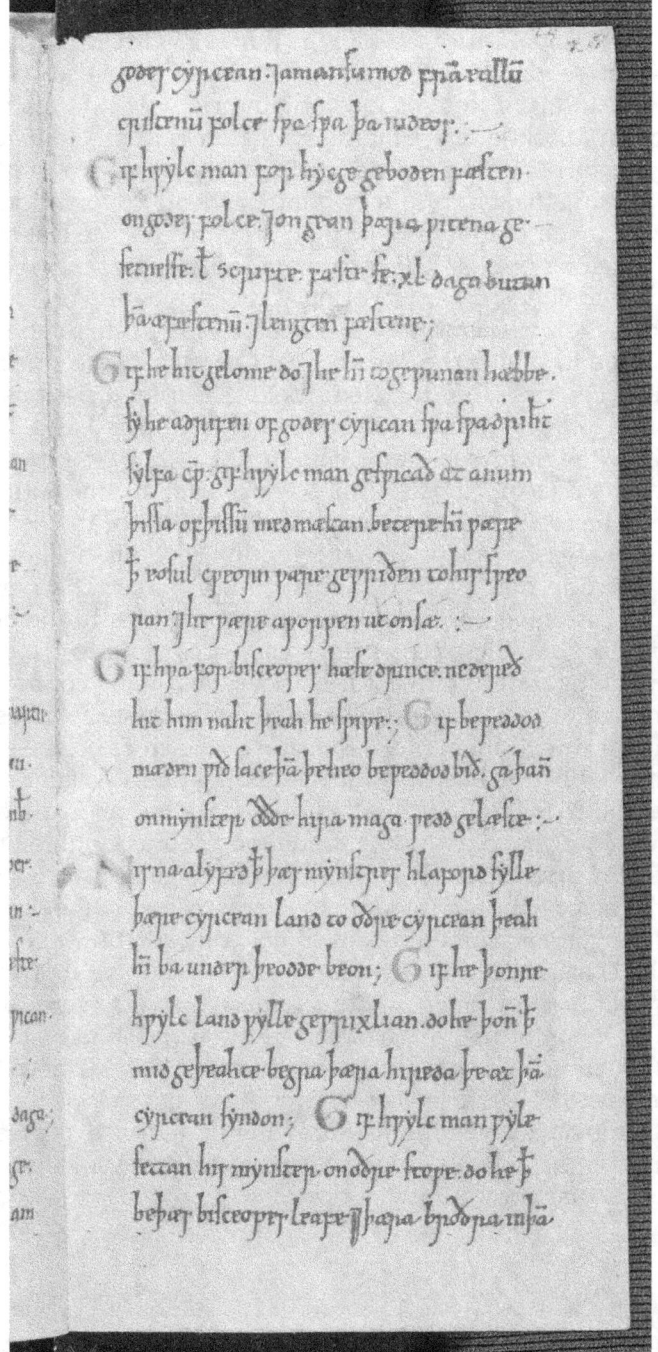

Plate 8: Oxford, Bodleian Library, Laud Misc. 482, f. 28r.
Old English texts on confession and penance.

The purpose of the latter section of this manuscript is the performance of occasional offices, which in this period had not developed into the seven sacraments officially promulgated some 500 years later. The first few folios of this section contain brief texts about confession and absolution, while the remaining section contains *ordines* for the use of a priest in "visiting the sick, celebrating mass in a sick person's house, attending the dying, and burying the dead".[64] Additionally, this section was at some point longer than it is now, as the last folio ends in the middle of a prayer. The information from this section allows us to see this very personal form of pastoral care as it was likely practiced. When the priest arrived at the home of the infirm, the penitent and the home in which the rite was to take place were purified with holy water. The rite from the Red Book of Darley envisions a single priest coming to the home of the penitent, whereas Laud Misc. 482, along with rites from contemporary episcopal books, expect at least a priest and a deacon to be on the scene.[65] Psalms and Latin prayers would then be recited, followed by the confession of the penitent, for which the confessor was given specific instructions on how to deal with the attitude that a given penitent might take. The penitentials in this book also give guidance to the priest on the attitude he should take during confession, which might vary according to the contrition and forthcoming nature of the parishioner. Following confession, and depending on the severity of the penitent's illness, the priest would bless ashes and with them make the sign of the cross on the penitent's chest, followed by the blessing and sprinkling of holy water and ashes on the haircloth. Following this, "anthems, psalms, and collects" were sung, after which the parishioner would be anointed with oil, the location of which varied strongly by tradition. Some manuscripts leave the areas of the body to be anointed up to the discretion of the priest, while others specify areas, sometimes in direct contradiction to each other, such as the head, shoulders, eyes, and ears, or simply "in loco maximi doloris".[66] After anointment with oil, more prayers were to be said, followed by the administration of communion and, finally, ten collects and a benediction. The *ordo* preserved in Laud Misc. 482 goes on to say that the mass to be performed in the home of the sick or dying could be said for the next seven nights following this service, representing a significant commitment of time and personnel to the spiritual care of a priest's or secular community's flock.[67]

---

[64] Thompson, *Dying and Death*, 68.
[65] Ibid., 80.
[66] "In the place of the greatest pain." Ibid., 63–64, 77.
[67] Ibid., 77. This summary of a pastoral visit to the home of a sick or dying individual is largely drawn from Thompson.

It is clear from its contents that Laud Misc. 482 was written for and likely used in pastoral care for the sick and dying. Its confessional and penitential texts point to a concern for the soul of the penitent in case of or before death. The occasional offices contained in the final third of the manuscript transmit the liturgical rites necessary for this form of pastoral care, including the texts needed to celebrate mass in the house of a sick individual and the final leaves probably originally contained a burial mass and *ordo*.[68] Victoria Thompson has argued that this book, which scholars have often found difficult to categorize, should be understood as a manual designed for the training of Worcester priests in the rites and ministries pertaining to sickness and death.[69] This rationale for the creation of Laud Misc. 482 is not unreasonable, but perhaps places too much specificity on the ways in which this book might be used. Though it is less likely to be a book for a single priest in a local church, it could instead have been compiled and written for a clerical community as a general manual for confession and ministry to the sick and dying, as Frantzen has suggested.[70] While the presence of the Tremulous Hand in the manuscript implies that this book was at Worcester Cathedral in the later Middle Ages, this is not necessarily an indication that the book only saw pastoral use within the city of Worcester. The book might instead have been written at the cathedral for use at a secular minster under Worcester's control and reverted to the cathedral at a later date or left to the cathedral by a priest upon his death. Certainly the number of minster churches in Worcester in the eleventh century was greater than in most bishoprics and there is evidence for priests elsewhere in early medieval Europe leaving their books to a monastery or cathedral.[71]

But regardless of whether this book was used by the cathedral clergy or by others, Laud Misc. 482 is one of the most explicitly pastoral English manuscripts of the tenth and eleventh centuries and was certainly intended for use by a priest or a team of clerics. Additionally, the production of a manuscript of this kind at Worcester in the mid-eleventh century clearly indicates that the cathedral scriptorium had the necessary exemplars to produce pastoral volumes of this kind and

---

[68] Ibid., 67.
[69] Ibid., 70.
[70] Frantzen, "Tradition of Penitentials," 26.
[71] Julia Barrow, "Wulfstan and Worcester: Bishop and Clergy in the Early Eleventh Century," in *Wulfstan, Archbishop of York: The Proceedings of the Second Alcuin Conference*, ed. Matthew Townend (Turnhout: Brepols, 2004), 146; Thomas Kohl, "*Presbyter in parochia sua*: Local Priests and Their Churches in Early Medieval Bavaria," in *Men in the Middle*, 62–63; Gonzalo Martínez Díez, ed., *Colección documental del Monasterio de San Pedro de Cardeña* (Burgos: Caja de Ahorros y Monte de Piedad del Circulo Católico de Obreros de Burgos, 1998), no. 37.

in fact did so. Considering the episcopal commitment to pastoral care at Worcester under St Wulfstan, Laud Misc. 482 may have been one of many such pastoral books produced there in the eleventh century. What we can unambiguously draw from the witness of this book is the strong pastoral concern for the provision of confession, penance, and compassionate care for the dying in the diocese of Worcester in the eleventh century.

London, British Library, Cotton Vespasian D. XV, ff. 68–121

This book measures approximately 200 × 145 mm, a comfortably hand-sized volume, and as it currently stands is made up of three parts, of which one is a twelfth-century pontifical and two are late Anglo-Saxon. The first Anglo-Saxon portion, making up ff. 68–101 of the current volume, is a mid-tenth-century collection consisting of confessional prayers, the *Penitential of Theodore*, and other penitential texts, such as excerpts on sin, penance, and confession from Isidore's *Sententiarum*.[72] The second section, consisting of ff. 102–121, has been dated to about the turn of the eleventh century and contains part of the *Liber officialis* of Amalarius, texts on the *Pater Noster*, and a tract on the duties of a priest.[73] It is unclear if these two sections were bound together in the Anglo-Saxon period, but both have been bound with a later pontifical since Robert Cotton's aggregation of these leaves in the seventeenth century. The first section was written by at least three scribes practicing Anglo-Saxon Square Minuscule in the mid-tenth century. One scribe was responsible for copying the content of ff. 68–83, but the size and aspect of the writing changes significantly at 84r and the work of two scribal hands, neither of which is found in the earlier leaves, is detectable from ff. 84–101.[74] Further and more significant scribal change can be seen in the final section of the book, comprising ff. 102–121, which has been dated x/xi. David Dumville has tentatively suggested that the later folios may have been written at Worcester based on their similarity to manuscripts of eleventh-century date typically assigned

---

[72] Neil R. Ker, *Catalogue of Manuscripts Containing Anglo-Saxon* (Oxford: Clarendon Press, 1957), 277; Rob Meens, "Penitentials and the Practice of Penance in the Tenth and Eleventh Centuries," *Early Medieval Europe* 14, no. 1 (2006): 13, n. 31. Ker assigns a date of s. x med. to Vespasian D. XV, but Meens has given a somewhat later date of s. x/xi to this manuscript without comment. The Isidorean excerpts begin at f. 69v, starting with book 2, *caput* 13 of the *Sententiarum*. Jacques-Paul Migne, ed., *Sancti Isidori hispalensis episcopi opera omnia ...*, Patrologia Latina 83 (Paris, 1862), 614.

[73] David Dumville, *Liturgy and the Ecclesiastical History of Late Anglo-Saxon England: Four Studies* (Woodbridge: Boydell Press, 1992), 136.

[74] Ker, *Catalogue of Manuscripts Containing Anglo-Saxon*, 278.

to Worcester.⁷⁵ The entirety of the section in question (ff. 68–121) is exceedingly plain. There are no illustrations or illuminations of any kind; the only embellishments are the initials, which in many cases have been very simply colored in with a dark ink. This manuscript has never been explicitly associated with priestly use, though Sarah Hamilton has described it as one of several "practical manuscripts" relating to the administration of penance.⁷⁶ An analysis of the relevant sections of this manuscript will show that it is a witness to penitentials used in England before significant circulation of vernacular penitentials and that this book would have been very suitable for use by an Anglo-Saxon priest.

The mid-tenth-century portion of this manuscript is made up of two distinct sections. The first, consisting of ff. 68–83, contains confessional prayers and extracts from patristic writings, such as the *Sententiarum* of Isidore of Seville and a pseudo-Augustinian homily originally derived from Jerome. While this homily is not necessarily penitential in its theme, it does emphasize certain penitential practices, particularly fasting.⁷⁷ Interesting for this relatively early date, the Latin confessional prayer that begins this section is given an Old English title: "þis siondon ondetnessa to gode seolfum".⁷⁸ The second section contains a form of the *Penitentiale Theodori*, which, though not composed by Theodore, may have had some genuine content originating with the archbishop and in any case enjoyed significant influence and wide circulation in the early Middle Ages.⁷⁹

Though there are scribal differences between ff. 68–83 and 84–101, it is likely that these sections were bound together in the Anglo-Saxon period for three reasons. Firstly, the style of the handwriting is consistent throughout these two sections and all three scribes were practicing a form of Anglo-Saxon Square Minuscule. Though the handwriting of ff. 84–101 is quite different from the previous section in terms of aspect and size, the letterforms are generally similar: the Insular forms of both *g* and *f* are frequently used in both sections,

---

⁷⁵ David Dumville, *English Caroline Script and Monastic History: Studies in Benedictinism, A.D. 950–1030* (Woodbridge: Boydell Press, 1993), 55, n. 242, 149, n. 49.

⁷⁶ Hamilton, "Remedies for 'Great Transgressions'", 89–90.

⁷⁷ An edition of this homily can be found in Jacques-Paul Migne, ed., *Sancti Aurelii hipponensis episcopi opera omnia ...*, Patrologia Latina 40 (Paris, 1841), 1342–44. Though the *Sermones ad fratres in eremo* are clearly intended for a monastic audience and the version of Homily LX transmitted in Vespasian D. XV is generally very close to the original, it is intriguing that most references to "fratres" or "fratres charissimi" are not included in the version of the homily found in this book.

⁷⁸ "This is a confession to God himself." The prayer goes on to confess to others however, including a "man of God". Frantzen, *Literature of Penance*, 171.

⁷⁹ Frantzen, "Tradition of Penitentials," 30.

as is the "straight back" Caroline d. Secondly, the content of these two sections is complementary. The first section contains penitential prayers, Isidorean excerpts related to penance, and a sermon that emphasizes fasting, while the second contains the *Penitentiale Theodori*, clearly showing the interrelation of the purpose of these two sections. Finally, some physical aspects of these sections suggest their connection in the late Anglo-Saxon period. The recto of f. 68 is significantly darker than the surrounding folios, suggesting that this folio was at one time the beginning of a book or booklet. Similarly, f. 101v, while less worn than f. 68r, still exhibits some wear as well as staining of the parchment, which appears to be the product of water damage. As Pamela Robinson has pointed out in an important article, soiling or rubbing on the outside leaves of a section within a manuscript is one indication of the presence of a "self-contained unit" within a bound collection, potentially indicating that ff. 68–101 were an independent book or booklet prior to their binding into this volume by Robert Cotton.[80] Considering the sum of the evidence here for the conjunction of these two sections, it is probable that ff. 68–101 of Cotton Vespasian D. XV were bound together in the Anglo-Saxon period and furthermore that this may in fact be an example of the type of penitential booklet that might have been used by an Anglo-Saxon priest in the tenth century.

The content of this book certainly suggests a penitential purpose. This recension of the *Penitentiale Theodori* is generally known as the *Iudicia Theodori* and is an early recension of this penitential, circulating in the British Isles and on the continent in the eighth century and later.[81] The text transmitted by this manuscript is a particular version of the *Iudicia* known as the *Canones Cottoniani*, which is loosely organized and intermixes canons on clerical conduct with penances for sins such as fornication and homicide.[82] However, the organization of the penitential found in this volume is well suited for pastoral use. The various sections of the penitential are rubricated with the types of offences that a particular section contains, with headings such as "De homicidiis diuersisque malis mulieris" and "De iuramento".[83] Many of the Latin penitentials as well as the Old English *Scrift boc* are organized in a similar way, providing headings for the various classes of

---

[80] Pamela R. Robinson, "Self-Contained Units in Composite Manuscripts of the Anglo-Saxon Period," *Anglo-Saxon England* 7 (1978): 232.

[81] Thomas Charles-Edwards, "The Penitential of Theodore and the *Iudicia Theodori*," in *Archbishop Theodore: Commemorative Studies on His Life and Influence*, ed. Michael Lapidge (Cambridge: Cambridge University Press, 1995).

[82] Frantzen seems to have misidentified the recension of the *Iudicia* in this manuscript by associating it with the *Capitula Dacheriana*. Frantzen, "Tradition of Penitentials," 39.

[83] London, British Library, Cotton Vespasian D. XV, ff. 95v, 98r.

sins contained in a particular section to aid a confessor in finding the right category for a confessed offense.

As has been discussed above, most penitentials of this period are found in the commonplace books of cathedrals, but in this book we find a penitential of Insular origin in a collection of texts well suited for use by a priest. The types of material that we find in ff. 68–101 may indeed be what the writers of early prescriptive booklists had in mind when writing that priests should own a *penitentiale*. Unlike Laud Misc. 482, which postdates this book by a century, this manuscript transmits a Latin penitential of the kind reimported during the Benedictine reform of the later tenth century. But the date of this manuscript, the use of Anglo-Saxon Square Minuscule rather than Caroline Minuscule – a script with monastic association in this period – combined with the evidence for penitential practice in the late ninth- and early tenth-century law codes could indicate that rather than an early product of monastic reform, this manuscript is instead a late product of a pre-existing English penitential tradition. Frantzen has suggested that penitential texts imported from the continent may have been available decades prior to the Benedictine reform and Vespasian D. XV may be a link between these proposed early copies and the products of later monastic scriptoria.[84]

The later material in this manuscript is also of some interest for the study of priests' books. The texts found in Cotton Vespasian D. XV, ff. 102–121 were copied around the turn of the eleventh century and may not have originally been bound with the preceding folios.[85] Much of this section consists of extracts from Amalarius of Metz's *Liber officialis*, particularly the recension known as the *Retractio prima*, which probably came to England in the early tenth century. Dumville has argued that the excerpts copied into this book were selected "by the scribe as he wrote, and second thoughts – leading to additional excerpting – are apparent".[86] Through significant condensation of the text, the copyist primarily selected material from the *Liber officialis* on the mass, though there is significant disorder in the way the selections have been copied. Christopher Jones notes that the scribe began copying in relative concordance with the order of the Mass, but then doubled back to copy material from the preface before returning "to those parts of the Mass passed over in the earlier round of compilation and conclud[ing] with a sequence of comments on the canonical

---

[84] Frantzen, "Tradition of Penitentials," 49.
[85] This may be suggested by wormholes that are found in ff. 102 and 103, but are not found in the adjoining folios of the earlier section.
[86] Dumville, *Liturgy and the Ecclesiastical History of Late Anglo-Saxon England*, 136.

hours".[87] Considering the way this was excerpted, a priest might have assembled and copied these texts for his own use, in a similar, though far more conventional, fashion to the marginal scribe of Corpus 41. Additionally, an exposition on the Pater Noster is included, which is not unexpected, considering the episcopal exhortations to priests to ensure that those in their care both know and understand the Pater Noster and Creed.[88] Though these are uncommon in surviving priestly books from England, expositions on the mass, baptism, and the Pater Noster and Creed are common in manuscripts belonging to priests from the Carolingian period.[89] A short tract on priestly duties also appears on f. 121 and might be a further indication that the user of this section of the manuscript was a priest.

Folios 68–101 of Cotton Vespasian D. XV are important evidence for the practice of penance by the secular clergy in tenth-century England. Though it is impossible to say with certainty that this was indeed the book of a mid-tenth century Anglo-Saxon priest, the texts that Vespasian D. XV contains strongly align with those of need or interest to a secular priest. This may indeed allow a glimpse into a penitential tradition predating the influence of Benedictine monasticism on the types of penitential texts available in England. The types of texts available to a priest may also be represented by the contents of ff. 102–121; *expositio missae* and tracts on the *Pater Noster* were certainly available to priests in the Carolingian Empire in the ninth century and would have been no less useful to English priests. It is uncertain whether ff. 68–101 were bound with ff. 102–121 in the Anglo-Saxon period, but if this is the case, they might represent an addition made to the book by a subsequent generation of users. Though we are unfortunately ignorant of the original context of these two sections or their history prior to their acquisition by Robert Cotton, the types of texts in these Anglo-Saxon survivals in addition to their unpretentious and portable format make their use by secular priests a strong possibility. The form and content of ff. 68–101 are a particularly striking example of what might

---

[87] Christopher Jones, "The Book of the Liturgy in Anglo-Saxon England," *Speculum* 73, no. 3 (1998): 682, n. 105.
[88] Whitelock, Brett, and Brooke, *Councils and Synods*, 208, 322.
[89] Carine van Rhijn, "The Local Church, Priests' Handbooks and Pastoral Care in the Carolingian Period," in *Chiese locali e Chiese regionali nell'alto medioevo*, vol. 61, no. 2 of *Settimane di studio della Fondazione Centro italiano di studi sull'alto medioevo* (Spoleto: Fondazione Centro italiano di studi sull'alto medioevo, 2014), 699; Susan A. Keefe, *Water and the Word: Baptism and the Education of the Clergy in the Carolingian Empire*, vol. 1, *A Study of Texts and Manuscripts* (Notre Dame: University of Notre Dame Press, 2002), 13–16. Two examples, though both more extensive than the text in Vespasian D. XV, are Orléans, Bibliothèque municipale 116 and St Petersburg, National Library of Russia, Q.V.I.34. Both contain *expositio missae* and the former also contains an exposition on the Lord's Prayer.

have constituted a *penitentiale* for a mid-tenth-century Anglo-Saxon priest: confessional prayers, patristic excerpts related to the practice of penance, a related homily, and a practically organized penitential. Though few Anglo-Saxon manuscripts containing penitentials can be convincingly posited as those used in pastoral care, an examination of the evidence demonstrates that Cotton Vespasian D. XV should be regarded as a book for just such a purpose.

The Red Book of Darley (Cambridge, Corpus Christi College 422)

The last chapter discussed the Red Book of Darley in reference to its liturgical use and found that the conflicting internal evidence was too great to make a determination as to its use by the secular clergy. What is certain about this manuscript, however, is that it was designed for and likely utilized in pastoral ministry and therefore the evidence it offers in regard to the types of computistical texts copied into pastoral manuscripts makes it an invaluable resource. In addition, this manuscript contains a significant number of texts for the performance of occasional offices and is a particularly important source for late Anglo-Saxon baptismal rites. Thus both the computus and manual of this book will be discussed in turn below.

Prior to the binding of this book with the Old English poem *Solomon and Saturn*, the book opened with a relatively extensive computistical section that now occupies pages 27–49. Though this manuscript has received a great deal of scholarly attention, its computus has rarely been the subject of significant interest since Heinrich Henel's extensive use of the manuscript in his study more than eighty years ago.[90] The first few pages contain material related to the lunar cycle, including a lunar table and notes on the concurrents and epacts, along with short moon-related prognostics. The calendar follows this brief section, taking up half of the computus (pp. 29–40); the contents of this calendar have heavily influenced the attribution of this manuscript to Sherborne or Winchester.[91] In addition to the extensive list of saints' days recorded in the calendar, there are some indications of the dates of moveable feasts. The calendar notes the dates of the equinoxes and the winter solstice, which fall more or less consistently with regard to the solar calendar, and the limits of when the moveable feasts can occur. The calendar is followed by tables for calculating not only the date of Easter, but also the first Sunday in Lent, Rogationtide, and Pentecost in a nineteen-year cycle. The remaining pages of the computus give Old

---

[90] Heinrich Henel, *Studien zum altenglischen Computus* (Leipzig: Bernhard Tauchnitz, 1934), *passim*.
[91] Richard Pfaff, *The Liturgy in Medieval England: A History* (Cambridge: Cambridge University Press, 2009), 95.

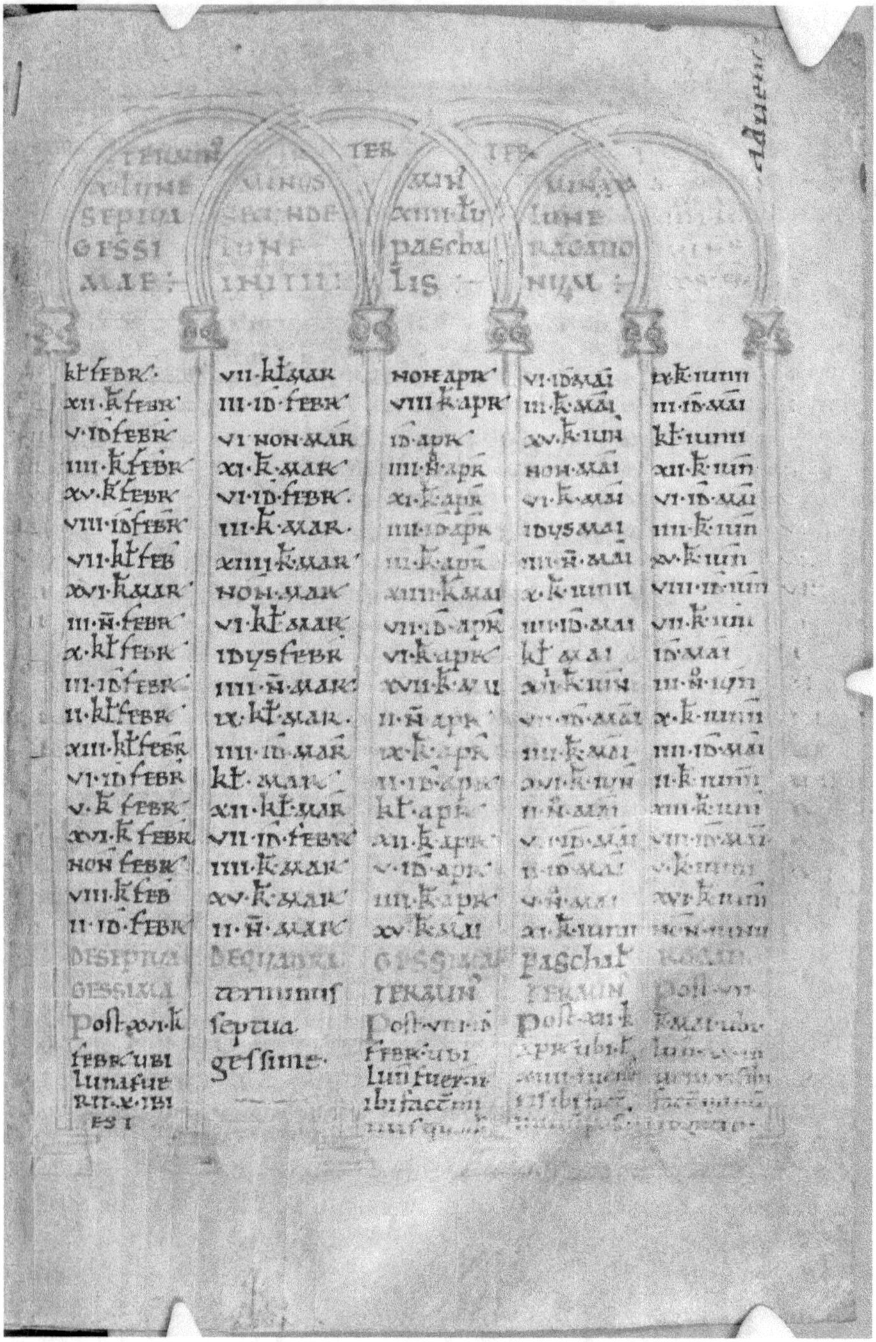

Plate 9: Cambridge, Corpus Christi College 422, p. 41. A computistical table of the *termini paschales*.

English instructions for determining the date of other festivals, such as the quarterly Ember fasts and the three Fridays on which people were expected to fast.

The computus extant in Corpus 422 is not precisely accordant with any one late Anglo-Saxon computus. Rather, it stands somewhere between the Leofric-Tiberius computus and the Winchester computus, both of which were composed in the second half of the tenth century and are practical computistical collections.[92] These computistical traditions are closely related, as the content of the Winchester computus is essentially drawn from Leofric-Tiberius, but the Winchester computus has been stripped of "redundancy" and "theoretical matter", leaving the end user with a brief and utilitarian computus.[93] The Sacramentary of Robert of Jumièges (Rouen, Bibliothèque municipale, 274, Y.6), produced at Christ Church, Canterbury in the first quarter of the eleventh century, similarly displays dependence on both computistical traditions, drawing its calendar and several tables from the Winchester computus, while most of the other material originated in Leofric-Tiberius.[94] A further characteristic of the Winchester computus, one that is shared by the Red Book of Darley, is the frequent use of Old English. The first half of the Corpus 422 computus contains only Latin aside from a handful of glosses to calendar entries, but the subsequent section contains Old English commentary on two of the five tables, followed by several full pages of vernacular computistical instructions. Despite the omission of this manuscript from the representatives of the Winchester computus, some of these vernacular instructions bear a strong resemblance to those in manuscripts identified by Baker and Lapidge as examples of the Winchester computus. For example, material in Corpus 422 concerning the lunar cycle and the determination of the limits of particular feasts may be compared with very similar material in the Vitellius Psalter (London, British Library, Cotton Vitellius E. XVIII), London, British Library, Harley 3271, London, British Library, Cotton Titus D. XXVII, and other manuscripts.[95]

The similarity of aspects of the computus in the Red Book of Darley to *computi* in manuscripts produced in cathedrals and monasteries may imply a certain degree of standardization in the types of computistical texts copied in these centers. Assuming major Anglo-Saxon scriptoria

---

[92] Baker and Lapidge, *Byrhtferth's* Enchiridion, xlviii; Roy Liuzza, "In Measure, and Number, and Weight: Writing Science," in *The Cambridge History of Early Medieval English Literature*, ed. Clare Lees (Cambridge: Cambridge University Press, 2012), 485.

[93] Baker and Lapidge, *Byrhtferth's* Enchiridion, xlix.

[94] Ibid., xlviii.

[95] Phillip Pulsiano, "The Prefatory Matter of London, British Library, Cotton Vitellius E. XVIII," in *Anglo-Saxon Manuscripts and Their Heritage*, ed. Pulsiano and Elaine Treharne (Aldershot: Ashgate, 1998), 87–88.

were providing pastoral manuscripts for the clergy that included *computi*, it seems likely that this material would resemble the computistical collections found in other manuscripts from these centers, especially the pastorally-oriented Corpus 422. If so, the Winchester and Leofric-Tiberius collections, as well as their variants and admixtures, may have been a common feature of English priestly books from the later tenth century onwards. More manuscript evidence would be needed to confirm this, but certainly the limited amount of computistical material in surviving practical manuscripts for priests is in stark contrast to the consistent emphasis on access to computus in prescriptive booklists.

In addition to its computus and mass and Office texts, the Red Book of Darley transmits an extensive collection of pastoral rites. These generally accord with the types of rituals needed in ministry in a parish church or small religious community, assumedly one with baptismal rights. Like Laud Misc. 482, this manuscript contains rites for the sick and dying, such as those for the visitation of the sick and extreme unction. In fact, some of the vernacular rubrics for the rites included in Corpus 422 strongly resemble a pared-down version of those presented in Laud Misc. 482, prompting Thompson to suggest the possibility of a "common history" for some portions of the manuals in these books.[96]

Despite the relative brevity of these rites compared to the previously discussed Laud Misc. 482, a significantly wider variety of texts for the performance of occasional offices are proffered by Darley, particularly for baptism. Baptism is a central focus of these offices, including a shortened form of baptism for "untrumnum cildum" and a service for the blessing of a baptismal font. This book is in fact "the only major vernacular witness for baptism" from Anglo-Saxon England and as such its contents provide significant insight into the performance of these rites at a local level.[97] The rite of baptism recorded in Darley in essence follows that of the Supplemented Hadrianum, but it is in the details of the rite that this manuscript significantly departs from other liturgical books. This departure is partially visible through the use of extensive and detailed Old English rubrics for the order of baptism. These not only smoothly guide the priest through the baptismal liturgy, but they also clarify the structure of the rite and even provide clear guidance for how laypersons are to participate in the ceremony.[98] For example,

---

[96] Thompson, *Dying and Death*, 78.
[97] Keefer, "Manuals," 102.
[98] R. I. Page, "Old English Liturgical Rubrics in Corpus Christi College, Cambridge, MS 422," *Anglia* 96 (1978); Timothy Graham, "The Old English Liturgical Directions in Corpus Christi College, Cambridge, MS 422," *Anglia* 111 (1993). The Latin content of the offices themselves is written in black ink, while the rubrics and directions for the priest are written in Old English with red ink. The degradation of this ink over time has caused great difficulty in

the priest is instructed at one point to "[a]xa nu þæs cildes naman and do of þisum gehalgodan sealte on þæs cildes muð", and this rubric is followed by the Latin text that is to be said after the giving of the salt.[99] Later in the rite, the godfather is to give responses to questions asked by the priest and the rubrics also give specific instructions for this, reproduced below with the Old English rubrics set in roman and the Latin responses in italics:

> Ahsige her se preost þæs cyldes naman. ðonne secge se godfær þæs cildes naman. Ðonne sette se preost his hand uppan þæs cildes heafod. 7 cweðe.
> *Credis in dominum patrem omnipotentem creatorem celi et terre. et in.*
> Ðonne andswarige se godfæder.
> *Credo.*
> Ðonne cweð se preost gyt oþre syðan.
> *Credis et in ihesum cristum filium eius unicum domiinum nostrum natum et passum.*
> Ðonne andswarige se godfæder.
> *Credo.*[100]

Additionally, as Gittos has pointed out, the baptismal liturgy here is unusual in a number of ways, such as the signing of the cross in the hand of the baptized child, the earlier position of the blessing of the font within the service, and the placing of a lit candle in the hand of the child after baptism.[101]

In addition to the significant material concerning baptism, we also find rites for the care of the sick and dying. Immediately following the section on baptism, there are rites for the visitation of a sick individual and extreme unction, a mass to be performed in the house of a sick person, as well as a burial office and masses for the dead. Rites for some of the same offices have been discussed above for Laud Misc. 482, but the texts for the care of the sick and dying included in the Red Book of Darley are less elaborate and detailed, with shorter rubrics

---

reading these vernacular texts, but the application of ultraviolet light has fortunately allowed their recovery.

[99] "Now ask the child's name and put this consecrated salt in the child's mouth." Page, "Old English Liturgical Rubrics," 151.

[100] "At this time the priest asks the child's name. Then the godfather is to say the child's name. Then the priest places his hand on the child's head and says, 'Do you believe in the Lord, Father Almighty, creator of heaven and earth?' Then the godfather answers, 'I believe.' Then the priest afterward says another: 'And do you believe in Jesus Christ, the only son of our Lord, and his birth and suffering?' Then the godfather answers, 'I believe.'" I have not translated the "et in." following "et terre"; this may be a scribal error. Ibid., 154; Graham, "Old English Liturgical Directions," 442.

[101] Gittos, "Is There Any Evidence for the Liturgy of Parish Churches," 71–73.

and less confessional material for the penitent layperson to recite.[102] Various other offices have also been included in the book, such as those for the making of catechumens; the exorcism of water and salt, which includes the account of the Passion from the Gospel of Matthew to be read over the exorcised elements; the blessing of ashes; the blessing of a marriage; and various ordeals.

What is most remarkable about the occasional offices in Corpus 422 is not their departure from forms found in other liturgical books, but their overt practicality for use in a pastoral setting. The fullness of the rubrics would leave little doubt in the mind of a priest concerning how a rite was to be conducted, and as shown above, there is even specific guidance for how laypeople were to be involved in the baptismal rite. Though we are unsure as to whether the Red Book of Darley was used by a monk-priest or secular priest after its production, there is little doubt that the book was intended for use in pastoral ministry and the vast majority of the content of the book would have been suitable for a secular cleric. In addition, the computus discussed above, derived from two practical computistical collections of the later tenth century, would have enabled a priest with limited education to determine not only the date of Easter and the feasts that depended on that date, but also the Ember fasts, important saints' days, and other liturgical occasions. The occasional offices included here are extensive and cover the full range that an eleventh-century priest would have been called on to perform, including baptism and care for the sick and dying. Despite the lack of penitential material of the kind found in Laud Misc. 482, the Red Book of Darley does provide for the confession of those who are sick, albeit less elaborately than its Worcester contemporary, and it may have been assumed that a proper penitential text would have been available to the user of the manuscript.

Conclusions

It is often challenging to assess the manuscript evidence for the type of priestly texts discussed above due to the ways in which they circulated. However, the above discussion has not only emphasized the importance of these texts to the practice of Anglo-Saxon pastoral care, but has also highlighted potential means of transmission as well as the limited but significant manuscript evidence. While penitentials, manuals, and computistical collections do not typically survive in the manuscript record independently, but are instead typically bound with other liturgical and pastoral texts, this may not reflect the context

---

[102] These rites are compared in Thompson, *Dying and Death*, 78–79.

in which shorter texts for priests often circulated. There is evidence that both penitentials and pastoral rites may have been copied into small books or booklets that were subsequently lost or destroyed, as was certainly the case for homilies; the vagary of unbound booklets of this kind may distort our view of the ways in which short but essential texts for priests circulated. It is in any case difficult to imagine how priests could assign penance without a penitential to guide them or go about the business of pastoral care without a collection of pastoral rites.

The evidence presented herein has suggested that penitentials were important to the practice of pastoral care even prior to their importation by the Benedictine reformers, as is implied by references to penance in late ninth- and early tenth-century law codes. Though most of the manuscript evidence for Anglo-Saxon penitentials comes to us from so-called commonplace books, this chapter has reviewed more practical books for use in pastoral care. The brief penitential handbook found in Vespasian D. XV, which contains a version of the *Penitentiale Theodori* along with a confessional prayer and excerpts relating to sin and penance from Isidore's *Sententiarum*, may point to the form of penitential handbooks prior to the composition and circulation of vernacular penitentials, supporting Thompson's view of an English penitential tradition with "a well-established tradition of confession".[103] Laud Misc. 482, containing both penitential texts and offices for the sick and dying, presents a view of English penitential practice almost a century later, at which time the written vernacular saw significant use, both in penitentials and in the rites of pastoral care.

Manuals of pastoral rites were essential for priests to perform their pastoral duties, yet locating practical manuscripts for pastoral care containing this type of text presents difficulties. We are aided in this to some degree by the occasional offices contained in the Red Book of Darley, which represent a very complete set of rites for use in pastoral care, and though the previous chapter has pointed out the uncertainty concerning the use of this volume by the secular clergy, vernacular rubrics that have been included with the rites for occasional offices testify to the suitability of this book or similarly produced books for use in a local church or small religious community for ministry to the laity. But whether this manuscript was used by secular priests or others, this book tells us that these pastoral rites were available to priests who received their books from episcopal centers, a trend for which evidence has been presented in chapter 3. This may be further supported by the form of the pastoral rites in Laud Misc. 482, a Worcester product that focuses on care for the sick and dying and displays material very

---

[103] Thompson, *Dying and Death*, 58.

similar to that in the Red Book of Darley, though the shorter book's content is more detailed than Darley's relatively abbreviated rites for the sick and dying.

We have seen from the computistical evidence that, as one might expect, similar computistical material circulated in pastoral manuscripts and in books strongly associated with monasteries and monastic cathedrals. Material from both the Winchester and Leofric-Tiberius *computi* was copied in these manuscripts, as is evident from both the Red Book of Darley and other Anglo-Saxon manuscripts. These practical collections of computistical material seem to have gained particular prominence in the late tenth and eleventh centuries, and their relative simplicity and ease of use must have made them ideal and desirable texts for secular priests. Though unambiguous manuscript evidence for the inclusion of computistical material in books for priests is rare, the importance of these sorts of texts to early medieval priests is attested to by the emphasis placed on computus in prescriptive booklists, texts on ordination, and computistical handbooks. Some priests may not have had a great deal of computistical knowledge, as both Bede and Byrhtferth intimate, but demonstration of one's ability to use the computus was a part of the process of ordination and it is certain that early medieval bishops saw availability and knowledge of computus as an essential part of the priestly curriculum.

Conclusions

A recent collection of essays has characterized early medieval priests as "men in the middle", and the characterization is apt.[1] Priests, particularly local priests, were interposed between the higher clergy and the laity, secular authority and local communities, and most importantly, between God and humanity. Priests' roles as spiritual mediators were integrally connected with the rites and ministries of pastoral care, and priests brought literacy and liturgical experience to this aspect of their vocation. This book has focused on one of the few ways to access this essential feature of priestly life: the books used by priests. Many of these books were humble, practical volumes for everyday use. Constant use and changing liturgical trends, combined with a lack of institutional stability in many minor churches, has led to poor rates of survival for priests' books, especially those from Anglo-Saxon England. In spite of this, the analysis of documentary and manuscript evidence for late Anglo-Saxon priests' books sheds new light on the early medieval clergy and the practice of pastoral care.

Fundamentally, the evidence analyzed in this book indicates that Anglo-Saxon priests were expected to have access to a core of priestly texts that would enable them to provide pastoral care as well as the ability to use these books in the performance of their duties. As demonstrated in the Introduction and chapter 1, early medieval bishops in England and on the continent saw access to books as essential to pastoral care and the education of the clergy. As a result, bishops frequently provided lists of the books that priests needed to own. These have in some ways acted as a guide for this study and they certainly point to the importance of considering priests' books as an integral part of understanding pastoral care. While some contemporary sources expressed doubts about priestly literacy in Latin, it is significant that they do not make similar pronouncements about a lack of essential books. Furthermore, the liturgical competence of secular priests was not commonly maligned, but rather assumed in high expectations of their liturgical capability. Various sources, such as accounts of priestly performance of the liturgy, scribal activity, and accounts of clerical training, testify to, at minimum, the possession of functional literacy on the part of Anglo-Saxon priests in performing their pastoral duties.[2] Certainly the greatest difficulty of studying

---

[1] Steffen Patzold and Carine van Rhijn, eds., *Men in the Middle: Local Priests in Early Medieval Europe* (Berlin: De Gruyter, 2016).

[2] This point has been argued in detail in chapter 2.

Anglo-Saxon priests' books is the limited nature of the manuscript evidence. Much has been lost and much has been obscured as a result of these losses. However, we have seen in the preceding chapters a limited but significant number of examples of priests' books, some produced in cathedrals and monasteries and some seemingly written in smaller, less well-provisioned centers of book production, which may have been secular minsters in some cases. These books were not only used, but also corrected, annotated, and added to in the course of their use. Memorization probably also played a role: priests would have known some texts by heart, particularly parts of the liturgy, but their rote knowledge was frequently supplemented by written texts, liturgical and otherwise.[3] Furthermore, two manuscripts probably utilized by Anglo-Saxon secular priests – London, British Library, Cotton Vespasian D. XV, ff. 68–121 and Warsaw, Biblioteka Narodowa, I. 3311 – have been identified in the course of this book and more are likely to be identified with concerted study.

The first of these manuscripts is a lectionary in two parts dated to roughly 1000 AD that unusually presents gospel lections in canonical order in the first section and in liturgical order in the second. Though the work of other scholars has precluded any liturgical use for the Warsaw Lectionary, chapter 5 has shown that this book contains musical notation for the feast of St Andrew and Palm Sunday and that the first and second parts of the books are complementary in providing the readings for Sundays and all the major festivals of the liturgical year. The presence of neumes in this book and the pattern of supplementation of the canonically ordered first section by the liturgically ordered latter section with readings for Sundays and major feast days indicate that this book was used liturgically rather than as a devotional book. This is the type of book that we would expect a small clerical community or local priest to own – a small, portable, and modestly decorated book that provides the pericopes needed for the performance of the mass. Cotton Vespasian D. XV on the other hand is a mid-tenth-century penitential handbook containing Isidore's *Sententiarum* and two patristic homilies in addition to the Latin *Penitentiale Theodori*. Like the Warsaw Lectionary, this book has received little scholarly attention and has thus been largely passed over, but the collection of texts presented in this book are eminently suitable for use by a priest. While the combination of ff. 68–101 with other medieval volumes by Robert Cotton has left this book bereft of a firm context, what is clear is that this book is a portable, low-status, and practical collection of texts that was copied prior to the Benedictine reform or in its early years. The relatively early

---

[3] Julia Barrow, *The Clergy in the Medieval World: Secular Clerics, Their Families and Careers in North-Western Europe, c. 800–c. 1200* (Cambridge: Cambridge University Press, 2015), 224.

Conclusions

date of this book may indeed point back to penitential practice in the secular church prior to the English Benedictine reform, which reached its apogee in the 960s and 970s. This book clearly could have been fruitfully used by a priest and chapter 6 has contended that this is its most probable context.

The addition of these manuscripts to the corpus of Anglo-Saxon priests' books leads us to examine the implications of the large number of unlocalized manuscripts in this group, particularly as neither Vespasian D. XV nor the Warsaw Lectionary have themselves been localized. In fact, of the manuscripts considered in detail, the majority have not been firmly localized, though it should be repeated that the manuscript case studies included in this study are not exhaustive. Dating and localization of manuscripts is most commonly established by paleographical methods and the paleographical means by which a manuscript's geographical origin is assigned relies on comparative evidence. The challenge of associating the script of many of these manuscripts with a particular center or region is a product of a lack of such evidence. Patterns of manuscript survival have perhaps even led to a paleographical overemphasis on particular centers of book production, which may have acted as "hubs of interconnecting networks", but these scriptoria alone cannot tell the whole story.[4] The proportion of unlocalized manuscripts considered here at the very least indicates the large gaps in our knowledge of book production in Anglo-Saxon England, particularly for the secular clergy. Difficulties of localization also suggest that the books produced for use by the secular clergy were often written locally and, as with many Carolingian priests' books, "outside the recognisable centres of book production".[5] Cathedral or monastic scriptoria from which little or no other material has survived are likely candidates for this and a priest might also have benefitted from connections to a local minster with the necessary resources to copy books. Caution should be taken to avoid overgeneralization about the origins of priestly books from this relatively small group of manuscripts, but the evidence most often points away from the more well-studied centers of Anglo-Saxon book production and toward what may be smaller, local scriptoria into which more investigation is needed.

---

[4] Elaine Treharne, "Scribal Connections in Late Anglo-Saxon England," in *Texts and Traditions of Medieval Pastoral Care: Essays in Honour of Bella Millett*, ed. Cate Gunn and Catherine Innes-Parker (York: York Medieval Press, 2009), 29.

[5] Carine van Rhijn, "Manuscripts for Local Priests and the Carolingian Reforms," in *Men in the Middle*, 181.

Changing strategies

While the basic practices and function of pastoral care remained the same throughout the early medieval period, the means of its delivery evolved in response to external political events and major institutional changes within the English church. The tenth and eleventh centuries in England saw the proliferation of local churches, the revitalization of English monasticism and rapid growth of its influence and power, and the influence of Norman conquerors on English ecclesiastical institutions. In some ways, priests' books are a barometer for these changes: their form, content, and even their language evolved to meet the needs of the late Anglo-Saxon church. Priests' books are not necessarily unique in this regard, but changes in these books are one indication of "confronting and processing internal and external changes".[6] For example, the increasing number of missals and missal fragments in late Anglo-Saxon England reflects the changing dynamic of English pastoral care, as all the texts necessary for the performance of mass had originally been separated into discrete books for different actors within the liturgy, but were combined for the use of the celebrant within the missal. Though examples of plenary missals are found in continental Europe in earlier centuries, it is not until the end of the tenth century that missals begin to appear in England, and this shift in the type of mass-books being produced is indicative of the demands of a changing pastoral infrastructure. Both archaeological and textual evidence attest to the exponential increase in the number of small, local churches, most of which probably lacked a clerical community, necessitating that one priest perform most or all of the liturgical roles within the mass and making the plenary missal singularly useful.

Another means by which we can witness change in pastoral strategies in the late Anglo-Saxon period is through the emergence of vernacular preaching texts. While preaching to the laity had been mandated in England since the mid-eighth century, almost all extant homiletic material prior to the second half of the tenth century is in Latin.[7] By the late tenth century however, manuscript evidence attests to the wide circulation of Old English homiletic texts. Particularly after the composition and circulation of Ælfric's homilies, large numbers of manuscripts and manuscript fragments containing vernacular hom-

---

[6] Carol Symes, "Liturgical Texts and Performance Practices," in *Understanding Medieval Liturgy: Essays in Interpretation*, ed. Helen Gittos and Sarah Hamilton (Farnham: Ashgate, 2015), 252.

[7] For the recently discovered exception to this trend, see Donald Scragg, "A Ninth-Century Old English Homily from Northumbria," *Anglo-Saxon England* 45 (2016).

ilies are in evidence. As has been argued in chapter 4, vernacular homilies were primarily intended to be preached within the context of the mass and may have formed a significant part of the catechetical material passed on to laypeople. It is unclear to what extent vernacular preaching to the laity took place prior to the later tenth century, but Donald Scragg's discovery of a ninth-century snippet of an Old English homily in Digby 63 is certainly suggestive of a vernacular preaching tradition that significantly predates the extant codices. The tenth and eleventh centuries nevertheless seem to mark a shift in the extent to which vernacular homilies were being circulated, and, presumably, preached. The composition and wide circulation of Ælfric's *Catholic Homilies* are indicative of the need for preaching texts; the adaptive processes that the work of Ælfric and others underwent is perhaps even more telling. That said, the surviving homiletic manuscripts that we can directly associate with pastoral use by the secular clergy are relatively few. But what has survived, along with episcopal exhortations enjoining preaching and the striking evidence of Anglo-Saxon homiletic booklets, shows the contemporary importance of preaching to pastoral care and a significant shift in textual strategies relating to pastoral care.

Another facet of this shift is the appearance of other, non-homiletic texts for priests in Old English in the later tenth century. Multiple penitentials, computistical collections, and sets of liturgical directions and rubrics were produced in the vernacular, representing a change in the texts available to priests and a stark contrast to the books of priests on the continent. As Mechthild Gretsch has contended, translations into Old English and the composition of new texts in the vernacular are not indications of slovenly unwillingness on the part of the Anglo-Saxons to engage with Latin texts, but rather a sign of the development of Old English "as a medium for scholarly and religious discourse on a par with Latin".[8] Helen Gittos has recently demonstrated that the statements in the prefaces of Old English texts that often define their audiences as lay, unlearned, or both, are "rhetorical conventions" that provided "a way of presenting them for use to the ecclesiastical and educated".[9] But how does the appearance of Old English pastoral texts reflect changes in the way pastoral care was provided? Firstly, the availability of these texts is largely due to the textual fecundity of the reformed monasteries and monastic bishops. The newly composed Old English penitentials seem to have come from this context

---

[8] Mechthild Gretsch, "Winchester Vocabulary and Standard Old English: The Vernacular in Late Anglo-Saxon England," *Bulletin of the John Rylands University Library of Manchester* 83, no. 1 (2001): 87.

[9] Helen Gittos, "The Audience for Old English Texts: Ælfric, Rhetoric and 'the Edification of the Simple'," *Anglo-Saxon England* 43 (2014): 232, 257.

as did the vernacular Winchester computus, and even the Old English portions of the manual in the Red Book of Darley were copied at a monastic cathedral. There also seems to have been a role for monasteries and monastic cathedrals in the production and distribution of these texts, indicating the significant influence of reformed monasticism on the pastoral texts that were circulating. Additionally, the production of vernacular texts for pastoral care is one facet of a growing cultural apprehension of the value and utility of the vernacular, and this was not at all confined to pastoral materials for the secular clergy. Texts like the *Rule of Benedict* and the *Regularis Concordia* were translated into Old English and utilized at Winchester, one of the most prominent centers of Anglo-Saxon learning. This, along with a variety of other evidence for the wide use of the vernacular in monastic contexts, suggests that vernacular pastoral texts were not supplied to the secular clergy due to laziness or inability to understand Latin, but were rather one of several ways in which the acceptance of Old English as a viable medium for wide use within the church manifested itself.

The opening chapter of this book discussed the study of priests' books on the continent, particularly those from the Carolingian Empire, as they relate to Anglo-Saxon priests' books. A brief comparison of the features of the priestly books from these regions can now be made. It has become clear through the course of this study that the books of Anglo-Saxon priests are distinct from many of the continental books that have been considered by scholars such as Yitzhak Hen and Carine van Rhijn. The priests' books from the late Anglo-Saxon period contain little of the material associated with Carolingian priestly handbooks, such as expositions of the mass, baptism, Creed, and *Pater Noster*, as well as abbreviated collections of canon law and episcopal legislation. Some tenth-century manuscripts, such as Cotton Vespasian D. XV and London, British Library, Royal 8 C. III, do contain some of these texts, but despite the greater degree of manuscript survival in the eleventh century, these appear to be relatively rare in late Anglo-Saxon England as opposed to contemporary priests' books from the continent as well as those from the Carolingian period.[10] Much of this is surely due to patterns of manuscript survival. However, we may well wonder if the content of Anglo-Saxon priests' books was significantly distinct from that of their continental counterparts. One distinction is a lack of the priestly handbooks addressed by Susan Keefe and Carine van Rhijn. Combing through the compendia of Anglo-Saxon manuscripts, one

---

[10] Christopher Jones, "The Book of the Liturgy in Anglo-Saxon England," *Speculum* 73, no. 3 (1998): 673–74. David Dumville has noted that there is manuscript evidence for only three *expositio missae* circulating in Anglo-Saxon England. Dumville, *Liturgy and the Ecclesiastical History of Late Anglo-Saxon England: Four Studies* (Woodbridge: Boydell Press, 1992), 116.

Conclusions

will find few manuscripts containing combinations of texts like penitentials, brief, often anonymous, expositions on Christian doctrine, episcopal statutes, a smattering of canon law, and a homily or two.[11] Of the manuscripts considered in detail here, Vespasian D. XV most closely resembles the continental handbooks and might indicate that earlier English priests' books conformed more to continental patterns. Whether due to vagaries in manuscript survival or differing methods of equipping priests, few books like Keefe's "instruction readers" are in evidence.[12] A second distinction is the use of the vernacular in Anglo-Saxon priests' books. While early medieval vernaculars were not absent from continental priests' books, Old English was employed in pastoral and liturgical manuscripts from late Anglo-Saxon England more widely and more frequently than any contemporary vernacular of Western Europe.[13] The clearest context for this is perhaps in preaching, where there is voluminous evidence for Old English homiletic texts and their wide currency. Though homiletic texts could not replace the sort of expositions commonly found in Carolingian priests' books, vernacular homilies and the theological ideas that they transmitted might have served to reduce the need for catechetical texts, which are typically absent from Anglo-Saxon priestly books. A further distinction is the overall survival of priests' books. As the result of a great deal of scholarly effort, dozens of early medieval priests' books from continental Europe have been identified. Priests' books from England, while not receiving an abundance of attention, have not been totally neglected, but the scope of the surviving evidence seems slim by comparison. However, I think it likely that more English priests' books will be identified with time and concerted study.

One route of expanding our understanding of these books may in fact be through the remains of dismembered codices. This book has primarily considered more or less whole codices with the exception of the Taunton Fragment, but fragments of liturgical books from the Anglo-Saxon period are plentiful and are deserving of consideration in their own right. Fragments may in fact better represent the bookholdings of the Anglo-Saxon period than the surviving codices, as the books that have survived intact often exhibit patterns of survival from particular types of institutions, skewing the evidence towards monasteries and

---

[11] Carine van Rhijn, "The Local Church, Priests' Handbooks and Pastoral Care in the Carolingian Period," in *Chiese locali e Chiese regionali nell'alto medioevo*, vol. 61, no. 2 of *Settimane di studio della Fondazione Centro italiano di studi sull'alto medioevo* (Spoleto: Fondazione Centro italiano di studi sull'alto medioevo, 2014), 696, 699.

[12] Susan Keefe, *Water and the Word: Baptism and the Education of the Clergy in the Carolingian Empire*, 2 vols. (Notre Dame: University of Notre Dame Press, 2002).

[13] Francesca Tinti, "Looking for Local Priests in Anglo-Saxon England," in *Men in the Middle*, 160–61.

cathedrals. A larger and perhaps more representative body of material might also aid in better understanding the geographical distinctions in pastoral texts for priests between England and continental Europe. Considering the remarkably valuable evidence from fragments that has come to light in recent years, a study of fragments of Anglo-Saxon liturgical manuscripts could prove to be an important resource for the study of priests' books and pastoral care.

This book has demonstrated the importance of priests' books both to early medieval ecclesiastical authorities and to the study of pastoral care, and despite their poor rate of survival, the study of these sources is vital to our understanding of the ministry and lives of the Anglo-Saxon clergy. Furthermore, the group of those books thought to have been used by the secular clergy has been significantly expanded through this study, showing the importance of reconsidering overlooked and marginalized manuscripts. The findings of this study, as informed by both documentary and manuscript evidence, indicate that priests did have access to pastoral texts, help to contextualize the growth of the local church in the tenth and eleventh centuries, and further elucidate the relationship of the Anglo-Saxon secular clergy to Benedictine monasticism. By studying these often-humble volumes, this study has brought the witness of the Anglo-Saxon priest and his tools to the fore, giving those intimately involved in pastoral care a voice and bringing us closer to the practice of medieval Christianity.

Appendix

Table 5. Tabulation of pericopes from Warsaw, Biblioteka Narodowa, I. 3311

Folio(s)	Scripture reference	Feast/notes[a]
First section		
2r–3r		Preface to the Gospel of Matthew
4v–5v	Matt. 1:1–16	Nativity of Mary
5v–6r	Matt. 1:17–18a	Vigil of Christmas (including next two readings)
6r	Matt. 1:18b–21	
6v	Matt. 1:22–25	
6v–7v	Matt. 2:1–12	Epiphany
8r–8v	Matt. 2:13–18	Holy Innocents
8v	Matt. 2:19–22a	Vigil of Epiphany (fragmentary)
9r–10v	Matt. 28:1–20	Vigil of Easter, Easter Sunday?
11r–12v		Preface to the Gospel of Mark
14r–14v	Mark 1:2–13	Weekday in Advent?
15r–16r	Mark 6:17–29	Beheading of John the Baptist
16r	Mark 13:33–37	St Clemens?
17r	Matt. 4:6–11	First Sunday in Lent (fragmentary)
17v	Matt. 4:18–22	St Andrew
17v–18v	Matt. 5:1–12a	All Saints
18v–18r	Matt. 9:9–13	St Matthew
19r–19v	Matt. 10:1–4	
19v–20v	Matt. 14:1–12	Beheading of John the Baptist
20v–21r	Matt. 16:13–19	Sts Peter and Paul
21r–21v	Matt. 16:24–28	Vigil of the feast of St Laurentius
21v–22v	Matt. 18:1–11	St Michael
22v–23r	Matt. 19:27–29	St Paul
23r–23v	Matt. 20:20–23	St James
23v–24v	Matt. 21:1–9	First Sunday in Advent
24v–25r	Matt. 23:34–39	St Stephen
25r–25v	Matt. 24:42–47	St Sylvester
25v–26v	Matt. 25:1–13	St Agatha, St Cecilia

Appendix

Folio(s)	Scripture reference	Feast/notes[a]
26v–27v	Matt. 25:14–23	St Marcellus, St Marcus
27v–39v	Matt. 26–27	Palm Sunday
40r–50v	Mark 14–16:7	Tuesday in Holy Week, Easter Sunday
51r–51v	Mark 16:14–20	Ascension
53v	Luke 1:1–4	
54r–55r	Luke 1:5–17	Vigil for the feast of John the Baptist
55r–56r	Luke 1:26–38	Lenten Ember day, the Annunciation
56r–57r	Luke 1:39–56	Lenten Ember day?
57r–58r	Luke 1:57–68	John the Baptist
58r–59r	Luke 2:1–14	Christmas
59r–59v	Luke 2:15–20	Christmas
59v–60r	Luke 2:21	
60r–60v	Luke 2:22–32	Candlemas
60v–61r	Luke 6:20–23	Martyrs?
61r–61v	Luke 9:1–6	Eighth Sunday after Epiphany, Thursday of Pentecost Week
61v–62r	Luke 10:1–7	St Luke?
62r–62v	Luke 10:21–22	
62v–63r	Luke 10:38–42	Assumption of Mary
63r–63v	Luke 11:5–13	*Litaniae minores*
63v–64r	Luke 11:33–36	Seven Holy Brothers
64r–65r	Luke 12:2–8	St James
65r	Luke 12:32–34	Translation of St Martin
65r–66r	Luke 12:35–44	Doctors of the Church
66r–67r	Luke 14:26–33	A martyr
67r	Luke 18:31–33	Tuesday of Holy Week?
67r–68r	Luke 21:9–19	Sts Marcellinus and Peter
68r–68v	Luke 21:25–33	Second Sunday in Advent
69r–79r	Luke 22:1–23:53	Wednesday of Holy Week
79r–81r	Luke 24:13–35	Easter Monday
81r–82v	Luke 24:36–53	Tuesday of Easter Week
83r–83v		Preface to the Gospel of John
84r–85r	John 1:1–14	Christmas
85r–86v	John 1:35–51	Vigil of the feast of St Andrew
86v–87v	John 3:1–15	Monday after Octave of Easter, Sunday after Pentecost

236

Appendix

Folio(s)	Scripture reference	Feast/notes[a]
88r	John 12:24–26	St Lawrence, St Vincent
88r–90v	John 13:1–32	Maundy Thursday
90v–92r	John 14:1–21	Sts Philip and Jacob, Vigil of Pentecost
92v–93r	John 14:23–31	Pentecost
93r–94r	John 15:1–11	Vigil of the feast of Sts Simon and Jude
94r–94v	John 15:12–16	Sts Primus and Felician, Sts Marcus and Marcellianus
94v–95r	John 15:17–25	Sts Simon and Jude, Sts Alexander, Eventius and Theodolus
95r–95v	John 15:26–16:4	Sunday before Pentecost
95v–96v	John 16:5–14	Fourth Sunday after Easter
96v–97r	John 16:16–22	Third Sunday after Easter
97r–97v	John 17:1–8a	Vigil for the Ascension (fragmentary)
98r–105r	John 18:3–19:42	Good Friday (fragmentary)
105r–106r	John 20:1–10	Saturday after Easter
106r–107r	John 20:11–18	Thursday after Easter
107r–108r	John 20:19–31	Octave of Easter
108r–109v	John 21:1–15a	Wednesday after Easter
109v–110r	John 21:15b–19a	Vigil of the feast of Sts Peter and Paul
110r–110v	John 21:19b–25	St John
Second section		
111r–111v	Luke 2:33–40	Sunday after Christmas
111v–112v	Luke 2:42–52	Sunday after Epiphany
112v–113r	Matt. 3:13–17	Octave of Epiphany
113r–113v	John 2:1–11	Second Sunday after Epiphany
113v–114v	Matt. 8:1–13	Third Sunday after Epiphany
114v–115r	Matt. 8:23–27	Fourth Sunday after Epiphany
115r–116r	Matt. 13:24–30	Fifth Sunday after Epiphany
116r–117r	Matt. 20:1–16	Septuagesima
117r–118r	Luke 8:4–15	Sexagesima
118r–119r	Luke 18:31–43	Quinquagesima
119r–119v	Matt. 6:16–21	Ash Wednesday
119v–120v	Matt. 17:1–9	Lenten Ember day
120v–121r	Matt. 15:21–28	Second Sunday in Lent
121r–122v	Luke 11:14–28	Third Sunday in Lent
122v–123v	John 6:1–14	Fourth Sunday in Lent

Appendix

Folio(s)	Scripture reference	Feast/notes[a]
123v–125r	John 8:46–59	Fifth Sunday in Lent
125r–125v	John 10:11–16	Week after Octave of Easter
125v–126r	John 16:23–30	Fifth Sunday after Easter
126r–126v	Matt. 20:29–34	Pentecost Ember day (mislabelled)[b]
126v–127v	John 17:17–26	Sunday after Pentecost (mislabelled)
127v–128v	Luke 16:19–31	Second Sunday after Pentecost (mislabelled)
129r–129v	Luke 14:16–24	Third Sunday after Pentecost (mislabelled)
129v–130v	Luke 15:1–10	Fourth Sunday after Pentecost (mislabelled)
130v–131v	Luke 16:36–42	Fifth Sunday after Pentecost
131v–132v	Luke 5:1–11	Sixth Sunday after Pentecost
132v–133r	Matt. 5:20–24	Seventh Sunday after Pentecost
133r–133v	Mark 8:1–9	Eighth Sunday after Pentecost
133v–134v	Matt. 7:15–21	Ninth Sunday after Pentecost
134v–135r	Luke 16:1–9	Tenth Sunday after Pentecost
135v–136r	Luke 19:41–47a	Eleventh Sunday after Pentecost
136r–136v	Luke 18:9–14	Twelfth Sunday after Pentecost
136v–137r	Mark 7:31–37	Thirteenth Sunday after Pentecost
137r–138v	Luke 10:23–37	Fourteenth Sunday after Pentecost
138v–139r	Luke 17:11–19	Fifteenth Sunday after Pentecost
139r–140r	Matt. 6:24–33	Sixteenth Sunday after Pentecost
140r–140v	Luke 7:11–16	Seventeenth Sunday after Pentecost
140v–141v	Luke 14:1–11	Eighteenth Sunday after Pentecost
141v–142r	Matt. 22:34–46	Nineteenth Sunday after Pentecost
142r–143r	Matt. 9:1–8	Twentieth Sunday after Pentecost
143r–144r	Matt. 22:1–14	Twenty-first Sunday after Pentecost
144r–144v	John 4:46–53	Twenty-second Sunday after Pentecost
144v–146r	Matt. 18:23–35	Twenty-third Sunday after Pentecost
146r–146v	Matt. 22:15–21	Twenty-fourth Sunday after Pentecost
146v–147r	Matt. 9:18–22	Twenty-fifth Sunday after Pentecost
147r–148r	John 6:5–14	Twenty-sixth Sunday after Pentecost
148r–148v	Matt. 11:2–10	Third Sunday in Advent
148v–149r	Luke 3:1–6	Advent Ember day
149r–150r	John 1:19–28	Fourth Sunday in Advent
150r–150v	John 11:21–27	Mass for the Dead
150v–151v	Luke 19:1–10	Dedication of a church

Appendix

Folio(s)	Scripture reference	Feast/notes[a]
151v	Luke 6:43–45	Dedication of the Lateran Basilica (fragmentary)

[a] The cross-referencing of pericopes with the appropriate feasts was done with reference to Ursula Lenker, *Die westsächsische Evangelienversion und die Perikopenordnungen im angelsächsischen England* (Munich: Wilhelm Fink, 1997), 298–383.

[b] These entries are labelled as *Dominica v, Dominica vi, Dominica vii, Dominica viii,* and *Dominica x,* respectively.

Bibliography

Unpublished primary sources

Berlin, Deutsche Staadtsbibliothek, Phillips 1667
Bern, Burgerbibliothek 671
Bloomington, Indiana University, Lilly Library, Poole 41
Boulogne-sur-Mer, Bibliothèque municipale 106
Cambridge, Corpus Christi College 41
Cambridge, Corpus Christi College 69
Cambridge, Corpus Christi College 162
Cambridge, Corpus Christi College 173 (The Parker Chronicle)
Cambridge, Corpus Christi College 190
Cambridge, Corpus Christi College 198
Cambridge, Corpus Christi College 201
Cambridge, Corpus Christi College 260
Cambridge, Corpus Christi College 265
Cambridge, Corpus Christi College 391
Cambridge, Corpus Christi College 422 (The Red Book of Darley)
Cambridge, Trinity College, B. 10. 4
Cambridge, University Library, Add. 3206
Dublin, Royal Irish Academy, D. II. 3
Durham, Cathedral Library, A. II. 17 (Durham Gospels)
Durham, Cathedral Library, A. IV. 19 (The Durham Collectar)
Durham, Cathedral Library, B. II. 2
Edinburgh, National Library of Scotland, Advocates 18. 7. 8
Esztergom, Archiepiscopal Library, s.n.
Exeter, Cathedral Library 3501 (The Exeter Book)
Karlsruhe, Badische Landesbibliothek, Aug. perg. 221
Le Havre, Bibliothèque municipale 330 (Missal of the New Minster)
Lincoln, Cathedral Library 158
Lincoln, Cathedral Library 182
London, British Library, Add. 37517 (The Bosworth Psalter)
London, British Library, Add. 47967 (The Lauderdale Orosius)
London, British Library, Add. 49598 (Benedictional of St Æthelwold)
London, British Library, Add. 56488, ff. i, 1–6 (The Muchelney Breviary Fragment)
London, British Library, Cotton Galba A. XVIII (The Æthelstan Psalter)
London, British Library, Cotton Nero D. IV (The Lindisfarne Gospels)
London, British Library, Cotton Tiberius A. III

Bibliography

London, British Library, Cotton Titus C. XV, f. 1
London, British Library, Cotton Titus D. XXVII
London, British Library, Cotton Vespasian A. I (The Vespasian Psalter)
London, British Library, Cotton Vespasian D. XV, ff. 68–121
London, British Library, Cotton Vitellius A. XV (The Beowulf Manuscript)
London, British Library, Cotton Vitellius A. XVIII (The Giso Sacramentary)
London, British Library, Cotton Vitellius E. XII
London, British Library, Cotton Vitellius E. XVIII (The Vitellius Psalter)
London, British Library, Harley 2961 (The Leofric Collectar)
London, British Library, Harley 3271
London, British Library, Royal 1 D. III
London, British Library, Royal 2. B. V (The Royal Psalter)
London, British Library, Royal 8 C. III
London, British Library, Royal 17 C. XVII, ff. 2–3, 163–166
London, British Library, Stowe 944
London, Lambeth Palace Library 487
London, Lambeth Palace Library 489
London, Society of Antiquaries 154
Orléans, Bibliothèque municipale 116
Orléans, Bibliothèque municipale 127 (The Winchcombe Sacramentary)
Oslo, Riksarkivet, Lat. fragm. 206 + 209, nos. 1–4 + 239, nos. 6–7
Oxford, Bodleian Library, Auct. D. 2. 14
Oxford, Bodleian Library, Auct. D. 2. 19 (The MacRegol Gospels)
Oxford, Bodleian Library, Auct. F. 4. 32, ff. 10–18
Oxford, Bodleian Library, Bodley 343
Oxford, Bodleian Library, Bodley 386, ff. 1, 174
Oxford, Bodleian Library, Bodley 579 (The Leofric Missal)
Oxford, Bodleian Library, Digby 63
Oxford, Bodleian Library, Hatton 115, ff. 140r–147r
Oxford, Bodleian Library, Junius 27 (The Junius Psalter)
Oxford, Bodleian Library, Junius 85 and 86
Oxford, Bodleian Library, Junius 121
Oxford, Bodleian Library, Laud Misc. 482
Oxford, Corpus Christi College 282
Paris, Bibliothèque nationale de France, lat. 1603
Paris, Bibliothèque nationale de France, lat. 8092
Princeton, New Jersey, Princeton University Library, Scheide Collection 71 (The Blickling Homilies)
Rome, Biblioteca Vallicelliana, E 15
Rome, Vatican City, Biblioteca Apostolica Vaticana, Pal. lat. 259
Rome, Vatican City, Biblioteca Apostolica Vaticana, Pal. lat. 554
Rouen, Bibliothèque municipale, 274, Y.6
SHC DD\SAS/C1193/77 (The Taunton Fragment)

Bibliography

St Petersburg, National Library of Russia, Q.V.I.34
Vercelli, Biblioteca Capitolare CXVII (The Vercelli Book)
Warsaw, Biblioteka Narodowa, I. 3311 (The Warsaw Lectionary)
Worcester, Cathedral Library, F. 173
York Minster, Minster Library, Add. 1 (The York Gospels)

Published primary sources

Ælfric Bata. *Anglo-Saxon Conversations: The Colloquies of Ælfric Bata*. Edited by Scott Gwara. Translated by David W. Porter. Woodbridge: Boydell Press, 1997.

Ælfric of Eynsham. *Ælfric's Catholic Homilies: The First Series*. Edited by Peter Clemoes. Early English Text Society Supplementary Series 17. Oxford: Oxford University Press, 1997.

———. *Ælfric's Catholic Homilies: The Second Series*. Edited by Malcolm Godden. Early English Text Society Supplementary Series 5. Oxford: Oxford University Press, 1979.

———. *Ælfric's* De Temporibus Anni. Edited by Martin Blake. Cambridge: D. S. Brewer, 2009.

———. *Ælfric's* Lives of Saints: *Being a Set of Sermons on Saints' Days Formerly Observed by the English Church*. Edited by Walter W. Skeat. Vol. 1. Early English Text Society Original Series 76 and 82. London: Oxford University Press, 1966.

———. *Ælfric's Prefaces*. Edited by Jonathan Wilcox. Durham: Durham Medieval Texts, 1994.

———. *Die Hirtenbriefe Ælfrics in altenglischer und lateinischer Fassung*. Edited by Bernhard Fehr. Hamburg: Henri Grand, 1914.

———. *The Old English Heptateuch and Ælfric's* Libellus de Veteri Testamento et Novo. Edited by Richard Marsden. Early English Text Society Original Series 330. Oxford: Oxford University Press, 2008.

Angelsächsische Homilien und Heiligenleben. Edited by Bruno Assmann. Kassel: G.H. Wigand, 1889.

Anglo-Saxon Charters: An Annotated List and Bibliography. Edited by Peter H. Sawyer. London: Royal Historical Society, 1968.

Anglo-Saxon Penitentials: A Cultural Database. Edited by Allen J. Frantzen. Accessed October 11, 2018. http://anglo-saxon.net/penance/.

Anglo-Saxon Wills. Edited and translated by Dorothy Whitelock. Cambridge: Cambridge University Press, 1930.

Asser. *Alfred the Great: Asser's* Life of King Alfred *and Other Contemporary Sources*. Translated by Simon Keynes and Michael Lapidge. London: Penguin Books, 1983.

Bede. *Bedae Opera De Temporibus*. Edited by Charles Williams Jones. Cambridge, MA: Mediaeval Academy of America, 1943.

Bibliography

———. *Bede: The Reckoning of Time*. Translated by Faith Wallis. Liverpool: Liverpool University Press, 1999.

———. *Bede's Ecclesiastical History of the English People*. Edited by Bertram Colgrave and R. A. B. Mynors. Oxford: Clarendon Press, 1969.

The Blickling Homilies (The John H. Scheide Library, Titusville, Pennsylvania). Edited by Rudolph Willard. Early English Manuscripts in Facsimile 10. Copenhagen: Rosenkilde and Bagger, 1960.

The Blickling Homilies: With a Translation and Index of Words together with the Blickling Glosses. Edited by Richard Morris. Early English Text Society Original Series 58, 63, and 73. London: Oxford University Press, 1967.

Boniface. *The Letters of Saint Boniface*. Translated by Ephraim Emerton. New York: Columbia University Press, 1940.

Burchard of Worms. *Burchardi vormatiensis episcopi opera omnia* .... Edited by Jacques-Paul Migne. Patrologia Latina 140. Paris: Garnier, 1880.

Byrhtferth. *Byrhtferth of Ramsey: The Lives of St Oswald and St Ecgwine*. Edited and translated by Michael Lapidge. Oxford: Clarendon Press, 2009.

———. *Byrhtferth's* Enchiridion. Edited by Peter S. Baker and Michael Lapidge. Early English Text Society Supplementary Series 15. Oxford: Oxford University Press, 1995.

Capitula episcoporum. Pt. 1, edited by Peter Brommer. *Monumenta Germaniae Historica*. Hanover: Hahnsche Buchhandlung, 1984.

Capitula episcoporum. Pt. 2, edited by Rudolf Pokorny and Martina Stratmann. *Monumenta Germaniae Historica*. Hanover: Hahnsche Buchhandlung, 1995.

Capitularia regum Francorum. Pt. 1, edited by Alfred Boretius. *Monumenta Germaniae Historica*. Hanover: Hahnsche Buchhandlung, 1883.

The Cartulary of St Mary's Collegiate Church, Warwick. Edited by C. R. Fonge. Woodbridge: Boydell Press, 2004.

Charters of St Albans. Edited by Julia Crick. Oxford: Published for the British Academy by Oxford University Press, 2007.

Charters of the Redvers Family and the Earldom of Devon, 1090–1217. Edited by Robert Bearman. Devon and Cornwall Record Society Publications, n.s., 37. Exeter: Devon and Cornwall Record Society, 1994.

Chronique de l'Abbaye de St-Hubert dite Cantatorium. Translated by A. L. P. de Robaulx de Soumoy. Brussels: Méline, Cans et Compagnie, 1847.

Coatsworth, Elizabeth. *Western Yorkshire*. Vol. 8 of *Corpus of Anglo-Saxon Stone Sculpture*. Edited by Rosemary Cramp. Oxford: Oxford University Press, 2008.

Concilia aevi Karolini. Vol. 2, pt. 1, edited by Albert Werminghoff. *Monumenta Germaniae Historica*. Hanover, 1906.

Bibliography

Councils and Ecclesiastical Documents Relating to Great Britain and Ireland. Edited by Arthur West Haddan and William Stubbs. Vol. 3, *English Church during the Anglo-Saxon Period: A.D. 595–1066*. Oxford: Clarendon Press, 1871.

Councils and Synods, with Other Documents Relating to the English Church, AD 871–1204. Edited by Dorothy Whitelock, Martin Brett, and Christopher N. L. Brooke. Vol. 1. Oxford: Clarendon Press, 1981.

Colección documental del Monasterio de San Pedro de Cardeña. Edited by Gonzalo Martínez Díez. Burgos: Caja de Ahorros y Monte de Piedad del Circulo Católico de Obreros de Burgos, 1998.

The Domesday Monachorum of Christ Church, Canterbury. Edited by David C. Douglas. London: Royal Historical Society, 1944.

Eadmer. *Eadmer of Canterbury: Lives and Miracles of Saints Oda, Dunstan, and Oswald*. Edited and translated by Andrew Turner and Bernard Muir. Oxford: Clarendon Press, 2006.

The Early Charters of the Augustinian Canons of Waltham Abbey, Essex, 1062–1230. Edited by Rosalind Ransford. Woodbridge: Boydell Press, 1989.

The Early Lives of St Dunstan. Edited and translated by Michael Winterbottom and Michael Lapidge. Oxford: Clarendon Press, 2012.

English Historical Documents. Edited by David C. Douglas. Vol. 1, *c. 500–1042*, edited by Dorothy Whitelock. 2nd ed. London: Eyre Methuen, 1979.

Die Gesetze der Angelsachsen. Vol. 1, *Text und Übersetzung*. Edited by Felix Liebermann. Halle: Max Niemeyer, 1903.

Gregory the Great. *Homiliae in Evangelia*. Edited by Raymond Étaix. Corpus Christianorum Series Latina 141. Turnhout: Brepols, 1999.

Isidore of Seville. *Sancti Isidori hispalensis episcopi opera omnia …*. Edited by Jacques-Paul Migne. Patrologia Latina 83. Paris, 1862.

John of Forde: The Life of Wulfric of Haselbury, Anchorite. Translated by Pauline Matarasso. Collegeville, MN: Liturgical Press, 2011.

John of Worcester. *The Chronicle of John of Worcester*. Vol. 2, *The Annals from 450 to 1066*, edited by R. R. Darlington and P. McGurk. Translated by Jennifer Bray and Patrick McGurk. Oxford: Clarendon Press, 1995.

Justin Martyr. *St Justin Martyr: The First and Second Apologies*. Translated by Leslie W. Barnard. New York: Paulist Press, 1997.

Lang, James. *York and Eastern Yorkshire*. Vol. 3 of *Corpus of Anglo-Saxon Stone Sculpture*. Edited by Rosemary Cramp. Oxford: Published for the British Academy by Oxford University Press, 1991.

The Leofric Missal I: Introduction, Collation Tables and Index. Edited by Nicholas Orchard. London: The Henry Bradshaw Society, 2002.

Liber Eliensis: A History of the Isle of Ely from the Seventh Century to the Twelfth. Translated by Janet Fairweather. Woodbridge: Boydell Press, 2005.

The Life of St. Chad: An Old English Homily. Edited by Rudolf Vleeskruyer. Amsterdam: North-Holland, 1953.

The Macregol Gospels or the Rushworth Gospels: Edition of the Latin Text with the Old English Interlinear Gloss Transcribed from Oxford Bodleian Library, MS Auctarium D. 2 19. Edited by Kenichi Tamoto. Philadelphia: John Benjamins, 2013.

Medieval Handbooks of Penance: A Translation of the Principal Libri Poenitentiales *and Selections from Related Documents*. Edited and translated by John T. McNeill and Helena M. Gamer. New York: Columbia University Press, 1965.

Munimenta Gildhallæ Londoniensis. Vol. 2, pt. 1, *Liber Custumarum with Extracts from the Cottonian MS. Claudius, D. II*. Edited by Henry Thomas Riley. Rerum Britannicarum medii aevi scriptores (Rolls Series) 12. London: Longman, Green, Longman, and Roberts, 1860.

Okasha, Elisabeth. *Handlist of Anglo-Saxon Non-runic Inscriptions*. Cambridge: Cambridge University Press, 1971.

The Old English Finding of the True Cross. Edited and translated by Mary-Catherine Bodden. Cambridge: D. S. Brewer, 1987.

The Old English Martyrology: Edition, Translation and Commentary. Edited and translated by Christine Rauer. Cambridge: D. S. Brewer, 2013.

The Old English Version of the Enlarged Rule of Chrodegang. Edited and translated by Brigitte Langefeld. Frankfurt: Peter Lang, 2003.

The Old English Vision of St. Paul. Edited by Antonette DiPaolo Healey. Cambridge, MA: Mediaeval Academy of America, 1978.

Orderic Vitalis. *The Ecclesiastical History of Orderic Vitalis*. Edited and translated by Marjorie Chibnall. Vol. 3, bks. 5 and 6. Oxford: Clarendon Press, 1972.

Poems and Prose from the Old English. Edited by Alexandra H. Olsen and Burton Raffel. Translated by Burton Raffel. New Haven: Yale University Press, 1998.

Preston, Todd. *King Alfred's Book of Laws: A Study of the* Domboc *and Its Influence on English Identity, with a Complete Translation*. Jefferson, NC: McFarland, 2012.

Regino of Prüm. *Das Sendhandbuch des Regino von Prüm*. Edited by Wilfried Hartmann. Darmstadt: Wissenschaftliche Buchgesellschaft, 2004.

Rumble, Alexander R. *Property and Piety in Early Medieval Winchester: Documents Relating to the Topography of the Anglo-Saxon and Norman City and Its Minsters*. Oxford: Clarendon Press, 2002.

Sancti Aurelii Augustini hipponensis episcopi opera omnia .... Edited by Jacques-Paul Migne. Patrologia Latina 40. Paris, 1841.

Select English Historical Documents of the Ninth and Tenth Centuries. Edited by F. E. Harmer. Cambridge: Cambridge University Press, 1914.

Scriptores rerum Merovingicarum. Vol. 1, pt. 1, edited by Bruno Krusch and Wilhelm Levison. *Monumenta Germaniae Historica*. Hanover: Hahnsche Buchhandlung, 1951.

Theodulfi Capitula in England: Die altenglischen Übersetzungen, zusammen mit dem lateinischen Text. Edited by Hans Sauer. Munich: Wilhelm Fink, 1978.

The Vercelli Homilies and Related Texts. Edited by Donald G. Scragg. Early English Text Society Original Series 300. Oxford: Oxford University Press, 1992.

Vetus registrum Sarisberiense alias dictum registrum S. Osmundi Episcopi: The Register of S. Osmund. Edited by W. H. Rich Jones. Vol. 1. Rerum Britannicarum medii aevi scriptores (Rolls Series) 78. Millwood, NY: Kraus Reprint, 1965.

The Waltham Chronicle: An Account of the Discovery of Our Holy Cross at Montacute and Its Conveyance to Waltham. Edited and translated by Leslie Watkiss and Marjorie Chibnall. Oxford: Clarendon Press, 1994.

William of Malmesbury. *Saints' Lives: Lives of SS. Wulfstan, Dunstan, Patrick, Benignus and Indract*. Edited and translated by Michael Winterbottom and R. M. Thomson. Oxford: Oxford University Press, 2002.

Wordsworth, Charles. Pontificale Ecclesiae S. Andreae: *The Pontifical Offices Used by David de Bernham, Bishop of S. Andrews*. Edinburgh: Pitsligo Press, 1885.

Wulfric of Haselbury, by John, Abbot of Ford. Edited by Maurice Bell. Frome and London, 1933.

Wulfstan of Winchester. *Life of St Æthelwold*. Edited and translated by Michael Lapidge and Michael Winterbottom. Oxford: Clarendon Press, 1991.

Wulfstan. *The Homilies of Wulfstan*. Edited by Dorothy Bethurum. Oxford: Clarendon Press, 1957.

———. *Wulfstan's Canons of Edgar*. Edited by Roger Fowler. Early English Text Society Original Series 266. London: Oxford University Press, 1972.

Secondary sources

Abrams, Lesley. *Anglo-Saxon Glastonbury: Church and Endowment*. Woodbridge: Boydell Press, 1996.

Amodio, Mark. *Writing the Oral Tradition: Oral Poetics and Literate Culture in Medieval England*. Notre Dame: University of Notre Dame Press, 2004.

Amos, Thomas L. "Monks and Pastoral Care in the Early Middle Ages." In *Religion, Culture, and Society in the Early Middle Ages: Studies in Honor of Richard E. Sullivan*, edited by Thomas F. X. Noble and

John Contreni, 165–80. Kalamazoo: Medieval Institute Publications, 1987.

———. "Preaching and the Sermon in the Carolingian World." In *De Ore Domini: Preacher and Word in the Middle Ages*, edited by Thomas L. Amos, Eugene Green, and Beverly Mayne Kienzle, 41–60. Kalamazoo: Medieval Institute Publications, 1989.

Backhouse, Janet. "Aldred (*fl.* c.970)." In *Oxford Dictionary of National Biography*. Oxford University Press, 2004. Accessed October 3, 2014. doi:10.1093/ref:odnb/312.

Baker, Nigel, and Richard Holt. *Urban Growth and the Medieval Church: Gloucester and Worcester*. Aldershot: Ashgate, 2004.

Baker, Peter S. "Textual Boundaries in Anglo-Saxon Works on Time (and in Some Old English Poems)." In *Studies in English Language and Literature: "Doubt Wisely", Papers in Honour of E. G. Stanley*, edited by M. J. Toswell and Elizabeth M. Tyler, 445–56. London: Routledge, 1996.

Barlow, Frank. *The English Church, 1000–1066: A History of the Later Anglo-Saxon Church*. 2nd ed. London: Longman, 1979.

Barrow, Julia. "Clergy in the Diocese of Hereford in the Eleventh and Twelfth Centuries." In *Anglo-Norman Studies XXVI: Proceedings of the Battle Conference 2003*, edited by John Gillingham, 37–54. Woodbridge: Boydell Press, 2004.

———. "The Clergy in English Dioceses c. 900–c. 1066." In *Pastoral Care in Late Anglo-Saxon England*, edited by Francesca Tinti, 17–26. Woodbridge: Boydell Press, 2005.

———. *The Clergy in the Medieval World: Secular Clerics, Their Families and Careers in North-Western Europe, c. 800–c. 1200*. Cambridge: Cambridge University Press, 2015.

———. "The Community of Worcester, 961–c. 1100." In *St Oswald of Worcester: Life and Influence*, edited by Nicholas Brooks and Catherine Cubitt, 84–99. London: Leicester University Press, 1996.

———. "English Cathedral Communities and Reform in the Late Tenth and Eleventh Centuries." In *Anglo-Norman Durham, 1093–1193*, edited by David Rollason, Margaret Harvey, and Michael Prestwich, 25–39. Woodbridge: Boydell Press, 1998.

———. "Grades of Ordination and Clerical Careers, c. 900–c. 1200." In *Anglo-Norman Studies XXX: Proceedings of the Battle Conference 2007*, edited by C. P. Lewis, 41–61. Woodbridge: Boydell Press, 2008.

———. "Survival and Mutation: Ecclesiastical Institutions in the Danelaw in the Ninth and Tenth Centuries." In *Cultures in Contact: Scandinavian Settlement in England in the Ninth and Tenth Centuries*, edited by Dawn M. Hadley and Julian D. Richards, 155–76. Turnhout: Brepols, 2000.

———. *Who Served the Altar at Brixworth? Clergy in English Minsters c. 800–c. 1100*. Brixworth: Friends of All Saints Church, Brixworth, 2013.

———. "Wulfstan and Worcester: Bishop and Clergy in the Early Eleventh Century." In *Wulfstan, Archbishop of York: The Proceedings of the Second Alcuin Conference*, edited by Matthew Townend, 141–59. Turnhout: Brepols, 2004.

Barton, David, and Mary Hamilton. "Literacy Practices." In *Situated Literacies: Reading and Writing in Context*, edited by David Barton, Mary Hamilton, and Roz Ivanič, 7–15. London: Routledge, 2000.

Bassett, Steven. "Anglo-Saxon Shrewsbury and Its Churches." *Midland History* 16 (1991): 1–23.

Bäuml, Franz H. "Varieties and Consequences of Medieval Literacy and Illiteracy." *Speculum* 55, no. 2 (1980): 237–65.

Baxter, Stephen. *The Earls of Mercia: Lordship and Power in Late Anglo-Saxon England*. Oxford: Oxford University Press, 2007.

Bedingfield, M. Bradford. *The Dramatic Liturgy of Anglo-Saxon England*. Woodbridge: Boydell Press, 2002.

———. "Public Penance in Anglo-Saxon England." *Anglo-Saxon England* 31 (2002): 223–55.

Berlin, Gail Ivy. "Memorization in Anglo-Saxon England: Some Case Studies." In *Oral Tradition in the Middle Ages*, edited by W. F. H. Nicolaisen, 97–113. Binghamton, NY: Medieval and Renaissance Text and Studies, 1995.

Bibire, Paul, and Alan S. C. Ross. "The Differences between Lindisfarne and Rushworth Two." *Notes and Queries* 28, no. 2 (April 1981): 98–116.

Billett, Jesse D. "The Divine Office and the Secular Clergy in Later Anglo-Saxon England." In *England and the Continent in the Tenth Century: Studies in Honour of Wilhelm Levison (1876–1947)*, edited by David Rollason, Conrad Leyser, and Hannah Williams, 429–71. Turnhout: Brepols, 2010.

———. *The Divine Office in Anglo-Saxon England, 597–c.1000*. London and Woodbridge: Henry Bradshaw Society and Boydell Press, 2014.

———. "*Sermones ad diem pertinentes*: Sermons and Homilies in the Liturgy of the Divine Office." In *Sermo Doctorum: Compilers, Preachers and Their Audiences in the Early Middle Ages*, edited by Maximilian Diesenberger, Yitzhak Hen, and Marianne Pollheimer, 339–73. Turnhout: Brepols, 2013.

Blair, John, and Richard Sharpe. Introduction to *Pastoral Care before the Parish*, edited by John Blair and Richard Sharpe, 1–10. Leicester: Leicester University Press, 1992.

Blair, John. "Bosham." In *The Wiley-Blackwell Encyclopedia of Anglo-Saxon England*, 2nd ed., edited by Michael Lapidge, John Blair, Simon Keynes, and Donald Scragg. Oxford: Wiley-Blackwell, 2014.

***. *The Church in Anglo-Saxon Society*. Oxford: Oxford University Press, 2005.

***. Introduction to *Minsters and Parish Churches: The Local Church in Transition, 950–1200*, edited by John Blair, 1–19. Oxford: Oxford University Committee for Archaeology, 1988.

***. "Saint Cuthman, Steyning and Bosham." *Sussex Archaeological Collections* 135 (1997): 173–92.

***. "Secular Minster Churches in Domesday Book." In *Domesday Book: A Reassessment*, edited by Peter Sawyer, 104–42. London: Edward Arnold, 1985.

Blake, Brett Elizabeth, and Robert W. Blake. *Literacy and Learning: A Reference Handbook*. Santa Barbara, CA: ABC-CLIO, 2002.

Boddington, Andy. *Raunds Furnells: The Anglo-Saxon Church and Churchyard*. London: English Heritage, 1996.

Bonner, Gerald. "St Cuthbert at Chester-le-Street." In *St Cuthbert, His Cult and His Community to AD 1200*, edited by Gerald Bonner, Clare Stancliffe, and David Rollason, 387–95. Woodbridge: Boydell Press, 1989.

Borst, Arno. *The Ordering of Time: From the Ancient Computus to the Modern Computer*. Translated by Andrew Winnard. Chicago: University of Chicago Press, 1993.

Boyd, W. J. P. *Aldred's Marginalia: Explanatory Comments in the Lindisfarne Gospels*. Exeter: University of Exeter, 1975.

Boynton, Susan. "The Bible and the Liturgy." In *The Practice of the Bible in the Middle Ages: Production, Reception, and Performance in Western Christianity*, edited by Susan Boynton and Diane Reilly, 10–33. New York: Columbia University Press, 2011.

***. "Training for the Liturgy as a Form of Monastic Education." In *Medieval Monastic Education*, edited by George Ferzoco and Carolyn Muessig, 7–20. Leicester: Leicester University Press, 2000.

Bredehoft, Thomas A. "Filling the Margins of CCCC 41: Textual Space and a Developing Archive." *The Review of English Studies* 57 (2005): 721–32.

Breeze, Andrew. "The Provenance of The Rushworth Mercian Gloss." *Notes and Queries* 43, no. 4 (1996): 394–95.

Brooke, Christopher N. L. *Churches and Churchmen in Medieval Europe*. London: Hambledon Press, 1999.

Brooks, Nicholas. "The Career of St Dunstan." In *St Dunstan: His Life, Times and Cult*, edited by Nigel Ramsay, Margaret Sparks, and Tim Tatton-Brown, 1–23. Woodbridge: Boydell Press, 1992.

***. *The Early History of the Church of Canterbury: Christ Church from 597 to 1066*. London: Leicester University Press, 1984.

***. "Introduction: How Do We Know about St Wulfstan?" In *St Wulfstan and His World*, edited by Julia Barrow and Nicholas Brooks, 1–21. Aldershot: Ashgate, 2005.

Brown, George. "The Dynamics of Literacy in Anglo-Saxon England." In *Textual and Material Culture in Anglo-Saxon England: Thomas Northcote Toller and the Toller Memorial Lectures*, edited by Donald Scragg, 183–212. Cambridge: D. S. Brewer, 2003.

———. "The Psalms as the Foundation of Anglo-Saxon Learning." In *The Place of the Psalms in the Intellectual Culture of the Middle Ages*, edited by Nancy van Deusen, 1–24. Albany: State University of New York Press, 1999.

Brown, Michelle. "'A Good Woman's Son': Aspects of Aldred's Agenda in Glossing the Lindisfarne Gospels." In *The Old English Gloss to the Lindisfarne Gospels: Language, Author and Context*, edited by Julia Fernández Cuesta and Sara M. Pons-Sanz, 13–36. Berlin: De Gruyter, 2016.

Brown, T. Julian. "The Boge-Aldred-Mantat Inscriptions." In *The Durham Gospels, Together with Fragments of a Gospel Book in Uncial, Durham, Cathedral Library, MS A. II. 17*, edited by Christopher Verey, T. Julian Brown, and Elizabeth Coatsworth. Early English Manuscripts in Facsimile 20. Copenhagen: Rosenkilde and Bagger, 1980.

Budny, Mildred. *Insular, Anglo-Saxon, and Early Anglo-Norman Manuscript Art at Corpus Christi College, Cambridge: An Illustrated Catalogue*. Kalamazoo: Medieval Institute Publications, 1997.

Bullough, Donald A. "The Educational Tradition in England from Alfred to Ælfric: Teaching *utriusque linguae*." In *Carolingian Renewal: Sources and Heritage*, 297–334. Manchester: Manchester University Press, 1991.

Butler, Lawrence. "All Saints Church, Harewood." *The Yorkshire Archaeological Journal* 58 (1986): 85–108.

———. "Church Dedication and the Cults of Anglo-Saxon Saints in England." In *The Anglo-Saxon Church: Papers on History, Architecture, and Archaeology in Honour of Dr. H. M. Taylor*, edited by Lawrence Butler and Richard Morris, 44–50. London: Council for British Archaeology, 1986.

Cambridge, Eric, and David Rollason. "Debate: The Pastoral Organization of the Anglo-Saxon Church: A Review of the 'Minster Hypothesis'." *Early Medieval Europe* 4, no. 1 (1995): 87–104.

Campbell, Alastair. *Old English Grammar*. Oxford: Clarendon Press, 1959.

Campbell, Anne, Irwin S. Kirsch, and Andrew Kolstad. *Assessing Literacy: The Framework for the National Adult Literacy Survey*. Washington, DC: US Department of Education, 1992.

Charles-Edwards, Thomas. "The Penitential of Theodore and the *Iudicia Theodori*." In *Archbishop Theodore: Commemorative Studies on His Life and Influence*, edited by Michael Lapidge, 141–74. Cambridge: Cambridge University Press, 1995.

Bibliography

Chazelle, Celia. "The Eucharist in Early Medieval Europe." In *A Companion to the Eucharist in the Middle Ages*, edited by Ian Christopher Levy, Gary Macy, and Kristen Van Ausdall, 205–50. Leiden: Brill, 2012.

Clanchy, M. T. "Did Mothers Teach Their Children to Read?" In *Motherhood, Religion, and Society in Medieval Europe, 400–1400: Essays Presented to Henrietta Leyser*, edited by Conrad Leyser and Lesley Smith, 129–53. Farnham: Ashgate, 2011.

Clayton, Mary. "Homiliaries and Preaching in Anglo-Saxon England." *Peritia* 4 (1985): 207–42.

Clemoes, Peter. "History of the Manuscript *and* Punctuation (from Ælfric's First Series of Catholic Homilies—British Library, Royal 7. C. XII, fols. 4–218)." In *Old English Manuscripts: Basic Readings*, edited by Mary P. Richards, 345–64. New York: Routledge, 1994.

Coates, Richard. "The Scriptorium of the Mercian Rushworth Gloss: A Bilingual Perspective." *Notes and Queries* 44, no. 4 (1997): 453–58.

Collins, Rowland L. *Anglo-Saxon Vernacular Manuscripts in America*. New York: Pierpont Morgan Library, 1976.

Conner, Patrick. *Anglo-Saxon Exeter: A Tenth-Century Cultural History*. Woodbridge: Boydell, 1993.

———. "Parish Guilds and the Production of Old English Literature in the Public Sphere." In *Intertexts: Studies in Anglo-Saxon Culture Presented to Paul E. Szarmach*, edited by Virginia Blanton and Helene Scheck, 257–73. Tempe, AZ: Arizona Center for Medieval and Renaissance Studies, 2008.

Constable, Giles. "Monasteries, Rural Churches and the *Cura Animarum* in the Early Middle Ages." In *Cristianizzazione ed organizzazione ecclesiastica delle campagne nell'alto medioevo: Espansione e resistenze*, 349–89. Vol. 28, no. 1 of *Settimane di studio del Centro italiano di studi sull'alto medioevo*. Spoleto: Presso la sede del Centro, 1982.

———. "Religious Communities, 1024–1215." In *The New Cambridge Medieval History Volume 4: c.1024–c.1198*, edited by David Luscombe and Jonathan Riley-Smith, 1:335–67. Cambridge: Cambridge University Press, 2004.

Conti, Aidan. "The Taunton Fragment and the Homiliary of Angers: Context for New Old English." *Review of English Studies* 60 (2008): 1–33.

Cooper, Janet M. *The Last Four Anglo-Saxon Archbishops of York*. York: St. Anthony's Press, 1970.

Cooper, Tracey-Anne. "Lay Piety, Confessional Directives and the Compiler's Method in Late Anglo-Saxon England." *Haskins Society Journal* 16 (2006): 47–61.

———. *Monk-Bishops and the English Benedictine Reform Movement: Reading London, BL, Cotton Tiberius A. iii in Its Manuscript Context*. Toronto: Pontifical Institute of Medieval Studies, 2015.

Corrêa, Alicia. "Daily Office Books: Collectars and Breviaries." In *The Liturgical Books of Anglo-Saxon England*, edited by Richard Pfaff, 45–60. Kalamazoo: Medieval Institute Publications, 1995.

———. "A Mass for St Birinus in an Anglo-Saxon Missal from the Scandinavian Mission-Field." In *Myth, Rulership, Church and Charters: Essays in Honour of Nicholas Brooks*, edited by Julia Barrow and Andrew Wareham, 167–88. Aldershot: Ashgate, 2008.

Cownie, Emma. *Religious Patronage in Anglo-Norman England, 1066–1135*. London and Woodbridge: The Royal Historical Society and Boydell Press, 1998.

Crawford, Sally. "Baptism and Infant Burial in Anglo-Saxon England." In *Medieval Life Cycles: Continuity and Change*, edited by Isabelle Cochelin and Karen Smyth, 55–80. Turnhout: Brepols, 2013.

Cross, James E. *Cambridge Pembroke College MS 25: A Carolingian Sermonary Used by Anglo-Saxon Preachers*. London: King's College, 1987.

———. "On the Library of the Old English Martyrologist." In *Learning and Literature in Anglo-Saxon England: Studies Presented to Peter Clemoes on the Occasion of His Sixty-Fifth Birthday*, edited by Michael Lapidge and Helmut Gneuss, 227–49. Cambridge: Cambridge University Press, 1985.

Crowley, D. A., ed. *A History of the County of Wiltshire: Volume 16, Kinwardstone Hundred*. Oxford: Oxford University Press, 1999.

Cubitt, Catherine. "Ælfric's Lay Patrons." In *A Companion to Ælfric*, edited by Hugh Magennis and Mary Swan, 165–92. Leiden: Brill, 2009.

———. "Bishops, Priests and Penance in Late Saxon England." *Early Medieval Europe* 14, no. 1 (2006): 41–63.

———. "The Clergy in Early Anglo-Saxon England." *Historical Research* 78 (2005): 273–87.

———. "Images of St Peter: The Clergy and the Religious Life in Anglo-Saxon England." In *The Christian Tradition in Anglo-Saxon England: Approaches to Current Scholarship and Teaching*, edited by Paul Cavill, 41–54. Cambridge: D. S. Brewer, 2004.

———. "Individual and Collective Sinning in Tenth- and Eleventh-Century England: Penance, Piety and the Law." In *Religion und Politik im Mittelalter: Deutschland und England im Vergleich*, edited by Ludger Körntgen and Dominik Waßenhoven, 51–70. Berlin: De Gruyter, 2013.

———. "Pastoral Care and Conciliar Canons: The Provisions of the 747 Council of *Clofesho*." In *Pastoral Care before the Parish*, edited by John Blair and Richard Sharpe, 193–211. Leicester: Leicester University Press, 1992.

———. "Pastoral Care and Religious Belief." In *A Companion to the Early Middle Ages: Britain and Ireland, c.500–c.1100*, edited by Pauline Stafford, 395–413. Oxford: Wiley-Blackwell, 2009.

———. "The Politics of Remorse: Penance and Royal Piety in the Reign of Æthelred the Unready." *Historical Research* 85 (2012): 179–92.
Cuesta, Julia Fernández and Sara M. Pons-Sanz, eds. *The Old English Gloss to the Lindisfarne Gospels: Language, Author and Context*. Berlin: De Gruyter, 2016.
Cutts, Edward L. *Parish Priests and Their People in the Middle Ages in England*. London: Society for Promoting Christian Knowledge, 1898.
Czock, Miriam. "Practices of Property and the Salvation of One's Soul: Priests as Men in the Middle in the Wissembourg Material." In *Men in the Middle: Local Priests in Early Medieval Europe*, edited by Steffen Patzold and Carine van Rhijn, 11–31. Berlin: De Gruyter, 2016.
Dalbey, Marcia. "Themes and Techniques in the Blickling Lenten Homilies." In *The Old English Homily and Its Backgrounds*, edited by Paul Szarmach and Bernard Huppé, 221–39. Albany: State University of New York Press, 1978.
Dales, Douglas. *Dunstan: Saint and Statesman*. Cambridge: Lutterworth Press, 1988.
Dalton, Paul, Charles Insley, and Louise Wilkinson. Introduction to *Cathedrals, Communities and Conflict in the Anglo-Norman World*, edited by Paul Dalton, Charles Insley, and Louise Wilkinson, 1–26. Woodbridge: Boydell Press, 2011.
Dance, Richard. "Sound, Fury, and Signifiers; or Wulfstan's Language." In *Wulfstan, Archbishop of York: The Proceedings of the Second Alcuin Conference*, edited by Matthew Townend, 29–61. Turnhout: Brepols, 2004.
Davies, Wendy. "Priests and Rural Communities in East Brittany in the Ninth Century." *Etudes Celtiques* 20 (1983): 177–97.
———. *Small Worlds: The Village Community in Early Medieval Brittany*. Berkeley: University of California Press, 1988.
De Hamel, Christopher. *A History of Illuminated Manuscripts*. London: Phaidon Press, 1986.
De Jong, Mayke. *In Samuel's Image: Child Oblation in the Early Medieval West*. Leiden: Brill, 1996.
———. "Power and Humility in Carolingian Society: The Public Penance of Louis the Pious." *Early Medieval Europe* 1, no. 1 (1992): 29–52.
Dockray-Miller, Mary. *The Books and the Life of Judith of Flanders*. Farnham: Ashgate, 2015.
Dohar, William J. "*Sufficienter litteratus*: Clerical Examination and Instruction for the Cure of Souls." In *A Distinct Voice: Medieval Studies in Honor of Leonard E. Boyle, O.P.*, edited by Jacqueline Brown and William Stoneman, 305–21. Notre Dame: University of Notre Dame Press, 1997.
Dudley, Martin. "Sacramental Liturgies in the Middle Ages." In *The Liturgy of the Medieval Church*, 2nd ed., edited by Thomas Heffernan

and E. Ann Matter, 193–218. Kalamazoo: Medieval Institute Publications, 2005.
Duffy, Eamon. *The Stripping of the Altars: Traditional Religion in England, c.1400–c.1580*. New Haven: Yale University Press, 1992.
Dumville, David. "Anglo-Saxon Books: Treasure in Norman Hands?" In *Anglo-Norman Studies XVI: Proceedings of the Battle Conference 1993*, edited by Marjorie Chibnall, 83–100. Woodbridge: Boydell Press, 1994.
———. *English Caroline Script and Monastic History: Studies in Benedictinism, A.D. 950–1030*. Woodbridge: Boydell Press, 1993.
———. *Liturgy and the Ecclesiastical History of Late Anglo-Saxon England: Four Studies*. Woodbridge: Boydell Press, 1992.
———. *Wessex and England from Alfred to Edgar: Six Essays on Political, Cultural, and Ecclesiastical Revival*. Woodbridge: Boydell Press, 1992.
Dyer, Joseph. "The Singing of Psalms in the Early-Medieval Office." *Speculum* 64, no. 3 (1989): 535–78.
Dyson, Gerald P. "Liturgy or Private Devotion? Reappraising Warsaw, Biblioteka Narodowa, I. 3311." *Anglo-Saxon England* 45 (2016): 265–84.
Eagles, Bruce. "The Area around Bedwyn in the Anglo-Saxon Period." In *The Romano-British Villa at Castle Copse, Great Bedwyn*, edited by Eric Hostetter and Thomas Howe, 378–93. Bloomington: Indiana University Press, 1997.
Étaix, Raymond. "L'homéliaire carolingien d'Angers." *Revue Bénédictine* 104, no. 1 (1994): 148–90.
Firey, Abigail, ed. *A New History of Penance*. Leiden: Brill, 2008.
Foot, Sarah. "'By Water in the Spirit': The Administration of Baptism in Early Anglo-Saxon England." In *Pastoral Care before the Parish*, edited by John Blair and Richard Sharpe, 171–92. Leicester: Leicester University Press, 1992.
———. *Monastic Life in Anglo-Saxon England, c. 600–900*. Cambridge: Cambridge University Press, 2006.
Forbes, Helen Foxhall. *Heaven and Earth in Anglo-Saxon England: Theology and Society in an Age of Faith*. Farnham: Ashgate, 2013.
Franklin, Michael. "The Cathedral as Parish Church: The Case of Southern England." In *Church and City, 1000–1500: Essays in Honour of Christopher Brooke*, edited by David Abulafia, Michael Franklin, and Miri Rubin, 173–98. Cambridge: Cambridge University Press, 1992.
Frantzen, Allen J. *Food, Eating and Identity in Early Medieval England*. Woodbridge: Boydell Press, 2014.
———. *The Literature of Penance in Anglo-Saxon England*. New Brunswick, NJ: Rutgers University Press, 1983.
———. "The Tradition of Penitentials in Anglo-Saxon England." *Anglo-Saxon England* 11 (1982): 23–56.

Gamble, Harry. *Books and Readers in the Early Church: A History of Early Christian Texts.* New Haven: Yale University Press, 1995.

Gameson, Richard. "Anglo-Saxon Scribes and Scriptoria." In *The Cambridge History of the Book in Britain Volume 1: c.400–1100*, edited by Richard Gameson, 94–120. Cambridge: Cambridge University Press, 2011.

———. "Book Production and Decoration at Worcester in the Tenth and Eleventh Centuries." In *St Oswald of Worcester: Life and Influence*, edited by Nicholas Brooks and Catherine Cubitt, 194–243. London: Leicester University Press, 1996.

———. "The Colophon of the Eadwig Gospels." *Anglo-Saxon England* 31 (2002): 201–22.

———. "Eadwig Basan (*fl.* c.1020)." In *Oxford Dictionary of National Biography.* Oxford University Press, 2004. Accessed February 17, 2018. doi:10.1093/ref:odnb/55374.

———. *The Earliest Books of Canterbury Cathedral: Manuscripts and Fragments to c. 1200.* London: Bibliographical Society and the British Library, 2008.

———. "English Manuscript Art in the Late Eleventh Century: Canterbury and Its Context." In *Canterbury and the Norman Conquest: Churches, Saints and Scholars, 1066–1109*, edited by Richard Eales and Richard Sharpe, 95–144. London: Hambledon Press, 1995.

———. "The Gospels of Margaret of Scotland and the Literacy of an Early Medieval Queen." In *Women and the Book: Assessing the Visual Evidence*, edited by Jane H. M. Taylor and Lesley Smith, 149–71. London: British Library and University of Toronto Press, 1996.

———. "The Origin of the Exeter Book of Old English Poetry." *Anglo-Saxon England* 25 (1996): 135–85.

———. *The Role of Art in the Late Anglo-Saxon Church.* Oxford: Clarendon Press, 1995.

———. *The Scribe Speaks? Colophons in Early English Manuscripts.* Cambridge: Department of Anglo-Saxon, Norse and Celtic, University of Cambridge, 2002.

———. "St Wulfstan, the Library of Worcester and the Spirituality of the Medieval Book." In *St Wulfstan and His World*, edited by Julia Barrow and Nicholas Brooks, 59–104. Aldershot: Ashgate, 2005.

———. "Why Did Eadfrith Write the Lindisfarne Gospels?" In *Belief and Culture in the Middle Ages: Studies Presented to Henry Mayr-Harting*, edited by Richard Gameson and Henrietta Leyser, 45–58. Oxford: Oxford University Press, 2001.

Ganz, David. "Anglo-Saxon England." In *The Cambridge History of Libraries in Britain and Ireland Volume 1: To 1640*, edited by Elisabeth Leedham-Green and Teresa Webber, 91–108. Cambridge: Cambridge University Press, 2006.

———. "The Annotation in Oxford, Bodleian Library, Auct. D. II. 14."

In *Belief and Culture in the Middle Ages: Studies Presented to Henry Mayr-Harting*, edited by Richard Gameson and Henrietta Leyser, 35–44. Oxford: Oxford University Press, 2001.

———. "Book Production in the Carolingian Empire and the Spread of Caroline Minuscule." In *The New Cambridge Medieval History Volume 2: c.700–c.900*, edited by Rosamond McKitterick, 786–808. Cambridge: Cambridge University Press, 1995.

———. "The Preconditions for Caroline Minuscule." *Viator* 18 (1987): 23–44.

Gatch, Milton. *Preaching and Theology in Anglo-Saxon England: Ælfric and Wulfstan*. Toronto: University of Toronto Press, 1977.

———. "The Unknowable Audience of the Blickling Homilies." *Anglo-Saxon England* 18 (1989): 99–115.

Giandrea, Mary Frances. *Episcopal Culture in Late Anglo-Saxon England*. Woodbridge: Boydell Press, 2007.

"'Gift of Unity': Will Pope Francis Change the Date of Easter?" *National Catholic Register*, June 19, 2015. Accessed January 18, 2018. http://www.ncregister.com/daily-news/gift-of-unity-will-pope-francis-change-the-date-of-easter.

Gittos, Helen, and Sarah Hamilton, eds. *Understanding Medieval Liturgy: Essays in Interpretation*. Farnham: Ashgate, 2016.

Gittos, Helen. "The Audience for Old English Texts: Ælfric, Rhetoric and 'the Edification of the Simple'." *Anglo-Saxon England* 43 (2014): 231–66.

———. "Is There Any Evidence for the Liturgy of Parish Churches in Late Anglo-Saxon England? The Red Book of Darley and the Status of Old English." In *Pastoral Care in Late Anglo-Saxon England*, edited by Francesca Tinti, 63–82. Woodbridge: Boydell Press, 2005.

———. *Liturgy, Architecture, and Sacred Places in Anglo-Saxon England*. Oxford: Oxford University Press, 2013.

Gneuss, Helmut, and Michael Lapidge. *Anglo-Saxon Manuscripts: A Bibliographical Handlist of Manuscripts and Manuscript Fragments Written or Owned in England up to 1100*. Toronto: University of Toronto Press, 2014.

Gneuss, Helmut. "The Homiliary of the Taunton Fragments." *Notes and Queries* 52, no. 4 (2005): 440–42.

———. *Hymnar und Hymnen im englischen Mittelalter*. Tübingen: Max Niemeyer, 1968.

———. "Liturgical Books in Anglo-Saxon England and Their Old English Terminology." In *Learning and Literature in Anglo-Saxon England: Studies Presented to Peter Clemoes on the Occasion of His Sixty-Fifth Birthday*, edited by Michael Lapidge and Helmut Gneuss, 91–141. Cambridge: Cambridge University Press, 1985.

———. "More Old English from Manuscripts." In *Intertexts: Studies in Anglo-Saxon Culture Presented to Paul E. Szarmach*, edited by Virginia

Blanton and Helene Scheck, 411–21. Tempe, AZ: Arizona Center for Medieval and Renaissance Studies, 2008.

Godden, Malcolm. "Ælfric and the Vernacular Prose Tradition." In *The Old English Homily and Its Backgrounds*, edited by Paul Szarmach and Bernard Huppé, 99–118. Albany: State University of New York Press, 1978.

———, ed. *Ælfric's Catholic Homilies: Introduction, Commentary and Glossary*. Early English Text Society Supplementary Series 18. Oxford: Oxford University Press, 2000.

———. "Ælfric's Library." In *The Cambridge History of the Book in Britain Volume 1: c.400–1100*, edited by Richard Gameson, 679–84. Cambridge: Cambridge University Press, 2011.

———. "Literacy in Anglo-Saxon England." In *The Cambridge History of the Book in Britain Volume 1: c.400–1100*, edited by Richard Gameson, 580–90. Cambridge: Cambridge University Press, 2011.

———. "The Relations of Wulfstan and Ælfric: A Reassessment." In *Wulfstan, Archbishop of York: The Proceedings of the Second Alcuin Conference*, edited by Matthew Townend, 353–74. Turnhout: Brepols, 2004.

Godding, Robert. *Prêtres en Gaule mérovingienne*. Brussels: Société des Bollandistes, 2001.

Gorman, Michael. "A List of Books Lent by the Cathedral Library in Verona in the Eleventh Century." *Scriptorium* 56 (2002): 320–23.

———. "Manuscript Books at Monte Amiata in the Eleventh Century." *Scriptorium* 56 (2002): 225–93.

Graham, Timothy. "The Old English Liturgical Directions in Corpus Christi College, Cambridge, MS 422." *Anglia* 111 (1993): 439–46.

Gretsch, Mechthild. "Æthelwold's Translation of the *Regula Sancti Benedicti* and Its Latin Exemplar." *Anglo-Saxon England* 3 (1974): 125–51.

———. "Cambridge, Corpus Christi College 57: A Witness to the Early Stages of the Benedictine Reform in England?" *Anglo-Saxon England* 32 (2003): 111–46.

———. *The Intellectual Foundations of the English Benedictine Reform*. Cambridge: Cambridge University Press, 1999.

———. "The Junius Psalter Gloss: Its Historical and Cultural Context." *Anglo-Saxon England* 29 (2000): 85–121.

———. "The Taunton Fragment: A New Text from Anglo-Saxon England." *Anglo-Saxon England* 33 (2004): 145–93.

———. "Winchester Vocabulary and Standard Old English: The Vernacular in Late Anglo-Saxon England." *Bulletin of the John Rylands University Library of Manchester* 83, no. 1 (2001): 41–87.

Griffith, Mark. "How Much Latin Did Ælfric's Magister Know?" *Notes and Queries* 46, no. 2 (1999): 176–81.

Gullick, Michael and Susan Rankin. Review of *Catalogue of Manuscripts*

Written or Owned in England up to 1200 Containing Music, by K. D. Hartzell. *Early Music History* 28 (2009): 262–85.

Gullick, Michael. "Professional Scribes in Eleventh- and Twelfth-Century England." *English Manuscript Studies* 7 (1998): 1–24.

Hadley, Dawn M. "Conquest, Colonization and the Church: Ecclesiastical Organization in the Danelaw." *Historical Research* 69 (1996): 109–28.

———. *The Northern Danelaw: Its Social Structure, c. 800–1100.* London: Leicester University Press, 2000.

Haggenmüller, Reinhold. *Die Überlieferung der Beda und Egbert zugeschriebenen Bußbücher.* Frankfurt: Peter Lang, 1991.

Hall, Thomas N. "The Early English Manuscripts of Gregory the Great's *Homiliae in Evangelia* and *Homiliae in Hiezechihelem*: A Preliminary Survey." In *Rome and the North: The Early Reception of Gregory the Great in Germanic Europe*, edited by Rolf H. Bremmer, Jr., Kees Dekker, and David Johnson, 115–36. Paris: Peeters, 2001.

Hamilton, Sarah. *Church and People in the Medieval West, 900–1200.* London: Routledge, 2013.

———. *The Practice of Penance, 900–1050.* London and Woodbridge: The Royal Historical Society and Boydell Press, 2001.

———. "Remedies for 'Great Transgressions': Penance and Excommunication in Late Anglo-Saxon England." In *Pastoral Care in Late Anglo-Saxon England*, edited by Francesca Tinti, 83–105. Woodbridge: Boydell Press, 2005.

———. "Rites of Passage and Pastoral Care." In *A Social History of England, 900–1200*, edited by Julia Crick and Elisabeth van Houts, 290–308. Cambridge: Cambridge University Press, 2011.

———. "The *Rituale*: The Evolution of a New Liturgical Book." In *The Church and the Book*, edited by R. N. Swanson, 74–86. Woodbridge: Boydell Press, 2004.

Hammer, Carl. "Country Churches, Clerical Inventories and the Carolingian Renaissance in Bavaria." *Church History* 49, no. 1 (1980): 5–17.

Hardie, Jane. "Salamanca to Sydney: A Newly-Discovered Manuscript of the *Lamentations of Jeremiah*." In *Music in Medieval Europe: Studies in Honour of Bryan Gillingham*, edited by Terence Bailey and Alma Santosuosso, 11–22. Aldershot: Ashgate, 2007.

Hare, Michael. *The Two Anglo-Saxon Minsters of Gloucester.* Gloucester: Friends of Deerhurst Church, 1993.

———. "Wulfstan and the Church of Hawkesbury." In *St Wulfstan and His World*, edited by Julia Barrow and Nicholas Brooks, 151–66. Aldershot: Ashgate, 2005.

Harper, John. *The Forms and Orders of Western Liturgy from the Tenth to the Eighteenth Century: A Historical Introduction and Guide for Students and Musicians.* Oxford: Clarendon Press, 1991.

Hartzell, K. D. *Catalogue of Manuscripts Written or Owned in England up to 1200 Containing Music*. Woodbridge: Boydell Press, 2006.

———. "An Eleventh-Century English Missal Fragment in the British Library." *Anglo-Saxon England* 18 (1989): 45–97.

Hase, P. H. "The Mother Churches of Hampshire." In *Minsters and Parish Churches: The Local Church in Transition, 950–1200*, edited by John Blair, 45–66. Oxford: Oxford University Committee for Archaeology, 1988.

Haslam, Jeremy. "Parishes, Churches, Wards and Gates in Eastern London." In *Minsters and Parish Churches: The Local Church in Transition, 950–1200*, edited by John Blair, 35–44. Oxford: Oxford University Committee for Archaeology, 1988.

Heffernan, Thomas J. "The Liturgy and the Literature of Saints' Lives." In *The Liturgy of the Medieval Church*, 2nd ed., edited by Thomas J. Heffernan and E. Ann Matter, 65–94. Kalamazoo: Published for the Consortium for the Teaching of the Middle Ages by Medieval Institute Publications, Western Michigan University, 2001.

Heighway, Carolyn, and Richard Bryant. "A Reconstruction of the Tenth-Century Church of St Oswald, Gloucester." In *The Anglo-Saxon Church: Papers on History, Architecture, and Archaeology in Honour of Dr. H. M. Taylor*, edited by Lawrence Butler and Richard Morris, 188–95. London: Council for British Archaeology, 1986.

Hen, Yitzhak, and Rob Meens, eds. *The Bobbio Missal: Liturgy and Religious Culture in Merovingian Gaul*. Cambridge: Cambridge University Press, 2004.

Hen, Yitzhak. "A Liturgical Handbook for the Use of a Rural Priest (Brussels, BR 10127–10144)." In *Organizing the Written Word: Scripts, Manuscripts, and Texts*, edited by Marco Mostert. Turnhout: Brepols, forthcoming.

———. "Educating the Clergy: Canon Law and Liturgy in a Carolingian Handbook from the Time of Charles the Bald." In De Sion exibit lex et verbum domini de Hierusalem: *Essays on Medieval Law, Liturgy and Literature in Honour of Amnon Linder*, edited by Yitzhak Hen, 43–58. Turnhout: Brepols, 2001.

———. "Knowledge of Canon Law among Rural Priests: The Evidence of Two Carolingian Manuscripts from around 800." *The Journal of Theological Studies* 50, no. 1 (1999): 117–34.

———. "Priests and Books in the Merovingian Period." In *Men in the Middle: Local Priests in Early Medieval Europe*, edited by Steffen Patzold and Carine van Rhijn, 162–76. Berlin: De Gruyter, 2016.

———. "Review Article: Liturgy and Religious Culture in Late Anglo-Saxon England." *Early Medieval Europe* 17, no. 3 (2009): 329–42.

Henel, Heinrich. *Studien zum altenglischen Computus*. Leipzig: Bernhard Tauchnitz, 1934.

Heslop, T. A. "The Production of *de luxe* Manuscripts and the Patronage of King Cnut and Queen Emma." *Anglo-Saxon England* 19 (1990): 151–95.

Heyworth, Melanie. "The 'Late Old English Handbook for the Use of a Confessor': Authorship and Connections." *Notes and Queries* 54, no. 3 (2007): 218–22.

Hiley, David. *Western Plainchant: A Handbook*. Oxford: Clarendon Press, 1993.

Hill, Francis. *Medieval Lincoln*. Cambridge: Cambridge University Press, 1948.

Hill, Joyce. "Ælfric: His Life and Works." In *A Companion to Ælfric*, edited by Hugh Magennis and Mary Swan, 35–65. Leiden: Brill, 2009.

———. "Authorial Adaptation: Ælfric, Wulfstan and the Pastoral Letters." In *Text and Language in Medieval English Prose: A Festschrift for Tadao Kubouchi*, edited by Akio Ōizumi, Jacek Fisiak, and John Scahill, 63–75. Frankfurt: Peter Lang, 2005.

———. "Leofric of Exeter and the Practical Politics of Book Collecting." In *Imagining the Book*, edited by Stephen Kelly and John J. Thompson, 77–98. Turnhout: Brepols, 2005.

———. "Monastic Reform and the Secular Church: Ælfric's Pastoral Letters in Context." In *England in the Eleventh Century: Proceedings of the 1990 Harlaxton Symposium*, edited by Carola Hicks, 103–17. Stamford: Paul Watkins, 1992.

———. "Reform and Resistance: Preaching Styles in Late Anglo-Saxon England." In *De l'homélie au sermon: Histoire de la prédication médiévale*, edited by Jacqueline Hamesse and Xavier Hermand, 15–46. Louvain-la-Neuve: Université catholique de Louvain, 1993.

Hohler, Christopher. Review of *Cambridge, Corpus Christi College 41: The Loricas and the Missal*, by Raymond Grant. *Medium Ævum* 49 (1980): 275–78.

———. "Some Service-Books of the Later Saxon Church." In *Tenth-Century Studies: Essays in Commemoration of the Millennium of the Council of Winchester and* Regularis Concordia, edited by David Parsons, 60–83. London: Phillimore, 1975.

Holden, E. W. "New Evidence Relating to Bramber Bridge." *Sussex Archaeological Collections* 113 (1975): 104–17.

Hughes, Andrew. *Medieval Manuscripts for Mass and Office: A Guide to Their Organization and Terminology*. Toronto: University of Toronto Press, 1982.

Huglo, Michel, and J. W. McKinnon. "Gospel (i)." *Grove Music Online. Oxford Music Online*. Oxford University Press, 2007. Accessed February 15, 2018. http://www.oxfordmusiconline.com/subscriber/article/grove/music/11500.

Huglo, Michel. "The Cantatorium: From Charlemagne to the Fourteenth Century." In *The Study of Medieval Chant: Paths and Bridges, East and West, in Honor of Kenneth Levy*, edited by Peter Jeffery, 89–103. Woodbridge: Boydell Press, 2001.

Hunt, John. "Piety, Prestige or Politics? The House of Leofric and the Foundation and Patronage of Coventry Priory." In *Coventry's First Cathedral: The Cathedral and Priory of St Mary, Papers from the 1993 Anniversary Symposium*, edited by George Demidowicz, 97–117. Stamford: Paul Watkins, 1994.

Innes, Matthew. "'A Place of Discipline': Carolingian Courts and Aristocratic Youth." In *Court Culture in the Early Middle Ages: The Proceedings of the First Alcuin Conference*, edited by Catherine Cubitt, 59–76. Turnhout: Brepols, 2003.

Insley, Charles. "Charters and Episcopal Scriptoria in the Anglo-Saxon South-West." *Early Medieval Europe* 7, no. 2 (1998): 173–97.

Jaeger, C. Stephen. *The Envy of Angels: Cathedral Schools and Social Ideals in Medieval Europe, 950–1200*. Philadelphia: University of Pennsylvania Press, 1994.

James, M. R. "Manuscripts from Essex Monastic Libraries." *Transactions of the Essex Archaeological Society*, n.s., 21 (1933): 34–46.

Jayatilaka, Rohini. "King Alfred and His Circle." In *The Cambridge History of the Book in Britain Volume 1: c.400–1100*, edited by Richard Gameson, 670–78. Cambridge: Cambridge University Press, 2011.

John, Eric. *Orbis Britanniae and Other Studies*. Leicester: Leicester University Press, 1966.

Jolly, Karen. *The Community of St. Cuthbert in the Late Tenth Century: The Chester-le-Street Additions to Durham Cathedral Library A.IV.19*. Columbus: The Ohio State University Press, 2012.

———. "The Process of Glossing and Glossing as Process: Scholarship and Education in Durham, Cathedral Library, MS A.iv.19." In *The Old English Gloss to the Lindisfarne Gospels: Language, Author and Context*, edited by Julia Fernández Cuesta and Sara M. Pons-Sanz, 361–76. Berlin: De Gruyter, 2016.

Jones, Christopher. "Ælfric and the Limits of 'Benedictine Reform'." In *A Companion to Ælfric*, edited by Hugh Magennis and Mary Swan, 67–108. Leiden: Brill, 2009.

———. "Ælfric's Pastoral Letters and the Episcopal *Capitula* of Radulf of Bourges." *Notes and Queries* 42, no. 2 (1995): 149–55.

———. "*Meatim Sed et Rustica*: Ælfric of Eynsham as a Medieval Latin Author." *The Journal of Medieval Latin* 8 (1998): 1–58.

———. "The Book of the Liturgy in Anglo-Saxon England." *Speculum* 73, no. 3 (1998): 659–702.

Jungmann, Josef. *The Mass of the Roman Rite: Its Origins and Development*. Translated by Francis A. Brunner. Vol. 1. New York: Benziger, 1951.

Kabir, Ananya Jahanara. *Paradise, Death and Doomsday in Anglo-Saxon Literature*. Cambridge: Cambridge University Press, 2001.

Kato, Takako. "Exeter Scribes in Cambridge, University Library, MS Ii.

2. 11 + Exeter Book Folios 0, 1–7." *New Medieval Literatures* 13 (2011): 5–21.

Keefe, Susan A. *Water and the Word: Baptism and the Education of the Clergy in the Carolingian Empire*. 2 vols. Notre Dame: University of Notre Dame Press, 2002.

Keefer, Sarah Larratt. "Manuals." In *The Liturgical Books of Anglo-Saxon England*, edited by Richard Pfaff, 99–109. Kalamazoo: Medieval Institute Publications, 1995.

———. "Margin as Archive: The Liturgical Marginalia of a Manuscript of the Old English Bede." *Traditio* 51 (1996): 147–77.

———. "Use of Manuscript Space for Design, Text and Image in Liturgical Books Owned by the Community of St Cuthbert." In *Signs on the Edge: Space, Text and Margin in Medieval Manuscripts*, edited by Sarah Larratt Keefer and Rolf H. Bremmer, Jr., 85–115. Paris: Peeters, 2007.

Kelly, Susan. "Anglo-Saxon Lay Society and the Written Word." In *The Uses of Literacy in Early Medieval Europe*, edited by Rosamond McKitterick, 36–62. Cambridge: Cambridge University Press, 1990.

Ker, Neil R. *Catalogue of Manuscripts Containing Anglo-Saxon*. Oxford: Clarendon Press, 1957.

———. "The Handwriting of Archbishop Wulfstan." In *Books, Collectors and Libraries: Studies in the Medieval Heritage*, edited by Andrew Watson, 9–26. London: Hambledon Press, 1985.

Kerff, Franz. "Libri paenitentiales und kirchliche Strafgerichtsbarkeit bis zum Decretum Gratiani. Ein Diskussionsvorschlag." *Zeitschrift der Savigny-Stiftung für Rechtsgeschichte. Kanonistische Abteilung* 75 (1989): 23–57.

Keynes, Simon. "An Abbot, an Archbishop, and the Viking Raids of 1006–7 and 1009–12." *Anglo-Saxon England* 36 (2007): 151–220.

———. "Regenbald the Chancellor *(sic)*." In *Anglo-Norman Studies X: Proceedings of the Battle Conference 1987*, edited by R. Allen Brown, 185–222. Woodbridge: Boydell Press, 1988.

———. "Royal Government and the Written Word in Late Anglo-Saxon England." In *The Uses of Literacy in Early Medieval Europe*, edited by Rosamond McKitterick, 226–57. Cambridge: Cambridge University Press, 1990.

———. "The West Saxon Charters of King Æthelwulf and His Sons." *English Historical Review* 109 (1994): 1109–49.

Knappe, Gabriele. "The Rhetorical Aspect of Grammar Teaching in Anglo-Saxon England." *Rhetorica: A Journal of the History of Rhetoric* 17, no. 1 (1999): 1–34.

Knowles, David. *The Monastic Order in England: A History of Its Development from the Times of St. Dunstan to the Fourth Lateran Council 940–1216*. 2nd ed. Cambridge: Cambridge University Press, 1963.

Bibliography

Kohl, Thomas. "*Presbyter in parochia sua*: Local Priests and Their Churches in Early Medieval Bavaria." In *Men in the Middle: Local Priests in Early Medieval Europe*, edited by Steffen Patzold and Carine van Rhijn, 50–77. Berlin: De Gruyter, 2016.

Kotake, Tadashi. "Did Owun Really Copy from the Lindisfarne Gospels? Reconsideration of His Source Manuscript(s)." In *The Old English Gloss to the Lindisfarne Gospels*, edited by Julia Fernández Cuesta and Sara M. Pons-Sanz, 377–96. Berlin: De Gruyter, 2016.

Lapidge, Michael. "Ælfric's Schooldays." In *Early Medieval Texts and Interpretations: Studies Presented to Donald Scragg*, edited by Elaine Treharne and Susan Rosser, 301–10. Tempe, AZ: Arizona Center for Medieval and Renaissance Studies, 2002.

———. *The Anglo-Saxon Library*. Oxford: Oxford University Press, 2005.

———. "Artistic and Literary Patronage in Anglo-Saxon England." In *Anglo-Latin Literature, 600–899*, 37–91. London: Hambledon Press, 1996.

———. "B. and the *Vita Sancti Dunstani*." In *Anglo-Latin Literature, 900–1066*, 179–91. London: Hambledon Press, 1993.

———. "The Hermeneutic Style in Tenth-Century Anglo-Latin Literature." *Anglo-Saxon England* 4 (1975): 67–111.

———. "Latin Learning in Ninth-Century England." In *Anglo-Latin Literature, 600–899*, 409–54. London: Hambledon Press, 1996.

———. "Schools." In *The Wiley-Blackwell Encyclopedia of Anglo-Saxon England*, 2nd ed., edited by Michael Lapidge, John Blair, Simon Keynes, and Donald Scragg. Oxford: Wiley-Blackwell, 2014.

———. "Schools, Learning and Literature in Tenth-Century England." In *Anglo-Latin Literature, 900–1066*, 1–48. London: Hambledon Press, 1993.

———. "Some Old English Sedulius Glosses from BN Lat. 8092." *Anglia* 100 (1982): 1–17.

———. "Surviving Booklists from Anglo-Saxon England." In *Learning and Literature in Anglo-Saxon England: Studies Presented to Peter Clemoes on the Occasion of His Sixty-Fifth Birthday*, edited by Michael Lapidge and Helmut Gneuss, 33–89. Cambridge: Cambridge University Press, 1985.

Leach, A. F. *The Schools of Medieval England*. London: Methuen, 1915.

Lees, Clare. "Theme and Echo in an Anonymous Old English Homily for Easter." *Traditio* 42 (1986): 115–42.

Lenker, Ursula. *Die Westsächsische Evangelienversion und die Perikopenordnungen im Angelsächsischen England*. Munich: Wilhelm Fink, 1997.

———. "The West Saxon Gospels and the Gospel-Lectionary in Anglo-Saxon England: Manuscript Evidence and Liturgical Practice." *Anglo-Saxon England* 28 (1999): 141–78.

Lerer, Seth. *Literacy and Power in Anglo-Saxon Literature*. Lincoln: University of Nebraska Press, 1991.

Levy, Ian Christopher, Gary Macy, and Kristen Van Ausdall, eds. *A Companion to the Eucharist in the Middle Ages*. Leiden: Brill, 2012.

Lewis, C. P. "Communities, Conflict and Episcopal Policy in the Diocese of Lichfield, 1050–1150." In *Cathedrals, Communities and Conflict in the Anglo-Norman World*, edited by Paul Dalton, Charles Insley, and Louise Wilkinson, 61–76. Woodbridge: Boydell Press, 2011.

Lionarons, Joyce Tally. "Another Old English Text of the *Passio Petri Et Pauli*." *Notes and Queries* 45, no. 1 (1998): 12–14.

———. *The Homiletic Writings of Archbishop Wulfstan: A Critical Study*. Woodbridge: D. S. Brewer, 2010.

Liuzza, Roy. "In Measure, and Number, and Weight: Writing Science." In *The Cambridge History of Early Medieval English Literature*, edited by Clare Lees, 475–98. Cambridge: Cambridge University Press, 2013.

———. "Who Read the Gospels in Old English?" In *Words and Works: Studies in Medieval English Language and Literature in Honour of Fred C. Robinson*, edited by Peter S. Baker and Nicholas Howe, 3–24. Toronto: University of Toronto Press, 1998.

Love, Rosalind. "Wars of the Word." *Cambridge Alumni Magazine* 73 (2014): 34–37.

Lowe, Kathryn. "Lay Literacy in Anglo-Saxon England and the Development of the Chirograph." In *Anglo-Saxon Manuscripts and Their Heritage*, edited by Phillip Pulsiano and Elaine Treharne, 161–204. Aldershot: Ashgate, 1998.

Loyn, H. R. *The English Church, 940–1154*. New York: Pearson, 2000.

Madan, Falconer, H. H. E. Craster, and N. Denholm-Young. *A Summary Catalogue of Western Manuscripts in the Bodleian Library at Oxford* …. Vol. 2, pt. 2. Oxford: Clarendon Press, 1937.

Magennis, Hugh. "Audience(s), Reception, Literacy." In *A Companion to Anglo-Saxon Literature*, edited by Phillip Pulsiano and Elaine Treharne, 84–101. Oxford: Blackwell, 2001.

Mann, Gareth. "The Development of Wulfstan's Alcuin Manuscript." In *Wulfstan, Archbishop of York: The Proceedings of the Second Alcuin Conference*, edited by Matthew Townend, 235–78. Turnhout: Brepols, 2004.

Marsden, Richard. "'Ask What I Am Called': The Anglo-Saxons and Their Bibles." In *The Bible as Book: The Manuscript Tradition*, edited by John Sharpe and Kimberly van Kampen, 145–76. London: British Library, 1998.

Martin, Lawrence. "Bede and Preaching." In *The Cambridge Companion to Bede*, edited by Scott DeGregorio, 156–69. Cambridge: Cambridge University Press, 2010.

McGurk, Patrick, and Jane Rosenthal. "The Anglo-Saxon Gospelbooks of Judith, Countess of Flanders: Their Text, Make-Up and Function." *Anglo-Saxon England* 24 (1995): 251–308.

McGurk, Patrick. "Anglo-Saxon Gospel-Books, c. 900–1066." In *The Cambridge History of the Book in Britain Volume 1: c.400–1100*, edited by Richard Gameson, 436–48. Cambridge: Cambridge University Press, 2011.

McKitterick, Rosamond. *The Carolingians and the Written Word*. Cambridge: Cambridge University Press, 1989.

———. *The Frankish Church and the Carolingian Reforms, 789–895*. London: Royal Historical Society, 1977.

Meeder, Sven. "The Early Irish Stowe Missal's Destination and Function." *Early Medieval Europe* 13, no. 2 (2005): 179–94.

Meehan, Bernard. "Book Satchels in Medieval Scotland and Ireland." In *A Crannog of the First Millennium AD: Excavations by Jack Scott at Loch Glashan, Argyll, 1960*, edited by Anne Crone and Ewan Campbell, 85–92. Edinburgh: Society of Antiquaries of Scotland, 2005.

Meens, Rob. "The Frequency and Nature of Early Medieval Penance." In *Handling Sin: Confession in the Middle Ages*, edited by Peter Biller and A. J. Minnis, 35–61. York: York Medieval Press, 1998.

———. "Penitentials and the Practice of Penance in the Tenth and Eleventh Centuries." *Early Medieval Europe* 14, no. 1 (2006): 7–21.

Milfull, Inge B. *The Hymns of the Anglo-Saxon Church: A Study and Edition of the "Durham Hymnal."* Cambridge: Cambridge University Press, 1996.

Murray, Alexander. "Confession before 1215." *Transactions of the Royal Historical Society*, 6th ser., 3 (1993): 51–81.

Nees, Lawrence. "Reading Aldred's Colophon for the Lindisfarne Gospels." *Speculum* 78, no. 2 (2003): 333–77.

Newton, Francis L., Francis L. Newton, Jr., and Christopher R. J. Scheirer. "Domiciling the Evangelists in Anglo-Saxon England: A Fresh Reading of Aldred's Colophon in the 'Lindisfarne Gospels'." *Anglo-Saxon England* 41 (2012): 101–44.

Norton, Christopher. "York Minster in the Time of Wulfstan." In *Wulfstan, Archbishop of York: The Proceedings of the Second Alcuin Conference*, edited by Matthew Townend, 207–34. Turnhout: Brepols, 2004.

O'Brien O'Keeffe, Katherine. *Visible Song: Transitional Literacy in Old English Verse*. Cambridge: Cambridge University Press, 1990.

O'Leary, Aideen. "An Orthodox Old English Homiliary? Ælfric's Views on the Apocryphal Acts of the Apostles." *Neuphilologische Mitteilungen* 100, no. 1 (1999): 15–26.

Orchard, Andy. *A Critical Companion to Beowulf*. Cambridge: D. S. Brewer, 2001.

———. "Crying Wolf: Oral Style and the *Sermones Lupi*." *Anglo-Saxon England* 21 (1992): 239–64.

Orchard, Nicholas. "An Eleventh-Century Anglo-Saxon Missal Fragment." *Anglo-Saxon England* 23 (1994): 283–89.
Ott, John. *Bishops, Authority and Community in Northwestern Europe, c. 1050–1150.* Cambridge: Cambridge University Press, 2015.
Owen, Dorothy. "The Norman Cathedral at Lincoln." In *Anglo-Norman Studies VI: Proceedings of the Battle Conference 1983*, edited by R. Allen Brown, 188–99. Woodbridge: Boydell Press, 1984.
Page, R. I. "Old English Liturgical Rubrics in Corpus Christi College, Cambridge, MS 422." *Anglia* 96 (1978): 149–58.
Palazzo, Eric. *A History of Liturgical Books from the Beginning to the Thirteenth Century.* Collegeville, MN: Liturgical Press, 1998.
Parkes, Malcolm. "A Fragment of an Early-Tenth-Century Anglo–Saxon Manuscript and Its Significance." *Anglo-Saxon England* 12 (1983): 129–40.
———. "The Palaeography of the Parker Manuscript of the Chronicle, Laws and Sedulius, and Historiography at Winchester in the Late Ninth and the Tenth Centuries." In *Scribes, Scripts and Readers: Studies in the Communication, Presentation and Dissemination of Medieval Texts*, 143–69. London: Hambledon Press, 1991.
Parsons, David. "Odda's Chapel, Deerhurst: Place of Worship or Royal Hall?" *Medieval Archaeology* 44, no. 1 (2000): 225–28.
Patzold, Steffen and Carine van Rhijn, eds., *Men in the Middle: Local Priests in Early Medieval Europe* (Berlin: De Gruyter, 2016).
Paxton, Frederick. "*Bonus liber*: A Late Carolingian Clerical Manual from Lorsch (Bibliotheca Vaticana MS Pal. Lat. 485)." In *The Two Laws: Studies in Medieval Legal History Dedicated to Stephan Kuttner*, edited by Laurent Mayali and Stephanie Tibbetts, 1–30. Washington, DC: Catholic University of America Press, 1990.
———. *Christianizing Death: The Creation of a Ritual Process in Early Medieval Europe.* Ithaca: Cornell University Press, 1990.
Pelle, Stephen. "The Seven Pains of Hell: The Latin Source of an Old English Homiletic Motif." *The Review of English Studies* 62 (2010): 167–80.
———. "Source Studies in the Lambeth Homilies." *The Journal of English and Germanic Philology* 113, no. 1 (2014): 34–72.
Pfaff, Richard. "Liturgical Books." In *The Cambridge History of the Book in Britain Volume 1: c.400–1100*, edited by Richard Gameson, 449–59. Cambridge: Cambridge University Press, 2011.
———. *The Liturgy in Medieval England: A History.* Cambridge: Cambridge University Press, 2009.
———. "Massbooks." In *The Liturgical Books of Anglo-Saxon England*, edited by Richard Pfaff, 7–34. Kalamazoo: Medieval Institute Publications, 1995.
Pickles, Thomas. "*Biscopes-tun, muneca-tun and preosta-tun*: Dating, Significance and Distribution." In *The Church in English Place-Names*,

edited by Eleanor Quinton, 39–107. Nottingham: English Place-Name Society, 2009.

———. "Church Organization and Pastoral Care." In *A Companion to the Early Middle Ages: Britain and Ireland, c.500–c.1100*, edited by Pauline Stafford, 160–76. Oxford: Wiley-Blackwell, 2009.

Powell, Kathryn. "Viking Invasions and Marginal Annotations in Cambridge, Corpus Christi College 162." *Anglo-Saxon England* 37 (2008): 151–71.

Pratt, David. "Kings and Books in Anglo-Saxon England." *Anglo-Saxon England* 43 (2014): 297–377.

———. *The Political Thought of King Alfred the Great*. Cambridge: Cambridge University Press, 2007.

Pulsiano, Phillip. "Jaunts, Jottings, and Jetsam in Anglo-Saxon Manuscripts." *Florilegium* 19 (2002): 189–216.

———. "The Prefatory Matter of London, British Library, Cotton Vitellius E. XVIII." In *Anglo-Saxon Manuscripts and Their Heritage*, edited by Phillip Pulsiano and Elaine Treharne, 85–116. Aldershot: Ashgate, 1998.

———. "Psalters." In *The Liturgical Books of Anglo-Saxon England*, edited by Richard Pfaff, 61–85. Kalamazoo: Medieval Institute Publications, 1995.

Rahtz, Philip, and Lorna Watts. "Three Ages of Conversion at Kirkdale, North Yorkshire." In *The Cross Goes North: Processes of Conversion in Northern Europe, AD 300–1300*, edited by Martin Carver, 289–309. York: York Medieval Press, 2003.

Rankin, Susan. "An Early Eleventh-Century Missal Fragment Copied by Eadwig Basan: Bodleian Library, MS. Lat. Liturg. D. 3, Fols. 4–5." *Bodleian Library Record* 18 (2004): 220–52.

———. "From Memory to Record: Musical Notations in Manuscripts from Exeter." *Anglo-Saxon England* 13 (1984): 97–112.

———. "Music Books." In *The Cambridge History of the Book in Britain Volume 1: c.400–1100*, edited by Richard Gameson, 482–506. Cambridge: Cambridge University Press, 2011.

———. "Neumatic Notations in Anglo-Saxon England." In *Musicologie médiévale: Notations et Séquences*, edited by Michel Huglo, 129–40. Paris: Champion, 1987.

Rasmussen, Niels. "Célébration épiscopale et célébration presbytérale: Un essai de typologie." In *Segni e riti nella Chiesa altomedievale occidentale*, 581–607. Vol. 33, no. 2 of *Settimane di studio del Centro italiano di sull'alto medioevo*. Spoleto: Presso la sede del Centro, 1987.

Reynolds, Roger. "Ordinatio and the Priesthood in the Early Middle Ages and Its Visual Depiction." In *A Companion to Priesthood and Holy Orders in the Middle Ages*, edited by Greg Peters and C. Colt Anderson, 43–69. Leiden: Brill, 2016.

Riché, Pierre. *Education and Culture in the Barbarian West, Sixth through*

Eighth Centuries. Translated by John Contreni. Columbia: University of South Carolina Press, 1976.

Riedel, Christopher. "Praising God Together: Monastic Reformers and Laypeople in Tenth-Century Winchester." *The Catholic Historical Review* 102, no. 2 (2016): 284–317.

Roberts, Jane and Christian Kay, with Lynne Grundy. *A Thesaurus of Old English in Two Volumes*. Vol. 1, *Introduction and Thesaurus*. London: King's College London, Centre for Late Antique and Medieval Studies, 1995.

Robertson, Nicola. "Dunstan and Monastic Reform: Tenth-Century Fact or Twelfth-Century Fiction?" In *Anglo-Norman Studies XXVIII: Proceedings of the Battle Conference 2005*, edited by C. P. Lewis, 153–67. Woodbridge: Boydell Press, 2006.

Robinson, Pamela R. "Self-Contained Units in Composite Manuscripts of the Anglo-Saxon Period." *Anglo-Saxon England* 7 (1978): 231–38.

Rogers, Nicholas. "The Waltham Abbey Relic-List." In *England in the Eleventh Century: Proceedings of the 1990 Harlaxton Symposium*, edited by Carola Hicks, 157–81. Stamford: Paul Watkins, 1992.

Rollason, David. "Lists of Saints' Resting-Places in Anglo-Saxon England." *Anglo-Saxon England* 7 (1978): 61–93.

Romano, John. "Priests and the Eucharist in the Middle Ages." In *A Companion to Priesthood and Holy Orders in the Middle Ages*, edited by Greg Peters and C. Colt Anderson, 188–216. Leiden: Brill, 2016.

Rosser, Gervase. "The Anglo-Saxon Gilds." In *Minsters and Parish Churches: The Local Church in Transition, 950–1200*, edited by John Blair, 31–34. Oxford: Oxford University Committee for Archaeology, 1988.

———. "The Cure of Souls in English Towns before 1000." In *Pastoral Care before the Parish*, edited by John Blair and Richard Sharpe, 267–84. Leicester: Leicester University Press, 1992.

Rowley, Sharon M. *The Old English Version of Bede's* Historia Ecclesiastica. Cambridge: D. S. Brewer, 2011.

Rudolf, Winfried. "The Homiliary of Angers in Tenth-Century England." *Anglo-Saxon England* 39 (2010): 163–92.

Rusche, Philip. "The Glosses to the Lindisfarne Gospels and the Benedictine Reform: Was Aldred Trained in the Southumbrian Glossing Tradition?" In *The Old English Gloss to the Lindisfarne Gospels*, edited by Julia Fernández Cuesta and Sara M. Pons-Sanz, 61–78. Berlin: De Gruyter, 2016.

Rushforth, Rebecca. "Annotated Psalters and Psalm Study in Late Anglo-Saxon England: The Manuscript Evidence." In *Rethinking and Recontextualising Glosses: New Perspectives in the Study of Late Anglo-Saxon Glossography*, edited by Patrizia Lendinara, Loredana Lazzari, and Claudia Di Sciacca, 39–66. Porto: Fédération Internationale des Instituts d'Études Mediévales, 2011.

———. "The Prodigal Fragment: Cambridge, Gonville and Caius College 734/782a." *Anglo-Saxon England* 30 (2001): 137–44.

Sánchez Sánchez, Manuel Ambrosio. "Vernacular Preaching in Spanish, Portuguese and Catalan." In *The Sermon*, edited by Beverly Mayne Kienzle, 759–858. Typologie des Sources du Moyen Âge Occidental 81–83. Turnhout: Brepols, 2000.

Sauer, Hans. "The Transmission and Structure of Archbishop Wulfstan's 'Commonplace Book'." In *Old English Prose: Basic Readings*, edited by Paul Szarmach, 339–93. New York: Garland, 2000.

Sawyer, Peter H. *Anglo-Saxon Lincolnshire*. Lincoln: Committee for the Society for Lincolnshire History and Archaeology, 1998.

Scragg, Donald G. "The Corpus of Vernacular Homilies and Prose Saints' Lives." In *Old English Prose: Basic Readings*, edited by Paul E. Szarmach and Deborah A. Oosterhouse, 73–150. London: Garland, 2000.

———. *Dating and Style in Old English Composite Homilies*. Cambridge: University of Cambridge, Department of Anglo-Saxon, Norse and Celtic, 1998.

———. "The Homilies of the Blickling Manuscript." In *Learning and Literature in Anglo-Saxon England: Studies Presented to Peter Clemoes on the Occasion of His Sixty-Fifth Birthday*, edited by Michael Lapidge and Helmut Gneuss, 299–316. Cambridge: Cambridge University Press, 1985.

———. "A Ninth-Century Old English Homily from Northumbria." *Anglo-Saxon England* 45 (2016): 39–49.

———. "An Old English Homilist of Archbishop Dunstan's Day." In *Words, Texts and Manuscripts: Studies in Anglo-Saxon Culture Presented to Helmut Gneuss on the Occasion of His Sixty-Fifth Birthday*, edited by Michael Korhammer, with Karl Reichl and Hans Sauer, 181–92. Cambridge: D. S. Brewer, 1992.

Sharpe, Richard. "Latin and Irish Words for 'Book-Satchel'." *Peritia* 4 (1985): 152–56.

———. "The Medieval Librarian." In *The Cambridge History of Libraries in Britain and Ireland Volume 1: To 1640*, edited by Elisabeth Leedham-Green and Teresa Webber, 218–41. Cambridge: Cambridge University Press, 2006.

Sheerin, Daniel. "The Liturgy." In *Medieval Latin: An Introduction and Bibliographical Guide*, edited by F. A. C. Mantello and A. G. Rigg, 157–82. Washington, DC: Catholic University of America Press, 1996.

Shinners, John and William Dohar, eds. *Pastors and the Care of Souls in Medieval England*. Notre Dame: University of Notre Dame Press, 1998.

Singer, Mark Alan. "Evidence for an Early English Plenary Missal: The Flyleaves of MS Bodley 386." *Manuscripta* 57, no. 1 (2013): 112–48.

Sisam, Celia. "The Scribal Tradition of the Lambeth Homilies." *Review of English Studies* 2 (1951): 105–13.
Smetana, Cyril. "Ælfric and the Early Medieval Homiliary." *Traditio* 15 (1959): 163–204.
Smith, Mary Frances. "The Preferment of Royal Clerks in the Reign of Edward the Confessor." *The Haskins Society Journal* 9 (1997): 159–73.
———. "Regenbald (*fl.* 1050–1086)." In *Oxford Dictionary of National Biography*. Oxford University Press, 2004. Accessed February 18, 2018. doi:10.1093/ref:odnb/23312.
Spear, David. "The Norman Empire and the Secular Clergy, 1066–1204." *Journal of British Studies* 21, no. 2 (1982): 1–10.
Spinks, Bryan D. *Early and Medieval Rituals and Theologies of Baptism: From the New Testament to the Council of Trent*. Aldershot: Ashgate, 2006.
Stanley, Eric. "Karl Luick's 'Man schrieb wie man sprach' and English Historical Philology." In *Luick Revisited: Papers Read at the Luick-Symposium at Schloss Liechtenstein, 15.–18.9.1985*, edited by Dieter Kastovsky and Gero Bauer, with Jacek Fisiak, 311–34. Tübingen: Gunter Narr, 1988.
———. "The Lindisfarne Gospels: Aldred's Gloss." In *The Lindisfarne Gospels: New Perspectives*, edited by Richard Gameson, 206–17. Leiden: Brill, 2017.
Stanton, Robert. *The Culture of Translation in Anglo-Saxon England*. Cambridge: D. S. Brewer, 2002.
Stephenson, Rebecca. "Ælfric of Eynsham and Hermeneutic Latin: *Meatim Sed et Rustica* Reconsidered." *The Journal of Medieval Latin* 16 (2006): 111–41.
———. "Byrhtferth's *Enchiridion*: The Effectiveness of Hermeneutic Latin." In *Conceptualizing Multilingualism in England, c.800–c.1250*, edited by Elizabeth M. Tyler, 121–43. Turnhout: Brepols, 2011.
———. *The Politics of Language: Byrhtferth, Ælfric, and the Multilingual Identity of the Benedictine Reform*. Toronto: University of Toronto Press, 2015.
———. "Scapegoating the Secular Clergy: The Hermeneutic Style as a Form of Monastic Self-Definition." *Anglo-Saxon England* 38 (2009): 101–35.
Stevens, Wesley. "Cycles of Time: Calendrical and Astronomical Reckonings in Early Science." In *Cycles of Time and Scientific Learning in Medieval Europe*, edited by Wesley Stevens, 27–51. Aldershot: Variorum, 1995.
———. "Sidereal Time in Anglo-Saxon England." In *Cycles of Time and Scientific Learning in Medieval Europe*, edited by Wesley Stevens, 125–52. Aldershot: Variorum, 1995.
Stokes, Peter. "The Vision of Leofric: Manuscript, Text and Context." *The Review of English Studies* 63 (2012): 529–50.

Swan, Mary. "Cambridge, Corpus Christi College 198 and the Blickling Manuscript." *Leeds Studies in English* 37 (2006): 89–100.

———. "Memorialised Readings: Manuscript Evidence for Old English Homily Composition." In *Anglo-Saxon Manuscripts and Their Heritage*, edited by Phillip Pulsiano and Elaine Treharne, 205–17. Aldershot: Ashgate, 1998.

———. "Preaching past the Conquest: Lambeth Palace 487 and Cotton Vespasian A. XXII." In *The Old English Homily: Precedent, Practice, and Appropriation*, edited by Aaron Kleist, 403–24. Turnhout: Brepols, 2007.

Symes, Carol. "Liturgical Texts and Performance Practices." In *Understanding Medieval Liturgy: Essays in Interpretation*, edited by Helen Gittos and Sarah Hamilton, 239–67. Farnham: Ashgate, 2016.

Szarmach, Paul. "MS Junius 85 F. 2r and Napier 49." *English Language Notes* 14, no. 4 (1977): 241–46.

———. "Pembroke College 25, arts. 93–95." In *Via Crucis: Essays on Early Medieval Sources and Ideas in Memory of J. E. Cross*, edited by Thomas N. Hall, with Thomas D. Hill and Charles D. Wright, 295–325. Morgantown, WV: West Virginia University Press, 2002.

———. "The Vercelli Prose and Anglo-Saxon Literary History." In *New Readings in the Vercelli Book*, edited by Samantha Zacher and Andy Orchard, 12–40. Toronto: University of Toronto Press, 2009.

Temple, Elżbieta. *Anglo-Saxon Manuscripts, 900–1066*. London: Harvey Miller, 1976.

Teresi, Loredana. "Mnemonic Transmission of Old English Texts in the Post-Conquest Period." In *Rewriting Old English in the Twelfth Century*, edited by Mary Swan and Elaine Treharne, 98–116. Cambridge, Cambridge University Press, 2000.

Thacker, Alan. "Monks, Preaching and Pastoral Care in Early Anglo-Saxon England." In *Pastoral Care before the Parish*, edited by John Blair and Richard Sharpe, 137–70. Leicester: Leicester University Press, 1992.

———. "Priests and Pastoral Care in Early Anglo-Saxon England." In *The Study of Medieval Manuscripts of England: Festschrift in Honor of Richard W. Pfaff*, edited by George Brown and Linda Voights, 187–208. Turnhout: Brepols, 2010.

Thomas, Hugh M. *The Secular Clergy in England, 1066–1216*. Oxford: Oxford University Press, 2014.

Thompson, Augustine. *Cities of God: The Religion of the Italian Communes, 1125–1325*. University Park, PA: Pennsylvania State University Press, 2005.

Thompson, Victoria. *Dying and Death in Later Anglo-Saxon England*. Woodbridge: Boydell Press, 2004.

———. "The Pastoral Contract in Late Anglo-Saxon England: Priest and Parishioner in Oxford, Bodleian Library, MS Laud

Miscellaneous 482." In *Pastoral Care in Late Anglo-Saxon England*, edited by Francesca Tinti, 106–20. Woodbridge: Boydell Press, 2005.

Tibbetts, Sidney. "*Praescriptiones*, Student Scribes and the Carolingian Scriptorium." In *La collaboration dans la production de l'écrit médiéval: Actes du XIIIe colloque du Comité international de paléographie latine*, edited by Herrad Spilling, 25–38. Paris: École des chartes, 2003.

Timofeeva, Olga. "Anglo-Latin Bilingualism before 1066: Prospects and Limitations." In *Interfaces between Language and Culture in Medieval England: A Festschrift for Matti Kilpiö*, edited by Alaric Hall, Olga Timofeeva, Ágnes Kiricsi, and Bethany Fox, 1–36. Leiden: Brill, 2010.

Tinti, Francesca. "Benedictine Reform and Pastoral Care in Late Anglo-Saxon England." *Early Medieval Europe* 23, no. 2 (2015): 229–51.

———. "Looking for Local Priests in Anglo-Saxon England." In *Men in the Middle: Local Priests in Early Medieval Europe*, edited by Steffen Patzold and Carine van Rhijn, 145–61. Berlin: De Gruyter, 2016.

———, ed. *Pastoral Care in Late Anglo-Saxon England*. Woodbridge: Boydell Press, 2005.

———. *Sustaining Belief: The Church of Worcester from c.870 to c.1100*. Farnham: Ashgate, 2010.

Tollerton, Linda. *Wills and Will-Making in Anglo-Saxon England*. York: York Medieval Press, 2011.

Toswell, M. J. "The Codicology of Anglo-Saxon Homiletic Manuscripts, Especially the Blickling Homilies." In *The Old English Homily: Precedent, Practice, and Appropriation*, edited by Aaron Kleist, 209–26. Turnhout: Brepols, 2007.

Treharne, Elaine. "The Bishop's Book: Leofric's Homiliary and Eleventh-Century Exeter." In *Early Medieval Studies in Memory of Patrick Wormald*, edited by Stephen Baxter, Catherine Karkov, Janet Nelson, and David Pelteret, 521–37. Farnham: Ashgate, 2009.

———. "Producing a Library in Late Anglo-Saxon England: Exeter, 1050–1072." *Review of English Studies* 54 (2003): 155–72.

———. "Reading from the Margins: The Uses of Old English Homiletic Manuscripts in the Post-Conquest Period." In *Beatus Vir: Studies in Early English and Norse Manuscripts in Memory of Phillip Pulsiano*, edited by A. N. Doane and Kirsten Wolf, 329–58. Tempe, AZ: Arizona Center for Medieval and Renaissance Studies, 2006.

———. "Scribal Connections in Late Anglo-Saxon England." In *Texts and Traditions of Medieval Pastoral Care: Essays in Honour of Bella Millett*, edited by Cate Gunn and Catherine Innes-Parker, 29–46. York: York Medieval Press, 2009.

Upchurch, Robert. "Catechetic Homiletics: Ælfric's Preaching and Teaching during Lent." In *A Companion to Ælfric*, edited by Hugh Magennis and Mary Swan, 217–46. Leiden: Brill, 2009.

Uro, Risto. "Ritual, Memory and Writing in Early Christianity." *Temenos* 47, no. 2 (2011): 159–82.

Van Rhijn, Carine. "The Local Church, Priests' Handbooks and Pastoral Care in the Carolingian Period." In *Chiese locali e Chiese regionali nell'alto medioevo*, 689–706. Vol. 61, no. 2 of *Settimane di studio della Fondazione Centro italiano di studi sull'alto medioevo*. Spoleto: Fondazione Centro italiano di studi sull'alto medioevo, 2014.

———. "Manuscripts for Local Priests and the Carolingian Reforms." In *Men in the Middle: Local Priests in Early Medieval Europe*, edited by Steffen Patzold and Carine van Rhijn, 177–98. Berlin: De Gruyter, 2016.

———. *Shepherds of the Lord: Priests and Episcopal Statutes in the Carolingian Period*. Turnhout: Brepols, 2007.

Vogel, Cyrille. *Medieval Liturgy: An Introduction to the Sources*. Edited and translated by William George Storey, Niels Rasmussen and John Brooks-Leonard. Washington, D.C.: Pastoral Press, 1986.

Wack, Mary F., and Charles D. Wright. "A New Latin Source for the Old English 'Three Utterances' Exemplum." *Anglo-Saxon England* 20 (1991): 187–202.

Watkins, C. S. "Sin, Penance and Purgatory in the Anglo-Norman Realm: The Evidence of Visions and Ghost Stories." *Past and Present* 175, no. 1 (2002): 3–33.

Webber, Teresa. "Books and Their Use across the Conquest." In *Bury St Edmunds and the Norman Conquest*, edited by Tom Licence, 160–89. Woodbridge: Boydell Press, 2014.

———. "Cantor, Sacrist or Prior? The Provision of Books in Anglo-Norman England." In *Medieval Cantors and Their Craft: Music, Liturgy and the Shaping of History, 800–1500*, edited by Katie Bugyis, A. B. Kraebel, and Margot Fassler, 172–89. York: York Medieval Press, 2017.

———. *Scribes and Scholars at Salisbury Cathedral, c.1075–c.1125*. Oxford: Clarendon Press, 1992.

Wilcox, Jonathan. "Ælfric in Dorset and the Landscape of Pastoral Care." In *Pastoral Care in Late Anglo-Saxon England*, edited by Francesca Tinti, 52–62. Woodbridge: Boydell Press, 2005.

———. "The Audience of Ælfric's *Lives of Saints* and the Face of Cotton Caligula A. XIV, fols. 93–130." In *Beatus Vir: Studies in Early English and Norse Manuscripts in Memory of Phillip Pulsiano*, edited by A. N. Doane and Kirsten Wolf, 229–59. Tempe, AZ: Arizona Center for Medieval and Renaissance Studies, 2006.

———. "The Blickling Homilies Revisited: Knowable and Probable Uses of Princeton University Library, MS Scheide 71." In *The Genesis of Books: Studies in the Scribal Culture of Medieval England in Honour of A. N. Doane*, edited by Matthew T. Hussey and John D. Niles, 97–115. Turnhout: Brepols, 2011.

———. "The Dissemination of Wulfstan's Homilies: The Wulfstan Tradition in Eleventh-Century Vernacular Preaching." In *England in the Eleventh Century: Proceedings of the 1990 Harlaxton Symposium*, edited by Carola Hicks, 199–217. Stamford: Paul Watkins, 1992.

———. "The Use of Ælfric's Homilies: MSS Oxford, Bodleian Library, Junius 85 and 86 in the Field." In *A Companion to Ælfric*, edited by Hugh Magennis and Mary Swan, 345–68. Leiden: Brill, 2009.

Williams, Ann. "A Bell-House and a Burh-geat: Lordly Residences in England before the Norman Conquest." In *Medieval Knighthood IV: Papers from the Fifth Strawberry Hill Conference, 1990*, edited by Christopher Harper-Bill and Ruth Harvey, 221–40. Woodbridge: Boydell Press, 1992.

———. *Land, Power and Politics: The Family and Career of Odda of Deerhurst*. Gloucester: Friends of Deerhurst Church, 1997.

———. "The Spoliation of Worcester." In *Anglo-Norman Studies XIX: Proceedings of the Battle Conference 1996*, edited by Christopher Harper-Bill, 383–408. Woodbridge: Boydell Press, 1997.

———. "Thegnly Piety and Ecclesiastical Patronage in the Late Old English Kingdom." In *Anglo-Norman Studies XXIV: Proceedings of the Battle Conference 2001*, edited by John Gillingham, 1–24. Woodbridge: Boydell Press, 2002.

Windeatt, Barry. "1412–1534: Texts." In *The Cambridge Companion to Medieval English Mysticism*, edited by Samuel Fanous and Vincent Gillespie, 195–224. Cambridge: Cambridge University Press, 2011.

Wood, Susan. *The Proprietary Church in the Medieval West*. Oxford: Oxford University Press, 2006.

Wormald, Francis. "Decorated Initials in English Manuscripts from A.D. 900 to 1100." In *Collected Writings I: Studies in Medieval Art from the Sixth to the Twelfth Centuries*, edited by J. J. G. Alexander, T. J. Brown, and Joan Gibbs, 47–75. London: Harvey Miller, 1984.

———. "Fragments of a Tenth-Century Sacramentary from the Binding of the Winton Domesday." In *Winchester and the Early Middle Ages: An Edition and Discussion of the Winton Domesday*, edited by Martin Biddle, 541–49. Oxford: Clarendon Press, 1976.

———. "The 'Winchester School' before St. Æthelwold." In *Collected Writings I: Studies in Medieval Art from the Sixth to the Twelfth Centuries*, edited by J. J. G. Alexander, T. J. Brown, and Joan Gibbs, 76–84. London: Harvey Miller, 1984.

Wormald, Patrick. *How Do We Know So Much about Anglo-Saxon Deerhurst?* Deerhurst, Gloucester: Friends of Deerhurst Church, 1993.

———. *The Making of English Law: King Alfred to the Twelfth Century*. Oxford: Blackwell, 1999.

Bibliography

———. "The Uses of Literacy in Anglo-Saxon England and Its Neighbours." *Transactions of the Royal Historical Society*, 5th ser., 27 (1977): 95–114.

Wranovix, Matthew. "Ulrich Pfeffel's Library: Parish Priests, Preachers, and Books in the Fifteenth Century." *Speculum* 87, no. 4 (2012): 1125–55.

Wright, C. E. "The Dispersal of the Libraries in the Sixteenth Century." In *The English Library before 1700: Studies in Its History*, edited by Francis Wormald and C. E. Wright, 148–75. London: University of London, Athlone Press, 1958.

Wright, Charles D. "Old English Homilies and Latin Sources." In *The Old English Homily: Precedent, Practice, and Appropriation*, edited by Aaron Kleist, 15–66. Turnhout: Brepols, 2007.

———. "Vercelli Homilies XI–XIII and the Anglo-Saxon Benedictine Reform: Tailored Sources and Implied Audiences." In *Preacher, Sermon and Audience in the Middle Ages*, edited by Carolyn Muessig, 203–27. Leiden: Brill, 2002.

Yorke, Barbara. *Wessex in the Early Middle Ages*. London: Leicester University Press, 1995.

Young, Karl. *The Drama of the Medieval Church*. Vol. 1. Oxford: Clarendon Press, 1933.

Zacher, Samantha, and Andy Orchard. Introduction to *New Readings in the Vercelli Book*, edited by Samantha Zacher and Andy Orchard, 3–11. Toronto: University of Toronto Press, 2009.

Unpublished theses

Chadbon, John. "Oxford, Bodleian Library, MSS Junius 85 and 86: An Edition of a Witness to the Old English Homiletic Tradition." PhD thesis, University of Leeds, 1993.

Conti, Aidan. "Preaching Scripture and Apocrypha: A Previously Unidentified Carolingian Homiliary in an Old English Manuscript, Oxford, Bodleian Library, MS Bodley 343." PhD thesis, University of Toronto, 2004.

Dalbey, Marcia. "Structure and Style in the Blickling Homilies for the Temporale." PhD thesis, University of Illinois, 1968.

Drage, Elaine M. "Bishop Leofric and the Exeter Cathedral Chapter, 1050–1072: A Reassessment of the Manuscript Evidence." D.Phil thesis, University of Oxford, 1978.

Olson, Aleisha. "Textual Representations of Almsgiving in Late Anglo-Saxon England." PhD thesis, University of York, 2010. http://etheses.whiterose.ac.uk/1111/1/Textual_Representations_of_Almsgiving_-_Aleisha_Olson.pdf.

Schuler, Eric. "Almsgiving and the Formation of Early Medieval

Societies, A.D. 700–1025." PhD thesis, University of Notre Dame, 2010. https://curate.nd.edu/downloads/j9601z42v32.

Swan, Mary. "Ælfric as Source: The Exploitation of Ælfric's Catholic Homilies from the Late Tenth to Twelfth Centuries." PhD thesis, University of Leeds, 1993. http://etheses.whiterose.ac.uk/1949/1/uk_bl_ethos_394542.pdf.

Index

Adelard, master at Waltham Holy Cross 59–60, 91
Admonitio Generalis 114, 205
Ælfheah, St, archbishop of Canterbury 61
Ælfhelm, cleric at Ely 90
Ælfric Bata 105
Ælfric of Eynsham 53, 57, 128
   De temporibus anni 206
   Education 62–64
   Homilies 84, 95, 117–20, 123, 127
      Distribution 95, 129
   Pastoral letters 34–41, 49, 52, 56, 122
Ælfwold, nobleman 198–99
Æthelred, king 198
   VII Æthelred (lawcode) 17–18, 189
Æthelstan, king 58, 187, 195
Æthelstan, priest and father of St Wulfstan 52, 78
Æthelweard, ealdorman 64, 124
Æthelwold, bishop of Winchester 63, 94–95, 187–88, 191, 199
   Education 53, 58
Aldbrough sundial 99–100 n. 70
Aldred, glossator of the Lindisfarne Gospels 69–71, 74, 82–83
Alfred, king of the Anglo-Saxons 51, 62, 89, 169, 195
   Establishment of schools 58, 61
All Saints, Harewood 73–74, 90
All Saints, Warwick 60–61

B., author of *Vita Sancti Dunstani* 47, 53–54, 71, 75–76, 89 n. 36
Baptism 12, 29, 31, 39, 201–2, 222–23
Bede 55, 111–12, 118, 172, 206, 207
Bedwyn, Wiltshire 51, 67–69, 88–89
Benedictine reform 93, 128, 165, 231–32

Effects on secular churches 18, 86
Importation of texts 114, 120, 152, 153, 217
Beverley 94, 160
Bishops
   As fathers 52
   Connections with penance 30, 195, 200
   Episcopal books 4–5, 150 n. 12, 157–58
   Prescriptions for priests' books 12–13, 34–37, 40, 227
   Promotion of royal priests 24
   Provision of books 93–95, 96, 98–99
Blickling, Homily II 123
   Homily VI 135
   Homily IX 129, 139
Booklending *see* Lending
Booklets 126, 130–31, 138, 193
Booklists
   Inventories 87, 94, 96, 159–61, 166–67, 207
   Prescriptive lists 12–14, 34–37, 40, 200
Book production
   Commissioning 87–88, 104–7
   Funding 98–99, 101
   Liturgical books 84–87
   Material resources 83
   Specialization 87, 106–7
Book storage 33
Book theft 107–8
Bosham, Sussex 60, 91
Britheah, bishop of Worcester 86
Burhs 61, 77, 161
Bury St Edmund's 96–97, 160 n. 48
Byrhtferth of Ramsey 53–54, 205, 207

Index

Calendars 186–87, 219
Canons of Edgar 13, 40, 65, 146, 163, 191, 202
Canterbury 84, 95, 125, 127–29, 188
Cathedrals 18–19, 53–55, 74–75, 98, 155–58
  Book production *see under* Scriptoria
  Monasticization 26, 84–85
Charters 24, 66, 88, 198
Chester-le-Street 70–71
Chrism 202
Cirencester 24
Clergy
  Below the priesthood 18, 52
  Clerical grades 4, 55–56
  Priesthood *see* Priests
Clerical families 51–53, 64, 108
Clerical literacy 40–41, 44–45, 52, 69–71
  Definitions 46–48
  Functional literacy 48, 78, 227
  Monastic criticisms 27, 48–50, 78
Cnut, king 87, 103
  I Cnut (lawcode) 189
Colophons 69, 71–73, 104
Commonplace books 117, 196, 200, 210
Computus 194, 204–9, 219–22, 226
Council of *Clofesho* 111, 165
Cuthman, St 76–77
Cynesige, archbishop of York 94, 160

Deerhurst 61–62
Divine Office 28–29, 100, 164–69, 190–91
  Books used 39, 152–54, 175
  Lay involvement 167–69, 191
  Monastic practices 164–66
Domesday Book 19, 21, 45, 51, 73, 104
Dover 162
Dunstan, St, archbishop of Canterbury 53, 58, 71, 89

Dying and death, rites for 30–31, 203, 212–13, 222, 223

Eadmer of Canterbury 57
Eadmer the priest 104
Eadwig Basan 87, 106
Ealdred, archbishop of York 94
Earnwig, monk at Peterborough 106
Edgar, king 100, 166
  II Edgar (lawcode) 20
Edmund, king 195
Education
  At the royal court 57–58
  By local priests 62–65
  Curriculum 54–55, 65
  In monasteries and cathedrals 53–57
  In secular minsters 58–62, 77
  Liturgical training 59–60, 77–78
Ely 90
Emma of Normandy 87, 103
Exeter 94, 107, 157–58, 172, 200
  Scriptorium 66, 75, 83, 92

Farmon, glossator and priest at Harewood 71–74, 90
Fasting 198
Fécamp Abbey 76
Frithestan, bishop of Winchester 186, 187

Geþyncðo 164
Giso, bishop of Wells 24, 157
Glastonbury 53–54, 89
Glossing 69–74, 185–86
Goding, cleric and scribe 74
Godric, cleric at Twynham 162
Gregory the Great, homilies of 111–13, 118
Guilds 23, 124–25, 203–4

Harold Godwinson 59, 100–101, 167
Hawkesbury, Gloucestershire 86
Hemming, monk and author 30, 74

278

Index

Hermeneutic Latin 47, 75
Holy Trinity, Twynham 61, 161–63
Homiliary of Angers 116, 131–36, 145
Homilies
  Anonymous 116–17, 127–30
  In Old English 28, 112–13, 230–31
  Latin homiliaries 111–12, 113–14
  Performance 125–26
  Transmission 95, 129–31
Hurstmonceaux (Herstmonceux), Sussex 104

Isidore of Seville 214, 215

Judith of Flanders 102–3, 106
Justin Martyr 121

Kirkdale 99–100 n. 70

Law, Anglo-Saxon 17–18, 20, 195
Lending 96–98
Lent 30, 125, 140, 168, 198
Leofric, bishop of Exeter 24, 92, 94, 157–58
Leofric, earl of Mercia 76, 100, 163, 168
Leofric-Tiberius computus *see* Computus
Liber officialis 218–19
Lichfield 18
Lincoln 142–43
Literacy *see* Clerical literacy
Liturgical books 38–40, 147–54, 156–58
  Containing Old English 203–4, 209, 222–23, 231–32
  Evolution of 14 n. 35, 147, 189–90, 230
  For the Office *see under* Divine Office
  Gospelbooks 5–6, 151, 178
  Graduals 150
  Lectionaries 38, 151, 176–85
  Manuals 39, 194, 200–201, 225

Mass-books 105, 149–50, 169–71, 174–75, 189, 230
  Distinctions 149
  Psalters 97–98, 152, 166, 185–88
Local churches 147, 149, 163–64, 189–90
  Proliferation 41–42
Louis the Pious, Carolingian emperor 198

Manorial churches 20–21, 99, 102, 164
Manuscript fragments 15, 147, 154, 189–90, 233–34
Manuscripts
  Berlin, Deutsche Staadtsbibliothek, Phillips 1667 199 n. 25
  Bern, Burgerbibliothek 671 67–68, 88–89
  Cambridge, Corpus Christi College 41 91, 92, 105 n. 92, 107, 129–30, 172–76, 191–92
  Cambridge, Corpus Christi College 69 113
  Cambridge, Corpus Christi College 162 120, 125, 127, 135
  Cambridge, Corpus Christi College 173 (The Parker Chronicle) 185
  Cambridge, Corpus Christi College 190 168, 200, 210
  Cambridge, Corpus Christi College 191 158 n. 38
  Cambridge, Corpus Christi College 198 142–43
  Cambridge, Corpus Christi College 265 196 n. 14
  Cambridge, Corpus Christi College 422 (The Red Book of Darley) 26, 85, 154, 169–72, 182, 191, 202, 207, 211, 219–24
  Cambridge, University Library, Add. 3206 196
  Dublin, Royal Irish Academy, D. II. 3 105

Index

Durham, Cathedral Library,
A. II. 17 (Durham Gospels) 82
Durham, Cathedral Library
A. IV. 19 (The Durham
Collectar) 69, 82, 153–54
Durham, Cathedral Library,
B. II. 2 118 n. 35
Exeter, Cathedral Library 3501
(The Exeter Book) 92
Le Havre, Bibliothèque
municipale 330 (Missal of the
New Minster) 156–57 n. 34
Lincoln, Cathedral Library
158 118 n. 35
London, British Library, Add.
37517 (The Bosworth
Psalter) 187
London, British Library, Add.
47967 (The Lauderdale
Orosius) 185
London, British Library, Add.
56488 (The Muchelney
Breviary Fragment) 154
London, British Library, Cotton
Galba A. XVIII 186
London, British Library, Cotton
Nero D. IV (The Lindisfarne
Gospels) 69, 73–74
London, British Library, Cotton
Tiberius A. III 26
London, British Library, Cotton
Titus D. XXVII 221
London, British Library, Cotton
Vespasian D. XV 214–19,
228–29
London, British Library, Cotton
Vitellius A. XV (The Beowulf
Manuscript) 81, 92
London, British Library, Cotton
Vitellius A. XVIII (The Giso
Sacramentary) 157
London, British Library, Cotton
Vitellius E. XVIII (The
Vitellius Psalter) 221
London, British Library,
Harley 2961 (The Leofric
Collectar) 154
London, British Library, Harley
3271 221
London, British Library, Royal
1 D. III 85 n. 19, 103
London, British Library, Royal
8 C. III 232
London, British Library, Royal
17 C. XVII 154
London, Lambeth Palace Library,
489 83
London, Society of Antiquaries
154 156–57 n. 34, 201
Orléans, Bibliothèque municipale
116 218 n. 89
Orléans, Bibliothèque municipale
127 (The Winchcombe
Sacramentary) 201
Oslo, Riksarkivet, Lat. fragm. 206
+ 209, nos. 1–4 + 239, nos.
6–7 156 n. 34
Oxford, Bodleian Library, Auct.
D. 2. 14 96–97
Oxford, Bodleian Library, Auct.
D. 2. 19 (The MacRegol
Gospels) 71–74, 90
Oxford, Bodleian Library, Auct.
F. 4. 32 126, 130
Oxford, Bodleian Library, Bodley
343 132
Oxford, Bodleian Library, Bodley
386 182
Oxford, Bodleian Library,
Bodley 579 (The Leofric
Missal) 157–58
Oxford, Bodleian Library, Digby
63 112–13, 128, 231
Oxford, Bodleian Library, Hatton
115 130, 135
Oxford, Bodleian Library, Junius
27 (The Junius Psalter) 166,
185–88, 191
Oxford, Bodleian Library, Junius
85 and 86 125–26, 136–42

Index

Oxford, Bodleian Library, Junius 121 196 n. 14, 200
Oxford, Bodleian Library, Laud Misc. 482 12, 31, 85, 168, 196, 203, 209–14, 222
Oxford, Corpus Christi College 282 105 n. 92, 174–75
Paris, Bibliothèque nationale de France, lat. 1603 84–85 n. 16
Paris, Bibliothèque nationale de France, lat. 8092 104
Princeton, New Jersey, Princeton University Library, Scheide Collection 71 (The Blickling Homilies) 115–16, 138, 142–44
Rome, Biblioteca Vallicelliana, E 15 199 n. 25
Rome, Vatican City, Biblioteca Apostolica Vaticana, Pal. lat. 554 193
Rouen, Bibliothèque municipale, 274, Y.6 204 n. 44, 221
SCH, DD\SAS/C/1193/77 (The Taunton Fragment) 92, 131–36
St Petersburg, National Library of Russia, Q.V.I.34 218 n. 89
Vercelli, Biblioteca Capitolare CXVII (The Vercelli Book) 115–16
Warsaw, Biblioteka Narodowa, I. 3311 (The Warsaw Lectionary) 91, 176–85, 191, 228, 235–39
York, Minster Library, Add. 1 (The York Gospels) 159–60
Marriage 201 n. 32
Mass
  Celebration of 27–28, 155–64
  Expositio missae 217–18, 232
  Mass liturgy 148, 155
Memorization 14–15, 54, 121–22, 147–48
Minsters *see* Secular minsters

Monks
  As scribes 106
  Influence on pastoral texts 231–32
  Monk-priests 4, 25, 87
  Relationship to secular clergy 7–8, 26–27, 48–49
  Role in pastoral care 19, 26–27, 86–87, 165–66
Musical notation 175, 181–85

Oda, archbishop of Canterbury 24, 65, 78
Old English martyrologist, the 113
On the Examination of Candidates for Ordination 40, 65, 205
Orderic Vitalis, monk and chronicler 64
Ordination 56
Osbern, priest at Haselbury 52
Oswald, bishop of Worcester 57
Ovid 69–70
Owun, glossator of the MacRegol Gospels 71–74

Passio Apostolorum Petri et Pauli 119
Pastoral care 31, 115
  By monks *see under* Monks
  Definitions 10
  In towns 19, 26
Patronage
  Of local churches 101–3
  Of secular minsters 5–6, 99–101, 162–63, 168
Paul, abbot of St Alban's 101
Paul the Deacon 112, 114, 118–19
Penance 29–31, 195, 197–99
  Public penance 197 n. 16
Penitentials 194–96, 199–200, 210, 216–17
  Carolingian texts 195
  Old English Handbook 196, 197, 209
  Old English Penitential 209, 210
  Penitential of Egbert 13, 35–39, 41 n. 81, 193, 200

281

Penitential of Halitgar 197, 210
Penitential of Theodore 215, 216
Scrift boc 202, 210
Pershore Abbey 86–87
Peterborough 95, 106
Peter Damian 199
Preaching
  As a priestly duty 111, 114–15, 121
  To the laity 118, 132–34, 230–31
  Within the mass 28, 122–23
Priests
  As authors 8 n. 16, 75–77
  As educators 24 n. 36, 62–65
  As glossators *see* Glossing
  As homilists 127–28, 145
  As scribes 66–68, 74–75, 88–90
  Household priests 24–25, 65, 76, 103, 124
  Illegal activity 17
  In cathedral communities 18–19
  In property transactions 108 n. 103
  Royal priests 23–24, 52 n. 33, 104
Priests' books
  As an inheritance 108
  Carolingian influence 13, 34, 42, 218
  Distinctions from continental books 232–33
  Survival 15–16, 85, 95, 131, 169
  Terminology 32, 38–40
  Typology 3–5
Pseudo-Augustine 215

Ramsey Abbey 54, 57, 93
Raunds, Northamptonshire 20–21
Redon Abbey 101
Regenbald, royal priest 24
Royal minsters 67, 88–89, 92–93
Rule of Chrodegang 34, 36–39, 158

Salisbury 75, 81
Scribal training 82–83, 89
Scriptoria 80–81
  In monasteries and cathedrals 84–88, 95, 103, 213–14
Secondhand books 107–8
Secular minsters 19–20, 162–63, 190, 202
  Competition with other institutions 22–23, 49
  Early minsters 10, 111–12
  Manuscript production 88–93
Sherborne 85, 169
Sherburn-in-Elmet 159–61, 166
Shrewsbury 64
Siward the priest 64
Steyning, Sussex 76–77
St Helen's, Darley Dale, Derbyshire 170–71
St Mary Magdalen's, London 61
St Mary's, Castlegate, York 99 n. 70
St Oswald's, Gloucester 61
Stow, Lincolnshire 100, 168

Theodulf of Orléans 30, 34, 69
  Episcopal statutes 64, 116
Twynham, Hampshire 61

Unlocalized manuscripts 81, 91, 229

Vercelli homilies 127–28
Vision of Leofric 76, 164
Visio Pauli 119, 139

Waltham Chronicle, the 58–59, 167–68
Waltham Holy Cross 5–6, 91, 100–101, 167
  School 58–60
Wells 18, 174
Westbury-on-Trym 93–94
Wills 99, 102
Winchester 19, 25, 26, 63, 75, 84–85, 156–57
  Expulsion of secular clerics 84, 166
  Scriptorium 84–85, 103, 169, 185, 187
Winchester computus *see* Computus

Index

Worcester 18, 19, 26, 107, 209, 213
   Scriptorium 84–85, 213–14
Wulfstan, archbishop of York 56, 88, 128, 146, 196
   Homilies 117–20

Wulfstan, St, bishop of Worcester 25, 26, 52, 53, 86, 93–94
   Pastoral care 30, 202, 214

York 112

ANGLO-SAXON STUDIES

Volume 1: The Dramatic Liturgy of Anglo-Saxon England,
M. Bradford Bedingfield

Volume 2: The Art of the Anglo-Saxon Goldsmith: Fine Metalwork in Anglo-Saxon England: its Practice and Practitioners, *Elizabeth Coatsworth and Michael Pinder*

Volume 3: The Ruler Portraits of Anglo-Saxon England, *Catherine E. Karkov*

Volume 4: Dying and Death in Later Anglo-Saxon England,
Victoria Thompson

Volume 5: Landscapes of Monastic Foundation: The Establishment of Religious Houses in East Anglia, c. 650–1200, *Tim Pestell*

Volume 6: Pastoral Care in Late Anglo-Saxon England, *edited by Francesca Tinti*

Volume 7: Episcopal Culture in Late Anglo-Saxon England,
Mary Frances Giandrea

Volume 8: Elves in Anglo-Saxon England: Matters of Belief, Health, Gender and Identity, *Alaric Hall*

Volume 9: Feasting the Dead: Food and Drink in Anglo-Saxon Burial Rituals,
Christina Lee

Volume 10: Anglo-Saxon Button Brooches: Typology, Genealogy, Chronology, *Seiichi Suzuki*

Volume 11: Wasperton: A Roman, British and Anglo-Saxon Community in Central England, *edited by Martin Carver with Catherine Hills and Jonathan Scheschkewitz*

Volume 12: A Companion to Bede, *George Hardin Brown*

Volume 13: Trees in Anglo-Saxon England: Literature, Lore and Landscape,
Della Hooke

Volume 14: The Homiletic Writings of Archbishop Wulfstan,
Joyce Tally Lionarons

Volume 15: The Archaeology of the East Anglian Conversion, *Richard Hoggett*

Volume 16: The Old English Version of Bede's *Historia Ecclesiastica*,
Sharon M. Rowley

Volume 17: Writing Power in Anglo-Saxon England: Texts, Hierarchies, Economies, *Catherine A. M. Clarke*

Volume 18: Cognitive Approaches to Old English Poetry, *Antonina Harbus*

Volume 19: Environment, Society and Landscape in Early Medieval England: Time and Topography, *Tom Williamson*

Volume 20: Honour, Exchange and Violence in *Beowulf*, *Peter S. Baker*

Volume 21: *John the Baptist's Prayer* or *The Descent into Hell* from the Exeter Book: Text, Translation and Critical Study, *M.R. Rambaran-Olm*

Volume 22: Food, Eating and Identity in Early Medieval England, *Allen J. Frantzen*

Volume 23: Capital and Corporal Punishment in Anglo-Saxon England, *edited by Jay Paul Gates and Nicole Marafioti*

Volume 24: The Dating of *Beowulf*: A Reassessment, *edited by Leonard Neidorf*

Volume 25: The Cruciform Brooch and Anglo-Saxon England, *Toby F. Martin*

Volume 26: Trees in the Religions of Early Medieval England, *Michael D.J. Bintley*

Volume 27: The Peterborough Version of the Anglo-Saxon Chronicle: Rewriting Post-Conquest History, *Malasree Home*

Volume 28: The Anglo-Saxon Chancery: The History, Language and Production of Anglo-Saxon Charters from Alfred to Edgar, *Ben Snook*

Volume 29: Representing Beasts in Early Medieval England and Scandinavia, *edited by Michael D.J. Bintley and Thomas J.T. Williams*

Volume 30: Direct Speech in *Beowulf* and Other Old English Narrative Poems, *Elise Louviot*

Volume 31: Old English Philology: Studies in Honour of R.D. Fulk, *edited by Leonard Neidorf, Rafael J. Pascual and Tom Shippey*

Volume 32: 'Charms', Liturgies, and Secret Rites in Early Medieval England, *Ciaran Arthur*

Volume 33: Old Age in Early Medieval England: A Cultural History, *Thijs Porck*

Volume 34: Priests and their Books in Late Anglo-Saxon England, *Gerald P. Dyson*

Volume 35: Burial, Landscape and Identity in Early Medieval Wessex, *Kate Mees*

Volume 36: The Sword in Early Medieval Northern Europe: Experience, Identity, Representation, *Sue Brunning*

Volume 37: The Chronology and Canon of Ælfric of Eynsham, *Aaron J Kleist*

Volume 38: Medical Texts in Anglo-Saxon Literary Culture, *Emily Kesling*

Volume 39: The Dynastic Drama of *Beowulf*, *Francis Leneghan*

Volume 40: Old English Lexicology and Lexicography: Essays in Honor of Antonette diPaolo Healey, *edited by Maren Clegg Hyer, Haruko Momma and Samantha Zacher*

Volume 41: Debating with Demons: Pedagogy and Materiality in Early English Literature, *Christina M. Heckman*

www.ingramcontent.com/pod-product-compliance
Lightning Source LLC
Chambersburg PA
CBHW051603230426
43668CB00013B/1967